Intention and Identity

Works of John Finnis available from Oxford University Press

Reason in Action
Collected Essays: Volume I

Intention and Identity
Collected Essays: Volume II

Human Rights and Common Good
Collected Essays: Volume III

Philosophy of Law
Collected Essays: Volume IV

Religion and Public Reasons
Collected Essays: Volume V

Natural Law and Natural Rights
Second Edition

Aquinas
Moral, Political, and Legal Theory

Nuclear Deterrence, Morality and Realism
with Joseph Boyle and Germain Grisez

INTENTION AND IDENTITY

Collected Essays: Volume II

John Finnis

OXFORD
UNIVERSITY PRESS

OXFORD
UNIVERSITY PRESS

Great Clarendon Street, Oxford, OX2 6DP,
United Kingdom

Oxford University Press is a department of the University of Oxford.
It furthers the University's objective of excellence in research, scholarship,
and education by publishing worldwide. Oxford is a registered trade mark of
Oxford University Press in the UK and in certain other countries

First published 2011

Published in the United States of America by Oxford University Press
198 Madison Avenue, New York, NY 10016, United States of America

British Library Cataloguing in Publication Data
Data available

Library of Congress Cataloging in Publication Data
Data available

ISBN 978-0-19-958006-4

PREFACE

The earliest of the essays collected in these five volumes dates from 1967, the latest from 2010. The chronological Bibliography of my publications, near the end of each volume, shows how the collected essays are distributed across the volumes. But each volume also contains some essays previously unpublished.

Many of the essays appear with new titles. When the change is substantial, the original published title is noted at the beginning of the essay; the original can of course always also be found in the Bibliography.

Revision of previously published work has been restricted to clarification. Where there seems need for substantive qualification or retractation, I have said so in an endnote to the essay or, occasionally, in a bracketed footnote. Unless the context otherwise indicates, square brackets signify an insertion made for this Collection. Endnotes to particular essays have also been used for some updating, especially of relevant law. In general, each essay speaks from the time of its writing, though the dates given in the Table of Contents are dates of publication (where applicable) not composition which sometimes was one or two years earlier.

I have tried to group the selected essays by theme, both across and within the volumes. But there is a good deal of overlapping, and something of each volume's theme will be found in each of the other volumes. The Index, which like the Bibliography (but not the 'Other Works Cited') is common to all volumes, gives some further indication of this, though it aspires to completeness only as to names of persons. Each volume's own Introduction serves to amplify and explain that volume's title, and the bearing of its essays on that theme.

CONTENTS

LIST OF ABBREVIATIONS

AAS	*Acta Apostolicae Sedis* (Rome)
AJJ	American Journal of Jurisprudence
All ER	All England Law Reports
Aquinas	1998d: John Finnis, *Aquinas: Moral, Political and Legal Theory* (OUP)
CCC	*Catechism of the Catholic Church* ([1994] rev edn, 1999)
CL	H.L.A. Hart, *The Concept of Law* ([1961] 2nd edn, OUP, 1994)
CLR	Commonwealth Law Reports (of decisions of the High Court of Australia)
CUP	Cambridge: Cambridge University Press
DS	H. Denzinger, *Enchiridion Symbolorum Definitionum et Declarationum de rebus fidei et morum* (ed. A. Schönmetzer) (34th edn, Barcelona and New York: Herder, 1967)
EJP	H.L.A. Hart, *Essays in Jurisprudence & Philosophy* (OUP, 1983)
EPD	Joseph Raz, *Ethics in the Public Domain* (OUP, 1994)
FHG	Mary Geach and Luke Gormally (eds), *Faith in a Hard Ground: Essays on Religion, Philosophy and Ethics by G.E.M. Anscombe* (Charlottesville, VA and Exeter, UK: Imprint Academic, 2008)
FoE	1983b: John Finnis, *Fundamentals of Ethics* (OUP; Washington, DC: Georgetown University Press)
HLAE	Mary Geach and Luke Gormally (eds), *Human Life, Action and Ethics: Essays by G.E.M Anscombe* (Charlottesville, VA and Exeter, UK: Imprint Academic, 2005)
HUP	Harvard University Press
In Eth.	Aquinas, *Sententia Libri Ethicorum* [Commentary on *NE*] (ed. Gauthier) (1969)
LCL	Germain Grisez, *The Way of the Lord Jesus*, vol. 2, *Living a Christian Life* (Quincy: Franciscan Press, 1993)
LE	Ronald Dworkin, *Law's Empire* (HUP; London: Fontana, 1986)
LQR	Law Quarterly Review

MA	1991c: John Finnis, *Moral Absolutes: Tradition, Revision, and Truth* (Catholic University of America Press)
MoP	Ronald Dworkin, *A Matter of Principle* (HUP, 1985)
NDMR	1987g: John Finnis, Joseph Boyle, and Germain Grisez, *Nuclear Deterrence, Morality and Realism* (OUP)
NE	Aristotle, *Nicomachean Ethics*
NLNR	1980a: John Finnis, *Natural Law and Natural Rights* (2nd edn, OUP, 2011)
OUP	Oxford: Oxford University Press (including Clarendon Press)
Pol.	Aristotle, *Politics*
ScG	Aquinas, *Summa contra Gentiles* [A Summary against the Pagans] (c. 1259–65)
Sent.	Aquinas, *Scriptum super Libros Sententiarum Petri Lombardiensis* [Commentary on the Sentences [Opinions or Positions of the Church Fathers] of Peter Lombard] (c. 1255)
ST	Aquinas, *Summa Theologiae* [A Summary of Theology] (c.1265–73)
TRS	Ronald Dworkin, *Taking Rights Seriously* ([1977] rev edn with Reply to Critics) (HUP; London: Duckworth, 1978)
US	United States Reports [decisions of the Supreme Court of the United States]

THE COVER PICTURE

Bethany, a village of German settlers, depicted in watercolour by George French Angas in the early evening of a late-summer day in February of 1844 or 1845.

Bethany was established by twenty-four German families in 1842, just over five years after South Australia's founding. These families had emigrated to the new British colony from Prussia via Hamburg, wanting to escape the deviations from Lutheran church order that were being imposed by the King of Prussia so as to unite his Lutheran and Calvinist subjects in a single state church.†

Bethanien village was built below (and west of) the Barossa Range, forty miles north-east of Adelaide, on nine 80-acre sections leased and later bought from the artist's father; by 1844 the villagers had about 500 acres under cultivation. Three Old Lutheran congregations near Adelaide had convened in 1839 at Glen Osmond (below the Adelaide Hills: see cover of Volume III) and contracted to acquire over 2,000 acres of Angas land in the Barossa Valley. Though the village seems higgledy-piggledy here, it took the customary form of a Prussian farmlet-village (*Hufendorf*), and already had its church and associated school. Each farming family's cottage along the north-side of the government road stood near the head of its own cultivable strip, some hundreds of yards deep, intended for vegetables, orchard, crops, and pasture. Beyond lay common pastureland bordering the south bank of the near-perennial creek, which flows down from the Kaiserstuhl hills and was called by the aborigines Tanunda and by the Christian settlers Kedron.

Among many scarcities in New Silesia (the Barossa Valley) was timber; felling on public (Crown) land was forbidden. In the foreground, part of a red gum trunk is being split.

NOTE

† *German Lutheran settlers in South Australia, 1838–41*...Some of those who settled at Bethany had arrived in South Australia in 1838–9, most of the rest in 1841. They had set out by barge from the district of Züllichau in Brandenburg (about 100 miles east-south-east of Berlin, and now part of Poland). After a 300-mile, three-week journey along the Oder, the Spree, the Havel, and the Elbe,

they reached the independent city-state of Hamburg, whence they sailed for Adelaide. On the 1841 voyage about one-fifth of the passengers died of illness and were buried at sea.

The Prussian authorities had only reluctantly and after delays granted the emigrants licence to leave, a licence which involved loss of citizenship. The negotiations with the Prussian government, and the financing of the voyage, were facilitated and assisted by the artist's father (George Fife Angas, in some ways the founding father of the colony), by his English agent in Germany and South Australia, and by other English persons of Baptist or similar Protestant faith. The deliberations and intentions of the two pastors who led the two early, religiously motivated voyages of German emigrants to South Australia can be studied in their letters, appended to Iwan, *Because of Their Beliefs*.

The Barossa Valley, whose first vineyard was probably planted at Bethany in 1847, was for long called New Silesia, and though most Germans became naturalized British subjects within a couple of years of arrival, German language and culture survived for generations there and in one or two other areas nearer Adelaide.

INTRODUCTION

Practical reason's subject is not the basic human goods, but the human persons and communities that flourish in those goods and are harmed by being deprived of them. Practical reasoning and deliberation are supremely personal acts of individuals and groups, and practical reasonableness in deliberate choice and action is the decisive virtue, without which human rights will not be respected and no common good will be secured. Virtues, like vices, go to make up a kind of self-constituted second nature; they shape up the identity that, as part author and wholly owner, each of us, and each of our communities, is responsible for keeping oriented rightly, towards human fulfilment. So the topics of this volume's essays are foundational stepping stones on the way between Volume I's essays on reason in action (practical reason) and the volumes on human rights and common good (III), law (IV), and religion (V). They are topics not handled with sufficient explicitness or depth, or in some cases even clearly noticed, in *Natural Law and Natural Rights*, and the essays here are no older than 1987.[1]

I. NATURE AND FREEDOM IN PERSONAL IDENTITY

Ought implies *can*. One is under no obligation to do the impossible. Or even to attempt it (though there can sometimes be an obligation to fight against overwhelming odds, so that other possibilities are realized—that others get away, or learn, or…). But this oft-explored thought is less interesting than: *Ought* implies can *not*. Norms and normative claims (including 'I should not have done…') make sense only as addressed to those who have, or had, a choice. That is, a choice *between*…. Call the alternatives (there can be more than two at a time) options. Choosing (opting) is preferring one option to the other(s), terminating one's deliberation about the alternatives, which

[1] *FoE* makes substantial progress over *NLNR* by its attention to the intransitivity of action and to the reality and undeniability of free choices.

fall away as if dismissed, and treating the preferred option as now *what is to be done*—what I am going to do.[2] And choosing is the exercise of freedom, freedom 'of will', 'of choice'—not simply the freedom from being blocked, or chained, or pinned down. *Our* nature includes this freedom of choice: more precisely, we can and sometimes do make free choices, though most of what we freely do is the carrying out of unrevoked and still relevant free choices we made back in the past. And some of what we freely do is done with such spontaneity that the need to choose (or to have earlier chosen) does not arise.

Of course, to say that capacity to choose is part of our nature is to say (among other things) that this capacity of ours to choose between options is not something we chose to have. In that respect it is like our circulatory and digestive systems, not subject to choice nor matter for deliberation (which is reasoning *towards* choice).

An option always has two elements or aspects: some benefit, for the sake of which it may be preferred to alternatives, and something that may be done for the sake of that benefit. Call these *end* and *means*, respectively. The benefit may of course be multiple, and the something done may be 'doing nothing' (as when one votes for a proposal by sitting still, not moving at all). And the benefit envisaged may of course be, in truth, no benefit at all; but if this becomes apparent to the deliberating person, the option ceases to seem choiceworthy, ceases to be choosable (as that option). And each means, all the way in from 'ultimate end' (say, restoring one's health) to the point where one is first exerting oneself (say, to get up to go to the doctor), is also an end, something promising the benefit of making more nearly attainable the end(s) (health and return to work) for the sake of which the chosen option was preferred (say, to going back to sleep). Equally, of course, all the way to the end(s) just mentioned, the ends wanted, pursued, and attained (say, catching the daily bus to the doctor's town) are also means.[3]

There is deliberating and choosing wherever there is both a comparison of benefits (and of obstacles, burdens, and bad side effects) and a preferring (in the decisive way that clears the decks for, even if it does not initiate, action). These may involve scant extension in time: one may decide to reply to the interrogator's question with an evasion—or to give a mathematically ambitious answer to the pupil's question—and do so (and then change

[2] This resolution, articulated in what Aquinas calls one's *imperium* (order) to oneself (*NLNR* 337–42) can be conditional: 'This is what I will do if (or when) X' (as with choice and *imperium* with immediate effect, this 'will' is not a prediction): see essay 11.

[3] On this philosophically neglected feature of action, hidden but implicit in the word 'means', see essay 9, sec. II and essay 14 at pp. 273–4.

one's mind again!), without pause or hesitation, as quick as thought. There need be no sense or experiencing of the choice, but just a comparing and a preferring, such that from a certain point one's explanations of what one is doing (or preparing to do) have—or would have, if they were sought—a new content. But whether it's like that, or there is a sense of choosing and relief from the tension of comparing, there is always this: to the extent that one can analytically distinguish between the option as being compared and the option as chosen, one can call the former a proposal[4] (a kind of synonym for an option) and the latter one's intention *in doing* (or being resolved to do) what one has chosen to do.[5]

Deliberating is a rational process, though like all human thinking it is (and we need it to be) accompanied by images, which may or may not be memories or modifications of the remembered. Images are not ideas (nor are ideas a refined form of image), but they help us to shape and deploy our ideas, even when the idea in some respect contradicts the image, as the idea of a line (length with no breadth) contradicts any drawn line (which cannot be seen, remembered, or imagined unless it has some breadth). The images that accompany the ideas with which we are concerned in our practical reasoning towards the shaping up of choiceworthy options can support the intelligible attractiveness (desirability) of the respective benefits at stake; memories of feelings of well-being and of enjoyably vigorous activity in health, or of miseries of sickness, support one's interest in the intelligible good of life and health. Or the images—say, of nauseating medicine or pains of treatment—can deflect and disrupt the intelligent appreciation of those benefits or of the opportunities for and obstacles in the way of attaining them. For emotions respond especially to images, and emotional desire, aversion, and inertia operate not only to support but also to deflect or disrupt. Still, what we call *will* is that aspect of our rational capacities

[4] Anscombe, 'Thought and Action in Aristotle' at 69 says: '... [Aristotle] says [this man] will get what he "proposes" (*protithetai*); and this verb expresses a volition, or perhaps rather an intention. Aristotle ought, we may say, to have seen that he was here employing a key concept in the theory of action, but he did not do so; the innocent unnoticeable verb he uses receives no attention from him.' Germain Grisez put 'proposal' to work as the key concept in the theory of freely chosen action: see e.g. his 'Choice and Consequentialism', which also provides a highly comprehensible account of choosing.

[5] What is intended, in this sense of 'intend', 'intent', etc., is the whole set of means and end(s) included in the proposal and adopted by opting for (choosing) that proposal in preference to the alternative option(s). But 'intent', etc. may be given a more specialized sense by speaking of the intent(ion) *with which* something is done, meaning the end for which the relevant means are being (or were) carried out. And in a stabilized and partly stipulative vocabulary, one may distinguish intention and object in just the same way, so that 'object' signifies the means (the close-in end) and 'intention' the (further-out) end(s)—even though 'object(ive)' is a word also available for use, with precisely the opposite nuance, to signify the end as distinct from the means!

which consists in responding, with interest, willingness, intent, and so forth, to prospective *intelligible* benefits.

That is why the tradition which most attentively investigated the process of deliberating and choosing—the process of willing—summed up a basic aspect of these realities with the saying: will is within reason (*voluntas in ratione*). And this did not apply just to those options and choices which directly concern reasoning—choices to investigate, reason things out, reflect, and so on (all of which are kinds of action)—but also to the many choices in which such choices to reason are in the service of one's interest in actions and benefits outside reason, such as driving, typing, reading, maintaining life and health, producing, clearing away physical obstacles, and countless other activities engaging with the world outside reasoning.

But though its working is all within our rational capacities, willing is distinguishable from reasoning because it is the factor whereby we move towards choice, and eventually terminate deliberation by choice and terminate it even though reason (and understanding of the intelligible benefits available) did not *require* the interest, the willingness, or the choice.[6] Reason as such, going beyond its first phase, understanding, looks for necessities, for compelling evidence, for valid arguments which, granted the premises, necessitate the conclusion, and so forth. Practical reasoning, in the countless situations where free choice is possible, does not compel or necessitate. So the responsiveness to intelligible benefits which is called *will* supplies what reason alone cannot: decision (choice) and action: trying, doing, accomplishing...

Such are some main elements of the structure of human freedom. It can be called an ontological structure, because it belongs to the way we find we *are*, the kind of *being* we find ourselves to be in a world of diverse kinds of being. It is a fundamental aspect of our nature, and one—perhaps the one—that distinguishes us from every other kind of being of which we have experience. It is utterly familiar to us, yet deeply strange compared with physical realities. This strangeness has two aspects. (i) There is the strangeness of the immaterial, the spiritual—that kind of reality that we find manifested in words, where material marks or sounds are freighted with meaning, which on the one hand cannot be communicated without materiality (signs, visible marks, audible sounds, etc.) but on the other hand can be detached from any particular material reality whatsoever and be precisely the same in meaning, be the same proposition or expression, constant through indefinitely many different material realities (different signs, sounds, marks) and sharable across vast distances of time and space.

[6] On understanding and reason as motivator (*pace* Hume), see essay I.1, secs II and III.

We have well-grounded confidence that we can understand precisely what Plato, Thucydides, Cicero, Ulpian, Luther, or John F. Kennedy meant, in at least some of their utterances. (ii) And there is the strangeness of the freedom we find we have, in choosing between intelligibly attractive options offering different, partly incommensurable benefits—a freedom such that, on those occasions when one does make a choice, nothing except the choosing itself settles which option is chosen.

Wittgenstein spoke about the first kind of strangeness, and indirectly about the second, when he wrote (in his pupil Elizabeth Anscombe's summary):

> In *Zettel* 608–610... Wittgenstein says: 'No supposition seems to me more natural than that there is no process in the brain correlated with associating or with thinking', and further on asks 'Why should there not be a psychological regularity to which *no* physiological regularity corresponds?' He remarks 'If this upsets our concepts of causality, then it is high time they were upset.'[7]

Anscombe's sinewy explorations of thinking clear the ground for getting Wittgenstein's point here. She makes clear, example after example, how far and how ordinarily it is the case that thinking something, or thinking of something, or associating something with something else, is not a matter of having a kind of experience: 'This [thinking *of*, or *that*, such and such] is an event, but not an experience; what we call its content is given by words which do not describe an inner experience (unless that is what the thought was about) but which have their primary application'[8]—such as in 'There's a snowy landscape', 'I haven't sent the card I meant to send to John', or 'If Kennedy pressed the button, then luckily someone interfered with the connections between Kennedy and the thermonuclear missiles'—not the secondary application the words *can* have when what is considered is an image or experience ('I see a snowy landscape in my mind's eye', 'I had a sudden image of Kennedy pressing the button').[9] And the same is true of intending, which 'after all needn't be a thought, for one can intend

[7] Anscombe, 'Ludwig Wittgenstein' at 406. [8] Anscombe, 'Events in the Mind' at 63.

[9] 'Events in the Mind' begins (57) with the case of realizing one hasn't sent the card, and argues (59) that:

> May it not be that there was absolutely nothing which occurred in one and meant 'Oh heavens I haven't yet sent that card', but that one simply had the thought in a flash, which would be expressed by those words, and that is what one remembers: it's no use asking what it consisted in because it didn't consist in anything or have any vehicle, it was only the thought itself. Yet, deprived of a vehicle, of the slightest flicker which should signify it, the naked thought seems like a nothing when one tries to recall what it was—which in another sense one can say perfectly well: one simply gives the words which express it.

(And, she might have said, those could be any words, in any language, that express it.) Her general conclusion (63) is that 'one thing that is not a "thought" in the sense Descartes gave to the Latin [*cogitatio*] and French for "thought", is: a thought.'

what one is not thinking of, as when one intends over a whole period to make a certain journey, but in fact seldom thinks of it, and when one even thinks of it, one's thoughts aren't to the effect that one is going to make that journey';[10] rather, they are thoughts about (to illustrate her point by reference to the story behind this volume's cover picture) whether the ship is ready or the Prussian government will grant an emigration licence, and so forth. But always one *could*, if asked or if reflecting, say (and think!) what one intends—and thus tell just what one is up to, is doing. Not spying, or fleeing, or touring, but emigrating (and with the ultimate intention of educating one's children in one's own faith).

And the strangeness of our familiar, homely freedom of choice can be expressed starkly in the passage from Aquinas which Anscombe doubtless had in mind to test, and support, in her explorations of causality and freedom,[11] the passage where he says (a) that to actively think about something requires an *intentio* of one's will (a wanting and trying to think about it, to focus on the matter and order or set about (re)ordering or amplifying one's ideas about it), and (b) that such 'movements of [human] will are *not dependent on or connected with any natural cause*'.[12] As to (a): though such an intending to think about X does not entail that there was either deliberation or choice (for one can and often does just spontaneously set about thinking something out), it does involve the freedom which Aquinas will starkly assert in (b), and which becomes freedom *of choice* whenever some alternative possibility, incompatible with thinking (or thinking about such-and-such), comes to mind and seems attractive, so that one needs to choose whether or not to think about X. As to (b): Aquinas here asserts what Wittgenstein only suggests. Neither philosopher thinks that our thinking has no natural causal and indeed physical (chemical, electrical, etc.) preconditions—a well-functioning brain—any more than either of them thinks that we can communicate without marks or sounds, which are brutely physical. They are pointing out, after searching reflections on the phenomena of thought (and of intention), that what is decisive about our thoughts (and intentions)—that they make sense, are relevant, are argumentatively sound, are true, and so forth—simply transcends, escapes, surpasses the natural, material causality that we sum up as 'physiological'

[10] *Ibid.* at 59.

[11] Essay 3, pp. 71–2. For example, see Anscombe's inaugural lecture in Cambridge, 'Causality and Determination' esp. at 145–7; Anscombe, 'Soft Determinism' (esp. at 172: '...the soft determinist...does think freedom compatible with physical impossibility...since, being a determinist, he thinks that everything except what actually happened was always impossible.... I am at liberty to say that I believe a "can of freedom" which holds in face of physical impossibility is pure nonsense'.)

[12] *De Veritate* q.8 a.13c: 'motus autem voluntatis non habet dependentiam nec connexionem ad aliquam causam naturalem'; and texts cited in essay 3, n. 12.

and the like: the criteria of intelligibility, soundness, and so forth are entirely distinct from, and could not be improved by knowledge of, any natural, material causes. The immaterial reality in play in one's *meaning* something, publicly or privately, is the reality we call mental or spiritual. The freedom from natural causality in free choices, when we make them, is only the most obvious manifestation of the difference in kind between the spiritual and what one might call the rest of creation, or the nature and natural causality with which natural sciences (including neurophysiology and empirical psychology) are concerned.

Less specialized than the meaning of 'nature' that is in play in the natural sciences is the metaphysical sense of 'nature' that is implicit in the epistemological axiom deployed by Aristotle and, more extensively, by Aquinas: a being's nature is what you understand by understanding its capacities, which you understand by understanding its activities, which you understand by understanding their objects (objectives). The axiom is epistemological because it sets out the order in which we come to know. In that order, nature comes last, because real knowledge of something's nature is the end of a process of inference. In the ontological order—that is, the structure of reality (being)—the order is the opposite: it is because something has the nature it has that it has the capacity to act in the way it does for the objects its activity has.

One of the implications of this axiom, as it bears on human free choices and intentions, is that we will not understand what kind of being human persons are unless we take with full seriousness the capacity for free choice, a capacity which we become aware of, intimately and securely, both in being aware of attractive alternative incompatible options (objects shaped up in deliberation) each fully available for our choosing, and in the choosing itself, whether experienced as a distinct event or identified only in retrospect. That awareness is awareness that nothing—not reasons, not internal forces, nor any external pressures—*settled* our choice except the choosing itself. (*Ought* implies can *not*: even when rational considerations are not under-determined, but rather deliver a resounding *You ought* or, in another case, a resounding *You ought not*, the rationally inferior option may well have some intelligible attraction, some desirability not present in the superior option; and thus one can really, albeit wrongly, choose it.) The so-called law of sufficient reason is not in truth a metaphysical or ontological law, but just an epistemological presumption which turns out not to be irrebuttable—a rationality norm.[13] For its universal

[13] On the illusory Leibnizian 'law', and sound rationality norms, see *NLNR* 384–5, 412. To the texts there, add the first of Leibniz's letters to Arnauld of 14 July 1686, arguing that only ignorance induced by complexity prevents us from knowing that it is part of the very concept of himself

applicability is negated by free choices. In free choice, when it occurs, there is no motivating factor of any kind sufficient to exclude the not-chosen alternative, or to prevent it from being chosen then and there, in preference to the chosen alternative.

So the human person, as is evident in health and maturity, is not submerged in that realm of nature in which the principle of sufficient reason can reasonably be taken to be universally applicable (as Newtonian natural sciences fruitfully take it to be). And the healthy maturity of persons is just that, the actualizing of capacities which were present from the outset, as radical (at-the-root) capacities, the presence of which from the outset of this or that human being's existence can be securely inferred from the unbroken course of their (and the being's) development, and is confirmed by the distinctive human genomic constitution.

These remarkable aspects of human nature are explored in the two wide-ranging essays with which this volume opens. The first was written for a collection of essays on jurisprudence, and so considers the many-faceted reality and status of the person as a foundation of law, in which subjects are never properly (justly) reduced to objects. The essay does not use the term 'spirit(ual)', except in a special context where 'spirit-person' signifies an unacceptable, dualist conception in which the body-spirit unity of the human person is split and *person* is assimilated to spirit rather than body. Such a dualism is attacked with one set of argumentative strategies by Anscombe and with another, complementary strategy deployed in essay 1, sec. VII, in essay 2, secs II and IX, in essay 5, sec. I, and in other essays. Essay 2, at nn. 66–7, suggests that the form : matter account of soul : body (the account accepted in essay 1) may underplay the difference between human nature and the nature of beings more completely immersed in the realm of material nature. 'Formal cause'—which is not correlated merely with 'matter'—might have been a better category to deploy here, if any such category is going to serve as the account of what it is that unifies the human person's existing. For that, so remarkably, is an existing not only in the order of nature but also in the order of logic (in which we *mean* and set

(G.W. Leibniz) [or (see my account of the cover picture): of several hundred Prussian Old Lutherans in 1839)] that he would make a certain journey to Paris [and that they would emigrate to Bethanien in the Barossa], and that if he [those Germans] did not make it, it would not be him [them] not making it but someone else [some other people]: Montgomery (ed.), *Leibniz... Correspondence with Arnauld*, 125–7; Leibniz's notes of May 1686, *ibid.*, 105–19 esp. at 112–13, make clear both the connection with his conception of sufficient reason and his awareness of the paradox of his thesis, in which freedom of choice is saved only at the expense of subsisting personal identity (and vice versa). And notice, at 105, his associated incomprehension of our freedom's relation to the moral 'ought', when he speaks of 'the principle of morality... that every mind *will* pursue that which appears to it the best' (emphasis added). Since Leibniz's concerns were theological, see Grisez, *Christian Moral Principles*, ch. 2 ('Free Choice, Self-Determination, Community, and Character', esp. app. 2 'The compatibility of God's causality with free choice').

in order meanings), the order of technique (in which we master materials, including the materials of our own psychosomatic make-up), and the order of morally significant choice (in which we act as self-determining through undetermined choices which last in our character unless, if ever, negated by a contrary choice). (See essay 2, sec. I for these four kinds of order and sec. IX for our existing in all of them.)

Engaging with an empiricist philosophical culture in which it was widely assumed that progress would be made in understanding human understanding by scrutinizing 'I see a red patch before me', Anscombe's challenges to materialist, behaviourist, and other reductivist misapprehension of reality deploy examples like someone's pointing to something's shape rather than its colour (essay 3, sec. I).[14] The strategy has its efficacy, as does the comparable (relative) simplicity of the example of interpretation (*Mannai Investment*) analysed in essay 1, sec. VI. However, one of the purposes of essay 2's panoramic survey of philosophical issues around personal identity was to show how, and how diversely, spirit's forming up of the simply material and simply animal into the human is exemplified in the vastly more elaborate and refined ways of intending and meaning that are found in human conduct of the realistically complex kind which provides matter for dramatic and/or poetic (re)presentation. And such representation is itself an intending, meaning, and communicating of a kind the calculated complexity of which doubles up, so to speak, on the spiritual acts and dispositions represented, expressively or allusively. *Samizdat* writing, intended both to elude and tease the censor and to encourage, console, and inform the threatened, is a particularly rich trebling of intentionality, and is a spiritual-bodily reality facilitating one's understanding of how much is implied by *Mannai Investment*'s simple affirmation that *people mean*. The poem and the riddling touched upon in essay 2, sec. V, the issues of self-consciousness, authenticity, humiliation, and repentance taken up in secs IV, VI, and VII, and the dramatic affirmations (repeatedly noticed in the same essay) that commitment is possible, intelligible, and often reasonable—these are all reminders of the heavy freight of meaning in the traditional tags: we are *rational animals* and each of us is an *individual substance of a rational nature.*

For, as Aquinas says in his mature treatment of the phrase *individua substantia* in Boethius' succinct definition (just given) of a person, there are individual substances of many kinds but if the substance is not merely organically developing, as animals do, but has the self-mastery that is

[14] Essays 3 and 8 in this volume were written for publications with theological interests, though this affects only the range of topics treated in the essays, and the treatment of theological topics when they do arise (in each case rather peripherally).

entailed by being able to make *free* choices, choices made and carried out not by one's being acted upon but on one's own initiative and intention and responsibility, then we have that more special and perfect kind of substance that we call a *person*.[15] The full significance of this excellence of the person, compared with all that is sub-personal in the animal and organic realm, is only understood when account is taken of its manifestations in intentional action of every kind, including acts expressing irony, commitment, shame, hope, love, deception, fidelity, and so forth. But the capacity to act like this *in due course* already distinguishes the early human being from embryonic life in every other species of which we know.

One implication of this excellence in freedom and self-mastery is that Aquinas errs in his own account of *habitus*, the (vicious or virtuous) dispositions that one acquires in choosing and acting. For he accepts too easily the traditional account of habituation, of dispositions acquired by repeated acts or actions, as other animals are trained by patterned repetition. In human choosing and acting, the choice's lasting in one's character—as the perduring intransitive aspect of an action whose transitive, outer world-affecting performance has been completed—can constitute a 'habit', an enduring disposition, without or before any repetition whatever of the choice or its execution.[16] This is one of the relatively few cases where Aquinas does not have fully in view, or at least follow through fully from, the strangeness of our human nature by virtue of our capacity to mean and to choose meanings and other deeds and accomplishments.

II. GROUP IDENTITY AND GROUP ACTS

Drawing on Honoré's clarifying discussion of group identity and action, *Natural Law and Natural Rights* explained the existence of a community, big or small, by reference to shared activity with a view to a shared objective.[17] The book did not altogether neglect the substrata of shared nature, understanding, symbols, sympathies and dispositions usually prerequisite to the sharing of objectives and coordination of action which are constitutive of groups. But its explicit consideration of those substrata, in this context, took as its exemplar the more or less nuclear family. And its analysis of coordinated actions, though in no way restricted to or even focused on group actions *qua* acts precisely *of* the

[15] *ST* I q.29 a.1c; cf. *Sent.* I d.25 q.1 a.1. On being master of one's own acts, and its strategic place in his ethical thought, see *Aquinas* 20.

[16] See *FoE* 138–42; essay 8 at n. 10 and sec. III.

[17] *NLNR* 150–3, 160.

group, was silent, or at least hesitant in what it suggested, about them. This hesitancy or silence stemmed, on the one hand, from a justified denial that any group is ontologically a person, an individual substance of a rational nature with the organic unity and remarkable dignity or nobility that non-metaphorical personality entails; and, on the other hand, from my account's failure to bring shared or coordinated activity and shared objective or aim into a sufficiently precise relationship. For in reality, in many contexts, that relationship is so close and direct that it is proper to speak of the group itself acting, albeit not at all independently of the acts of its members.

What I was missing was the proposal. The analysis of deliberations towards free choices, when it is fully attentive, draws attention to the strategic role of the proposal, the option which, when competing with alternative proposals (options), must be chosen or rejected, preferred or not preferred, if anything is to be settled and done. The proposal, as I have indicated in the preceding section, picks out an object(ive) which is a means or set of means to an end or set of ends; the proposal is to pursue the end(s) it specifies, by the means it specifies; choice is precisely the adoption of this proposal—this whole specific set of end(s) and means—in preference to that or those alternatives. This articulated structure of ends and means, which could also be called a plan (usually in an informal sense), is essentially propositional in form, and can be communicated, formally or informally, to other persons, for their adoption. Just insofar as it is communicated (published) to them, the proposal can be called—as in essays 4 and 5—a public proposal. The unity of action coordinated according to this adopted proposal is the unity of a group act distinguishable (albeit inseparable) from the activities of individuals (or sub-groups) pursuant to the single, public proposal (which of course may, in advance, be wholly secret vis-à-vis non-members or members whose cooperation is not needed for the accomplishing of the group proposal).

Essays 4 and 5 spell this out, in each case by reflection, at a crucial point, on the (im)possibility of there being a group bluff by or in any community too large for a secret shared among its members to be kept secret from non-members. The normative context for this non-normative point of social ontology (reality) is in both essays the nuclear deterrents amply dissected and documented in *Nuclear Deterrence, Morality and Realism*, written with Germain Grisez and Joseph Boyle not long before those essays. The normative conclusions of that book are discussed in essay V.20 (1988b) and in the Introduction to that volume. Their profoundly disturbing character has only increased in the decades between then and now, as our countries have grown less and less fit for action even in 'passive' resistance, under the stress of the moral and cultural revolutions discussed in essay IV.11 (2009b), secs III and IV, and of the multicultural and multiethnic immigration touched upon in essays 6 and 7 below.

Those two essays each consider the aspects of group identity that are presupposed by the complex, coordinated dispositions without which the members of a political community are unlikely to accept that for them—taken one by one or sub-group by sub-group—there is sufficient reason to adopt and help carry out public proposals for group action such as the action of constituting and maintaining a constituted legal system, a welfare state, a national border, and so forth. Essay 6 focuses on shared language, and does so in a highly normative context. Debated questions about the proper sources and structure of the content of a decent legal order are serially reviewed, and inappropriate solutions identified, until the issue bearing most narrowly on language in the national community is reached. Here, the essay argues, is an issue not well resolved by demands for respect and denunciations of insult which misunderstand the intentions involved in proposals defending the country's identity as factually indispensable for preserving its common good and promoting politically or economically the common good of other peoples. Such defensive public proposals are ancillary manifestations of deeper, less articulated proposals: to be *this* people, making its own self-determined and self-determining choices of its own constitutional order and order of civil decencies and rights.

Like all practical reasoning, the argument just mentioned has premises of two different kinds, one kind normative but the other factual (including contingent states of affairs—'risks' as well as 'opportunities'—considered as more or less likely to become actual). Given an end, what means are needed, and their availability for and serviceability of attaining it, are largely matters of fact, prediction, empirically educated guesswork, and the like. The factual premises at stake in multicultural immigration are given some further consideration in essay 7's discussion of the national state's reality and propriety in the writings of Karol Wojtyla (John Paul II) and in John Rawls's contemporaneous late work, *The Law of Peoples.* Among other issues essential to an understanding of the properly political community (the state, in the more fundamental meaning of that term), the essay touches on the family in one of its inevitable political aspects: as a source of menace, injustice, and disintegration—a Platonic theme in an essay to which Plato is central, as he is in the original essay's other fragments, now essays I.5 and V.8.

III. ACTS AND INTENTIONS

These seven essays have normative settings. Some of these settings are theological, some legal, some simply moral. But all are concerned with a non-normative truth: the structure of human freedom as it is known to us in deliberation and choice, as much when these head towards immorality, crime, or delict as when they witness to and consolidate the humanly excellent in private or public conduct. Anscombe's great work *Intention* made readily available to philosophers much of that reality and philosophical tools for understanding it, tools such as a better understanding of the 'practical syllogism' recalled in the preceding paragraph, or again the idea of choosing and acting 'under a description' which is not a mere rationalization but a genuine step in one's deliberation about means suitable for one's purposes, about what to do in order to, or for the sake of, or with a view to, or simply *to* achieve the benefit one hopes for and (along with those means) intends. The variety of essentially synonymous idiomatic phrases just deployed witnesses that the structure in question is real, not a mere shadow or projection of surface grammar.

But the actions, and reasoning towards the choice(s) whose carrying out is what human action centrally is, are complex and often subtle. Transparent to a really clear-headed chooser,[18] they are for observers always more or less a matter of inference or of belief in testimony, and that in turn tempts judges and legislatures to replace truth about intention with fictions much more distorting in their effect than the doctrine that courts should in many (not all) fields be concerned only with 'objective' intention. For, as is explained in *Mannai Investment* and later cases, what lawyers call 'objective intention' is nothing other than what a reasonable observer, apprised of the context but eschewing testimony from the parties about what they had in mind, would judge or have judged that the parties really ('subjectively') intended.[19] But the lawyers' doctrine that what is foreseen as morally certain is intended imposes on the law a sheer fiction. And those theological traditions about 'double effect' in which causality and immediacy substitute for an understanding of means to ends, and of action as the carrying out of a chosen proposal, are equally untrue to the reality of the vital difference between side effects and intended effects.

For philosophers willing to consider an illustrative segment of criminal law, essay 10 provides a fairly foundational treatment of these realities. Essay 13, written with Germain Grisez and Joseph Boyle, provides a fund of illustrations and close, fundamental analysis, concluding with an intense

[18] See e.g. essay IV.10 (2007b), sec. II.

[19] See essay 1, n. 64.

consideration of the particular moral-theological teaching that attracted the critical attentions of both H.L.A. Hart and Philippa Foot. That issue, transposed to the famous hypothetical about the fat man stuck in the mouth of the underground cavern, also earned Anscombe's close attention, in a passage with which I critically engage, and firmly disagree, in essay 10, pp. 189–93 ('But doing X *just is* doing Y!').

Anscombe's *Intention* and related work of hers took its visible inspiration from Aristotle. My treatment of intention fields as a telling philosophical witness Aquinas, who had understood Aristotle, to be sure, and so much else in our main tradition, but who shows again and again that he has closely attended to the structure of deliberation, choice, and action in his own astonishingly active[20] life. The literary complexity of his mature treatment of action left his disciples struggling, however, and the neo-scholastic tradition lost its grip on some of the main lines. Essay 9 is work of historical-philosophical retrieval and reflection, fundamental for almost everything else in this part, though not, of course, indispensable, since the realities are as available to us from experience as they were to any philosophical master. Essays 11, 12, and 14 are exercises in testing the foundational analysis by reference to our law's fund of experience and reflection under normative stress. But as essay 12 also shows, conscientious reflection on great questions such as participation in nuclear deterrence cannot dispense with an understanding of what one is *choosing* in assenting to this policy or that, of public proposals which go under the same generic name but differ strategically.

IV. PERSONS BEGINNING AND DYING

The volume's last five essays look to some of the material substrata of human existence. They scrutinize various kinds of spiritualist dualism with which the reality of human persons is misdescribed—not least under the stress of normative motivations—by basically materialist philosophers. The axiom that nature is known only in capacities, and capacities in acts and acts by their objects finds here a new field of application in relation to persons who, by immaturity, illness, or decay, cannot now pursue objects in action. Only essay 19 has normative issues as its primary focus (and those

[20] See *Aquinas* 5–10. Voegelin, no follower of his faith or philosophy but competent over vast fields of political thought and history, says:

> Saint Thomas could achieve this incredible concentration of the past and the future of high civilization through the miracle of his personality...equally distinguished by sensorial receptivity, range of soul, intellectual energy, and sublimeness of spirit.... Nobody after him has represented in the same grandiose style the spiritually and intellectually mature Western man. (*History of Political Ideas* II, 231, 207, 232.)

issues are more thematic in essays III.14–19). The others grapple with facts about development, decay, and injury. It is a common saying, and brush-off, that these essays' theses about those facts are religious, rooted in faith not evidence or philosophy. The truth, I think, is quite opposite. The religion blamed for these theses earns the attention of open-minded outsiders—as I myself found when one of them—by its openness to investigating and acknowledging these realities for what they are, and just what and who is at stake in satisfying the interests, desires, or convenience of others.

Part One

Nature and Freedom in Personal Identity

1

THE PRIORITY OF PERSONS*

> So, since all law is made *for the sake of human beings*, we should speak first of the status of persons.[1]
>
> Justinian, *Digest* 1. 5. 2
>
> Knowledge of law amounts to little if it overlooks the *persons for whose sake* law is made.[2]
>
> Justinian, *Institutes* 1. 2. 12

What it is to be a person, and why it matters that one is, are issues no longer thematic in general accounts of law. But the very concept of law, of an existing and projected reality profoundly, and deliberately, different from both anarchy and tyranny, is shaped by the recognition that: (i) we human beings are all persons and each other's equals in that respect even if in no other; (ii) persons of sufficient maturity and health can understand and communicate what they and other persons mean, and can intend and choose many other ways of behaving, too; and (iii) persons, their well-being, and their intentions matter in ways that nothing else in our environment does. This essay outlines some reasons for bringing these issues, rather neglected in modern jurisprudence, back into focus.

I. LAW IS 'FOR THE SAKE OF . . .'

Hart's rejection of 'the positivist thesis' that 'law may have any content' appealed to the 'natural necessity' of 'the minimum forms of protection for persons, property, and promises which are . . . indispensable features of municipal law', 'if it is to serve the minimum purposes of beings constituted

* 2000a (for *Oxford Essays in Jurisprudence, Fourth Series*).

[1] '*Cum* . . . hominum causa *omne ius constitutum sit, primo de personarum statu* . . ., *dicemus*' (emphasis added, here and elsewhere unless otherwise indicated).

[2] '*Nam parum est ius nosse si* personae quarum causa *statutum est ignorentur.*'

as men are'.[3] A 'natural' necessity of this kind is in the first instance a *rational* necessity. As Hart himself remarks, his discussion of the minimum content of law[4] is trying to identify 'the distinctively *rational* connection between natural facts and the content of legal and moral rules'.[5] And this 'connection' is 'rational' given the 'minimum purposes' or 'natural aims' of 'beings constituted as men are'. The rationality, then, is that of practical reasoning—reasoning along the following lines (for example): we want to survive; but, given that we are vulnerable and the altruism of others is limited, we cannot survive without rules prohibiting the free use of violence; *so* such rules are necessary and other rules are worthless without these.

Though Hart spoke often enough of human beings' natural aims, plural, his official list of them famously admitted only the aim just mentioned: 'survival'.[6] Fortunately for jurisprudence, his real list of the minimum purposes which give law and legal system their complex, shaping point tacitly went wider. It included the aims or purposes relative to which people—not least Hart and the readers he anticipated—count certain aspects of 'pre-legal' conditions as 'defects', defects to which the minimally adequate response is, as Hart argues, the 'amenity' of power-conferring rules and the 'remedy' of 'secondary rules', the amenities and remedies which make law what it essentially is.[7]

Law, then, is for the sake of serving certain purposes of 'beings constituted as men are', and Hart speaks of serving these purposes as law's *point*. For Ronald Dworkin, on the other hand, 'the most abstract and fundamental *point* of legal practice' is:

to guide and constrain the power of government [by insisting that] force not be used or withheld...except as licensed or required by individual rights and

[3] *CL* 199. The word omitted is 'similarly', referring to the same 'setting of natural facts and aims, which make sanctions both possible and necessary in a municipal system' (*ibid.*). The Postscript, *ibid.*, 248–9, seems to retreat from the book's clear and well-argued rejection of the above-described 'positivist thesis'; '[l]ike other forms of positivism my theory makes no claim to identify the point or purpose of law and legal systems as such... In fact I think it quite vain to seek any more specific purpose which law as such serves beyond providing guides to human conduct and standards of criticism of such conduct.' But *CL* 251 reverts to speaking of 'aims [besides certainty] which law should cherish'.

[4] He called it 'the minimum content of natural law' but meant, rather, the minimum content of positive law (content which, being necessary, one can call natural law).

[5] *Ibid.*, 193, where the treatment of the minimum content begins: 'it is important to observe that in each case the facts mentioned afford a *reason* why, given survival as an aim, law and morals should include a specific content' (Hart's emphasis).

[6] *Ibid.*, 191. On his argument here, see *NLNR* 30–1, 82.

[7] See *CL* 28, 41–2, 196–7 (on the 'huge and distinctive amenity' conferred by the institution of power-conferring rules, 'one of the great contributions of law to social life' and 'a step forward as important to society as the invention of the wheel'); 91–9 (on the remedies required to overcome the defects of a social structure of primary rules of obligation restricting the free use of violence, theft and deception); and 155 (on the union of primary and secondary rules as 'the "essence" of law').

responsibilities flowing from past political decisions about when collective force is justified.[8]

And Dworkin favours a specific conception of that point, 'law as integrity'; 'law insists', he holds, that collective force be licensed by rights and responsibilities 'flowing from' past decisions, in order that the law will thereby benefit 'society' precisely 'by securing a kind of equality among citizens'.[9] And rights and responsibilities only 'flow from' a political community's decisions if that community's practices 'show not only concern but an *equal* concern for all members'.[10]

So law's point, on Dworkin's conception, is to serve the interests of 'citizens' or (equivalently, it seems) 'members of the group'—and if it fails to try to do so, it lacks legitimacy, authority, and obligatory force, and fails to justify the coercion it pretends to justify. Dworkin's restriction of the point to citizens or members of the community seems deliberate. True, one of his summaries of the equality condition says that the 'command of integrity assumes that each *person* is as worthy as any other, that each must be treated with equal concern',[11] and there is mention of the concept of 'general duties [a group's] members owe equally to persons outside it'.[12] But no such general duty is affirmed as having a place in the account of law's empire, and in its context the summary's reference to 'persons' seems to be no more than shorthand for 'members'. Moreover, membership is said to be a matter of 'genetic or geographical or other historical conditions identified *by social practice*'.[13] (Some elements of American legal history which I recall in sec. IV make these restrictions noteworthy.)

Thus there are telling differences in the conceptions of law's point proposed by Hart and Dworkin as internal to the very idea of law. For Dworkin, 'securing' an equality understood as incompatible with counting 'some members as inherently less worthy than others'[14] is central to law's point and idea. For Hart, concern for any such kind of equality, though 'deeply embedded in *modern* man'[15] and '*now* generally accepted as a statement of an ideal of obvious relevance in the criticism of law',[16] is extrinsic to the concept of law, and the question whether such concern or criticism is warranted 'cannot be investigated'[17] in his book on that concept. But the contrast between these two theorists is softened by Dworkin's

[8] *LE* 93. [9] *Ibid.*, 95–6. [10] *Ibid.*, 200 (Dworkin's emphasis). [11] *Ibid.*, 213.
[12] *Ibid.*, 199. [13] *Ibid.*, 201. [14] *Ibid.*, 201. [15] *CL* 162. [16] *Ibid.*, 206.
[17] *Ibid.*, 206. Notice that in his *Punishment and Responsibility* he is willing to say things like (at 22):

> [j]ustice simply consists of principles...which (i) treat all *alike as persons* by attaching special significance to human voluntary action and (ii) forbid the use of the human being for the benefit of others except in return for his voluntary actions against them.

noticeable unwillingness to affirm that the equality intrinsic to law's point is the equality of all human beings or of all persons or of any other class of beings identifiable prior to a social practice—a practice, such as the law's, of defining the membership whereby moral and legal rights are 'given'.[18]

II. ON LAW AS FOR THE SAKE OF ALL

To the thought that the primary element in law's point is not merely promoting 'survival' but respecting and appropriately promoting the survival of *all* human beings within its jurisdiction, Hart has a simple response, tirelessly deployed throughout his work. Legal systems, he reminds us, 'have long endured though they flouted these principles of justice'.[19] Moreover, 'it is conceivable that there might be a moral outlook which did not put individuals on a footing of reciprocal equality'.[20] Well, neither the facts nor the logical possibilities are in doubt. But Hart's own strategy of displaying law as a kind of *reason* apt for being counted as a *common standard* for action undercuts this response. Just as fallacious arguments earn a place in a treatise on argumentation only as instances of what, despite appearances and popularity, is really *not an argument*, so unreasonable kinds of law and legal system should be attended to in legal theory precisely as instances of law diluted with the effluents of what law *essentially opposes*: the arbitrary exercise of one person's or group's power over other persons and groups. Dworkin is right to hold that 'any full theory of law'[21] will go beyond Hart's explicit and tacit accounts of the benefits which differentiate law from the commands of powerful people, and will include a reference to equality and its moral entailments, 'principles of justice, fairness, and procedural due process'.[22] But, as we have seen, he leaves in shadow the question *who* is equal, and should be treated as equal, to whom.

Roman law, which long endured though flouting some of the principles of justice, gave its students and practitioners a better account of law's point. The opening sentence of the *Institutes* directs us towards it: justice, understood precisely as a disposition to act for a certain kind of purpose: 'Justice is the stable and lasting willingness *to give to each his right*'.[23] 'Each' who? The Birks translation quite properly renders this object as 'to acknowledge all men's rights'. For the closing words of the introductory sections (titles 1–3 of Book 1) tell us that law exists 'for the sake of persons', and the following sentence, opening the whole treatise on the law of persons, stakes out the

[18] See Dworkin, *Life's Dominion*, 23. [19] *CL* 206. [20] *Ibid.*, 165.
[21] See *LE* 110. [22] See *ibid.*, e.g. 225. [23] *Digest* 1. 1. pr.; *Institutes* (*Inst.*) 1. 1. pr.

essential position: all men are persons.[24] Slavery is bluntly defined as the subjection of 'someone' to another's ownership and mastery 'contrary to nature',[25] indeed, more precisely, 'contrary to natural law/right'.[26] 'For by natural law/right, from the beginning, all human beings were born free.'[27]

The requirements of justice-for-persons are thus affirmed and flouted in almost the same breath. No attempt is made to deny that slaves are persons and are their owners' equals in human nature. The institution is presented not as justified but as a fact of life and a product of the arbitrament of war—of sheer power. The frankness, to be sure, has its limits; the fact is here veiled that slavery as an institution of the law is maintained by sheer power, long after any war or war-captivity, and is imposed upon persons who were never party to war. Law's point is stated by Roman law's self-interpretative doctrines, but its implications are not pursued with undeflected practical reasonableness.

Law's point—what, or better, whom it is for the sake of—is identified in the opening words of Article 1 of the Universal Declaration of Human Rights (1948), adapting the phraseology of the Roman jurists: '[*a*]*ll human beings* are born free and equal in dignity and rights'. Article 1's subject, 'all human beings', is equated with the preamble's 'all members of the human family' and 'the human person', so that the reference of the remaining articles,[28] 'everyone', 'all', and 'no one', is clear. So it is all human beings who are 'equal before the law' and entitled to its 'equal protection' (Article 7); and 'everyone' has the 'right to recognition everywhere as a person before the law' (Article 6).

III. ON RULES AS RELATIONSHIPS OF THE DELIBERATING PERSON TO OTHER PERSONS

What is a rule of law? It is certainly not well defined as an 'assemblage of signs declarative of a volition', as Bentham supposed. It is not, indeed, to be defined as any kind of assemblage of signs, for rules of law are no more than evidenced and, in some instances, performatively *effected* by the assembling of such signs. Nor is it, ultimately, the meaning of a set of signs or of an act of signifying, for, while meaning remains constant, validity

[24] *Inst.* 1. 2. 12; 1. 3. 1: '[t]he main classification in the law of persons is this: all men are either free or slaves' (*summa itaque divisio de iure personarum haec est, quod omnes homines aut liberi sunt aut servi*).

[25] *Inst.* 1. 3. 2. [26] *Inst.* 1. 2. 2.

[27] *Ibid.*: '*servitutes . . . sunt iuri naturali contrariae—iure enim naturali ab initio omnes homines liberi nascebantur.*'

[28] There is one exception, Art. 16, which has as its subject 'men and women of full age', to signify that marriage is between persons of opposite sex (gender).

and obligatoriness may come and go. In my general account of law, I tried to answer the question:

> legal thinking (i.e. the law) brings what precision and predictability it can into the order of human interaction by a special technique: the treating of (usually datable) past acts (whether of enactment, adjudication, or any of the multitude of exercises of public and private 'powers') as giving, *now*, sufficient and exclusionary reason for acting in a way *then* 'provided for'. In an important sense the 'existence' or 'validity' of a legal rule can be explained by saying that it simply is this relationship, this continuing relevance of the 'content' of that past juridical act as providing reason to decide and act in the present in the way then specified and provided for.[29]

The explanation is, I think, sound. But we will get still closer to the bottom of the matter if we say that a rule is a relationship between persons. To say that a rule of positive law exists is to say: (a) that its subjects (those upon whom it imposes duties or confers powers, etc.) stand in a certain relationship to the class of person whose—interests—would be served by the rule-subjects' adherence to their duties or exercise of their powers, etc.; and (b) that those rule-subjects stand in that relationship to persons of that class because they (and in some way also the persons whose interests are thus to be served) stand in a certain relationship to the person(s) whose 'past juridical act' therefore provides 'reason to decide and act in the present in the way then specified and provided for'.

Why give explanatory priority, thus, to the relationship between persons? Well, nothing short of an acknowledgement of the reality and value ('dignity') of other persons, as my equals in reality and value, will suffice to make sense of law's most elementary claims on my attention: its claim to *direct* certain choices of mine, to *override* my self-interest in certain respects, to stipulate *conditions* for lending me its assistance in pursuing my purposes, and so forth.

The history of jurisprudence since Bentham is, in some important respects, the history of failure and regression. The Benthamite strategy of describing, analysing, expounding law as a kind of mechanism supposed to be fully intelligible by reference exclusively to its origin in a 'volition'—excluding, that is to say, all reference to its point (that is, its rationale)—was pursued with unsurpassable pertinacity and ingenuity, across more than half the twentieth century, by Kelsen. Its *dénouement* was the spectacular débâcle in which Kelsen, rightly acknowledging the failure of his legal philosophy from 1911 to 1960[30] to explain or even coherently describe law's validity, its normativity, its elementary particle (the norm), and its

[29] *NLNR* 269.

[30] On the phases of Kelsen's work, see e.g. Paulson, 'Four Phases in Hans Kelsen's Theory?', 154–66 at 161.

coherence, severed all links between law and practical reasonableness, embraced even the most open contradiction between legal norms,[31] denied the possibility of legal reasoning even by subsumption of an uncontroversial instance under the corresponding norm,[32] and proposed an admitted fiction as the 'scientific' explanation of validity.[33] Kelsen's lifelong aversion from any resort or reference to practical reasonableness to understand, describe, and interpret law became, in the end, a headlong flight. It was, in the last analysis, an aversion from understanding law as a set of implications of one's seeing the point of serving—respecting and promoting—other persons, and so their interests or well-being, as equal in dignity and value to oneself and one's own. But there is, I am suggesting, no other way of understanding law's claims and directives, their grounds and origins, their force, their limits, and their pathological forms.

IV. CONSEQUENCES OF CONSIDERING LAW WITHOUT ACKNOWLEDGING PERSONS AS ITS POINT

Kelsen's refusal to treat human persons and their interests and well-being as the point of law, a refusal generally shared by analytical jurisprudence from Bentham on, is plainest in his treatment of persons in the law, in the first instance 'physical (natural) persons'.[34] To say that a human being A has a right 'means only that certain *conduct of* the individual A is the object of a legal right... that certain conduct of the individual A is, in a specific way, the contents of a legal norm'.[35] Likewise, of course, with A's duties. Hence: '[i]n juristic considerations we are concerned with man only insofar as his *conduct* enters into the contents of the legal order'.[36] 'The person exists only insofar as he "has" duties and rights' (these rights pertaining, remember, only to that same person's own conduct); 'apart from them the person has no existence whatsoever'.[37] So:

That man and person are two entirely different concepts may be regarded as a generally accepted result of analytical jurisprudence.... [T]he physical (natural) person is the personification of a set of legal norms which by constituting duties and rights containing the conduct of one and the same human being regulate

[31] Hans Kelsen, *General Theory of Norms*, 214 ('[a]s far as conflicts between general norms are concerned, it is not the case—as I claimed in my *Pure Theory of Law*—that a conflict of norms which cannot be resolved by the principle *Lex posterior derogat legi priori* makes no sense... Each of the two general norms makes sense and both are valid'), 223–5.

[32] *Ibid.*, 232–8.

[33] *Ibid.*, 256 ('the assumption of a Basic Norm—for instance... the Basic Norm of a legal order, "Everyone is to behave as the historically first constitution specifies"—not only contradicts reality, since there exists no such norm as the meaning of an actual act of will, but is also self-contradictory.... The cognitive goal of the Basic Norm... can be attained only by means of a fiction').

[34] Kelsen, *General Theory of Law and State*, 95. [35] *Ibid.*, 94. [36] *Ibid.* [37] *Ibid.*

the conduct of this being. The relation between the so-called physical (natural) person and the human being with whom the former is often erroneously identified consists in the fact that those duties and rights which are comprehended in the concept of the person all refer to the behavior of that human being.[38]

In short: juristic thought as such knows nothing of any human person save that person's conduct as specified in legal norms, and does not have as its primary or any concern the interests and well-being of this or any other person.

In the decades of Kelsen's greatest influence, judges confronted by the practical problems of identifying law and rights after revolution turned to Kelsen's account of revolutionary transition. They found no guidance, but some material for rationalizing conclusions reached on other grounds.[39] So too, Kelsen's treatment of the person has been called upon to rationalize judicial abdication from such disciplined and critical concern with the interests and well-being of real people.

Of course, such an abdication can and has, from time to time, occurred without the aid or encouragement of analytical jurisprudence. Among the most striking examples is the justly infamous judgment of the US Supreme Court in *Dred Scott v Sandford* (1857), holding that members of 'the African race' imported into or born in the United States (whether or not they had become free) were not citizens of the United States, and could never be made citizens by Congress even under its undoubted power of naturalization.[40] The decision rested on the fact that, at the time of the Declaration of Independence (1776) and the founding of the Constitution (1789), public opinion—real enough though the Court vastly exaggerates its unanimity—considered that 'the negro might justly and lawfully be reduced to slavery' as 'beings of an inferior order'.[41] At the time of the framing and adoption of the Constitution, 'neither the class of persons who had been imported as slaves, nor their descendants, whether they had become free or not', had any 'rights or privileges but such as those who held the power and the Government might choose to grant'.[42] And 'the duty of the court is... to administer [the instrument they have framed] as we find it, according to its true intent and meaning when it was adopted'.[43] The Court's radical failure, then, was to approach its duty of doing justice according to law without recognizing that law, the whole legal enterprise, is for the sake of persons, and that the founders' intentions were therefore to be interpreted—not, as the Court did, so as to promote their background

38 *Ibid.*, 94–5.

39 See 1968b at 83, 91–5; 1969b at 75, 112; (1970d) at 76–7.

40 60 US 393 at 417, 420, per Taney CJ for the Court (7:2).

41 60 US at 407, per Taney CJ.

42 60 US at 405, per Taney CJ.

43 *Ibid.*

prejudices (from which the Court dissociated itself) against the people they wished to treat as mere property, but rather—in favour of the basic interests and well-being of every person within the jurisdiction so far as was possible without contradicting the Constitution's provisions.

A post-Kelsenian version of *Dred Scott* can be found in the judgment of the New York Court of Appeals in *Byrn v New York City Health and Hospitals* (1972). Discussing the status of children before birth, the Court says:

> What is a legal person is for the law, including, of course, the Constitution, to say, which simply means that upon according legal personality to a thing the law affords it the rights and privileges of a legal person (e.g. Kelsen, General Theory of Law and State, pp. 93–109; Paton, Jurisprudence [3rd ed.], pp. 349–356, esp. pp. 353–354 as to natural persons and unborn children; Friedmann, Legal Theory [5th edn], pp. 521–523; Gray, The Nature and Sources of the Law [2nd edn] ch. II). The process is, indeed, circular, because it is definitional. Whether the law should accord legal personality is a policy question which in most instances devolves on the Legislature, subject of course to the Constitution as it has been 'legally' rendered.... The point is that it is a policy determination whether legal personality should attach and not a question of biological or 'natural' correspondence.[44]

The judgment concludes: 'There are, then, real issues in this litigation, but they are not legal or justiciable. They are issues outside the law unless the Legislature should provide otherwise.'[45] Like the Supreme Court's presumptionless positivism in *Dred Scott*, this New York judgment foreshadows the Supreme Court's holding, six months later, in *Roe v Wade* (1973), that children *en ventre sa mère* are not persons 'within the meaning of the Fourteenth Amendment'.[46] The Court's reasoning to this holding simply recites the uses of 'person' in the Constitution, remarks that 'none indicates, *with any assurance*, that it has any possible pre-natal application', adds (quite misleadingly)[47] that 'throughout the major portion of the 19th century prevailing legal abortion practices were far freer than they are today', and then simply says that these two facts 'persuade us' of the conclusion.[48]

What we see in these cases is a notable failure of judicial reasoning, of intellectual and moral responsibility in face of the law's most fundamental point and meaning: the service of persons. Here, where juristic thought should be most fully and carefully deployed, we find abrupt ukase. The failure and the abruptness are not peculiar to the Court's dealings with

[44] 286 NE 2d 887 at 889, per Breitel J for the Court (5:2). [45] 286 NE 2d at 890.

[46] 410 US 113 at 157, per Blackmun J (7:2). At 162 Blackmun J quotes verbatim, though without acknowledgement, a whole sentence from *Byrn* at 888.

[47] See 1994d at 1–18, 36–7. [48] 410 US at 157–8.

the unborn. In 1886 the Supreme Court was asked to settle the question whether the Fourteenth Amendment's provision forbidding any state to deny the equal protection of the laws to any *person* within its jurisdiction applies to corporations. Its judgment in *Santa Clara County v Southern Pacific Railroad Co.* is prefaced by the answer: '[t]he court does not wish to hear argument on the question.... We are all of opinion that it does.'[49] As Justices Black and Douglas observed in 1949, 'there was no history, logic, or reason given to support that view. Nor was the result so obvious that exposition was unnecessary.'[50] But though this dissenting judgment of Black and Douglas JJ deploys powerful reasons against that 'result', developing the reasons deployed many years earlier in another dissent by Black J,[51] neither the Court itself nor any Justice supporting the result has ever added even a single sentence of justification to the ukase of 1886. Perhaps we should not be surprised, though we are entitled to be dismayed, that no Justice has ever tried to reconcile the 'conclusion' in *Roe* with the 'result' in *Santa Clara.*

As Black and Douglas JJ remark, after demonstrating the arbitrariness of the Court's checkerboard rulings about the application to corporations of the Fourteenth Amendment's several uses of 'person' and 'citizen', and the good sense of a finding that the Amendment's protection is of human beings, natural not artificial persons: '[h]istory has gone the other way'. To which they add, however, that it is not too late for the Court to overrule its error on 'a question of vital concern to the people of the nation'.[52] It is increasingly accepted, by legislative and judicial authorities in most US states,[53] that the unborn child is entitled to protection and remedies in tort even if born dead, and likewise to the protection of the criminal law. These developments, though restricted rather arbitrarily by the constitutional maternal rights declared by the Supreme Court in *Roe,* mark a retreat from simple refusal to take account of the realities of personal existence before birth.

V. ON NATURAL AND ARTIFICIAL PERSONS IN LAW

In a realistic moral, political, or legal analysis of human associations and their actions, 'personality' is a distracting metaphor. For it is a metaphor always tugged between its two historic sources. On the one hand, there is

49 118 US 394 at 396.
50 *Wheeling Steel Corporation v Glander* 337 US 563 at 577.
51 *Connecticut General Legal Insurance Co. v Johnson* 303 US 77 (1938) at 85–90.
52 337 US at 580, 581.
53 See e.g. Forsythe, 'Human Cloning and the Constitution' at 497–502.

persona as mask; to this corresponds the law's carefree attribution of legal personality to *anything* that figures as subject (topic) of legal relations, particularly of property and/or litigious relationships: idols, funds, parcels of property on the quayside, the Crown, and so forth. On the other hand, there is *persona* as individual substance, of a rational nature;[54] to this corresponds nothing (save metaphorically) in the many orderings of human interaction and association which we call groups[55]—nothing except the people who are members. Still, there is a link between these two sources and poles of meaning of 'person'. For the actor's mask is or creates an assumed identity. But a being of a rational nature can, with sufficient health and maturity, make choices (because understanding different kinds of benefit and different ways to one and the same benefit), and by making choices one shapes one's character/identity—one comes to have, and in that sense assumes, a personal identity (one's character). A day-old baby has—*radically*, albeit not yet in actually usable form—this capacity to choose (with such self-determining, intransitive effects). A mouse, whether day-old or mature, lacks that radical capacity, though even as a day-old embryo it has the radical capacity, unlike an acorn or an oak seedling, to run.

Hart recommended that we 'put aside the question "What is a corporation?", and ask instead "Under what types of conditions does the law ascribe liabilities to corporations?"', since this would, he thought, clarify 'the precise issues at stake' in 'extension to corporate bodies of rules worked out for individuals'.[56] The advice to look for the truth conditions of propositions, to understand analogies, and to seek for the principle upon which rules are extended from one context to another was sound. But it was mistaken to assume that such techniques of analysis would dissolve the underlying question whether corporations are entities in the same plane of reality as the human persons whom Hart referred to by his term 'individuals'. The suppression of that question, a suppression implicitly defended if not proposed by Hart, opens the way to the agnosticism,

[54] '*Persona est rationalis naturae individua substantia*': Boethius, *De Duabus Naturis*, c. 3 (Migne, *Patrologia Latina* 64, 1,343); see *ST* I q.29 a.1.

[55] Here and elsewhere in this essay I use 'group' in the second, more specified sense of that highly ambiguous term, the two basic poles of meaning of which are (a) class or category, regardless of cohesiveness, cooperation, or interaction, e.g. all women in Pakistan (held to be a 'particular social group' for the purposes of Art. 1A(2) of the Convention relating to the Status of Refugees (1951): *R v Immigration Appeal Tribunal, ex parte Shah* [1999] 2 AC 629)), and (b) a number of persons who coordinate their activity over an appreciable span of time by interactions with a view to a shared objective (see *NLNR* 150–3; Honoré, 'What is a Group?' in his *Making Law Bind*).

[56] 'Definition and Theory in Jurisprudence' (1953) in *EJP* at 43, also 45, 47. [The advice referred to in the next sentence of the text is at 22.]

arbitrariness, and consequent injustice of cases such as *Byrn v New York City Health and Hospitals*.

Without doubting or challenging the legal rules which distinguish a corporation's rights and liabilities from those of its members, one can make more progress in understanding the relevant realities and interests by first going beyond and behind Hart, to Hohfeld's masterly demonstration that

> transacting business under the forms, methods, and procedure pertaining to so-called corporations is simply another mode by which *individuals* or *natural persons* can enjoy their property and engage in business.[57]

One does not well understand corporate[58] liability (or rights, duties, etc.) until one understands how the liabilities, etc. of human persons, such as shareholders, directors, employees, and other agents, are implicated and affected. The same will be true of the rights and liabilities of other juristic entities such as idols, parcels of goods, etc.; these rights and liabilities are not well understood until one can point, directly or through corporate intermediaries, to individuals with control over ascertainable funds, and so forth.

Hohfeld's more famous analysis of jural relations, though making possible (with a few further specifications) a complete analysis of such relations between persons at any given moment, still leaves something to be explained in terms of the continuity and rationale of rights.[59] Similarly, his demonstration that a corporation's rights, etc., as they exist at any moment, are analysable without remainder into individuals' rights, etc. should not be understood as showing that a group of persons has no reality. A human group or community has all the reality of group action, as well as of the group's members'—human persons'—acts and dispositions to act, dispositions which are manifested in the members' readiness to participate in, and emotional responsiveness to, the group's action, for the sake of the good(s) which give(s) point to that action. That is to say, the reality of a group is the reality of an order of human, truly personal acts, an order brought into being and maintained by the choices (and dispositions to

[57] Hohfeld, 'Nature of Stockholders' Individual Liability for Corporation Debts', in Hohfeld, *Fundamental Legal Conceptions* at 197. Hart's partly critical remarks about Hohfeld's account of corporations ('Definition and Theory in Jurisprudence', *EJP* at 42 n. 22) seem beside the point.

[58] Note that, as Hohfeld incidentally makes clear, the distinction between bodies formally incorporated and unincorporated associations is in many respects much less clear-cut than is often supposed. There is evidence of this in the provisions of the Interpretation Act 1978, s. 5 and Sch. (adapted from the Interpretation Act 1889, s. 19); '[i]n any Act, unless the contrary intention appears…"Person" includes a body of persons corporate or unincorporated.' Notice also that this definition would be mired in an infinite regress but for the fact that the term 'person' also 'includes' individual persons such as those who are the paradigmatic members of bodies, corporate or unincorporated, of persons.

[59] See e.g. *NLNR* 201–2.

choose, and responses to choices) *of persons*. A group's act is defined by its 'public' proposal—that is, by the form in which it is proposed to members of the group, for them to participate in or not. Social acts, though irreducible to the acts of people in the acting group, are constituted exclusively by those acts—acts of individual human persons.[60]

VI. ON PERSONS AS PRIMARY BEARERS OF MEANING AND OBJECTS OF INTERPRETATION

Interpretation is primarily and focally a matter of trying to understand the person or persons whose utterance or other significant performance is under consideration.

Decided entirely by Oxford members of the House of Lords, *Mannai Investment Co. Ltd v Eagle Star Life Investment Co.*[61] might be deemed an Oxford essay in jurisprudence. Does '12th' mean 13th? At large, it clearly does not. But someone who uses the word '12th' may in fact mean 13th, and a proper interpretation of that person's use of the word, in the relevant and properly admissible circumstances of the utterance, may determine that that, being what the person meant to convey and would reasonably have been understood to mean to convey, was the utterance's real meaning, properly construed. As Lord Hoffmann says, 'It is a matter of constant experience that people can convey their meaning unambiguously although they have used the wrong words.' It is true, he adds, that:

> the law is not concerned with the speaker's subjective intentions. But the notion that the law's concern is therefore with the 'meaning of his words' conceals an important ambiguity. The ambiguity lies in the failure to distinguish between the meaning of words and the question of what would be understood as the *meaning of a person* who uses words ...
>
> When ... lawyers say that they are concerned, not with subjective meaning but with the meaning of the language which the speaker has used, what they mean is that they are concerned with what he would objectively have been understood to mean. This involves examining not only the words and the grammar but the background as well. So, for example, in *Doe d. Cox v Roe* (1802) 4 Esp 185, 170 ER 685 the landlord of a public house in Limehouse gave notice to quit 'the premises which you hold of me ... commonly called ... the Waterman's Arms'. The evidence showed that the tenant held no premises called the Waterman's Arms; indeed, there were no such premises in the parish of Limehouse. But the tenant did hold premises of the landlord called the Bricklayer's Arms. By reference to the background, the notice was construed as referring to the Bricklayer's Arms.

[60] See essay 5 (1989a).

[61] [1997] AC 749, [1997] 3 All ER 352. The Lords divided 3:2, with the two University College judges in the majority (supported by a Scot from Corpus Christi College).

The meaning was objectively clear to a reasonable recipient, even though the landlord had used the wrong name... There was no need to resort to subjective meaning.[62]

In an academic essay in jurisprudence, there is no need to employ the rather misleading lawyers' jargon of 'subjective' and 'objective'. But Lord Hoffmann's meaning emerges clearly despite that lawyerly opacity. As he put it later: 'words do not in themselves refer to anything; it is people who *use* words to refer to things'.[63] And again: '[i]n this area [commercial contracts] we no longer confuse the meaning of words with the question of what meaning the use of the words was intended to convey'.[64] The decision of the House was that, similarly, a notice to terminate a lease 'on 12 January 1995' unambiguously conveyed, in all the circumstances of the giving of the notice (including such circumstances as the terms of the lease itself)—as they would have been apparent to and considered relevant by a reasonable bystander at the time—the intention to terminate the lease on 13 January 1995. For that was what a reasonable person aware of the relevant background would have understood to have been the intention and therefore the meaning of the person giving the notice.

Since the law is for the sake of persons, and its rules are fundamentally relationships between persons, it is a mistake to try to understand legal interpretation on the model of the creation and representation, recital, or rendering of works of art.[65] So, if jurists seeking to understand the place of interpretation in law were obliged to choose between 'conversational' and 'artistic' models, they would be well advised to choose the conversational. But the alternatives are not exhaustive.

[62] At 376. Lord Goff, dissenting, accepts that *Doe d. Cox v Roe* was rightly decided—i.e. that the court in that case 'properly construed' the notice—and he does not succeed in explaining satisfactorily why the majority's construction of the notice in *Mannai* itself is not equally 'proper'.

[63] At 378 (emphasis in original).

[64] At 380. On interpreting commercial contracts, see also *Investors' Compensation Scheme Ltd v West Bromwich Building Society* [1998] 1 WLR 896 at 912–13, [1998] 1 All ER 98 at 114e–16f, per Lord Hoffmann; [and now *Chartbrook Ltd v Persimmon Homes Ltd* [2009] UKHL 38 at paras 33, 37–41, per Lord Hoffmann; contrast *A-G of Belize v Belize Telecom Ltd* [2009] UKPC 10 at para. 16, per Lord Hoffmann. More generally, *R (Godmanchester Town Council) v Secretary of State for the Environment* [2007] UKHL 28 at para. 32, per Lord Hoffmann:

> I think that upon the true construction of s. 31(1) [of the Highways Act 1980], 'intention' [in the phrase 'there was no intention... to dedicate [the way over land as a highway]'] means what the relevant audience, namely the users of the way, would reasonably have understood the landowner's intention to be. The test is... objective: not what the owner subjectively intended nor what particular users of the way subjectively assumed, but whether a reasonable user would have understood that the owner was intending... to 'disabuse him' of the notion that the way was a public highway.... Outside the criminal law and parts of the law of torts, it is common to use the word intention in an objective sense, as in the intention of Parliament, the intention of the parties to a contract and even, in Latin, the *animus possidendi* which a squatter must have to acquire a title by limitation.'

[65] See essay I.14, secs III–IV (= 1992a at 139–43).

Like participants in conversation, legal interpreters seek to understand the author who, in making some statement, has exercised a private power or public authority. But legal interpreters are entitled and required to treat that statement, especially when made in the exercise of the public powers of legislation or adjudication, as taking its place in the legal system as a whole—in a complex of persons and their institutions, as well as of principles and rules, including techniques and conventions of drafting and interpreting, all presumptively oriented towards justice and common good. Dworkin has proposed that the political, legally organized community be personified, so that such cohering with a larger whole, like integrity of personal character, be taken as axiomatically required.[66] The proposal shows vividly enough that his general assimilation of legal with artistic rather than conversational interpretation is a choice of the less fitting of the two models he puts forward as the alternatives. True, in legal interpretation as in conversation the intent of the author really matters, as the very concept of authority to make or declare law entails.[67] But a properly juridical interpretation will not be as ready to consider authoritative an unjust as it will a just meaning. Thus it differs from sensible conversationalists, who like good historians are quick to detect, and not too ready to overlook, their interlocutors' perhaps vicious purposes and deficiencies of personal character.

VII. ON THE NATURE OF PERSONS AND THE GROUND OF THEIR RADICAL EQUALITY

What, then, are the 'natural facts' which should inform juristic thought about the persons whom law exists to serve? What is this human nature, which in its bodiliness is known to lawyers as injured in crimes and torts, and sustained by the resources always somehow disposed of in property rights (howsoever artificial); and which in its irreducible intellectuality is known to us as the maker of signs, signatures, and meanings, and subject of intentions? Here jurisprudential reflection can helpfully go back to its origins, perhaps in Plato's reflections on the trial and execution of Socrates.

In the act of, say, speaking to my partner in discourse—perhaps, the court I am addressing as advocate, or the client I am advising as

[66] *LE* 167–75; see also e.g. 225:

> [t]he adjudicative principle of integrity instructs judges to identify legal rights and duties, so far as possible, on the assumption that they were created by a single author—the community personified—expressing a coherent conception of justice and fairness.

[67] See Raz, *Between Authority & Interpretation*, 285.

jurisconsult—I understand my utterance as the carrying out of a choice *which I made*, and in the same act I am aware of my audible uttering, see the hearers register their comprehension, feel, say, confidence or anxiety, remember a past misunderstanding, and hope my statement will make my point. This experience of the *unity (including continuity)* of my being—as a feeling, willing, observing, remembering, understanding, physically active, and effective mover or cause of physical effects and equally an undergoer and recipient of such effects—is a datum which philosophical exploration of human and other natural realities can account for adequately only with great difficulty and many a pitfall. Still, prior to all accounts of it, this intelligible presence of my many-faceted acting self to myself is a datum of *understanding*, one and the same I—this human being—who am understanding and choosing and carrying out my choice and sensing, etc., is a reality I already truly understand, albeit not yet fully (explanatorily, with elaboration). (Indeed, it is only given this primary understanding of one's understanding, willing, and so forth, that one can and typically does *value* such understanding, freedom, voluntariness, unity of being, and so forth.)

So, as Aristotle and (more clearly) Aquinas argue more or less explicitly,[68] any account proposing to explain these realities must be consistent with the complex data it seeks to explain, data which include the proposer's performance, outward and inward, in proposing it. It will not do to propose (as many today propose) an account of personhood such that spirit-person and mere living body are other and other, for 'spirit-person' and 'mere living body' are philosophical constructs neither of which refers to the unified self, the person who had set out to explain his or her own reality. Both of these constructs purport to refer to realities which are other than the unified self yet somehow, inexplicably, related to it.[69]

The only account which meets the condition of consistency with the explainer's own reality and performances will be an account along the lines argued for by Aristotle and Aquinas: the very *form* and lifelong *act(uality)* by which the matter of my bodily make-up is constituted the unified and active subject (me myself) is a factor, a reality, which Aristotle (after Plato) calls *psychē* and Aquinas calls soul (*anima*). In the human animal—the very same animal whose interests in every individual case are to be taken equally into account, in Plato's as in present-day ethics aspiring to be 'post-metaphysical'—from the very outset of his or her existence as human, it is this one essentially unchanging factor, unique to each individual, which explains (a) the unity and complexity of the individual's activities, (b) the

[68] See Aquinas, *De Unitate Intellectus*, III.3 [79]; *Aquinas* 177–9.

[69] See essay 19 at 318.

dynamic unity in complexity—in one dimension, the programme—of the individual's growth as embryo, fetus, neonate, infant...and adult, (c) the relatively mature individual's understanding of universal (for example generic) immaterial objects of thought (for example classes of entities, or truth and falsity of propositions, or soundness/unsoundness in reasoning), and (d) this unique individual's generic unity with every other member of the species. In members of our species the one factor unifying and activating the living reality of each individual is at once vegetative, animal (sentient and self-locomotive), and intellectual (understanding, self-understanding, and, even in thinking, self-determining by judging and choosing). Of course, the manifold activations of these bodily and rational powers are variously dependent upon the physical maturity and health of the individual. But the essence and powers of the soul seem to be given to each individual complete (as wholly undeveloped, *radical* capacities) at the outset of his or her existence as such. And this is the root of the dignity we all have as human beings. Without it claims of equality of right would be untenable in face of the many ways in which people are unequal.

This metaphysics of the activity of discourse, advocacy, adjudication, lecturing, and writing[70] enables jurisprudence to stabilize its most fundamental concepts: the good which, because it is the good of members of a group who all are persons, can and should be a *common* good; and the rights which justice essentially consists in respecting and promoting unyieldingly.

[70] On personal unity and identity as actuated in activities such as writing, see essay 5, sec. I.

2

PERSONAL IDENTITY IN AQUINAS AND SHAKESPEARE*

I. FOUR IRREDUCIBLY DISTINCT EXPLANATIONS OF PERSONAL IDENTITY

Questions about identity are questions about what some object of attention and inquiry is and whether it is the same as, or different from, another object of attention and inquiry. So, for example, one might attend to the uttering of this paragraph, on some occasion, by a speaker. Considering the speaking source of the beginning of the utterance and the speaking source of the end of it, one might ask whether—and if so how and why—one and the same object, this speaking person, was the source of the whole utterance. Explanatory affirmations or denials of identity will be as irreducibly various as the kinds of explanation that, in any field of inquiry whatever, are available for fruitfully answering pertinent questions.

At the beginning of his commentary on what in fact, though not in name, is Aristotle's main treatise on persons, the *Nicomachean Ethics*, Aquinas set out what he considered the four irreducibly distinct kinds of explanation (that is, of *scientia*), corresponding to four irreducibly distinct aspects of reality or, more precisely, real kinds of order.[1] Followers of Aquinas have, to their cost, paid scant attention to this foundational analysis. More generally, many of the failures that mark the history of philosophy and learned discourse involve neglect of the fundamental complexity of reality and the corresponding necessity of diverse kinds of explanation. And as will be immediately obvious, the four kinds of order, understood in the four kinds of explanation, are instantiated paradigmatically in the human person, whose *what-it-is* includes being a *who-(s)he-is*, being an object that is also a subject.

The first kind of order is that of nature, of things that are what they are independently of our considering them and understanding them to

* 2005c ('"The Thing I Am": Personal Identity in Aquinas and Shakespeare').

[1] I have given an account of this part of the prologue to Aquinas's commentary in *Aquinas* 20–3; see also *NLNR* 135–9.

be so—the kind of order that is the subject of all the natural sciences in the broadest sense of that term (which will include a philosophical explanation of the kind being pursued here). Each of us, each human person, is by nature an animal with the naturally given capacity not only for all the kinds of activity found in other animals but also for the kinds of understanding, reflection, explanatory judgment, language, and community with other persons that open up to us in and by being understanding speakers (and readers) of the linguistically communicated—for example, of this sentence. In this order and its corresponding mode of explanation, one has one's identity, one's personal identity, as a given (independently of one's thinking about it, or at all), as one's subsisting and continuity as this animal.

The second kind of order is that of thought itself, of consciousness, observation, attention, consideration, inquiring, understanding, reasoning, and judging. In this order, one has one's identity, one's personal identity, in and by subsisting as knowing, as conscious of one's remembered childhood ignorance, one's present improved but incomplete understanding, and one's envisaged and intended future increase of knowledge. So the primary aspect of one's identity in this order is one's identity as the *subject* of knowing (and erring), who knows (and errs about) oneself along with other objects (as what Shakespeare, as we will see, regularly calls 'the thing I am'). The secondary aspect, then, is precisely one's identity as *object* of one's knowing (and erring), as something of which one has reflexive knowledge both immediate and inferential, in and in respect of one's awareness (and inattention), observing (and oversight), knowing (and erring), choosing and character, self-expressive activity (and ineptitude), and one's whole make up as someone whose given capacities and exercise of them in activities include all this, remembered, present in consciousness, and anticipated. In this order there can be self-awareness, self-deception, and more or less (un)perceptive self-consciousness. Grasp of oneself as object is difficult. Even great philosophers—but not Aquinas—have often failed to notice themselves adequately as objects within the subject-matter of their general propositions, and have thus fallen into the self-referential inconsistency that disqualifies so many philosophical theories. That is why one's identity as object of one's understanding is secondary to one's identity as the subject of coming to know whatever, in all orders of explanation, one knows and intends to come to know.

The third kind of order is that which is anticipated and shaped in deliberation, choice, intentional actions, and thus—because choices last in the chooser until negated by a contrary choice—is instantiated in one's subsisting character as self-centred or generous, constant or treacherous, converted or perverted, and so forth. In this order one has one's personal identity both as self-determining and as self-determined. The latter, the identity that has the content of one's unrepented choices, is the more important: what counts is what one becomes in choosing *what one chooses.* Self-determination, the fact of autonomy and its exercise, is not itself, as such, a good but rather is simply the fact that one can and does make oneself good or evil, and that this freedom is a necessary condition for the moral goodness which is the proper measure deployed (even if only implicitly) in fully adequate explanations and explanatory descriptions in this third order.

The fourth of the four irreducibly distinct kinds of order is that of culture, or mastery over materials (in the broadest sense of material), every kind of *technē*. This order includes not only language but also all (or important elements in all) the crafts of self-expression—of rhetoric, poetry, drama, lectureship, conference-paper writing, and auditing—and not only these as crafts but also the adopting of a *persona* (or *personas*) whereby one communicates to others some truth or falsehood about oneself. Of course, the adoption of such a 'personal identity' is a morally significant act in, and to be assessed by, the third order. (So, too, is a choice to attend to one's health, or to engage in intellectual activity, or to exercise self-discipline in one's choosing.) But the *persona* is an artefact, intelligible and assessable as a means of communication, and by all the criteria applicable to the arts.

In this essay, I shall elaborate and illustrate these four senses of personal identity by pointing out some of the consideration given to them by two great masters of reflective openness to and appropriation of the complexity and depths of human nature and existence. Most if not all the aspects of reality that are alluded to, since the late seventeenth century, with the phrase 'personal identity' are central to Shakespeare's work. Very many of the thoughts his plays and poems are intended to convey and/or do in fact suggest are conveyed or suggested in the resonant opening words of *Hamlet*: 'Who's there?', when those words are heard or read in the context not only of the whole of that play but also of the entire Shakespearean corpus. Shakespeare is a writer who conveys his own understanding of human existence, nature, and personality not didactically like Aristotle, Aquinas, Locke, or Hume, or even dialogically like Plato, but for the most part dramatically. Characters in a play, such as those I shall recall and discuss a little in this essay, are not persons we could bump into and who could make free choices. Everything they are presented as doing is necessitated by their playmaster's choice to make them so. But when the playwright has made us appreciate something of the force and depth of his understanding of human persons, we can reasonably make his characters and their doings material for reflection comparable to the material we find in biographies and autobiographies, which also, after all, present us with a kind of drama in which the reality of the life stories narrated is more or less overlaid by masks, misunderstandings, fabrications, and various (other) principles of selection of parts from a whole known adequately, no doubt, to no one.

II. BODILINESS, CHOICE, AND IDENTITY IN AQUINAS AND SHAKESPEARE

In Aquinas's account, the foundation of one's[2] identity as an individual person is one's material, bodily reality as this body, something which is both distinct from other bodies (human or non-human, animal or inanimate) and a subsisting thing in virtue of its physical, chemical, and biological unity and continuity as an organism. Organic existence is life or living existence. The principle—*principium*, fundamental element, and source—of this life, giving unity and continuity to the shifting material components of the organism, is the factor which Aquinas like Aristotle calls soul: the very *form* and lifelong *act(uality)* by which the matter of one's bodily make-up is constituted the unified and active subject/object, this organism, this human being, this person, from one's outset until one's death.[3]

In her vapid infatuation with Bottom, the weaver magically given an ass's head visible to all but himself, Titania, queen of the fairies in *A Midsummer Night's Dream*, promises him that she 'will purge thy mortal grossness so, / That thou shalt like an airy spirit go' (3.1.153–4). But she doesn't, and even when imaging the fantasy of magical transformations, Shakespeare

[2] The English (as opposed to American) semantics of 'one'—taken always in the first person singular—is highly convenient for expounding the philosophy of personal existence, of action, and of social reality as a function of the existence, activity, and dispositions to act, of individual human persons.

[3] Taking his natural science (biology, embryology, etc.) largely from Aristotle's empirical studies, Aquinas was unaware of the role of the male and female gametes in human generation. He envisaged it as resulting from the active, formative influence of male semen on essentially passive and inanimate (though not formless) female menstrual blood. He therefore supposed that it must naturally take some time (about 40 to 60 days from the outset of conception) for the process of generation to yield a body sufficiently elaborated (*complexionatum*) and organized (*organizatum*) to receive and be organized anew by the rational, specifically human soul. See e.g. *ScG* II c.30 n.12 [1074]; c.89 n.6 [1740]; IV c.44 n.5 [3814]. It seems clear that, had he known of the extremely elaborate and specifically organized structure of the sperm and the ovum, their chromosomal complementarity, and the typical, wholly continuous self-directed growth and development of the embryo or embryos from the moment of insemination of the ovum, Aquinas would have concluded that the specifically human, rational (and sensitive and vegetative) animating form and act (soul)—and therefore personhood (*personalitas*: *ScG* IV c.44 n.3 [3812])—can be and doubtless is present from that moment. If in some cases a single embryo divides to become twins, he would equally have understood this as an unusual (though not in any other sense unnatural) form of generation, either of two new embryos from one now deceased or of one new one from the older one which began a few days earlier and now continues as the newer one's sibling-parent. (On non-sexual generation by division in some animals, see *ScG* II c.86 n.3 [1708(b)].)

never loses hold of the personal identity that each of his characters has by being this living body rather than that. 'What I am' is (includes) for each of us, even the most elevated in rank, the corporeal susceptibility to 'the icy fang / And churlish chiding of the winter's winds, / Which ... bites and blows upon my body / Even till I shrink from cold ...'[4] Of course, Shakespeare has his characters enunciate the common Christian belief in souls surviving death in a life—perhaps heavenly, perhaps purgatorial, or even hellish—after death but prior to the miracle of bodily resurrection. So Lorenzo uses a Pauline-sounding image and conception of the relation between body and soul in his rhapsody for his young Jewish lover Jessica: 'Such harmony is in immortal souls, / But whilst this muddy vesture of decay / Doth grossly close it in, we cannot hear it' (*The Merchant of Venice* 5.1.63–5).[5] And in four plays there is a ghost or ghosts, a kind of reappearance of someone lately living but now dead.[6]

But the ghost in *Hamlet*, the only Shakespearean ghost visible to more than one character on stage, has no part in the play's resolution—and may even be a devil who has assumed the appearance of Hamlet's father, rather than a genuine remnant or reappearance, from Purgatory, of the father himself.[7] And all in all, there is little reason to think that Shakespeare would object to Aquinas's radical insistence on the unity of soul and body, and on one's body—with all its aspects and dynamisms—as the principle of one's soul's individuality. This insistence is very firm: Aquinas maintains that

> my soul is not me (*anima mea non est ego*); and so, even if [my] soul attained salvation in another life, still neither I nor anybody else would have attained it.[8]

A human soul is not a human person. (So between death and resurrection there can survive of me only a remnant, a remnant of a person.[9]) Or

[4] *As You Like It* 2, 1, 6–9: this famous speech by the exiled Duke goes on:

Even till I shrink from cold, I smile, and say
'This is no flattery. These [icy winds] are counsellors
That feelingly persuade me *what I am*.'
Sweet are the uses of adversity ...'

Note: all emphases in quotations have been added.

[5] Cf. 1 Corinthians 15: 42, 53 (Geneva Bible) ('The body is sown in corruption and is raised in incorruption.... For this corruptible [body] must put on incorruption, and this mortal [body] must put on immortality.' The Vulgate Latin for 'put on' is *induere*, to clothe or vest oneself or another; *indumentum* means a garment = vesture.) Note that Aquinas sums up the body-soul dualism which (not unfairly: see *Alcibiades* 129d–30c) he ascribes to Plato (and rejects) in the metaphor of the soul using the body as one uses a garment (*homo utens indumento*): *ScG* II, c.57 n.4 [1329].

[6] *Richard III*, *Julius Caesar*, *Hamlet*, and *Macbeth*.

[7] See e.g. Morris, *Last Things in Shakespeare*, 19–33.

[8] Aquinas, *In I Corinthians*, 15.2 on v.19 [924]). See further *Aquinas* 318n, 179n.

[9] We should not expect to understand this remnant until we understand better than we do the interrelation between time and eternity. Compare Geach, *God and the Soul*, 17–29 with Geach, *The Virtues*, 57–66.

again: 'Bodiliness [*corporeitas*], since it is the substantial form in a human being, cannot be other than the rational soul, which—since it is the act of some *body*—requires that its own matter have three dimensions' and have the make-up not merely of a substantial thing, and a living organism, and an animal, but of a particular thing of the human kind (nature and species).[10] In short, one's bodiliness is the foundation of one's personal identity, a subsisting identity which precedes consciousness and lasts through even protracted terminal unconsciousness until death.

Neither in Aquinas nor Shakespeare does this stress on bodiliness blunt their acute, meditated, and appropriated awareness of one's capacity to be uniquely, particularly ('personally') present to oneself in one's perceiving other things, as also in one's reflecting, deliberating, choosing, and carrying out one's choices in acting. At the very outset of his work, in the first pages of his youthful *Commentary on the Sentences*, Aquinas articulates a datum of our conscious life: 'in one and the same operation I understand something intelligible and understand that I understand'.[11] This he calls one's presence (*praesentia*) to oneself,[12] and of course it is an experience,[13] and understanding,[14] not only of one's acts of understanding narrowly understood, but also of one's active existence as someone feeling,[15] perceiving with one's senses, inquiring, deliberating, judging, choosing, and physically[16] carrying out one's choices. But one must be cautious about the word 'experience' here, lest it be taken to connote that one's consciousness of, say, choosing (at the moment of choice) is passive, a matter of undergoing something like a dream or a feeling of dizziness; rather it is an awareness

[10] *ScG* IV c.81 n.7 [4152a]; see further *Aquinas* 178n. A spirit which is not the form and act of a body—an angel—cannot both share its nature with and yet be an individual distinct from other individuals of the same nature: so each angel is of a different species from every other angel: *ST* I q.50 a.4.

[11] *Sent.* I d.1 q.2 a.1 ad 2; see further *Aquinas* 177n.

[12] *Sent.* I d.3 q.4 aa.4c and 5c; see further *Aquinas* 177–8.

[13] 'Experitur enim unusquisque seipsum esse qui intelligit'—each of us experiences that [i.e. is conscious that] it is he himself that understands: *ST* I q.76 a.1c.

[14] Thomas Wright SJ, who in or before 1597, while associated with the Earl of Essex, wrote an English treatise, *The Passions of the Mind*, clearly following Aquinas, and dedicated its second edition (1604) to the Earl of Southampton (close friend of the late Earl of Essex), says at the end of Ch. 1 that what the ancient injunction 'Know thyself' tells us to seek is a knowledge which 'principally consisteth of a perfect experience every man hath of himself in particular, and an universal knowledge of men's inclinations in common. The former is greatly helped by the latter, the which knowledge is delivered in this treatise.' Aquinas treats what Wright calls 'experience [of oneself]' as itself an understanding, albeit an understanding that can be enhanced by reflection and a philosophical anthropology based on information and reflection on human beings and their inclinations and actions in general.

[15] 'ipse idem homo est qui percipit se et intelligere et sentire'—one and the same human person [man] perceives himself both to understand and to have sensations/feelings: *ST* I, q.76 q.1c.

[16] Thinking/contemplating, too, is a physical act, even if it is also much more than a physical act. So too is mental prayer, whether or not it is divided and distracted as when 'my words fly up, my thoughts remain below' (*Hamlet* 3.3.97).

(a comprehending awareness) of one's own doing something, of acting in the precise sense of making the choice one is making. The 'mastery of [or over] one's own acts' that Aquinas makes so central to his entire philosophy of human matters[17] is not to be understood as if some ghost or homunculus were controlling the parts of some body (and their movements) 'from within', but is rather one's being in a position to adopt, and adopting, a proposal for action—one's own action—in preference to some alternative action(s) (of one's own) which one has envisaged and been interested in.

One has no direct, unmediated, non-inferential knowledge of oneself (as distinct from knowledge of characteristics of human beings in general) other than of what one experiences as happening to one corporeally (which includes psychologically) and of what one is doing or actively inclined to do, whether spontaneously or compulsively, or by one's free choices.[18] This knowledge is of a being extended in time, who can decide to respond to a question with reflective search for an answer, discover what seems to be the answer, communicate it to the questioner, and when it has been communicated *know* that the question was given a relevant answer—that I who heard the question found and gave an answer, and that it is not the same answer as I gave or would have given when I first came across a question of that content in another country forty-eight years ago. *All's Well that Ends Well*, the Shakespeare play on which I shall be focusing, is saturated, from its title and its opening page all the way to its last, with reference, explicit and implicit, to time and the passing of human existence in time, that necessary condition for all my opportunities of commitment and achievement, and all the perils of deflating failure, discredit, and humiliation. The experience of all this is made possible only by memory, prime witness, and testimony to one's personal identity. But from Aquinas's striking readiness to appeal to personal consciousness, his, yours, and mine, as the very pivot of his argument[19] for the radical unity of the animal human person as *corpore et anima unus*,[20] and from his readiness to affirm the consequences of this unity (*anima mea non est ego*) notwithstanding the obvious difficulties this sets up for talking of immortality, we can infer that he would not have been impressed by the thought-experiments which

[17] *ST* I–II prol. and q.1 a.1.

[18] That thesis is an implication of Aquinas's pervasive thesis that one understands (comes to know) the nature of something only by understanding its capacities, and understands its capacities only by understanding its act(ivitie)s: see *Aquinas* 29–33.

[19] *ST* I q.76 a.1c.

[20] 'by/in body and soul one [human being/human person]'. The phrase does not occur in Aquinas but is used by the Second Vatican Council, Pastoral Constitution *Gaudium et Spes* (1965), sec. 14, as a compressed formulation rightly judged to convey the essence of Aquinas's position (a position rejected by virtually all theologians when first articulated by Aquinas).

tempted Locke and his followers to take memory, 'consciousness of the past', to be not merely a witness and testimony to one's subsisting personal identity but its very reality, that in which that identity consists.[21]

Especially when taken as an account of one's subsisting identity as one and the same human being, rather than, as Locke often claims,[22] an account only of one's 'forensic' responsibility, Locke's position defies our most elementary knowledge of ourselves and others as beings who subsist and can and must acknowledge our authorship of our own acts notwithstanding decay or destruction of memories.[23] Locke's radical evasiveness about whether his accounts of *personal identity* are metaphysical (ontological) or merely forensic (moral) lends plausibility to the thought that *personal identity* is perhaps a pseudo-concept.[24] Whatever should be said about the character of residual existence as an intelligence separated from the body of which it was the very form and act(uality), or about a cobbler equipped by a philosophical magus with the memories of a prince,[25] must remain a speculation incapable of undermining one's primary experience and understanding of one's identity as someone who was born on a day one knows only by testimony, verifiably did things both forgotten and remembered, began this inseparably past and present, conscious, intelligent, and physical act of reading, listening to,

[21] John Locke, *An Essay concerning Human Understanding* (1690), II, xxvii.

[22] e.g. *ibid.*, II, xxvii:

> 21. ... whatsoever to some men makes a man, and consequently the same individual man, wherein perhaps few are agreed, personal identity can by us be placed in nothing but consciousness (which is that alone which makes what we call self) ...
>
> 26. Person, as I take it, is the name for this self. Wherever a man finds what he calls himself, there I think another may say is the same person. It is a forensick term appropriating actions and their merit; and so belongs only to intelligent agents capable of a law, and happiness and misery. This personality extends itself beyond present existence to what is past, only by consciousness, whereby it becomes concerned and accountable, owns and imputes to itself past actions, just upon the same ground, and for the same reason that it does the present. All which is founded in a concern for happiness, the unavoidable concomitant of consciousness; that which is conscious of pleasure and pain, desiring that that self that is conscious should be happy. And therefore whatever past actions it cannot reconcile or appropriate to that present self by consciousness, it can be no more concerned in, than if they had never been done.

[23] The classic critiques of Locke on personal identity: George Berkeley, *Alciphron* [1732], VII. viii; Joseph Butler, Dissertation I, 'Of Personal Identity,' appended to *The Analogy of Religion, Natural and Revealed, to the Constitution and Course of Nature* (2nd edn, London, 1736); Thomas Reid, *Essays on the Intellectual Powers of Man* (Edinburgh, 1785), 319–20, from essay III, ch. 4, 'Of Identity'. A recent restatement of them is Wiggins, *Sameness and Substance Renewed*.

[24] That it is a pseudo-concept is argued, without explicit reference to Locke, but drawing on Aquinas and Geach (who however does use the phrase) by Martin, 'Thomas de Aquino y la Identidad Personal'. Cf. also Sokolowski, 'Language, the Human Person, and Christian Faith', taking up the thought that 'person' is not a sortal noun.

[25] Locke, *Essay concerning Human Understanding*, II, xxvii, 15:

> ... should the soul of a prince, carrying with it the consciousness of the prince's past life, enter and inform the body of a cobbler, as soon as deserted by his own soul, every one sees he would be the same person with the prince, accountable only for the prince's actions: But who would say it was the same man?

or writing this sentence, and should regard oneself as responsible (in due measure)[26] for everything one has ever chosen to do.

III. NATURE, INCLINATIONS, CHARACTER, AND HONOUR IN *ALL'S WELL THAT ENDS WELL*

At the most obvious level, mistaken identity is the hinge of plots, subplots, and countless scenes in most of Shakespeare's comedies and romances and many of his tragedies.[27] The ways in which particular characters respond to, and under, their own and others' mistakes of identity convey much of what the dramatist wishes to say about what is most personal[28] to each of them. Shakespeare does not use 'identity' or 'individual' or their cognates. The phrase quoted in my title, 'the thing I am', is from *All's Well that Ends Well.* This remarkable comedy—one of the three known to twentieth-century critics as Shakespeare's 'problem plays'—thematizes many aspects of personal identity, both structurally, through a highly patterned set of personal humiliations induced by or involving mistakes of identity,[29] and discursively, through the articulations of several philosophically and theologically lucid characters whose statements are richly supplemented by the author's own linguistic and imagistic patternings.

Like almost all Shakespeare's drama, this comedy takes for its core a story well known to many in the sophisticated courtly audiences and

[26] Being responsible is one thing; being held responsible is another, even when everyone concerned knows all the facts of the case and is currently acting reasonably.

[27] As Wright, *Hearing the Measures*, 75, observes:

> Compared with earlier Elizabethan playwrights, Shakespeare complicates and multiplies the false supposes under which his gullible characters labor; like theatrical audiences—like *us*—they seem hungry for supposes. Throughout his work characters adopt disguises, change costumes, are misidentified, misread visual or political clues, make verbal mistakes, play-act, pretend to beliefs or affections they do not hold, or are miraculously transformed into other creatures or into people they never supposed they could become. Lies, deceptions, mistakes, and impersonations make his characters' dramatic lives treacherous for them and appealing or appalling to his audience.... Mistakes by the deceived and maskings by their deceivers mirror their counterparts in life and in the theater and are followed at some point in most of the plays by unmaskings, by moments in which the masking personages resume their original identities, disclose or discover their true ones, undeceive their victims, or adopt new masks.

[28] 'Personal' is used by Shakespeare in a variety of relevant senses, e.g. 'no mightier than thyself or me in personal action' (*Julius Caesar*, 1.3.77); 'I know no personal cause to spurn at him' (*ibid.*, 2.1.11). He does not use 'character' in the modern sense of personal individuality.

[29] Price, *The Unfortunate Comedy* is a valuable account of the many misunderstandings of this play down to 1964, and a fine vindication (133–72) of its many excellences, showing how 'the play is tightly knit through parallels, parodies, anticipations, and commentaries' and unified through its theme of honour, or rather, the 'nobility of virtue' (171). The introductory essay in the New Cambridge Shakespeare edition shows that this 'is a great play whose time has come round': Fraser, *All's Well That Ends Well*, 8. Neither Price nor Fraser, however, understands Parolles as fully as may be desired.

well-educated readership for which the plays were obviously intended. Here the tale derives from Boccaccio's *Decameron* (1353), and Shakespeare copies enough of the story's main lines, and of its characters' names, to keep it in the reader's mind, thereby pointing up the substantial changes he makes to both plot and character, and the wholly new (and evidently original, unsourced) subplot he introduces; that subplot will be the focus of sec. V below). Boccaccio's tale is set in that part of the *Decameron* which tells of people who win what they want through their personal initiative and ingenuity. The daughter of a physician falls in love with a young man of much higher social status, a young count. Following him to the French court, she uses one of her late father's secret prescriptions to heal the king, who accordingly keeps his promise to bestow her in marriage to whomever she nominates. She nominates the young count, but he bitterly objects to being married to a woman of such inferior origin and, when the king insists on the marriage, refuses to consummate it. Instead, he goes away to the Italian wars, stating that he will never live with her until she possesses the ring on his finger and bears him a son—two 'things impossible' because of his deliberate absence far away. But she follows him from France to Florence, where she finds him courting a poor but honest young Florentine woman. The abandoned wife reveals her identity to this young woman and her impoverished mother, and arranges with them to allow the count to have intercourse, in a dark room, with someone he supposes is the young woman he loves but in fact is his wife. And they make it a precondition of these liberties that he send ahead his ring as a token of his love. In this way, his wife both obtains his ring and conceives by him a son, indeed twin sons. So, when he has returned to his stately home in France, she is able, in due course, when he is holding a great feast, to confront him with the ring and his offspring. In admiration for her 'good wit', he acknowledges her as his wife and they live happily ever after.

All's Well that Ends Well retains (while subtly changing) all these elements except the twin sons and the great feast at the end. That is replaced by an immensely more elaborate scene in which the young count, Bertram, is comprehensively humiliated in the presence of the king and court and his own mother. The young Florentine woman Diana, whom he thought he had brought to bed with insincere promises of marriage, confronts him at the French court with the ring he gave away as his love-game, or purchase price. As he had mistaken his wife Helena for Diana, in a dark room in Florence, so in the broad daylight of the crowded French court Bertram takes Diana to be the woman to whom he made love and gave his ring. He lies to the king repeatedly about both woman and ring, representing

Diana as a mere camp follower who could be bought at market rate. His multiplying and excruciatingly public[30] lies are soon enough exposed by Helena's appearance on the scene, carrying her (one) child (of unknown sex) in her womb rather than, as in Boccaccio, her arms. Utterly discredited, the young count repents,[31] and declares emphatically that when all has been explained to him, he will love her dearly, ever dearly.

All's Well's philosophically minded interest in the interrelation of nature and virtue (or vice) in personal identity is opened up early in its first scene. Helena's father's skill as a physician 'was almost as great as his honesty', says the count's mother, using 'honesty' in the sense in which it is still close to *honestus*, worthy, virtuous; if his skill had 'stretched so far [as his moral worth, it] would have made nature immortal' (1.1.19–21). And this man's daughter Helena, says the old countess her guardian, is having an education which

> promises her dispositions [that] she inherits, which [education] makes fair gifts fairer: for where an unclean mind carries virtuous qualities, there commendations go with pity; they are *virtues and traitors too.* In her they are the better for their simpleness. She derives her honesty and achieves her goodness. (1.1.39–45)

Recent Oxford and Arden editors have thought that the 'virtuous qualities' which can be carried by an unclean mind ('virtues and traitors too') are accomplishments of 'learning without reference to morality', as contrasted with 'the inborn bad disposition'. But much more probably the playwright is resuming the classical and mediaeval problematic of the unity of the virtues (*connexio virtutum*): as Aquinas explains, virtues like courage, whether 'in us by nature' or by usage (*sive a natura sive ex assuetudine*), are radically imperfect unless the individual person who has them has no vices but rather *all* the virtues, especially the unifying and directing virtue of practical reasonableness, *prudentia*.[32] In Helena, says the countess, all the virtues are to be found unmixed with vice, and thus 'the better for their simpleness'. And this theme the countess interweaves with that of heredity and accomplishment: Helena 'derives [from her father] her honesty and achieves [through her

[30] The play's audience knows what Bertram's courtly audience does not, that Diana was poor but honest and that Bertram's various stories about how he parted with the ring are false.

[31] Some deny this, and certainly everything essential in the play's last minutes is compressed to the barest minimum. But the reality of his repentance is made more plausible for the audience by the play's thesis that Helena's cure of the king's ailment was miraculous and the choice to wager herself on achieving it was divinely approved: Price, *The Unfortunate Comedy*, 152, 161. E.M.W. Tillyard, speaking as 'a modern', reaches the same conclusion in his *Shakespeare's Problem Plays*, 117:

> when Bertram goes on to say that he will love Helena 'dearly, ever dearly', we should believe him implicitly. Helena has got her man; and he needs her moral support with such pathetic obviousness that she never need fear his escape.

[32] *ST* I–II q.65 a.1c.

education, understood in the broadest sense of that word] her goodness', that is her being an unqualifiedly good person (not merely someone good *at*..., or good *as*...).[33] Moments later the countess applies the same analysis, optatively, to her son the young count: 'Be thou bless'd, Bertram, and succeed thy father / In manner as in shape. Thy *blood and virtue* / Contend for empire, and thy *goodness / Share with thy birthright*' (1.1.57–60). This theme—inherited qualities must be appropriated and nurtured by personal choices ('adoption')[34]—is then taken up by the king, after his healing: confronted by the young count's refusal to marry a 'poor physician's daughter', the king judges that the young man is confusing names with realities. The social rank, standing, and repute ('title' and 'honour') that Helena lacks can be bestowed upon her by the king, but what *merits* honour depends upon her own gifts of nature and then, decisively, upon her own acts:

> The property [= quality of character] by what it is should go,
> Not by the title. She is young, wise, fair;
> In these to nature she's immediate heir,
> And these breed honour....
> ... Honours thrive
> When *rather from our acts we them derive*
> *Than our foregoers*....
> Virtue and she
> Is her own dower; honour and wealth from me.

As the play shows, the king's characterization of Helena as 'young, *wise*, fair', like the old countess's assumption that Helena has complete *prudentia*, is simplistic. Nature, her own nature (personality) as a rational animal of strong appetite, makes her susceptible to the infatuation which disables her

[33] The property of being 'good alone'—that is, good *simpliciter*, i.e. without qualification—is taken up, again in relation to Helena, by the King in 2.3.122–30, who equates it with her being 'all that is virtuous'. A recent Cambridge editor, in a generally illuminating commentary, says:

> we are told how Helena inherits her 'dispositions', and also her 'honesty'. She achieves her goodness, though (1.1.30–5). Evidently, natural disposition makes an antithesis to goodness. The papist and the puritan come down hard on this antithesis, but their psychology is disabling, and they fail to grasp what it means. Goodness involves a return on the talents which a provident man puts out at interest... (Fraser, *All's Well That Ends Well*, 24).

Whatever Russell Fraser may mean by 'come down hard on', it is clear that neither the play nor the central ('papist') tradition suggests an 'antithesis' between natural disposition and the human goodness *simpliciter* of perfect virtue (being simply 'a good person'). The gifts *dispose* one to virtue, but only by one's free choices and acts is one actually virtuous, straightforwardly good. The play emphasizes the priority of grace to freedom, and the gratuity and transcendence of grace and Providence: see sec. IV below, though in this essay I largely abstract from this important dimension of the play.

[34] In relation to the adoption of children into a family, the countess declares (1.3.145–6) that 'Adoption strives with nature, and choice breeds /A native slip to us from foreign seeds.' In the context of her moral-anthropological analyses, this remark casts the light of analogy onto the problematic of becoming a good person, even when one has admirably virtuous parentage and gifts and natural dispositions.

judgment of the count, 'a bright particular star ... so above me in his bright radiance and collateral light ... the lion ... his arched brows, his hawking eye, his curls ...' (1.1.88–98). Indeed, the play sets out, it seems, to show from many angles the commingling of good and bad dispositions in each of the persons in whose character it takes an interest. This commingling, and its universality, is articulated by two French noblemen, captains in the count's French regiment fighting in support of the Florentines, who reflect like a chorus on the count's seduction of—as he and the two commentators suppose—Diana, the young Florentine gentlewoman 'of most chaste renown', in the 'spoil of [whose] honour' he 'fleshes his will':

> FIRST LORD Now, God delay our rebellion! *As we are ourselves, what things are we*!
>
> SECOND LORD Merely our own traitors. And, as in the common course of all treasons we still see them reveal themselves till they attain their abhorred ends, so *he* [the count] *that in this action contrives against his own nobility, in his proper stream o'erflows himself.*
>
> (4.3.19–26)

And then, more generally:

> The web of our life is of a mingled yarn, good and ill together. Our virtue would be proud if our faults whipped them not, and our crimes would despair if they were not cherished by our virtues.
>
> (4.3.71-3)

The play looks to ends, and tells that Heaven, using weak human instruments, is capable of great works of healing and restoration and—why not?—conversion, especially when such results were least expected.[35] The ending well which the play projects (without guaranteeing) is the happy marriage that Helena's energetic and ingenious self-possession deserves, a marriage that truly remedies the urges of the flesh not by suppressing them or by following them where they drive, but by taking them up into the integrity of love's person-to-person commitment—no longer a yearning love pouring like water through a sieve,[36] nor yet the lust that makes a person overflow his proper stream.

[35] See Helena's speeches to the king, 2.1.134–43, 146–50, ratified by the king (2.1.173–6), by events, and by Lafeu and Parolles (2.3.1–39).

[36] 'I know I love in vain, strive against hope;
Yet *in this captious and inteemable sieve*
I still pour in the waters of my love
And lack not to lose still: thus, Indian-like,
Religious in mine error, I adore
The sun, that looks upon his worshipper,
But knows of him no more.'
(1.3.196–202)

IV. SELF-CONSCIOUSNESS AND COMMITMENT IN AQUINAS AND SHAKESPEARE

When one tries to extend one's awareness of one's identity, beyond the awareness of one's psychosomatic unity and continuity of being, to an understanding and knowledge of one's own character as formed by one's commitments and other choices, the way to knowledge is beset by pitfalls at least as much as any other kind of search for knowledge. Shakespeare spends much of his play *Richard II* showing this. King Richard is strongly interested in himself, at once self-conscious and self-regarding in the idiomatic senses of those terms—indeed, self-centred. Yet he shows himself to be a man who never understands that he is being deposed in response to his own and his henchmen's crimes, negligences, and injustices—misconduct which he never admits to himself, nor even really denies. For all his regrets, he never approaches or even contemplates repentance. In *Richard III*, his successor, awakening from a dream of visitation by the ghosts or visible souls of associates and friends whom he has murdered, articulates with utter clarity the difficulties, indeed the incoherence, inherent in the self-determining[37] commitment he had made years before 'to have his way',[38] to make the Crown and winning it 'my heaven'.[39] The division within himself, in the end suppressed, is wonderfully articulated in his dialogical soliloquy:

> O coward Conscience! how dost thou afflict me?
> The Lights burn blue. It is no[w] dead midnight.
> Cold fearful drops stand on my trembling flesh.
> What? do I fear my Self? There's none else by;
> Richard loves Richard, that is, I am I.
> Is there a Murderer here? No; Yes, I am:
> Then fly; What from my Self? Great reason: why?
> Lest I Revenge. What? my Self upon my Self?
> Alack, I love my Self. Wherefore? For any good
> That I my Self, have done unto my Self?
> O no. Alas, I rather hate my Self,
> For hateful Deeds committed by my Self.
> I am a Villain: yet I Lie, I am not.
> Fool, of thy Self speak well: Fool, do not flatter.
> My Conscience hath a thousand several Tongues,
> And every Tongue brings in a several Tale,

[37] 'and therefore, since I cannot prove a lover / To entertain these fair well-spoken days, / I am determined to prove a villain ...' (*The Tragedy of Richard III* 1,1, 28–30),

[38] *3 Henry VI* 3, 2, 139. [39] *Ibid.*, 3, 2, 168.

> And every Tale condemns me for a Villain;
> Perjury, in the high'st Degree,
> Murder, stern murder, in the dir'st degree,
> All several sins, all us'd in each degree,
> Throng all to'th' Bar, crying all, Guilty, Guilty.
> I shall despair, there is no Creature loves me;
> And if I die, no soul shall pity me.
> Nay, wherefore should they? Since that I my Self,
> Find in my Self, no pity to my Self.[40]

So Richard III, too, fails to repent, or even to consider repentance as a serious option. Indeed, it would be more accurate to say: he refuses to repent; he does not really try, and his non-repentance is an(other) (guilty) exercise of his self-determination. But at least he understands himself rather well, if not fully.

In the soliloquy just quoted, the typographer of the First Folio (1623) has maximized the apparent reference to a 'self', or even two 'selves', within oneself. Latin syntax is less open to the illusions that English syntax and orthography may generate hereabouts. Take, for example, Aquinas's treatment of one's first free choice(s). Until one reaches a certain age, the 'age of reason' as we say, one cannot make free choices. When one does reach it, one is immediately confronted, Aquinas says, with the rational necessity of deliberating *about oneself* [*de seipso*], and about the direction, the integrating point, of one's whole life [*salus sua*], so that in that choosing one (a) treats oneself like an end in oneself to which other things are related as quasi-means [*de seipso cogitet, ad quem alia ordinet sicut ad finem*], and (b) either does or fails to do 'what is in oneself' [*quod in se est*].[41] This thesis has sometimes been understood as asserting that one's first choice is somehow uniquely dispositive or self-determining, and/or as asserting that there are choices the precise object of which is to dispose of 'one's whole self' in a 'fundamental option', for example for or against God. Both of those readings are mistaken, I believe. Aquinas, in these passages, is pointing to the self-determining character of any significant choice, at any stage of one's life; the precise object of such a choice can be quite ordinary.[42] Aquinas holds that every particular choice one makes, even a choice to do something morally neutral in *kind*, is either morally good or morally bad, because of the place or role it has in contributing to or detracting from one's orientation towards wider purposes (ends) which are not morally

[40] *Richard III* 5, 3, 179–203.

[41] *ST* I–II q.89 a.6c ad 3; *Sent.* II d.42 q.1 a.5 ad 7; *de Veritate* q.28 a.3 ad 4; and see *de Malo* q.7 a.10 ad 8.

[42] Essay IV.1 at pp. 25–7 (= 2003a at 109–111) discusses one such kind of choice.

neutral.[43] And he understands the intransitivity of every chosen act, that is, the fact that it remains *in one*, as part of one's character: this, after all, was the basic Aristotelian distinction between the ethical and the technical in one's doings.

Still, it may be that Aquinas exaggerated the extent to which acting persons integrate their choices around relatively or absolutely 'ultimate' purposes (ends). He may have underestimated, or at least understated, the extent to which such integration does not take place without more or less explicit *commitment*—of a kind that not everyone makes, not even every healthy and active adult—to wide-ranging, open-ended ways of thinking and acting: ways of life like a religious faith, a marriage, a vowed religious (for example, monastic) state, a profession embraced as a vocation. Such character-shaping commitments, by which one constitutes, we can say, a distinct personal identity, are made by choices, and such choices have in a straightforward way the characteristics that Aquinas spoke of in relation to the child's first choice. Such choices are *de seipso*, about oneself, and by them one does *quod in se est*, 'what is in one'.

This last phrase might, of course, be taken to allude to some idea of intrinsically good and virtuous authenticity by fidelity to a somehow given 'real self', which it is one's business to discover and follow, as if it were some supra-moral standard of right judgment and action. But by 'what is in one' Aquinas surely has in mind nothing other than the capacities, inclinations, and dispositions one has, in the first instance as givens of one's make-up, that is, 'by nature', as 'seeds of the virtues'—capacities, that is, to pursue and do *good* and avoid evil (which is never more than good's negation). Love of neighbour has as its standard and measure love of self, but this normativity of love of self would be unintelligible unless love of self means wanting for oneself what is truly good, the fullness of virtue(s) in action.[44] As Shakespeare's choric French captains put it, in response to their own question ('As we are ourselves, what things are we?'), we 'merely are our own traitors', each in rebellion against himself, and 'in his proper stream o'erflow[ing] himself', when he 'contrives against his own *nobility*'. Against one's faults and crimes, one's vices, one should indeed contrive. One's true self, if we wish to speak like that, one's proper self, is the changing self that it is appropriate for one to choose to be, in all the circumstances of one's existence. The *standard* of appropriateness in those circumstances is always the same: simply the moral law: love of neighbour *as* oneself—that is, by the same sense of worth, of intrinsic goods, as makes intelligible one's choices

[43] *ST* I–II q.18 a.9 and parallel passages from *Sent.* (early) and *De Malo* (late).

[44] On the tightly inter-defined circle of practical reasonableness (*prudentia*), justice, flourishing (*beatitudo*), virtue, and love of self and neighbour, see *Aquinas*, ch. IV.

for oneself. Richard Earl of Gloucester, later Richard III, tried to integrate himself around an end that, in the interests of his self-love, involved treating his 'neighbours' as other than what they truly are: persons of intrinsically equal dignity with himself. The attempt was transitively effective enough, but resulted intransitively not in real integration of his own character but in the incoherence of self-love and self-hate, a self-pitying awareness of a paralysing inability—but (whatever he tells himself) this inability is not radical or ineluctable—to take pity on himself or others by repenting and renouncing the path of slaughterous injustice.

Aquinas is quite clear that one's individual nature may contain flaws, such as proneness to anger or lust or sloth, in a form or measure particular to oneself.[45] The fact that there are flaws such as these in my nature, present in my make-up as givens, not as the result of my own or even others' free choices, does not make them other than flaws to be overcome by the choice of (prospectively) self-discipline and (retrospectively) repentance, reform, conversion. Still less is it the case that such givens are to be taken to be a greater part of, or to have a greater influence in, my developed character than the vices or virtues—the settled and ready dispositions to make and carry out morally bad or good choices—by which, as master of my own acts and of my own willingness to act, I constitute myself the developed, decent, or misshapen, thing I am.

Though he does not, I think, articulate it, Aquinas would not have dissented from the summary thesis that (to put it in slogan form) 'faith is the fundamental option'—that the most fundamental and pervasively self-determining, identity-shaping option and commitment one can make is faith, understood not in the classic Protestant sense of an awareness of having been saved, but as the choice, lived out in action and constantly reaffirmed, to believe in God's self-disclosure and offer of adoption into the divine household, and to accept his love as object, and living in it as motive, of all one's most basic orientations to action in which one's neighbour is as valued as oneself.[46] In reaction against the misunderstandings encapsulated in the Reformers' *sola fide*, Catholic contemporaries of Shakespeare preferred to frame their practical theology in terms of love, and Shakespeare too makes no explicitly articulated theme of religious faith. But theme it is, for

[45] *ST* I–II q.41 a.3c; q.78 a.3c; q.31 a.7c; *De Malo* q.16 a.2c; *Aquinas* 93.

[46] See Aquinas's explanation of the virtue of faith (informed by *caritas*), and of its primacy, *ST* II–II q.4. That faith is the fundamental option is proposed, within a broadly Thomist tradition, by Germain Grisez, *Christian Moral Principles*, secs 16-E–G, 23-C, 25-A–F, 26-B, 27-E, 32-D; John Paul II, Encyclical *Veritatis Splendor*, 6 August 1993, sec. 66; see also sec. 65: 'freedom is not only the choice for one or another particular action; it is also, within that choice, a *decision about oneself* [*de seipso*] and a setting of one's life for or against the Good, for or against the Truth, and ultimately for or against God.'

all that. Without the thematizing of belief in divine intervention through human agents by Helena and the count's mother (and by other characters we shall meet, Lafeu and Parolles), the moral conversion of the count, without which nothing can end well, would be too abrupt to carry the play's conclusion. With that thematizing, it does—which does not make the thematizing mere machinery:

HELENA He that of greatest works is finisher
Oft does them by the weakest minister.
Holy writ in babes hath judgment shown,
When judges hath been babes. Great floods have flown
From simple sources, and great seas have dried
When miracles have by the great'st been denied.
...
KING I must not hear thee...
HELENA Inspired merit so by breath is barr'd.
It is not so with [H]im that all things knows
As 'tis with us that square our guess by shows;
But most it is presumption in us when
The help of heaven we count the act of men.
Dear sir, to my endeavours give consent;
Of heaven, not me, make an experiment...

(2.1.135–54)

The king's 'health shall live free, and sickness freely die' on the presupposition, she says (159), of 'the greatest [G]race lending grace...' And grace was so lent, the play seems to say. But the heavenly promised reward, a husband of her choice, remained more nominal than real until she had demonstrated in action the partial truth of her earlier statement about the relation between human freedom and divine providence:

Our remedies oft in themselves do lie,
Which we ascribe to heaven; the fated sky
Gives us free scope; only backward pull
Our slow designs when we ourselves are dull.

(1.1.212–15)

None of Helena's formulations captures the subtle truth about the relation(s) between grace and freedom, but they straddle the truth like a salvo.

V. COMMITMENT AND IDENTITY IN MARRIAGE

Comparable to the identity-shaping commitment of religious faith is the commitment of marriage, a commitment to which, once made, Aquinas and the tradition for which he speaks gives the same name, *fides*—understood not in the thin modern sense of avoiding 'infidelity' but rather as the disposition of this man and this woman, the spouses, to be maritally united to each other and to no other creature in that unique *societas* and friendship, their marriage.[47] This uniquely personal kind of union of two human persons—a union procreative in kind if not in the event—is celebrated by Shakespeare in most if not all his comedies, plays the concern of which to intimate serious truths, ethical, metaphysical, or theological, is clear to careful readers. But the most remarkable of his reflections on the implications of true marriage for personal identity are in his untitled poem known as *Phoenix and Turtle*. It has recently been shown, as I think, that this enigmatic and unparalleled piece memorializes the marriage and death of a young husband and his widow, shortly after her execution for religion, her ever-devoted husband having earlier died in exile for religion.[48] But this only confirms what should be clear from the poem, that it is a married couple whose unity is affirmed,[49] not without hyperbole, but with high seriousness:

Love and Constancy is dead,
Phoenix and the Turtle fled,
In a mutual flame from hence.

So they loved as love in twain,
Had the essence but in one,
Two distincts, Division none:
Number there in love was slain.

Hearts remote, yet not asunder;
Distance, and no space was seen,[50]
'Twixt this Turtle and his Queen;
But in them it were a wonder.

So between them Love did shine,
That the Turtle saw his right
Flaming in the Phoenix sight;
Either was the other's mine.

[47] *Aquinas* 143–54. [48] 2003e.

[49] The poem's final lament ('threne') says that they now rest to eternity 'Leaving no posterity / 'Twas not their infirmity, / It was married chastity.'

[50] Here, it seems, is the poem's disclosure, for some of its original readers, of the identity of the two 'birds'; the Euclidean definition of a line—length and no breadth—points via 'Distance and no space' to Roger and Anne Line, whose name is then echoed in the next stanza's 'shine' and 'mine'. There are many other pointers to this young couple in the poem and the circumstances of its origin. Anne Line was executed in London in February 1601 for having a priest perform a religious ceremony in her house.

Property[51] was thus appalled,
That the self was not the same:
Single Nature's double name
Neither two nor one was called.

Reason in itself confounded,
Saw Division grow together,
To themselves yet either neither,
Simple were so well compounded

That it cried, how true a twain,
Seemeth this concordant one,
Love hath Reason, Reason none,
If what parts, can so remain.

Whereupon it made this Threne
To the Phoenix and the Dove,
Co-supremes and stars of Love ...

Abstractly (at least on the surface) but with an intensity that gives substance to its hyperbole, the poem articulates the philosophical and theological understanding of interpersonal love as a thoroughgoing unity (amounting even to a shared 'single nature') without, however, any loss of personal identity—'neither two nor one', a twain, concordant, of *co*-supremes: a union initiated and maintained, until death, by free choice and the willed virtue of constancy, of being 'true', in a measure which Reason itself affirms, 'as Chorus', but which is far beyond reason in its attaching of this person to that, compounding this 'simple' with that 'simple'. All this is the more remarkable if it affirms, as I think it does, that there can be, and concretely has been, such a unity of spouses even though they have chosen to renounce the sexual intercourse, open to procreation, which is the rationale for this *form* of union.

At the end of *All's Well*, Diana brings to its close her extended *tour de force* of riddling allusion to the substitution of Bertram's supposedly dead wife Helena for Diana in the latter's supposedly 'unchaste composition' with Bertram in Florence:

So there's my riddle: one that's dead is quick,
And now behold the meaning.
Enter Widow, Helena

[51] i.e. individuality (though the word is also punning, I believe, on the disinheritance—for his religion—of the husband allusively referred to throughout, Roger Line—and 'appalled' alludes to the pall, the cloth that hides the chalice before and after the canon of the mass). In such a totally true marriage, the original individuality of husband and wife is so clothed and hidden 'that the self [is] not the same' (a line that equally bears further meanings). In the background throughout is a metaphysical theology like the Friar's in *Romeo and Juliet* (2.6.37): in sacramental marriage, 'holy Church incorporate[s] two in one'.

KING Is there no exorcist
Beguiles the truer office of mine eyes?
Is't real [w]hat I see?
HELENA No, my good lord;
'Tis but the shadow of a wife you see;
The name and not the thing.
COUNT BERTRAM Both, both, O pardon!

(5.3.297–302)

'The greatest Grace lending grace', and human choices responding as they ought—not least with Bertram's 'dearly, ever dearly'—this suffices to make the marital union of Helena and Bertram begin to be real and live, and, as Helena declares by indirection, makes fanciful any prospect that 'deadly divorce' will 'step between me and you'. Her direct response to Bertram's plea for pardon is an allusion (her second) to what she discovered in what was, in fact, the consummation, highly anomalous but not incontestably unreal, of their marriage: 'O my good lord, when I was like this maid / I found you wondrous kind.'[52] As I have already said: though the play's (happy) ending carefully disclaims the fixity of a Last Judgment, it affirms the prospect that, as Helena's love will no longer be poured away as in a sieve, so Bertram, in loving her ever dearly, will no longer o'erflow his stream. Rather—so we are encouraged at least to hope—he will have the quiet strength of a self-contained and virtuous identity, as a man and a husband.

VI. HUMILIATION AND IDENTITY IN *ALL'S WELL THAT ENDS WELL*

The humiliation of Count Bertram has, as I said, its artful parallel in a brilliantly comic subplot. The playwright has provided the count with a flamboyant and eloquent personal assistant, Parolles ('Words'). Upset at the loss of the regimental drum in the Sienna-Florence wars, Captain Parolles boastfully undertakes to recapture it by a lone mission behind the enemy lines. Other French officers in the count's regiment, anticipating that Parolles will lack what it takes to accomplish such a difficult mission, ambush him as he is excogitating some deceitful cover story to explain away his failure. They blindfold him, and then act—albeit farcically—as

[52] 'Kind' means both affectionate/generous and nature/species, and both meanings are here in play. 'Found/find' is one of the play's theme-words (used more than twice the average rate for Shakespeare's plays, and its primary reference is to discovering what or who someone *really* is, in their personal/individual nature. So Helena's words here directly echo the words of the chastened Parolles to his new master, Count Lafeu: 'O my good lord, you were the first that found me' (5.2.41); Parolles' 'every braggart shall be found an ass' (4.3.40); and many other instances in the play.

if they were a foreign military unit, perhaps Muscovites, and with threats of death and torture interrogate him about the dispositions of the French forces and the personal character of the very officers who, unrecognized by him, are interrogating him—and who now include the count his master. Just as in a dark bedroom the count will mistake the identity of the woman he is lying with, so Parolles in the darkness of a blindfold mistakes the identity of his interrogators and, in love with his own life, acts the traitor—or at least, enacts the identity of a traitor. He betrays (so it seems) the dispositions of the forces and extravagantly defames his master and the other principal officers until, pretending to be about to execute him, they take off his blindfold and let him experience, not death but crushing humiliation. Mocking him with politesse and irony, they all depart, leaving him alone on stage:

> Yet am I thankful: if my heart were great
> 'Twould burst at this: Captain *I'll be no more*,
> But I will eat and drink and sleep as soft
> As captain shall. *Simply the thing I am*
> *Shall make me live*: who *knows himself* a braggart,
> Let him fear this; for it will come to pass
> That every braggart *shall be found* an ass.
> Rust sword, cool blushes, and Parolles live
> Safest in shame: being fooled, by foolery thrive;
> There's place and means for every man alive.
>
> (4.3.333–43)

The scene immediately shifts back to the main plot; Helena, having accomplished her purpose in doing what was necessary to conceive by her husband (and obtain his ring), is conferring with Diana and her mother about the next phase in her 'business'. Many earlier plays in the European repertoire had involved the bed-trick, as does Shakespeare's *Measure for Measure* (probably a couple of years before *All's Well*). The biblical prototypes of this substitution ruse[53] were well known. But *All's Well*, perhaps uniquely, seeks to give us a glimpse of the inwardness of it, of what it is like to go through with it. Shakespeare prepares for this, much earlier, when underlining the humiliation for Helena in her husband's rejection of her, and introducing—as an element unknown to Boccaccio—Helena's own sense that she ('poor thief') has stolen the position of wife, that her doing so is cause of the count's imperilling himself in the wars (3.2.112–16),

[53] Leah and her father play the bed-trick on Jacob (Genesis 29: 21–4). One of Leah's sons, Judah, has the bed-trick played on him by his widowed daughter-in-law Thamar (Genesis 38: 14–26) in circumstances which include getting his ring as a precondition, and conception of twins from one act of intercourse.

and that her 'ambitious love hath so in me offended' that she must go on barefoot pilgrimage 'my faults to have amended'. The direct humiliation that was involved, along with much else, in the successful bed-trick is now conveyed with compression and delicacy in two sentences, prefaced by Helena's characteristic expression of faith in providential order; speaking to Diana's widowed mother, she says:

> Doubt not but heaven
> Hath brought me up to be your daughter's dower,
> As it hath fated her to be my motive
> And helper to a husband. But O, strange men,
> That can such sweet use make of what they hate
> When saucy trusting of the cozened thoughts
> Defiles the pitchy night! So lust doth play
> With what it loathes for that which is away.

(4.4.18–25)

'Sweet use' alludes directly to the pleasure of what, for her, was (as well as was not) a *usus matrimonii*, marital intercourse;[54] 'defile', 'saucy' (in Elizabethan, lascivious), and 'lust doth play with what it loathes' allude with equal directness to the painful indignity of her involvement, her presence to the act as if by proxy, as someone as radically misidentified as can be—subject of the deception in which her own husband in his very thoughts (and acts!) is 'cozened', that is deceived and betrayed,[55] and thus

[54] Her prospective first *usus matrimonii* was floridly evoked by Parolles (2.4.39–44) as go-between excusing the count's purportedly initial and temporary refusal to participate in it:

> The great prerogative and rite of love,
> Which, as your due, time claims, he does acknowledge;
> But puts it off to a compell'd restraint;
> Whose want, and whose delay, is strew'd with sweets,
> Which they distil now in the curbed time,
> To make the coming hour o'erflow with joy
> And pleasure drown the brim.

Notice also that Shakespeare takes great care to depart from Boccaccio by having Helena arrange that Bertram receive letters informing him of her death—information which arrives just before their tryst. So, though his intent in courting Diana was probably adulterous, his eventual act of intercourse did not involve him willing to go through with adultery; it was at least open to him to be willing the marriage he probably but not certainly insincerely promised Diana in order to get her agreement (as her thought) to surrender to him her virginity. Notice, thirdly, that Aquinas would doubtless point out the equivocation or error in '*both* not sin' in Helena's on the whole remarkably clear-headed moral analysis of the bed-trick as '... wicked meaning [Bertram's] in a lawful deed, / And lawful meaning [hers] in a lawful act, / Where both not sin, and yet a sinful fact' [Bertram's probable intent to fornicate] (3.7.45–7).

[55] The deception/betrayal is, on a first level, by the ruse of Diana and Helena, but on a second level is by the count's own desire/lust/'will'. This becomes clearer when one notices the association of ideas and images—so characteristic of Shakespeare's works—between this passage (taken with the parallel cozening of Parolles, the 'hoodman' (4.3.115) deceived behind a blindfold) and the passage in *Hamlet* where Hamlet denounces, in a series of hyperboles, the decision of his mother to go in marriage to the bed of Claudius. The hyperboles are constructed for the relish of readers familiar with a philosophical vocabulary, and conclude that in Gertrude 'reason panders will'. The thesis is that in preferring Claudius to her true husband Gertrude has acted on 'compulsive ardure' [ardour]

reduced to object even as she is made (albeit by making herself) the object of his 'use' in an act which should be but is not (even while, at the level of behaviour, it is) the height of inter-*subject*ivity.

The wintriness of this personal experience beneath its sweetness is suggested two sentences later, in a passage like a patch of colour in this most monochrome of Shakespeare's plays—a passage further emphasized by its explication of the play's own title, as Helena turns away from Italy towards her home country:

> But with the word the time will bring on summer,
> When briars shall have leaves as well as thorns,
> And be as sweet as sharp: we must away,
> Our wagon is prepared, and time revives us;
> All's well that ends well; still the fine's the crown;
> Whate'er the course, the end is the renown.[56]
>
> (4.4.31–6)

'As sweet as sharp': this is one of several metaphors for the play's motif (see sec. IV above), the commingling of good and bad dispositions in a single character, the 'web of our life' being 'of a mingled yarn, good and ill together' (4.3.71).

How does this evocation of mingled yarn apply to Parolles? There can be no other character in Shakespeare who is the object of more unbridled denigration—denigration first at the hands of every substantial character in the play, and thereafter by virtually every critic. As he enters for the first time, Act 1 scene 1, Helena says to herself and the audience 'I know him a notorious liar, / Think him a great way fool, solely a coward.... fixed evils... superfluous folly.'[57] In Act 2, not very long after he has engaged in a remarkable dialogue with good old Lord Lafeu, an aria in duet which shows them as of one mind about the miraculous nature of Helena's cure of the King,[58] Parolles is rounded upon by Lafeu who apparently all unprovoked unleashes a torrent of insults, writing Parolles off as 'my good window of

and her 'judgment' or 'sense' has been and is 'apoplex'd, for madness would not err, / Nor sense to ecstasy was ne'er so enthrall'd / But it reserv'd some quantity of choice / To serve in such a difference. What devil was't / That thus hath *cozen'd you at hoodman-blind*?' (3.4.70, 72, 73–77). The 'devil' or 'hell' is not, however, anything outside Gertrude, but is—this is Hamlet's argument—the lust that 'mutine[s] in' her 'matron's bones' (83), bringing her to 'live / In the rank sweat of an enseamed bed, / stew'd in corruption, honeying and making love ...' (91–3). (To note the parallel and its sense is not to assume that Hamlet's accusation is sound in relation to Gertrude.)

[56] This triplet of substantially identical saws seems to echo the Latin triplet near the end of (pseudo-)Aquinas's commentary on (pseudo-)Boethius, *In Boethii De Scholarium Disciplina*: '*exitus acta probat* et item *finis coronat* et insuper *a fine omnia denominari*'. There were sixteenth-century editions of this commentary available in England.

[57] However, Helena is the only one of his denigrators who does not condemn the man wholesale, for she goes on (1.1.106): 'Yet these fixed evils sit *so fit in him* / That *they take place when virtue's steely bones / Looks cold i'th' wind*.'

[58] A considerable shift from Boccaccio.

lattice ... Thy casement I need not open, for *I look through thee*' (2.3.214–16). Indeed, everyone (except for a time his master the count) claims to be able to *see through* and *find out* Parolles, and loudly declaims against what they 'find' and 'see'. The play's Clown writes Parolles off as a fool, and Lafeu returns to the charge: 'there can be no kernel in this light nut. The soul of the man is his clothes. Trust him not in matters of heavy consequence' (2.5.43–6). The count's distinguished mother's first words about Parolles are: 'A very tainted fellow, and full of wickedness. My son corrupts a well derived nature / With his inducement.' In Florence a citizen onlooker denounces him as he approaches on horseback alongside the count: 'one Parolles: a filthy officer he is in those suggestions for the young earl.' Diana, the object of the count's desire, likewise points to Parolles: 'Yonds that same knave / That leads him [the count] to these places. Were I his lady, / I would poison that vile rascal.... that jackanapes with scarves' (3.5.83–5). One of the French officer noblemen describes him to the count: 'he's a most notable coward, an infinite and endless liar, an hourly promise-breaker, the owner of no one good quality worthy of your lordship's entertainment' (3.6.7–12). The claims to know *what Parolles is* continue uninterrupted to the end: 'so bad an instrument', says Diana; 'I saw the man today, if man he be', says Lafeu; and now the young count himself, self-servingly, joins the chorus:

> What of him?
> He's quoted for a most perfidious slave
> With all the spots o'the' world taxed and debauched,
> Whose nature sickens but to speak a truth. Am I or that or this for what he'll utter, That will speak anything?
>
> (5.3.200–8)

What the play *shows* about Parolles is rather different. True, he is shown to be a braggart whose boasts trap him into attempting the impossible, and who is (he says) prepared to lie on oath to save face. And his letter to Diana, warning her against Bertram's unscrupulousness and immaturity is indeed 'tainted', addressing her as if she were willing to sell her favours, if not hinting that he would be a better beneficiary of them than his master. But the accusations that he leads Bertram into wickedness are never verified: the playwright makes it clear that it was the count's own decision to go to the Tuscan wars rather than attend to his wife, and the count's decision to pursue Diana. So far as the play indicates, Parolles does no more than second these decisions, and act as an agent and go-between (not wholly reliable) in carrying them out. When he is begging for his life he pours out purported details of the French and other pro-Florentine forces and of their officers' bad character. But nothing shows that the details are really military secrets of use to the enemy, or at all—his purported counting of the infantry asserts that numbers totalling 3,600 total 15,000—and the character sketches he offers are either fair enough (as when he says the count his master is 'a foolish idle boy but for all that very ruttish'), or so laughably exaggerated that no real enemy would give them a moment's notice. And whatever the truth about his character before his humiliation and self-knowledge, he afterwards acts as a teller of the truth, who at appropriate royal command says what he knows about Bertram's relationship with Diana, and does so without dishonouring him (or her). As the play reaches its benign resolution, his new master, wise old Lord Lafeu, weeping with joy, confers on Parolles a subtly new status, raised from the depths, by asking for a handkerchief for his own use from 'Good Tom Drum'.

We must conclude that Parolles' carefully constructed *persona*, his sartorial and rhetorical flamboyance, and his affectation of military zeal, was a failure of technique. As a means of achieving and keeping influence with the immature it was engaging and seductive, but as a means of gaining the confidence of the relatively mature, it was the failure that Lafeu encapsulates with his dismissive 'no kernel in this light nut; the soul of this man is his clothes. Trust him not ...'

The phrase 'The thing I am', in Parolles' meaning, signifies what was true about him all along (so to speak), underneath his bragging and overreaching of himself in foolhardy action and shame-faced deception. We, like so many of the play's leading characters, *suppose* we know the nasty truth about him, but perhaps, led on by all his critics, are mistaken about his real identity, that is, his true character. Certainly it seems that he does not confront or acknowledge the whole truth about himself, and his resolution to eat, drink, and sleep soft in a lower station—indeed, in 'foolery'—is neither morally uplifting nor true to his own manifest talents.[59] Still,

[59] These talents are first shown in the brilliance of his bawdy, philosophical, but crisp exposition of the case against virginity (and in favour of procreation rather than libertinism)—an exposition with echoes of Erasmus's colloquy on marriage and of William Gager's Latin Oxford play *Meleager* (see 2003m). They are soon shown again in his equally brilliant duet with Lafeu about the miraculous character of Helena's cure of the king, 'the rarest argument of wonder that hath shot out in our latter times'—a duet that ends:

PAROLLES Nay, 'tis strange, 'tis very strange; that is the brief and tedious of it; and he's of a most facinerious [abominable] spirit that will not acknowledge it to be the—
OLD LAFEU Very hand of heaven.
PAROLLES Ay, so I say.
OLD LAFEU In a most weak—
PAROLLES And debile minister, great power, great transcendence, which should indeed give us a further use to be made than alone the recov'ry of the king, as to be—
OLD LAFEU Generally thankful.

(2.3.28–38)

The play, moreover, seems to back this hypothesis against 'our philosophical persons [who] make modern [i.e. everyday] and familiar things supernatural and causeless' (2.3.2–3).

there is no reason to doubt what the play suggests, that the humiliation has induced in him a renunciation of his constructed social *persona*, and a kind of humbling that is an at least partial reshaping of his personal identity, under the description (we may suggest) of gaining or regaining *authenticity*. Two or three years earlier, in *As You Like It*, Shakespeare used the same phrase, 'thing I am', to mark a moral conversion—of the wicked eldest brother Oliver—a repentance which must, if that play is to make sense, be thoroughgoing. (The young count's conversion or repentance in the final moments of *All's Well* must equally be thoroughgoing, if that play is to end as its audience must unequivocally wish.) By recalling from its outset the parable of the prodigal son, *As You Like It* shaped itself towards the multiple conversions, moral and religious, with which it ended. And the murderously wicked elder brother revealed his own unanticipated moral transformation with the words:

> I do not shame
> To tell you *what I was*, since my conversion
> So sweetly tastes, *being the thing I am*.
>
> (4.3.135)

The thing I am thus stands over against *what I was*; more cautiously put, there has been a vital change—'my conversion'—in the one and the same *I*.

VII. REPENTANCE AND IDENTITY

So: to the radical shaping of personal identity by religious faith and by commitment to one's spouse in marriage can be added its shaping in conversion or repentance. Parolles' change of heart is left ambiguous, like his future relationship with his new master, Lafeu. Most critics take it at its surface appearance, a future as the old lord's fool, but Lafeu's 'I'll make sport with thee' may well envisage something much less unequal, such as riding together to the hunt. Be that as it may, Parolles' resounding 'simply the thing I am shall make me live' echoes two of Shakespeare's earlier articulations of a convert's change of personal identity. Oliver's we have just seen articulated by one who was the vicious would-be murderer of his own brother, and who, finding himself the beneficiary of that brother's generosity of spirit in action, is transformed by repentance into someone fit to love and marry a woman of high character and charm. Perhaps more well known is the new King Henry V's repudiation of Sir John Falstaff, entertaining enough but fundamentally vile, come up to Westminster on stolen horses to claim high office in the court of the new monarch, his long-time companion in low life:

HENRY V ...
Presume not that I am the thing I was;
For God doth know, so shall the world perceive,
That *I have turn'd away my former self;*
So will I those that kept me company.
When thou dost hear I am as I have been,
Approach me, and thou shalt be as thou wast,
The tutor and the feeder of my riots:
Till then, I banish thee, on pain of death,
As I have done the rest of my misleaders ...[60]

The new king does not deny that, as Falstaff's companion Prince Hal, he has been the kind of person that Falstaff happily assumed him to be—just the kind of person that the old king denounced him as being, an enemy of the kingdom's common good, a favourer of ruffians, wild dogs, scum. This 'dear and deep rebuke' by the dying king elicited from the Prince the same response as Bertram makes to his humiliation at the end of *All's Well*: 'O pardon me ...' The articulation of the new king's new identity in repudiating Falstaff affirms in act the repentance and reform that he chose, it seems, when he was at the king's deathbed, his conscience scoured by that rebuke. To all this we must add, however, that when this play is taken with its companion play *Henry IV, Part One*, the reality of this repentance, reform, conversion remains in doubt, along with the reality of the depravity that the Prince affected and appeared to share with Falstaff. For at the end of the first occasion when we are shown these two men together, the Prince discloses to us in soliloquy that in consorting with Falstaff in crime, he'll 'so offend to make offence a skill' so that in due course 'when this loose behaviour I throw off ... like bright metal on a sullen ground, / My reformation, glitt'ring o'er my fault, / Shall show more goodly and attract more eyes / Than that which hath no foil to set it off' (1.2.195–205). Yet the seriousness of Henry's reformation seems vouched for by much in the preceding scenes, including his testing by his dying father, and his own testing of and by the Chief Justice. The fact is that the playwright teases us, across three whole plays, with the possibility that Henry V was never really debauchee, never really convertite, and so, perhaps, never the authentic Christian king he ends up seeming. Dissipation and conversion, too, can be masks, *personae* in the word's oldest sense. The choice of masks

[60] *The History of King Henry IV, Part Two* 5.5.55–62. Modern audiences, directors, and readers tend to side with Falstaff, but are deeply and to some extent wilfully mistaken.

both shapes and reveals the person who chooses them, but only to one who knows that the choice has been made and persisted in. The Shakespearean soliloquy puts an audience in such a God-like position—or seems to.

VIII. MATURITY AND DECAY

Both *All's Well* and *As You Like It*, comedies of repentance or conversion, also make searching play of aging as maturation and decay. Early in *All's Well*, the king, who in his own long and apparently incurable illness has 'persecuted time with hope' (a hope he has by now abandoned), reports and seconds the saying of Helena's late father, the great physician whose skill, had it stretched as far as his honesty, would have 'made [his] nature immortal' (1.1.13, 19). Speaking to the young count Bertram, the king says:

> 'Let me not live,' quoth he,
> 'After my flame lacks oil, to be the snuff
> Of younger spirits, whose apprehensive senses
> All but new things disdain; whose judgments are
> Mere fathers of their garments; whose constancies
> Expire before their fashions.'[61] This he wish'd.
> I, after him, do after him wish[62] too,
> Since I nor wax nor honey can bring home,
> I quickly were dissolved from my hive
> To give some labourers room.
>
> (1.2.58–67)

This contrast between younger and older is part of the play's strong surface structure, in which old king, old countess, old lord Lafeu, and old Florentine widow are foils to the immaturities, ventures, achievements, follies, fecundity, and resource of Helena, Bertram, and Diana. And as the play's last act opens, the king is again speaking to Bertram, now returned from Florence, and both prematurely and casually asking forgiveness (for having gone away to the wars against a royal prohibition):

> KING The time is fair again.
> BERTRAM My high-repented blames
> Dear sovereign, pardon to me.
> KING All is whole,
> Not one word more of the consumed time;
> Let's take the instant by the forward top;

[61] Note the orderly philosophical sequence: 'apprehensive senses', 'judgment', 'constancy [of will]'.

[62] It now, regrettably, seems necessary to observe that this wish is not even conditionally an intent or willingness to commit suicide or accept euthanasia.

For we are old, and on our quick'st decrees
Th'inaudible and noiseless foot of time
Steals ere we can effect them.

(5.1.36–42)

As You Like It gives to its maverick melancholic Jaques a bravura rendering of late-sixteenth-century reflections on the 'seven ages of man', finishing up:

Last scene of all,
That ends this strange eventful history,
Is *second childishness and mere oblivion,*
Sans teeth, sans eyes, sans taste, sans everything.

(2.7.163–6)

The stagey morbidity of Jaques's reflections is undercut by the immediate entrance of the hero's aged servant, the venerable Adam, a man of unalloyed goodness and constancy. Almost 80, he has in an earlier scene declared himself, somewhat optimistically, 'strong and lusty': '... my age is as a lusty winter, / Frosty but kindly. Let me go with you, / I'll do the service of a younger man / In all your business and necessities.' However, the hungry journey into exile does prove too much for him, physically. And in any case, Jaques's depiction of decrepitude does tell a truth.

Does it tell the whole truth about the personal identity of someone thoroughly disabled by age? The question is difficult, and not directly answered, I think, by either Shakespeare or Aquinas. But just as neither believes that the dissolution of the person in death leaves no surviving remnant awaiting resurrection in heaven, purgatory, or hell, so neither believes that descent into the darkness of senility or other like disorder of mind expunges the identity shaped by free choices—by a freedom now lost. The choice to repent can cancel vice, but decay cannot cancel virtue or merit, the personal identity known to him who is 'the top of judgment'. As the heroine of another of Shakespeare's three 'problem plays' says:

ISABELLA How would you be,
If He, which is the top of judgment, should
But judge you as you are? O, think on that;
And mercy then will breathe within your lips,
Like man new made.

(*Measure for Measure* 2.2.88–95)

She is pleading for her brother's life with a man at the height of his powers, in the full pride of life, and of unshaken repute for his austerely virtuous character. She assumes that in the eye of God this man's character is nonetheless not free from vice—and so is in need of forgiving mercy—but she will be astounded and for a time incredulous when such vices, and very great ones, are disclosed to her later in their encounter. It is not too hazardous to think that Shakespeare and Aquinas, with the whole tradition in which they work, take for granted that what matters in divine judgment on human persons is not how weak they are through immaturity, illness, or senility at the time of their death, but *what they are* in the identity they have *made for themselves*. For: this identity they make (if they do) by their free choices, during the time, short or long, that they can freely choose. And: whereas God can remedy all deficiencies of nature such as immaturity or senility, giving to each the psychosomatic condition of a human being of the age Christ had at his death and resurrection,[63] even 'the greatest [G]race lending grace' (and by divine mercy making one 'new made') does not and cannot override the freedom by choice to make oneself what one's choices determine one to be, until (if ever) one chooses to repent or reverse them sometime later in this life.[64] Such seems to be Shakespeare's working assumption, too.

IX. CONCLUSION

As Germain Grisez, who took up and developed incipient elements of Aquinas's philosophical understanding of the person, rightly says:

> A person is in all four of the orders, and he embraces all of them in himself. In the person the four orders are distinct, irreducible, yet normally inseparable. The unity of the person is unlike the unity of any entity which is enclosed within one of the four orders. The unity of the person is mysterious and must remain so. This unity is immediately given in human experience, and it cannot be explained discursively, since reason cannot synthesize the distinct orders in a higher positive intelligibility.[65] The unity of the person is not an intelligible principle of a fifth order, distinct from the four, nor is it something like an entity belonging to one or another of the four orders hidden behind all of them. The four aspects of the person all involve and in a way include one another, as the four orders always do.... The person is the self who *unifies* these four distinct and irreducible but normally inseparable aspects. The self [which in the next paragraph Grisez speaks of, synonymously, as the soul] is a unifying principle ...[66]

Grisez's account seems intended to suggest that he does not accept Aquinas's account of the human soul as the substantial form of the human body, an account which looks as if the soul and thus too the human person as a whole is to be understood and explained as simply a reality in the first (natural)

[63] *ST* Supp. q.81 a.1; *ScG* IV c.88 n.5 [4231]—'by reason of the perfection of nature which is found in that age alone'.

[64] *ST* I–II q.113 aa.3 and 4. So until death ends the personal narrative, we can say no more of someone than what the king says in the play's last lines: 'All yet [so far] *seems* well ...'

[65] Grisez, *Beyond the New Theism*, 349.

[66] *Ibid.*, 350–1.

order. But in speaking of the soul as that which—we know not *how*—unifies all the irreducibly distinct but interpenetrated aspects of the person, including the bodily (that is, the psychophysical), Grisez retains the elements of Aquinas's account that I have emphasized, above all its insistence that that which is here and now producing physical and psychophysical effects by audibly speaking, and being acted upon physically and psychophysically by hearing, is identical—*qua* human person, I myself—with that which is reasoning logically (or perhaps correcting or failing to correct logical invalidity), *and* carrying out a choice to devote precious time to this act of communication, *and* using internalized technical resources, especially the English language and the techniques of effective utterance.[67]

In short: there is the identity I have as the particular human being I have been since I was formed in my mother's womb with all the radical capacities, and thus the nature, of a human person. There is the identity I have as a person conscious of much that I have experienced and thought since first I began to be aware of myself (my toes and my fears ...) in relation to other things including people, and began to inquire and assert and deny and argue. There is the identity I have as a person with the character I have made for myself by the choices I have made within the constraints, and between the opportunities, that have arisen from the nature of things, the choices of others, and the accidental conjunctions, by *all* of which factors, as Shakespeare and Aquinas each depict, divine providence 'shapes our ends, / rough hew them how we will' (*Hamlet* 5.2.11). And there is the identity I have as an object of cultural forms (a citizen of Australia) and a user of them (English-speaking, tie-wearing) and projecter of new and partly new *personas*.

Gary Taylor has recently suggested that Shakespeare errs in trying to 'flatter the would-be transcendentalism of the ego':

> Maybe we should not believe Hamlet, or Shakespeare, when he tells us 'I have that within which passeth show' [*Hamlet* 1.2.85]. Middleton did not believe him. Middleton answered Shakespeare ... 'You're the deed's creature.' What is within does not matter, if it does not come out; the secret subjectivity that you imagine

[67] On the philosophical significance of the distinction between *langue*, language as resource (found in dictionaries and in the competence of speakers), and *parole*, language as use of that resource in acts of communication (of inexhaustible variety and, often, novelty), see Braine, *The Human Person: Animal and Spirit*, 353–63, 461–5, etc. Braine's entire book is of great value as a thoroughgoing rethinking and restoration of an Aristotelian-Thomistic understanding of the human person and personal identity, making rich use of natural science and of recent English-language 'analytical' philosophy. Not unlike Grisez, he concludes that the soul is what gives nature, identity, unity, and operation to the human body and its parts, and that

> we can utilize the much more general Aristotelian conception of 'formal cause' and apply it to the soul, but it is...entirely optional whether we apply to the soul the separate (and in the development of Aristotle's thought, later) idea of 'form' as the correlate of 'matter' (527).

for yourself is irrelevant, by comparison to the substantive social and material identity created by what you have actually done. You are created by, and a slave to, your actions, not your self-regarding fantasies.[68]

Aquinas and Shakespeare, I have argued, would agree that we are each, in some respects, created by our actions, as well as by our experiences and skills, and scarcely by our self-regarding fantasies; and that as creatures of our actions we will be slaves to them unless we choose to reassert the mastery over them that we had when first we chose them. They would agree that 'the secret subjectivity that you imagine for yourself' matters far less than 'the substantive social and material identity created by what you have actually done'. But they would add that what one has actually *done* was the carrying out of intentions, proposals shaped, however rapidly, in deliberation and adopted by choices, and that one's deliberative shapings of intention, extended (by those choices and their execution) into one's actions, are one's real subjectivity, at once secret and made known. And, moreover, that one's 'social identity' may be a mask of which one might, in principle, be stripped as of a blindfold, revealing even to oneself something partly the same but partly different.

[68] Taylor, 'The Cultural Politics of Maybe' at 256. The allusion is to Thomas Middleton (1570–1627), *The Changeling* [first performed 1624] 3.4.140.

3

ANSCOMBE ON SPIRIT AND INTENTION*

I

Elizabeth Anscombe's work was, and is, a paradigm of Christian intellectual life. Since the faith has realities, not myth, for its object, and since everything that can be inquired into is what it is by virtue of God's actuality, one's inquiries and every other element in one's intellectual life—whether elements on which faith bears or elements remote from the faith—can be pursued with confidence that they will not contradict faith and if successful will have brought one a little closer to understanding what is really so. That is the free and diligent way in which Anscombe carried out the work that is widely and reasonably judged the twentieth century's outstanding English Catholic philosophical achievement. The two volumes of her essays[1] put together posthumously in 2005 and 2008 (with promise of yet more) by Mary Geach and Luke Gormally enable us to get a better sense of the paradigm.[2]

The introductions by Mary Geach, reflecting on the essays with a philosophical energy and style reminiscent of her mother's work, and imparting some valuable information both about the genesis of some of the notable essays and, especially in *FHG*, about the genesis of Anscombe's faith and philosophizing, and her approach to Aquinas, accompany shorter prefaces by Gormally, imparting helpful editorial information. The one philosophical remark Gormally allows himself is that Anscombe's understanding of the proper valuation of human life is of fundamental importance to her work in moral philosophy. This judgment must have guided the editors' decision to head up the essays in *HLAE* with seven papers under the heading Human Life, and to open with three remarkable

* 2009a, a review essay on the two books mentioned in n. 1. Reproduced here are secs I–III and V (part); the substance of the other portions is in essay V.21, secs IV and VIII, and an endnote to essay V.9.

[1] (1) Geach and Gormally (eds), *Human Life, Action and Ethics* (hereafter *HLAE*); (2) Geach and Gormally (eds), *Faith in a Hard Ground* (hereafter *FHG*).

[2] See Gormally, Kietzmann, and Torralba, *Bibliography of Works by G.E.M. Anscombe*.

lectures given at the University of Navarre in 1979, 1985, and 1988. There could have been no better beginning than the first of these, given by Anscombe under the title 'Analytical Philosophy and the Spirituality of Man', the great interest of which is only enhanced by the inclusion in *FHG* of a paper from two decades earlier, 'The Immortality of the Soul', wrestling with much the same matters. With these four essays, one should also take 'The Causation of Action', which has been put into *HLAE*'s second section (Action and Practical Reason).[3]

All these five essays attack the delusion, called by Anscombe Cartesian, that thinking and willing (say, intending) are to be taken to be events in an immaterial (spiritual) substance or medium: soul or spirit. Explicitly or implicitly, they all affirm the reality of the human soul and the spiritual nature of that human life, a spirituality that belongs to man's substance. They defend, that is, a 'metaphysics of the spirituality of man's nature'.[4] They do so with great resource: attentiveness alike to the history of philosophy and the contemporary physiology of movement, brain states, etc.; and a close-in and sinewy phenomenology, holding one closely to an awareness of what one's thinking and intending is really like—really is. But their point and thrust is always to instil and enforce an awareness, and some theoretical grasp, of just how radically *different* the immaterial and spiritual is from the material, including brain states, sensing, and mental imaging and other kinds of imagining. Of just how strange—relative to cause and effect in natural events, and to all that we can picture—our *everyday* thinking and intending (say, pointing to something's shape as opposed to its colour)[5] really is, when analysed philosophically.[†]

The proto-treatment ('Immortality of the Soul'), never published by Anscombe, proposes that 'the spirituality of the human soul is its capacity to get a conception of the eternal, and to be concerned with the eternal as an objective...',[6] and notes that from a certain point of view this non-reliance [only] 'on sensible things, physical probabilities, and purely conventional procedures', this 'acting as if something unseen were there', is a kind of 'insanity'.[7] The later treatment ('Analytical Philosophy and the Spirituality of Man') holds that 'the immateriality of the soul consists at bottom in the

[3] The twenty-three essays in *HLAE* are grouped into: (i) Human Life: seven essays, including two on the ontological status of human zygotes (papers which should be taken along with essay 20 in *FHG*, 'The Early Embryo: Theoretical Doubts and Practical Certainties'); (ii) Action and Practical Reason: four essays, among them the ambitious fifty-page 'Practical Inference'; and (iii) Ethics: twelve essays, on moral philosophy, intention, 'double effect', conscience, euthanasia, and non-treatment of controls in clinical trials. The twenty-five essays in *FHG* are not grouped, but about half are on faith and matters of, or proximate to, faith (such as immortality, transubstantiation, and sin) and about half are on matters of morals, including contraception, nuclear weapons, simony, and usury.

[4] *HLAE* 6; likewise *FHG* 76. [5] *HLAE* 7–15. [6] *FHG* 74. [7] *Ibid.*, 82.

fact that you cannot specify a material character or configuration which is equivalent to truth'.[8] Anscombe immediately adds, rightly:

> This thought is more like a chapter heading for many thoughts, the fruits of many investigations, than a conclusion of one. But it is already implicit in the consideration that the physical act of pointing, considered purely as a material event, is not even an act of pointing—it is just the fact that a finger, say, has a certain line.

At least this is so where the pointing is, say to colour *rather than* shape.

> Now if that is so we can say that man *qua* body can't be described as pointing to the colour rather than the shape. For his act of pointing is certainly a bodily act; but it is not *qua* bodily act that it is determined as pointing to the colour. This does not mean that we have to postulate a different, *another* act of pointing by a *different sort* of substance, an immaterial one... But we can say that this bodily act is an act of a man *qua* spirit.[9]

In these and various other respects the later paper is better, as well as being in its own right a superb introduction to Anscombe's thought, to its relationship to Wittgenstein's and the ancients', and to the strangeness that is at the root of human dignity.[10]

Still, the earlier essay provides a valuable clue to one of the several diverse springs of her thought, of her way of doing philosophy. The essay's one authorial footnote remarks that Christians, unless superstitious, do not believe that spirits (the angels) hear them, *nisi in Verbo*.[11] This is one of the relatively few references the editors have not identified, but it is certain that it alludes to Aquinas' argument in *De Veritate* q.8 a.13c that angels cannot know the secrets of our hearts, 'unless one or another *cogitatio* is revealed to an angel in the Word [*nisi in Verbo ei reveletur*]'. (Nowhere else does Aquinas use the phrase she quoted.) And this place in Aquinas, which Anscombe thus surely read with attention, is one which most strikingly asserts what I am calling this strangeness of commonplace human thinking and willing. For in the three sentences preceding the one she quotes from, Aquinas gives his reasons for taking angels to be naturally unable to read our thoughts; and the two key reasons are (1) that to think about something

[8] *HLAE* 15. [9] *Ibid.*, 15–16.

[10] I am not saying that Anscombe's view is strange. On the contrary, the author of the article on Action in the online Stanford Encyclopedia of Philosophy reports:

> many philosophers reject more than just reason-to-action laws. They believe, more generally, that there are no laws that connect the reason-giving attitudes with *any* material states, events, and processes, under purely physical descriptions. As a consequence, commonsense psychology is not strictly reducible to the neural sciences, and this means that reason explanations of action and corresponding neural explanations are, in the intended sense, 'independent' of one another (Wilson, 'Action').

[11] *FHG* 80.

requires an *intentio* of one's will (so as to focus on the matter and one's ideas about it), and (2) that such 'movements of [human] will have *no dependence on or connection with any natural cause*'. True, one's acts of will, as Aquinas explains here and in later writings,[12] are not independent of or unconnected with divine causality operating both as the creative and sustaining cause of everything and as the truly universal good that is the good to which one is responding when one['s will] responds to particular intelligible goods. But no chain of causality in the created world known to science and experience embraces or accounts for them.

In a lecture she gave in 1989 ('Sin: Voluntariness and Sins of Omission'), Anscombe resumes her critique of the 'quasi-Cartesian' 'doctrine of an act of the will, which is *willing*'.[13] She worries that Aquinas may hold this doctrine, but in the end is doubtful that he differs so widely from her about all this.[14] Be that as it may, this late lecture is one of the very rare occasions when she raises the question how far she agrees with or dissents from Aquinas. Overall, the influence of Aquinas on her thought was greater, I believe, than she made clear. Mary Geach says that Anscombe 'devised a method, which she recommended to me, of mining Aquinas for helpful philosophical points' and 'philosophically usable bits in the *Summa theologiae*' by 'considering to what Catholic doctrine her particular philosophical problem was relevant'.[15] Still: Anscombe set her own philosophical problems for herself, and even when her conclusions approximate to Aquinas's fairly closely, as in *Intention* and the essays I have mentioned, her argumentation is her own. It's just that she thought of Aquinas as 'a strikingly good philosopher',[16] from whom help is always on the cards albeit, like everything else in philosophizing as such, never guaranteed.[17]

The bearing on human dignity and worth of Anscombe's position about the radical difference between one's thinking and willing, on the one hand, and one's sensing, feeling, imagining, digesting, etc., on the other hand,

[12] *De Malo* q.16 a.8; *ST* I q.57 a.4; q.105 a.4; q.106 a.2; I–II q.9 a.6; *ScG* III. 88–91 (e.g. c.88 n.2: 'No created substance can act on the will, or be a cause of our choice, except by acting as a suasive [*nisi per modum persuadentis*]').

[13] *FHG* 129. [14] *Ibid.*, 137–8. [15] *FHG* xiv. [16] *FHG* 135.

[17] Much of Anscombe's philosophical effort is directed, at least implicitly, towards thinking through what is needed from philosophy in relation to faith, and the faith. In an address of 1975 she said that

> the only possible use of a learned clever man is as a *causa removens prohibens*. There are gross obstacles in the received opinion of my time and in its characteristic ways of thinking, and someone learned and clever may be able to dissolve these. (*FHG* 18; likewise *FHG* 91, in the fine essay-pamphlet on transubstantiation).

For an example of such obstacle-clearing, one may take not only the explications of human spirituality but also her devastating critique of Hume's very influential arguments against the possibility of miracles and prophecies (*FHG* 40–8).

is not extensively articulated. On the one hand, it seems in a sense clear: to possess dignity is to be somehow raised above a common level, and the considerations she brings out so well do show how each human being, just as having the *capacity* for the thinking and willing that are quite above the brain states and other natural processes that are this spirituality's human substrate, is raised above the other animals and creatures of every kind of which we have experience. We have all the levels of reality they have, and much more. In a sense, infinitely more, as knowers and choosers. On the other hand, if we ask how this dignity is also a worth, a matter of intrinsic and generic value, we reach considerations that Anscombe, especially perhaps in her writings from the mid-1970s and after, was wont to call *mystical*.[18]

In one essay she explores the ways in which knowing this worth is 'connatural'. As she says, this is not how St Thomas uses 'connatural'; rather, it is a (neo-)scholastic[19] application of the term, and one whose source she does not claim to know.[20] It denotes a kind of knowledge that 'is not unavailable to those of us who are not virtuous but may be restrained by shame from misusing people we have the power to misuse[, but] is strong only in good people'.[21] I heard her deliver that address in 1981 and thought then, as now, that this sort of taxonomizing of knowledge, while it has its truth, does little to convey the truth at issue, even when the categorizing is given the vigorous workout she does. She doesn't go in for it much. 'Mystical', though formally a category, and one taken from another context, has the advantage that it directs the mind to what I have called the strangeness of the spiritual, its radical difference from the material which nonetheless it forms and animates. This strangeness Anscombe also profitably calls wonderful. In doing so, she deliberately appropriates the prayer from the canon of the Tridentine mass: *Deus, qui humanae substantiae dignitatem* mirabiliter *condidisti*... [O God, who didst wonderfully create/establish the dignity of human substance/nature...].[22] In her most full-dress treatment of the issue she links this dignity to both origin and end:

But men, being spirit as well as flesh, are not the same as the other animals. Whatever blasphemes the spirit in man is evil, discouraging, at best trivializing,

[18] In 1975 she speaks of the mystical directly:

Sexual acts are not sacred acts. But the perception of the dishonor done to the body in treating them as the casual satisfaction of desire is certainly a mystical perception. I don't mean, in calling it a mystical perception, that it's out of the ordinary. It's as ordinary as the feeling for the respect due to a man's dead body: the knowledge that a dead body isn't something to be put out for the collectors of refuse to pick up. This, too, is mystical though it's as common as humanity (*FHG* 187).

[19] *FHG* 200. [20] *HLAE* 60. [21] *Ibid.*, 66; similarly *FHG* 100.

[22] *FHG* 197; see also *HLAE* 72.

> at worst doing dirt on life...It is irreligious, in a sense in which the contrasting religious attitude—one of respect before the mystery of human life—is not necessarily connected only with some one particular religious system...A religious attitude may be merely incipient...Or it may be more developed, perceiving that men are made by God in God's likeness, to know and love God....Such perception of what a human being is makes one perceive human death as awesome, human life as always to be treated with a respect which is a sign and acknowledgement of what it is for.[23]

II

Some main reviews of *HLAE*, and the publisher's blurbs for both *HLAE* and *FHG*, give special prominence to Anscombe's 'classic essay "Modern Moral Philosophy"', and one of its several theses got special attention. Simon Blackburn, a successor of hers in Cambridge University's chair of Philosophy, rightly pointed to the impact of two of the essay's theses: its

> influence initiated the return to the idea of virtues as the central concepts needed by moral thought. It was enormously influential, turning firstly most of her Oxford generation, and then probably a majority of philosophers worldwide, against utilitarianism as a moral and political theory, but also against the then-prevailing view that ethics is at bottom a matter of personal commitment or choice, a tool for voicing persuasions or exchanging social pressures.

Blackburn then turned to the further thesis, also emphasized by Michael Dummett's review; I would paraphrase it as: the modern sense of 'moral', 'moral duty', 'morally ought', and 'obligatory' are derived from an ethic of divine law, and ought not to be used by—because their meaning is essentially unavailable to—those who believe that we know of no such divine law.[24] Blackburn's paraphrase is: 'Anscombe's thought was a version of the Dostoievskian claim that if God is dead everything is permitted.' Blackburn comments that this is poppycock and was refuted by Plato.

Blackburn has badly misunderstood Anscombe. Her thesis and argument here entail that the idea of the 'permitted' is equally unavailable: if we know of no divine law, the question whether everything (or anything) is or is not *permitted* simply falls away. Doubtless, Anscombe is not confronting and explicitly repudiating what might be called the thought underlying Dostoyevsky's claim as commonly understood, the thought that distinctions between virtuous and vicious, just and unjust, deeds are all empty—if intelligible at all, have no grip on our reason—once we

[23] *HLAE* 269–70.

[24] See *HLAE* 175–94. Blackburn: TLS 30 Sept. 2005, 11–12; Dummett: Tablet 9 July 2005, 22.

take God to be non-existent (or, as Plato in his late work would add, to be unconcerned with or thoroughly indulgent about human affairs). But nor is Anscombe proposing or sponsoring or even insinuating that thought. On the contrary, her whole discussion assumes that any non-theistic moral philosopher who followed her advice and desisted from using the terms derived (she thought) from divine-law ethics could still find real distinctions to be drawn between the virtues and the vices, the just and the unjust, and more generally the reasonable and the unreasonable in action, and could still hold that 'it is in any case a disgraceful thing to say that one had better commit this unjust action'.[25]

But then I think it follows that this thesis of Anscombe's lacks what one might call working importance. If the issue is not about ethical scepticism as such, but only about the precise *force* of a negative ethical predicate such as 'is vicious and unreasonable', and if it is further accepted that this could extend to 'vicious and unreasonable whatever the circumstances', then I think the issue is quite marginal. And that seems to me confirmed by these essays. She never resiles from the thesis, and it makes occasional, low-key appearances,[26] but it plays little role, and in her 1989 lectures on sin she proceeds on the basis that 'against divine law' and 'against right reason' each define sin. True, she says that the two definitions are 'equivalent as far as concerns what they cover' only if reason dictates the worship of the true deity.[27] But this is far from saying that, if it failed to acknowledge *that* 'dictate', reason could have no concept of sin. I should add that I rather doubt the thesis, even when marginalized. I do not think Anscombe was right to say that *dei* in Aristotle (who, as she says,[28] did without a notion of divine law) is really different from the modern 'moral ought',[29] and I can't see that, for example, Gaius the second-century AD jurist is presupposing a divine law when he treats natural right and natural law as synonymous with what natural reason requires of us.

III

Mary Geach's preface to *HLAE* discloses that Anscombe's profoundly and rightly influential book *Intention* came from a course of lectures given as a result of her stand, in June 1956, against Oxford University's conferral of an honorary degree on the man who ordered the massacres at Hiroshima and

[25] *HLAE* 193 (= III 42). [26] e.g. *HLAE* 147 in 1974. [27] *FHG* 117–19.

[28] *Ibid.*, 148.

[29] See *NLNR* 297, 343. At *FHG* 148 she translates *dei athanatizein* 'should be on the side of the immortal', and if divine law is out of the picture, as it is for both Aristotle and modern moralists, that 'should' seems to me a moral ought, even though the object(ive) it, in this instance, directs us to (being on the side of the immortal—immortalizing) is an unusual, unfamiliar, and strategic one.

Nagasaki. But (in line with one of the theses or prescriptions in 'Modern Moral Philosophy') that book rigorously eschews any concern with moral reasoning or with the question what bearing the fruits of her analysis of intention would or should have for ethical analysis or moral judgment or assessment. The book ascribes a descriptive and explanatory priority to the description(s) which behaviour has in the practical reasoning (the deliberations) by which the acting person shaped up the proposal he or she adopted by choosing to behave (act or forbear) in this way. This shaping of description(s) in practical reasoning and deliberation is not a matter of finding a description under which the behaviour one is determined to carry out will be acceptable to oneself or others. Rather, it is settled by what one considers a necessary or helpful means to achieving an objective (usually a nested set of objectives) that one considers desirable, in view of the factual context as one understands its bearing on both one's end(s) and the means that one judges serviceable for achieving such end(s). In summarizing her book's main thesis in this way, I use terminology (for example, 'proposal', 'adopt') which is not altogether hers. But her favourable albeit informal and oral response to an exposition and analysis of intention which I gave in her presence in 1990 served, in my mind, to confirm my opinion that her main thesis was, or was in line with, what I have just set out.

However, her essays' discussions of intention in an *ethical* context tend to depart somewhat from that account. Characteristic is what she says (c. 1978) in judging immoral (simoniacal) the action of certain Catholic priests in Africa who have made it a condition of adult baptism that the convert first make a payment to the Church, their good motive or further intention in making this demand being to require the convert to 'show his good disposition', that is, his willingness to support the Church financially. She says:

> ...what determines what the intention is? Can you determine it by telling yourself and others 'I am not doing *this*, I am doing *that*'? No, you can't: the facts of the case, the conditions and consequences of one's act are mostly enough to determine *what* intentional act you are performing, they often declare it very loud and clear, and you cannot make it not be so by a story you tell or by inviting people to perform some little semantic exercise and *call* something a different name from the name that belongs to it from the facts of the case.[30]

This passage offers two alternative candidate-determinants of the action-defining intention-in-the-act: (1) telling yourself something, performing a little semantic exercise, etc.; and (2) the conditions and consequences of your act, 'the whole context that fixes and determines

[30] *FHG* 242–3.

the further description of the kind of act you are performing'.[31] But these alternatives omit what the *Intention* book had treated as decisive: your real practical reasoning, in which you identified the behaviour as a satisfactory means to the end(s) you were concerned to attain. Conditions, consequences, and context are surely determinants *as they figure in one's practical reasoning*, one's deliberating towards choice (not to be confused with some story one tells oneself or others in order to escape or attract some *moral* characterization of the act). Nor does it matter what words one uses in this reasoning. If, to take the case in hand, one judges that it would be good to make payment to the Church a condition of baptism, it doesn't matter whether one uses (thinks in terms of) the words 'payment' or 'condition' or their equivalent in any other language. Still less, of course, does it matter to the relevant description of what one is doing whether one knows the term 'simony' or is aware that hereabouts there is a class of acts judged by the Church to be seriously wrong.

In criticizing Anscombe's ethics-oriented analysis here for overlooking the act-analysis (intention-analysis) employed in her non-ethical writings,[32] I am resuming a criticism I have made before, especially in relation to her essay 'Action, Intention and "Double Effect"'.[33] But I do not dissent from her conclusion in relation to the clergy's well-motivated but wrongful demand in the African missions. And as Geach's preface remarks, the essay shows how far Anscombe was from being a party-line woman. One can add that it also shows that her interest in ethics was not simply apologetical, and like her paper on usury's injustice[34] witnesses that it was in no way limited to sex and killing.[35]

[31] *Ibid.*, 243.

[32] This distinction is not tight: in 'Practical Inference', mostly a revisiting in 1974 of *Intention*, Anscombe says by way of illustrating an inference: 'The British... wanted to destroy some German soldiers on a Dutch island... and chose to accomplish this by bombing the dykes and drowning everybody.' This she says is an instance of a decision 'to kill everyone in a certain place in order to get the particular people one wants'. But equally it may have been an instance of a decision to kill German soldiers by bombing the dykes, accepting the deaths of any Dutch civilians as a side effect, perhaps fairly, perhaps with vicious unfairness depending on the context and the planners' reasoning about its bearing on all affected. In her earlier account of this event, in 'Mr Truman's Degree' (1956) (*Collected Philosophical Papers*, vol. 3, 66), she recounts it in a way somewhat more open to the second version, in which there simply is no intent to kill everyone as a means to killing some but 'unscrupulousness in considering the possibilities'. One can agree with her that such unscrupulousness in considering side effects can 'turn it into murder', since 'murder' extends beyond its central paradigm—killing with intent to kill—to secondary cases such as intent to seriously wound, or recklessness about the lethal side effects of one's acts (especially, but not necessarily, unlawful acts) [see essay 10 at pp. 193–4].

[33] See essay 10 at pp. 189–93.

[34] And her notable papers on promising and on political authority in *Collected Philosophical Papers*, vol. 3. [On the former, see *NLNR* 298–308, 343; on the latter see essay IV.4 (1987d), sec. III.]

[35] There is in *HLAE* an essay on 'The Dignity of the Human Being' which shows how far Anscombe was open to new lines of ethical thought. The editors simply call it 'undated', but it surely dates from late 1985 or 1986. In it she articulates the argument worked up by English-speaking

IV

At a Dominican House of Studies in 1989, in public lectures on sin, Anscombe revisited in a remarkable way some themes I have pointed up in this review essay's first section. As her lectures end, she says that one of her purposes in giving them was 'to heighten my awareness of the amazing character of some of the things that we believe',[36] a purpose in line, as I have said, with much of her work in pure philosophy, too. Her final reflections are on the possibility of living here and now in the presence, the constant consciousness, of God. But here, too, part of her purpose is to wean us away from imagining some mental experience, some Cartesian *cogitatio* within a 'Cartesian consciousness'.[37] No, it is a matter of keeping in mind that God sees and hears us, and that there are divine commandments. And this keeping in mind is no more, in turn, than this: that a truthful account by us of the ultimate reasons for what we are at any time doing would mention those facts about divine knowledge and will. A reasonable mind ought always to have this form of divine presence to it. 'The absence of it, which is all but universal in the human race, is what I call "God's Exile".'[38] And then she adds, disclosing an amazing depth in all that she had elsewhere written about human spirit:

> Exile from what exists, even in Hell, is impossible for God. The exile of which I have been trying to speak is not an exile from our physical or mental existence: that too is impossible. It is an exile from our spiritual existence...

NOTE

† *Philosophical analysis of the spiritual aspect of pointing and other everyday acts*... (at nn. 4–6). See also the other works of Anscombe mentioned and briefly discussed in this connection in the Introduction to the present volume, at pp. 5–7.

Catholic philosophers after 1979, especially in the period 1982–83: 'making human zygotes in a dish or test-tube is an enormity because the operator is a manufacturer—even if he uses his own sperm—not a father... the child who is conceived by a mother, and who has a father, is not unequal to them' (*HLAE* 70–1). (In a letter to me in February 1983, clearly accepting the gist of the argument, she comments on its formulation.) This articulation of the argument from equality (the argument adopted as one amongst others in *Donum Vitae* in 1987 and then relied upon in the *Catechism of the Catholic Church*, para. 2377; and see essay 17, sec. III; and essay III.17) is incomplete, and too quick, no doubt, for most readers to take on board. But the argument is there, and there are even traces of the first part of it in an address she gave to clergy in Melbourne in 1978 ('children are to be begotten... not produced...': *FHG* 202).

[36] *FHG* 155. [37] *Ibid.*, 148. [38] *Ibid.*, 149.

Part Two

Group Identity and Group Acts

4

PURPOSES, PUBLIC ACTS, AND PERSONIFICATION*

Hart's inaugural lecture in 1954 virtually removed the issue of personification—'corporate personality'—from the agenda of Jurisprudence for a quarter of a century. The lecture teaches that statements about the rights and duties of corporations are statements about the rights and duties of those concerned in the affairs of the corporation (whether as members, officers, or agents)—though not simply *about* them, as former, abbreviationist, or collective name theories had supposed. Rather, such statements draw a conclusion of law from unstated legal rule-premises. This conclusion of law in each case discloses, summarily, the *reason* why those rights and duties of individuals *follow* from certain other dealings of individuals (whether of the individual members whose rights and duties are being affirmed, or perhaps of other individuals). The *reason* which the statement about corporate right or liability discloses is found in the bearing of those unstated rules of law on those facts and consequences.[1]

So 'X & Co.' does not name a fictitious entity, for in speaking of it we are not *pretending* that something exists to which those words apply in just the way that the name 'Smith' applies to Smith. But nor, of course, is X and Co. (or Smith & Co.) a real entity (with a real will and life but, mysteriously, no body).

So: we can and should use corporate, personifying language without any sense of mystery or embarrassment, since it does no more than pick out human individuals, not expressly but rather by signifying a special sort of reason why, given certain legal rules, these human beings have—in their capacities as members, officials, agents, etc.—certain duties, rights, etc. analogous to those they have as private individuals.

But what about when there are no legal rules controlling our interest? How can talk of corporations or other groups be accounted for *then*? Hart

* Unpublished: for a graduate seminar in political theory, with Ronald Dworkin, John Gray, Joseph Raz, and Bill Weinstein: Oxford, October 1987.

[1] See *EJP* 40–1.

does not shirk the question. He repeats his methodological prescription. This prescription he puts under the auspices of Bentham, but I would ascribe it to Aristotle[2]—for Bentham gravely abused the method, with damage to jurisprudence which had to wait until Hart to be undone. Anyway: Don't ask 'What is a group?', but rather 'Under what conditions do we refer to numbers and sequences of [individuals] [human beings] as aggregates of individuals, and under what conditions do we adopt instead unifying phrases extended by analogy from individuals?'[3] (Aristotle: 'What is an eclipse?' should be translated into 'Why is the moon now darkened?') Hart's response: Under many varieties of widely different conditions, some but not others significant for legal and political purposes. So: Hart did not shirk the question, but the response he gave to it is really no answer at all.

Now, if we skip forward more than thirty years, we find Ronald Dworkin proposing, with a touch of defiance, that in jurisprudence (political theory) we need to recognize a 'particularly deep personification of the community or state'.[4] *The community* has its own principles which need not be held by all or most or even any[5] of its individual members. It can act in accordance with them, or in defiance of them, or hypocritically or simply inconsistently. The community, or any lesser group such as a corporation, is a moral agent which can be at fault and whose responsibility should be ascertained as the *reason*, the *basis*, for ascribing certain responsibilities to its agents and members. In these cases, one fixes the responsibility of the members or agents by *first* fixing the responsibility of the group.[6] Again: we individuals have rights which are against the state; it is the community as a whole that has the duty, as a result of which certain of its officers or instrumentalities have duties. We have rights, in particular, to be treated equally and impartially by the state (and thus by officials in their official capacity)—a duty which no individual, or official in his private capacity, has.[7] Again, the community as a whole is *committed* to what the legislative process (as defined in that community) produces.[8] Integrity requires that a community (and *thus* its agents) act according to its commitments and its principles.[9]

Nonetheless, Dworkin is clear: the community is not a real person with a distinct interest or point of view or even welfare of its own, and the state cannot accept its principles freely or unfreely, or be misled, or misunderstand its own principles.[10]

[2] *Posterior Analytics* II.2: 90a5–20. [See now essay IV.1 (2003b), sec. I.]
[3] *EJP* 43. [4] *LE* 167. [5] *LE* 172. [6] *Ibid.*, 168.
[7] *Ibid.*, 173–5. [8] *Ibid.*, 343. [9] *Ibid.*, 166–7. [10] *Ibid.*, 168.

In short: if Hart took personification off the agenda, Dworkin has put it right back on. But both Hart and Dworkin leave unexplained *why*, when we ascribe official rights and responsibilities, etc. to officials, we do so *via* an ascription of rights and responsibilities to the group of which they are officials, agents, or representatives. Let me put this point another way. Granted that we should not ask simply 'What is a group?', still we can reasonably be puzzled to know *why*, or under what conditions, moral or legal predicates are to be applied to individuals precisely *because* such predicates are applicable 'to the group'.

In an essay which I found extremely helpful to my consideration of the existence of groups in *Natural Law and Natural Rights* (Chapter VI.7), an essay entitled 'What is a Group?', Hart's closest collaborator Tony Honoré tackles the question left so up in the air by Hart. (But he does not profess to be dealing with legal corporate personality, which remained and largely remains off the agenda.) Of course, Honoré translates the question into the proper Aristotelian form: What sort of links (interactions) between people make a collection of such people a social group?[11]

Answer: What distinguishes the active members of a group is that they coordinate their actions in the pursuit of a common enterprise (that is, a purpose or activity demanding coordination, and thus demanding a common understanding of how things are to be done in order to coordinate activity for that purpose). What is required to achieve and maintain coordination is explored by Honoré in that essay and in the essay which precedes it in *Making Law Bind*, 'Groups, Laws and Obedience'. And the content of practical reasoning about maintaining coordination can be stated in prescriptions. Then: the consequences of transgressing prescriptions, and the making of new prescriptions, can themselves become the subject of coordinative prescriptions. Such interlocking prescriptions also pick out 'officials' as having particular roles in maintaining and enhancing coordination. Honoré, in short, consciously recasts the whole Hartian account of law in terms of coordinative prescriptions and interactions which go to constitute the reality of group *existence*.

In *Natural Law and Natural Rights* (Chapter VI.2) I adopt much of this account, and add a methodological note about the four orders—or types of unifying real relationships—in which human existence is lived: the order of nature which is what it is whatever we choose (You hear the sound of my voice in that order of reality); the order which we can bring into our own understanding (You hear my analyses and arguments in this order); the order we bring into matter subject to our powers, to make food or

[11] Honoré, *Making Law Bind*, 54.

boats or symbols or poems (You hear the English language and a certain rhetoric in this order); and the order or unity we bring into our own actions and dispositions by intelligently deliberating and choosing (You hear me, conducting a seminar, in that order). The existence of community, interactive coordination, a group, is a reality in this fourth order.[12] *What is...?* questions are dangerous just insofar as they suggest that questions in, say, the second or fourth order are seeking some object properly studied in the first order; empiricist reductivism, as practised by Bentham, does just that.

But I want to turn now to the normative theory which underlies Dworkin's claims about the necessity to admit a personification of the community, the moral theory which is expounded by Thomas Nagel in the essay to which Dworkin refers in this context, 'Ruthlessness in Public Life'.[13]

Nagel starts by noting the widespread sense that people who act in public roles—and who participate in, commit, the great public crimes of modern life—are somehow insulated from culpability by their role (save in cases of exceptional originality such as Stalin, Hitler, Amin). Yet a public action, though diffused over many actors in its decision and execution,[14] *is* the action of the actor(s).[15] So if his responsibility (culpability) is different from when he acts privately, it must be because the moral requirements are different.[16] And so they are, though they are derived from the same common source-principles as private morality is.[17] The differences between, so to speak, private and public morality come down to two, according to Nagel.

First, public acts must be strictly impartial between the members of the public (the whole community in question)—and 'public' and 'community' here includes not only the state but also political parties, revolutionary movements, charitable organizations, universities, etc.[18] Public acts must look to the general good, in the sense of the good of each, and there is no room, as there is in private morality (Nagel says), for tending one's own personal space and indulging one's own interests (whims) regardless of the general (common) good. So: there is a requirement of impersonality in the sense of impartiality.

Secondly, *outcomes* are accorded a greater weight, because restrictions on means are loosened and public actors are permitted (morally) to act ruthlessly, get their hands dirty, and use coercive, manipulative, or obstructive methods not allowable for individuals—but not *à outrance*,

[12] [In publications since *NLNR* I have generally preferred to follow the order of Aquinas's original discussion of these four kinds of order, in which the order brought into our choices and actions (the order that is morality's domain) is listed third and the order of techniques, etc. is listed fourth. See e.g. essay I.14, sec. III (1992a at 134–42); *Aquinas* 21–2.]

[13] Now in Nagel, *Mortal Questions*. [14] *Ibid.*, 83. [15] *Ibid.*, 77. [16] *Ibid.*, 78.

[17] *Ibid.*, 82. [18] *Ibid.*, 82n.

as Nagel nervously says again and again; there are limits; 'the strongest constraints of individual morality will continue to limit what can be publicly justified even by extremely powerful consequentialist considerations'. So judicial murders and air force massacres of innocents remain out of bounds.[19]

Now the first of Nagel's two differences is a commonplace of classic western political philosophy: 'As regards the State, the interests of all, whether high or low, are equal': Leo XIII, *Rerum Novarum*, 15 May 1891. But the second is not; I think the position of common morality is summed up by John XXIII in *Pacem in Terris* (1963), para. 80:

> The *same* moral law of nature that governs the life and conduct of individuals must also regulate the relations of political communities with one another... Political leaders... are still bound by the natural moral law... and have no authority to depart from its slightest precepts.

Dialectically speaking, Nagel's position on this second point seems very insecure. Not only does he offer no hint of how or why a line is to be drawn restraining the degree and extent of the ruthlessness and dirty-handed manipulation which is morally permitted to his public officials. He also seems to me to be in no position to explain how or why the 'public officials' of political parties, universities, charitable organizations, etc. are morally licensed to be ruthless and dirty-handed in a way that, say, a parent is not with a child, or a doctor with a patient, or a private tutor with a tutee. Indeed, he never gives an example of licensed ruthlessness for our consideration. If I come downstairs to find a burglar rifling the expensive musical instruments, does the amount and type of coercion and manipulation I may rightfully apply to him depend upon whether I live alone, or have a family upstairs, or am the musician's security guard, or the musician's union's security guard? No, I should think. And if I'm a policeman? That does seem to make a difference, to some extent, just insofar as being a policeman is being the agent, ultimately, of the judicially supervised and enforced system of punitive reparation for injustice.

For, of course, those who are responsible—for example under the community's rules for coordination (including the negative coordination, as Honoré calls it, of not-cheating)—for maintaining that coordination and the equality of the members in the face of various schemes of unfair private self-preference, may rightly use coercive measures, with an impersonality one could call ruthless, to maintain the order of proportionate equality which law and morality establish[20] between weak and strong individuals; and to restore the order of fair distribution of benefits and burdens if it has

[19] *Ibid.*, 89. [20] As Hart points out when discussing justice: *CL* 164–5.

been or is being criminally violated.[21] Beyond that coerciveness and that willingness to override private sympathies with concern for common justice, I can see no case whatever for considering that the moral requirements holding for public (social) acts are different from those governing private (individual) actions.

But what I want to focus on in this essay is not the direct question what norms apply to which acts, but rather the question how moral and political theory should talk about the relation between social or public acts and private acts when applying whatever moral norms may be applicable to them. The example I want to consider is the one analysed in *Nuclear Deterrence, Morality and Realism*: the nuclear-deterrent system of, say, the United States.

The book's conclusion, which I shall not argue for now, we express thus:

> The deterrent is a public act, which comes to be in and through many individual choices which propose that act, or accept proposals to adopt, participate in, or in some other way support it. Everyone's fundamental responsibility is not to choose or do anything which itself adopts, participates in, or supports that public act or any of the subordinate acts by which it is constituted and sustained. For the public act includes an unacceptable proposal; to kill innocents in city swaps and/or final retaliation. Since that is a proposal one must never adopt, one must never accept any invitation to support the deterrent, or to help, however reluctantly, bring about its continuance.[22]

This conclusion gives effect to the methodological position we state at the end of our discussion of bluff:

> one cannot correctly understand the morality of anyone's participation in this deterrent threat without starting from the morality of the social act. That is why, throughout this book, we are primarily concerned with the deterrent as a unified social act, and only secondarily with the many acts of the various persons who participate in it.[23]

And this position—essentially Dworkin's in a very different context—is stated at the end of our analysis of the hypothesis that the deterrent is a bluff, precisely because that analysis shows, more clearly than any other that I know of, *why and how public acts are irreducible to private acts.*

Some people imagine that if the president is bluffing, or the president and a few high officials, the entire deterrent is a bluff. But the deterrent system is not some great machine at the disposal of one or a very few people, but a vast social undertaking which involves various forms of cooperation. It

[21] See the discussion of punishment in *NLNR* X.1 and *FoE* V.5 [and essays III.10–12].
[22] *NDMR* 343. [23] *Ibid.*, 123.

is an important part of the work of thousands; for millions of others it is shared in by their performance of civic duties as voters or otherwise. For all involved, participation in the deterrent is by personal moral choices for which each bears untransferable responsibility.

The deterrent system as a social undertaking does not exist independently of the multitude of personal moral acts of those who participate in it; there is no social person such as John Bull or Uncle Sam to deliberate and make choices on behalf of a nation. Still, there is a true sense in which a nation's deterrent system has the unity of a single social act. Though constituted through certain personal acts of members of the society, the social act is not reducible to the whole collection of those acts, or to any subset of them.

We offer a comparison: a team playing a game engages in a single social act. That act has no existence apart from the personal acts of the players. Yet the act of the team as a whole in playing, winning, or losing, cannot be reduced to the personal acts of the players. The purpose of the team is to win. Individual members have many other purposes, some, at times, more or less sharply at odds with winning. To understand the game as a social act, one must bear in mind the social purpose, and not be distracted by the irrelevant aspects of the individual players' purposes. Conceivably, every member of the team, for personal reasons, may secretly wish to lose the game (without being too obvious about it). Even so, the social act of the team's play retains its purpose: to win. And even if *some* members of the team conspire with each other to throw the game, the acts of *all* members of the team will be understood, by non-conspiring members and by the team's supporters and critics, as contributions to the social act of the team: playing to win.

The deterrent, too, is a social act. The US deterrent, for instance, came into being and is kept in being by acts of presidents, members of Congress, and others, in accord with their constitutional, statutory, or other public responsibilities. True, when public officials act, they act for personal reasons, and do personal acts. Yet through all these personal acts, carried out in fulfilment of their various social roles, these officials together give reality to a single social act: the US deterrent. This social act has its own purpose: to deter. And it involves a real communal choice: to carry out the threat under appropriate conditions.

That communal choice *cannot* be a bluff. A bluff is, so to speak, a gap between threat and intention or choice; but between the deterrent's threat and the communal choice to carry out the threat *if*...(the public choice that is stated *as* the threat on so many occasions) no wedge can be driven, any more than the purpose of winning can be separated from the team's playing of the game.

The moral quality of the deterrent is not defined or determined by the morally good or bad intentions of individuals. That moral quality would not change from day to day if the private resolve of a president and his inner circle swung from intent to bluff and back again. For the social act of nuclear deterrence is defined by its public proposal—for example, the proposal which members of Congress are called upon to support. And that proposal is not a proposal to bluff the Soviets. It is the proposal to deter them by a manifest capability *and will* to impose 'unacceptable losses'.

This social act, which members of Congress are called upon to share in by legislating, is the deterrent which certain other citizens are called upon to share in by performing their military duties, and which citizens at large are sometimes called upon to share in by their votes. Moral responsibility for this social act, with the moral character which really belongs to it, is shared by each and every clear-headed and uncoerced participant. Through their personal acts, all who deliberately do their part bear responsibility, not only for what they individually do, but for the social act to the extent that they participate (share) in it.

And so, one cannot correctly understand the morality of anyone's participation in this deterrent threat without starting from the morality of the social act. It is possible—imaginable—that many of those today participating in the deterrent *are* bluffing and that everyone else participating (or in any way involved) in it hopes that everyone else participating (involved) in the deterrent is bluffing. But even if this were so, *the deterrent* would not be a bluff, and participating in it would be participating in a public act which includes an immoral proposal, intention, and choice.

The point is not that there cannot be a group bluff. There can be. But if there is, it will not be because of the hidden interior decisions of one or more members of the group, but because the nature of the particular group is such that *it can act in secret*, and the group's make-up allows there to be sufficient group interiority (inconspicuous coordination, mutual trust, and trustworthiness, etc.) to make possible a group lie. The US Congress is a group whose only mode of action is public, and it is too big to have the interiority necessary for a group lie. The Soviet Politburo, on the other hand, is organized to act secretly; it can lie, and doubtless it sometimes does.

The group constituted of the participants in the deterrent cannot bluff. It is conceivable that, for their own part, the president and a few other high officials are personally bluffing. But consider the many classes of participants in the US deterrent: strategic planners, staff of the National Security Council and of the Joint Chiefs of Staff, budget officers of the Defense Department, members of Congress, targeters, service personnel trained to carry out the threat, and even citizens at large. (The latter become participants to the extent that they respond favourably to politicians who sometimes make an election issue of one or another aspect of the deterrent strategy, but who always assume that the threat of final retaliation is to be maintained.) Of all these various participants, very few could be in on the bluff. Yet insiders to the bluff would have to *intend the contributions* of those not in on the bluff whose participation is essential to the deterrent system.

'Intend those others persons' contributions'? Well, since this system cannot be maintained without the willing cooperation of so many participants of diverse kinds, bluffing insiders could not protect its credibility and effectiveness without *doing their best to ensure* that all other participants had the very same beliefs and intentions as they would if there were no bluff. So participants who were not insiders would have to cooperate just as they would if the insiders really intended to carry out the threat. (Thus, the moral responsibility of those not in on the bluff would be the same as if it were not a bluff.)

Nor would the insiders escape moral responsibility for the real intention to carry out the deterrent threat. While not personally sharing this intention, they would choose and do what was necessary to ensure that other participants shared it. By doing this, the insiders would be morally responsible for the intention of the others to carry out the threat. Those who deliberately bring others to will what is evil make themselves guilty, not only of the evil the others will, but also of leading them to become persons of evil will.

But could not the insiders avoid this awful responsibility by desiring that other participants play their part only with the same reservations as the insiders themselves? Of course, the insiders' desire that other participants also bluff could not be communicated to them. Still, could not the other participants, being upright, share each and all in the same basic attitude to the deterrent, and thus personally intend only to bluff, and wish others to do likewise?

This likely story, appealing as it is, cannot rescue the bluff theory. For there would remain a difference between what the insiders chose to do, when they led others to cooperate in the deterrent, and what they wished those others to do. By hypothesis, they would wish them to bluff. But they would have no good reason to expect that the cooperation they sought would in fact be carried out *as* a contribution to a bluff. Thus, the insiders would commit themselves to the wholehearted participation of the others. Such wholehearted participation would involve no bluff, but a real intention. Thus the insiders would be inciting the others to intend to kill the innocent.

But the story also breaks down in a more interesting way, when one looks more closely at the moral responsibility of those who are not insiders. For many of these cannot make their contribution while intending only to bluff. Some, even some whose contributions are indispensable, are not sufficiently involved to be in a position to bluff, because neither the making nor the executing of the threat is within their control. Ordinary citizens who lend their support to the deterrent strategy are in this position. Even some who are very actively involved, for example those who build or maintain nuclear weapon systems, are in the same position. Having done their part, they can at most hope that others will never execute the threat.

Others who are not insiders are too involved in making deterrent policy to be in a position to bluff. Some participants in the very making of the threat would not be involved in its execution, but, realistically, could not be let in on the bluff. For example: by sharing in the establishment of the policy and by providing the means for its execution, members of the US Congress who lend their support to the deterrent are partners with the president and other officials in making the threat. Yet they have no role in the apparatus which would execute the threat. Few if any of the 535 members of Congress could be in on the secret of the bluff. Most members of Congress, then, could not possibly separate the intention involved in making the threat from the threat itself and its execution. They cannot be bluffing. And theirs are the acts which define the public proposal which, when adopted by themselves and others, defines the social, public act in which they and everyone else, personally bluffing or not, participates: the proposal, not to bluff the Soviets, but to deter them by acquiring and maintaining the capability and will to destroy their cities if they destroy ours, and to destroy their society if they do what has the effect of destroying ours.

If Dworkin is right in saying that a group cannot accept its principles freely or unfreely, or be misled about or misunderstand its own principles, it is presumably because and just insofar as the group acts of adopting or interpreting the group's principles are acts constituted by acts of individuals who understand and adopt a proposal which, at least within the group, simply is and must be a *public* proposal; there is no group mind, behind the 'group mind' expressed in the public proposal, to be out of harmony (either in understanding or in willing) with the publicly expressed group mind.

So the question I propose for your consideration is this. Are we right to maintain that there is here a social act which has a reality not reducible to the individual behaviour and intentions of those who participate in it, and that the morality of such individual participation is to be judged by each potential or actual participant not by asking about his own intentions but by identifying first the intent involved in the social act and then asking whether that public intent is one that he can rightly make his own by choosing to participate in that social act?

5
PERSONS AND THEIR ASSOCIATIONS*

It would be hard to take seriously an inquiry into the personality of Roger Scruton's 'corporations'—committees, firms, churches, clubs, political parties, partnerships, universities and schools, farms and (aristocratic) families, states and Mafias, armies and trade unions—if one really considered individual people so 'metaphysically insecure' and 'inherently problematic' that we could 'see how to understand the human person' only by first studying 'the case of corporate personality'. Scruton professes to find people less securely persons than their associations, and grants if not concedes bad arguments for doubting the unity, identity, and wholeness of the rational animals he misnames 'embodied agents'. But in the end it is clear that for him, too, institutions and other associations are worth calling personal primarily because they enable individual human people to pursue shared purposes, fruitfully, in association with others who like them have had or will have lifetimes which last, in Scruton's words, from birth to grave. The thus persisting and organic unity, identity, and wholeness of each of these people provides us (for all its irreducible and puzzling complexity) with the paradigm of personhood.[1]

I

Because I am committed to writing this essay in time for printing, I am composing it straight onto a word processor; though I am feeling mildly rheumatic from a cold, I am exercising my fingers in tapping out this sentence, and am hoping that its multiple self-references will help convey

* 1989a, a comment on Scruton, 'Corporate Persons' (see endnote below on its theses).

[1] P.F. Strawson's arguments for the primitiveness of the concept of 'person', in *Individuals*, 87–116, seem successful but, as Germain Grisez argues, *Beyond the New Theism*, 348, fail to distinguish between people and other sentient organisms; Grisez remedies the failure of Strawson's argumentation to respond to the self/body, as distinct from mind/body, problem: *ibid.*, 347–53.

certain views which I formed years ago and am still sure of after some days reflecting on Scruton's paper.

Scruton speaks as if it were a 'huge and unwarranted assumption' that the 'I am' which occurs six times in the preceding sentence is a sign of the lasting and bodily identity of the one animal and rational substance (I myself) who moves, feels, cogitates, judges, chooses, makes commitments, and moves material objects in order to carry out his choice, fulfil his commitment, communicate his meaning, and report his feelings—and who equally is a reflexive subject, not only experiencing his being and acting in all these ways but also knowing himself both as object and subject of that experiencing, being, and doing. Now, certainly, the use of 'I am' is neither necessary nor sufficient to provide even a dialectical (in Aristotle's sense) 'proof' of that substantial identity. But I know no warrant for Scruton's assumption that neither this feature, nor the fact that that same sentence can be translated into many languages without significant loss of meaning, is a *sign* of such identity.[2] And, on the contrary, neither the experience of bodily (animal), rational, responsible, and self-conscious agency, nor the critical reflective judgment that such agency instantiates the several irreducible aspects of the personal identity of one of a natural kind of rational animal,[3] is an *assumption*.

This personal identity, which one both experiences and pace Kant and Scruton can critically affirm to be exemplified in one's responsible acting, is paradigmatic. If this is illusory, or even 'metaphysically problematic' (in the sense of open to reasonable doubt), we lack any basis upon which to raise any interesting question about whether or not associations or groups of us are (identifiable as) (corporate) persons.[4] Indeed, and as one would expect, Scruton's mode of analysing and arguing for the personality of groups, throughout his paper, belies his claim that corporate personality is epistemologically prior to, or in some similar way privileged in comparison with, the personhood of people.

[2] No such warrant is afforded by the various arguments of Vendler, Anscombe, and Strawson discussed in Mackie, 'The Transcendental "I"', in van Straaten, *Philosophical Subjects*, 48–61, on which see Strawson, *ibid.*, 266–71. The 'transparency' of the first-person singular has its importance, but not as a warrant for Scruton's assumption: see my *FoE* 3, 23, 70–4, 114, 117, 141, 143.

[3] Which kind? Well, that which includes at least all those whom I expect to read the first sentence of this section with sympathy. I need not say more, since Scruton accepts that the natural human person belongs to a natural kind.

[4] Equally, if one holds with Scruton that the discovery that one is a 'mere intelligent machine' should have 'no bearing whatever' on one's judgments about one's 'moral personality', one lacks any basis for raising interesting questions about personal responsibility, let alone about the distinction which Scruton wishes to make much of, between *thing*-institutions and personal-institutions.

II

The nature (explanatory account) of any active reality is best understood by identifying its capacities (potentialities), and these by attending to its activities.[5] People's personal reality is *fully* manifested only in their chosen actions. Where one's action is fully voluntary, one's 'prior' deliberation and choice can often be clearly identified and distinguished from the action itself only with some artificiality and for analytical convenience. *A fortiori*, a community's reality, its 'personal' character, is fully manifested and instantiated only by its corporate, collaborative, or cooperative *action*.[6]

In line with his tolerance of Kant's and other dualistic conceptions of personal reality, Scruton's case for attributing personality to certain human associations seems to give explanatory primacy to the fact that these associations *decide* matters 'as a result of common deliberation' (Section I), 'proceeding by rational discussion among its members' (Section VII). And he frowns on social-choice theory's incapacity, as he thinks, to mark the distinction between decision by collective deliberation and the emergence of, for example, prices as the side effect of 'choices which do not intend them'. But, in thus giving primacy to deliberation and decision in the account of corporations, he seems to overlook the fact that corporate decisions are often not unlike a market's pricing, in bearing only an accidental relation to any common deliberation and/or rational discussion which preceded them.

For: the 'social-choice' theory of voting demonstrates, for example, the easy possibility of cycles (intransitivity): a majority prefer A to B, a majority prefer B to C, and a majority prefer C to A—so that the outcome depends not so much upon any common deliberations as on accidents of process (for example, which vote is taken first). (The possibility of cycles is independent of, but their probability is much enhanced by, tactical voting.) So, even healthy groups often have to act collectively despite widespread knowledge or belief that the collective decision to be put into effect is only the accidental side effect of other decisions, collective and individual, and has only the appearance of analogy with the emergence of an individual's

[5] Cf. Aristotle, *de Anima*, II, 4: 415a 16–21.

[6] The primary meaning of *Genossenschaft* is 'a *cooperative*'. Ernest Barker when translating 'left *Genossenschaft* as "fellowship", following good authority', but speaking for himself identified it as a 'system of fellowship', paradigmatically

> the company of brothers, linked by the right hand of fellowship, and knit together by a spirit of fraternity, who pursued the common interest of their group (whether based on profession, or occupation, or the simple foundation of voluntary association) and vindicated its common honour with a common ardour. (Introduction to Gierke, *Natural Law and the Theory of Society 1500 to 1800* at xc, lviii.)

choice of action from his own deliberation.[7] In these cases, group action is undertaken in order to carry out a decision which has emerged from the 'black box' (invisible hand?) of formally correct process as a kind of side effect of any 'common deliberation', an effect which perhaps few of those deliberating about the decision, and none involved in executing it, either desired or even reluctantly intended.

The classic ground for denying that communities have a substantial identity is that their individual members, although parts of that whole which we rightly identify as a community, do and suffer things which are in no sense actions or experiences or events in the life *of the community*.[8] This seems right, though circular (and in need—and capable only—of dialectical explication and defence) in the way that definitions of primitive terms must be. In any case, Scruton I think concedes this denial, when he himself denies that groups are [members of] 'natural kinds', a matter he assimilates with animal life, unity, and duration.[9]

The consequence to be drawn from the position thus conceded is this. A human community's reality is no more and no less than the reality of group action, together with such acts and dispositions to act of the group's members as manifest their readiness to participate in, and emotional responsiveness to, the group's action, for the sake of the good(s) which give(s) point to that action.[10] That is to say: the reality of a community is the reality of an order of human, truly personal acts, an order brought

[7] Another consequence, also not of the first importance, of Scruton's emphasis on decision as the primary mark of personality is the prominence he gives to committees and their supposed personality, at the expense of the corporation within which, and on behalf of which, typically, a committee deliberates and decides. Committees, as their name implies, are characteristically commissioned to investigate and/or deliberate and/or decide on behalf of the body which committed this role to them. Scruton's elision of the two appears in his opening pages and recurs when listing the features of fully personal corporations: the list begins with three and ends with three or four features of the whole association ('It is voluntary', etc.), but in the middle switches without notice to features of a governing element ('It is deliberative/authoritative/a law-making body').

[8] See e.g. Aquinas, *in Eth*, intro., para. 5. This, not any notion that contract is prerequisite to group identity, is the reason why political theory in its central form is wont to reject the claim that groups are persons or bodies, and to treat such assertions as justified only if taken as metaphorical: *ST* III q.8 a.1 ad 2 ('in metaphoricis locutionibus ... similitudo ... non ... rei veritas'). Any Tridentine reference to the *compago spiritualis* will have nothing to do with theories that the Church is formed by contract [Scruton at 244] and everything to do with the Bible; for in the Vulgate, *compago* and its cognates signify, never a compact (agreement), but always a joint, frame, or bodily structure or structuring (see Daniel 5: 6, 10: 16; Job 10: 11; Ecclesiasticus 11: 5; Hebrews 4: 12; thus *compactum* in Ephesians 4: 16 means, as Knox appropriately translates, that the social body of the Church is 'organized [by the head, Christ]').

[9] The tradition uses 'natural' differently and says that some groups, such as the nuclear family and the *communitas perfecta* imperfectly exemplified by the modern state, are natural kinds, though still only 'accidental' rather than substantial wholes.

[10] For, if natures are understood by understanding capacities, and capacities by understanding their actuations, those actions are understood by knowing their objects (point): *de Anima* II, 4: 415a 16–21; n. 5 above.

into being and maintained by the choices (and dispositions to choose, and responses to choices) of persons.

III

Being constituted by, and having no existence independently of, the many individual acts of those people who participate in that action, the action and other reality of a community is properly understood only in that critical discourse which attends systematically to the 'existential', that is, to the intelligibilities which originate in personal choices to act. That critical discourse we call 'moral'.[11] And in a moral analysis of human affairs, a community's action is not reducible to the whole collection of those individuals' acts or any subset of them, nor even to that whole collection together with the common plan (so far as there is one). The action of the group itself—the group's action itself—can, as Scruton says, be rightly assessed as upright or immoral.

Sharing Scruton's judgments about certain particular acts of genocide, I shall discuss another (proposed) act of genocide. I do so in order to clarify the reasons for sharing Scruton's general claim: that such acts should indeed be ascribed to the group, as subject, though without prejudice to the moral responsibility of those people who participate in the social act.

Maintaining a nuclear deterrent is rightly said to be the act of the nation-state which does so: the act of credibly threatening to impose retaliatory nuclear destruction on some potential adversary nation-state. Not all members of the group participate in that act, and some have no moral responsibility for it. Those who have no moral responsibility for it could never be rightly punished for it; but as members they might be rightly called upon to contribute to compensating victims of the group's misdeeds.[12] As for those who participate in the social act of maintaining the deterrent, they do so by choosing to do something to further this act of the group, for example to authorize its funding, or to assist in the construction of weapons, or the elaboration of plans to use them, or the maintenance of systems for guiding or delivering them.

Now: anyone who both participates in communicating the deterrent threat and would be involved in executing it on the day can personally be bluffing (that is, can have the secret intention not to do anything, on the day, towards executing it). (Anyone who participates only in maintaining

[11] Hence, too, the justice of the old view that if one must speak of the personality of groups, one had better call it 'moral personality'—as Scruton comes round to doing.

[12] Here I differ from Scruton, who says (sec. III) that it is 'legally absurd and contrary to natural justice' to hold the present membership 'individually liable for the deeds of those to whom they have succeeded'. This is not clear to me; though English statute law prevents it, the law of other systems provides for the personal liability of partners for the debts and other liabilities of the partnership incurred before they joined. The position is not less complex than I have indicated it in the text.

the system but who would have no part in executing or not executing it on the day—for example a backbench MP voting to fund it—*cannot* be bluffing, however much he may hope that others are bluffing.) But the group act *cannot* be a bluff. For just as an individual's morally significant act is defined by the proposal which he adopts by choice, so a group's act is defined by its public proposal—that is, by the form in which it is proposed to members of the group, for them to participate in or not. And the public proposal of the deterrent is not a proposal to bluff our adversaries. It is the proposal to deter them by a manifest capability and will to impose on them 'unacceptable losses'. But the intentional imposition of such losses precisely satisfies the definition, in English as in international law and in sound morality, of genocide. Therefore, since the social act of maintaining the deterrent cannot be a bluff, but must involve the conditional intention to impose those losses, everyone who chooses to participate in that social act—including everyone who is personally bluffing, and everyone who hopes[13] that all who can be are—is choosing to participate in a real social choice: to commit genocide under certain foreseeable conditions.

The moral responsibility of all these individual participants is a real personal responsibility. But it is clearly various, as one individual is personally bluffing and another is not, one hopes that others are bluffing and another does not care, one participates for want of any other employment and another out of interest in maintaining our democratic order, and so forth. Yet the moral analysis of and judgment upon the social act of maintaining the deterrent can remain single and unvaried: *this* act involves the intention to commit genocide and so I may not participate in it in any way or for any reason. The difference summarized in the two preceding sentences affords the strongest reason I know for holding that social acts, though constituted by, are irreducible to the acts of people in the acting group.

IV

Scruton, having done what he could for it, finally drops the 'Hegelian claim…that individual personality requires for its fruition not only association, but also a personal relation to the corporation which is thereby formed' (Section IX). Indeed, as he says,

> there are associations founded in non-contractual obligation, and which are also ends in themselves, but which have no other features of corporate personality: love and friendship are the prime examples.

[13] Against all the evidence—but let that pass. For the full story, factual and conceptual, see *NDMR* ch. V.

To be improved by your associations, it is enough that you 'be joined in fellowship with others, assigning rights and duties to yourself and them' (*ibid.*). Thus Scruton accepts the core of the central tradition of moral and political reflection—in his paper incautiously given the same name ['Natural Law'] as currents which everywhere oppose it and for which Hobbes is a source and master.

'Personality' is a distracting metaphor in a realistic moral and political analysis of human associations and their actions. The metaphor is always tugged between its two historic sources. On the one hand, there is *persona* as mask; to this corresponds the law's carefree attribution of legal personality to *anything* that figures as the subject of legal relations, particularly litigious and/or property relations: idols, funds, parcels of property on the quayside, ships, the Crown... On the other hand, there is *persona* as individual substance, of a rational nature (Boethius); to this corresponds nothing (save metaphorically) in the many orderings of human association which we call groups—nothing except the people who are members.

Everything that Scruton wants to say about the injustices and inhumanity of Soviet social organizations can be said more precisely than the distinction[14] between 'thing-institution' and 'person-institution' allows. The distinction obscures its own point, since it diverts attention both from the reduction of people themselves to 'things' (mere means) in the machinations of their rulers, and from the status of the (Stalinist) Party as at once 'person' (agent) and 'thing' (tool). The injustices are all done to people, whose well-being and fulfilment is seriously injured by the restrictions upon, and manipulations of, the various forms of association which they have, or might otherwise have, with one another.

'Association' and 'community' (like 'organization' and even 'structure') are always best understood when considered as verbs, and suffice, I suggest, for all Scruton's legitimate purposes.

NOTE

Roger Scruton stated the programme of his paper, 'Corporate Persons', thus (239–41):

> *Introduction.* Prices in a market are determined by the choices of buyers and sellers; decisions in a committee are determined by the votes of members. In the first case, however, there is no decision as to what the price of anything should be. Prices arise by an 'invisible hand' from choices which do not intend them. In the second case a decision is taken by the committee as a result of common deliberation on the question before it. The difference between the two cases is hard to capture precisely, is barely noticed in the sociological theory of 'groups', and is strictly imperceivable to the theory of social choice, as this has been explored by Kenneth Arrow and his followers. Yet its political significance is enormous...

[14] Scruton, 'Corporate Persons' at 262, 265.

A first step towards understanding that distinction—but only a first step—is through the study of a concept that has been unjustly neglected by contemporary social and political philosophy: the concept of the corporate person. Committees, as a rule, are corporate persons; markets are not, and cannot be. That sentence may not be clear to the reader now; but I hope to explain it in the course of this paper.

Consideration of collective action in recent jurisprudence has tended to focus on something vaguely called the 'group', or else to offer some updated version of what Maitland called the 'bracket theory', but which we, with the hindsight of Russellian logic, might call the 'logical construction theory'. According to this theory—defended in a sophisticated form by H.L.A. Hart—the rights and duties of corporations are created by the law, in order to adjudicate the independent legal interests of individuals. The concept of the corporate person, with its own rights and duties, is a procedural device, whereby the business of adjudication is made more manageable.

Theories of responsibility rarely mention the liabilities of groups—even though more harm has been done, and wilfully done, by groups than by individuals; while theories of the person and of personal identity proceed as though human persons were the only persons that there are. Modern political philosophy usually makes no distinction between institutions with personality and those without it. Nor does it see the importance of that distinction, or the manifest catastrophe of a political order (such as that established and upheld by communism) in which all forms of corporate personality have been reduced to the 'masks' or 'fictions' which positivistic jurisprudence wrongly holds them to be. In this paper I shall outline a defence of the view—traditionally associated with Gierke, Maitland and Figgis—that human individuals derive their personality in part from corporations; and I shall indicate why it matters that corporate personality should be consecrated in our feelings, and acknowledged in our laws.

6

LAW, UNIVERSALITY, AND SOCIAL IDENTITY*

How should we understand this thesis[1] of St Thomas about law's *genus*: 'Laws are universal *propositiones*—propositions and premises—of practical reason'? And how should we respond to the thought, influential in many places and among some of the most eminent of my colleagues, that to prefer one set of forms of human character, relationship, and conduct to certain others, and accordingly to restrict the conduct of those persons who have these other preferences, is wrongfully to deny those persons' equality of entitlement to concern and respect, and/or to insult them?

I

A particular legal norm (rule, principle, standard...) is not the *text* (whether type or token) whose promulgation or pronouncement is the norm's formal source. More proximate to the norm is the text's *meaning*. But no meaning can correctly be said to *be* the norm unless it is the meaning which the text has when taken in conjunction with all the norms or meanings which properly affect its legally sound interpretation and its validity and authority as law. As every law teacher knows explicitly and every law student implicitly, the legal norm, adequately articulated, may never have been expressed precisely as it needs to be (should be) expressed. The challenge and goal for me as judge, teacher, or student is—is it not?—to find and set out that truly adequate expression of the norm, exactly as is made possible, and required of me, by a sound understanding of our law,

* Opening Address to III Congreso Sul-Americano de Filosofia do Direito and VI Colóquio Sul-Americano de Realismo Jurídico, Porto Alegre, Brazil, 4 October 2007.

[1] 'quia ratio etiam practica utitur quodam syllogismo in operabilibus...ideo est invenire aliquid in ratione practica quod ita se habeat ad operationes, sicut se habet propositio in ratione speculativa ad conclusiones. Et huiusmodi *propositiones universales rationis practicae ordinatae ad actiones*, habent rationem legis' ('and because practical reason, too, employs a kind of syllogism in relation to possible actions...so we should expect to find in practical reason some element which is related to actions as the propositional premise is related to conclusions in non-practical reason. And this kind of universal proposition of practical reason, bearing on actions, has the nature of law'): *ST* I–II q.90 a.1 ad 2.

all its relevant sources and principles of interpretation, and all its related norms. Only thus do I or anyone know what the norm is—what really is our law, the 'law of the land', the legal system, as it bears on that particular norm's subjects and subject-matter. (When I say 'our law', I of course refer and shall refer generically to a particular country's law, whether mine or yours.)

In that challenging exercise of mind and judgment which we summarily call interpretation, or understanding the law—*this* norm in the light of, in principle, all other norms of our law—I both find and put myself in relationship to all those people in the past of my political community whose acts of enactment or adjudication or of convention-following were legally decisive or relevant sources of the norm's present authority. I put myself into relationship too with all the people whose conduct is addressed by this norm adequately understood; and into relationship with everyone who ought to share my judgment about what our law is about this subject-matter. For that judgment of mine entails that anyone considering the legal question ought (in my judgment) to reach the same judgment, and under ideal epistemic conditions *would* reach it. The creation of legal norms conveys, expressively, the intentions of their creators, but legal norms transcend those particular acts of intellect(s) and will(s).

That transcendence has several aspects. One aspect is the subsistence of norms. They outlast the personal acts of uttering or making them, not only in the way that every word, sign, or symbol outlasts the event of uttering or making it, but also in a further way. Whatever is valid in law is held in being, retains its validity, by virtue of other norms of its legal system and—this is a basic principle of legal thinking—remains valid (unless its own terms provide otherwise) until it is repealed by some comparable act of intellect(s) and will(s).[2] So another aspect of legal norms' transcendence of the particular is their authoritativeness and normativity, the claim which each legal norm has to be counted part of our law in any discussion or application of law to members of our community, and the claim each of them presumptively has on the conscience of all these members. This claim makes its appearance within each norm's explicit or implicit content, in the use of such legal universals as 'ought', 'may', 'shall', 'is authorized', 'is required', and so forth.

[2] Where a legal system adopts a norm of *desuetudo* (expiry or nullification for long disuse), the principle of continuity or indefinite subsistence is qualified by that positive norm, which is itself a *determinatio* of the thought that application after long non-application will be unjust, whether as discriminatory or as inappropriate to current circumstances (*rebus haud sic stantibus*: things no longer being what they were when the disused rule was created).

The meaning of those legal universals—call them formal or structural legal universals—has aspects of universality and of particularity. That meaning shifts subtly as one moves from legal system to system, from Brazil to Australia to Byzantine Rome... and so forth. But—speaking only of these formal or structural legal universals—that shift, that particularity, is relatively marginal, I think, compared with the extensive overlap or commonality or shared identity in their meaning. This combination of universality and particularity is a part of what the Roman jurists called *ius gentium*. The other part of what they meant by *ius gentium* consists in its shared substantive content, that is, in the substantially identical kinds of human conduct picked out by all civilized legal systems as forbidden or required or authorized, and so forth. Of each legal system—more precisely, of each country or political community—it is true (1) that all of its norms are authoritative because they *are* part of *that* particular system, adopted by that particular country, and true (2) that some of those norms are authoritative for a further reason, that they not only are but *ought to have been* adopted by that country because they ought (at least in their substance) to be adopted by any and every country and more or less universally are adopted (at least 'on paper'). That pair of truths is the Roman juridical theory of *ius gentium* expounded, as you all know, at the beginning of Gaius's *Institutes* for law students. And it works well enough as an account of *just* law. Its supplementation by Gaius's thesis that *natural reason* (*ratio naturalis*) settles at least some relevant standards for our *ius civile* opens it up to realities over which the *ius gentium* theory or idealization stumbles, notably those unjust institutions, practices, and arrangements which are unjust in ways like Roman slavery's injustice, yet often found or even practically universal among the world's *gentes*.

The Roman jurists' understanding of the relation between natural reason and positive law needed, in any event, to be completed in two different ways, each accomplished, at least in principle, by Aquinas. One was the explanation of *naturalis ratio*, of *ratio* as the set of fundamental reasons for action, reasons which need no further reasons to explain their directiveness, a directiveness that consists in their pointing and directing us to genuine opportunities of flourishing, fulfilment of human nature, both in my life (my existence) and in the lives (existence) of, essentially and in principle, *anyone* else. The other necessary completion of the Roman jurists' theory was the demonstration that our country's laws, even those multitudes of norms of its *ius civile* which are not also part of the *ius gentium* but rather are simply *lex positiva*, are nonetheless all rationally connected with, indeed 'derived from', the universal principles and norms of *lex naturalis*, *naturalis ratio*, or *ius gentium*. To repeat: except for those particular norms, if any, which are truly *unjust*, all the norms of positive law are rationally connected to, that is, are (to use the key term in Aquinas's legal theory) *determinationes* of, the universal principles and norms of rational morality. But very many (not all!)[3] of those not-unjust legal norms have that rational connection only in the weak sense captured by the following pair of propositions: (i) each of these many norms is reasonable, but (ii) of each of these reasonable norms it is true that other, different, and also reasonable norms could reasonably have been adopted instead. So the adoption of these *leges latae*, these actual posited norms, was an act of self-determination by the political community that adopted them, self-determining and self-shaping in a stronger sense than the self-determination which every choice entails even when it is much more tightly constrained by reason(s) than are these choices to adopt 'purely positive' legal norms.

Though he does not speak of it as self-determination, my former long-time colleague Ronald Dworkin, in his theory of the nature of law, speaks of law's 'integrity' as being the content and character it has by virtue of being the law (legal system) of the particular society whose law it is, a society which correspondingly must be regarded as, or as if it is, a person. This communal person or personified entity is what it is because it has shaped a character that is its own; its acts of constitution-making, legislation, and superior-court adjudication are commitments that are its own, and to which it, and particularly the judges called upon to determine what its law is, can be faithful or (and this is presumptively wrongful) unfaithful.

We can think about all this more clearly if we step back to the point at which Aquinas stood as he thought about how to start off his vast discussion of morally (and therefore politically and legally) significant moral action, the *Prima-Secundae* of his *Summa Theologiae*. He decided to devote its preface, *prooemium*, to the fact that we image God by being, by and in our free choices, each of us the source (*principium*) and owner (*dominus*) of our own actions.[4] He will later add, in a text to which Maritain returned more than once, that the child at the outset of its free-willing, at the dawn of its age of reason, thinks and deliberates about, and makes a disposition of, *itself* (himself or herself: *de seipso*).[5] In a loose modern philosophical jargon, this could be called a reference, prominent and structural, to *autonomy*. And so, in a sense, it is, though Aquinas knows what many moderns do not, that the freedom of choice of the healthy human (adult) person is informed

[3] On the legal norms that ought to be, and normally are, posited as *conclusions* from or components of the universal requirements of moral decency (the natural moral law), see *NLNR* 282–4.

[4] *ST* I–II prol.

[5] *ST* I–II q.89 a.6c and ad 3; see also *Sent.* II d.42 q.1 a.5 ad 7; *De Veritate* q.28 a.3 ad 4. [And see essay 2 at p. 50.]

not only by the commitments he or she has chosen to make, or to accept from others' making, but also principles and norms that neither he nor she, nor any other human person, created but rather that everyone and anyone can and should understand, acknowledge, and accept—the requirements of practical reasonableness, in all their universality.

The late Pope, in his private philosophical work, made a close study of what he called (lending a word to a thought of Aristotle) the intransitivity of human action—a part or aspect of our actions that is as important as action's transitive effects on the world. One way of articulating this intransitivity is to observe that actions, even when transitively completed with success or failure, remain, *lasting* in the soul, personality, or character of the acting person unless they are, if ever, repudiated by repentance and resolution to amend. This is what, as Aristotle puts it, distinguishes *praxis*, morally significant action in the open horizon of one's own and one's communities' whole life, from *technē*, activity considered simply as a technique for mastering matter to achieve a specific kind of goal. So although Aristotle may not have the word self-determination, he has the concept (not perhaps fully adequately appropriated in his philosophy of human matters—*ta anthropina*). And self-determination is an essential element in one's reality as a unitary being, this person, me.

At the end of 'Personal Identity in Aquinas and Shakespeare' (essay 2) I offered the following summary:

> In short: there is the identity I have as the particular human being I have been since I was formed in my mother's womb with all the radical capacities, and thus the nature, of a human person. There is the identity I have as a person conscious of much that I have experienced and thought since first I began to be aware of myself (my toes and my fears ...) in relation to other things including people, and began to inquire and assert and deny and argue. There is the identity I have as a person with the character I have made for myself by the choices I have made within the constraints, and between the opportunities, that have arisen from the nature of things, the choices of others, and the accidental conjunctions, by *all* of which factors, as Shakespeare and Aquinas each depict, divine providence 'shapes our ends, / rough hew them how we will' (*Hamlet* 5. 2.11). And there is the identity I have as an object of cultural forms (a citizen of Australia) and a user of them (English-speaking, tie-wearing) and projecter of new and partly new *personas*.[6]

Here I wish to extend those reflections on identity, to bring into the picture some of what I there omitted to say about personal and, by analogy, communal identity. But the purpose of the present reflections is not so

[6] Essay 2, p. 67.

much to understand, for the sake of understanding, the metaphysics or ontology of identity. Rather it is to understand a little better, for the sake of *deliberation* towards right choice and action, what is good in identities and in forming and maintaining them: identity as opportunity, a *bonum honestum*, and as something to be grateful for. For this will bear closely upon the second of the two questions I posed at the outset, about equality of entitlement to concern and immunity from insult.

II

Besides 'the identity I have as the particular human being I have been since I was formed in my mother's womb with all the radical capacities, and thus the nature, of a human person', there is the identity I have as a male, not female. For we do not understand the category 'human nature' well unless we understand that in respect of the *full* range of capacities that define it, it cannot not be univocally predicated of anyone; rather, insofar as it includes capacities (especially of imagination and affect) which are generically different as between men and women, human nature is shared in according, I think, to a kind of analogy of proportionality, as between men and women. Neither sex is the paradigm, *simpliciter*, of human nature, which is only adequately understood across its full range of flourishing when the two sexes are understood in their complementarity.

One's understanding of one's 'gender identity', one's masculinity or femininity, as opportunity, as a form of flourishing to be respected and promoted, will be greatly enhanced (or, in unfortunate cases, impeded) by the example of one's parents. One's parentage, one's status as the child of these two parents and no others, is of course another identity which one finds rather than makes. By their difference as mother and father as well as their equality as human persons and spouses and parents, morally good parents are icons and nurturers of one's practical understanding of, and willingness to foster, one's opportunity to be a good person in a sisterly way or a brotherly way, as maiden or as man, as wife or as husband, in a maternal way or a paternal way. For, since the natural (physiological and psychological) preconditions are what they are, each of the ways of being I just listed is highly desirable and appropriate, if not strictly indispensable, for attaining and maintaining the form of life that helps both parents and children to their flourishing as individuals and as parts (members) of their familial community, such flourishing being in turn in part constituted by and in part dependent upon the family's willingness to draw from and contribute to the well-being and resources of wider communities, educative, commercial, defensive, and justice-enforcing.

A large part of what is shared amongst parents and children (and secondarily among uncles, aunts, cousins, and nephews) is language, that core of human culture. Again, there is no such thing as language. There are only languages—this one, that one, the other one, and so on. Each is highly particular—comprised of *determinationes* through and through, unlike the *ius gentium*—but is intelligible (to those to whom it is intelligible and usable) only because it is for them a kind of universal, both by being shareable amongst each other (their *langue*) and by being their gateway to universals *simpliciter*, their gateway, that is to say, to all the true propositions (practical as well as theoretical) which can be articulated in (in principle) any and every particular language. What I have just said is true paradigmatically of each person's native *langue*, mother tongue, for each of us an identity which we no more choose and opt into than we choose our parents, uncles, aunts, and siblings. Yet language, far more thoroughly and extensively than procreation, is culture—that is, one of the shareable realities that persons and their communities add, by choice and *technē*, to the naturally given.

This sketch of various natural and cultural realities does not seek to provide a taxonomy of stable realities or of aspects of human flourishing, but picks out examples perhaps sufficiently strategic to provide material for reflection on how the *determinationes* which constitute or result in these realities are made. In each kind of case, I think, the *determinatio* is, one way or another, the specifying and indeed particularizing of an opportunity understood as good for all who can share in the resultant benefits. In the case of a language, itself the resultant of countless unidentifiable options and acceptances, that opportunity of sharing—of sharing in a vehicle for understanding of each other's hopes and fears, belief and doubt, friendship or hostility, and so forth—is an open-ended opportunity, limited only by the preferences of other peoples for their own established languages. In the case of a marriage, on the other hand, the character of a procreative friendship which will respect and promote the equality of the spouses and potential parents requires that the *determinatio* involved in asking for and accepting the hand and commitment of one's spouse be radically and exclusively particular, this couple choosing to become the one husband and one wife who can be, lifelong, the father and mother to *their* children. The stringent limitation entails no contempt for others, 'eligible' or otherwise. Rather, it is an acknowledgement and anticipatory act of the particular love that will or would be needed if children of this marital union are to receive the dedicated nurture and care that their growth into flourishing will or would call for.

That growth into flourishing and self-determination will call for more than all that parents alone, or even a wider family, could provide. The language that good parents teach is the language of their own people, the people sufficiently numerous and differentiated to inter-marry safely, to divide and specialize their productive activities and their holdings and management of land and other natural resources well enough to prosper economically, and sufficiently concerned, fair-minded, and powerful to arrange for the doing and imposing of justice in contentions and injustices within or between families and for the defence of all families and neighbourhoods within a wide region against attacks and depredations. We know this Aristotelian ascent from family to political community with its government and law,[7] but my present point is that that ascent is made generally feasible by the sharing of a language, which in turn opens up all who share it to the whole treasury of experience, insight, and aspiration of *at least* one people whose existence and history far outreaches in extent and depth the concerns and activities of its present governmental structures or indeed its law. For this each member of this people can be grateful, with a gratitude that is accompanied by affection and zeal to retain, purify, and sustain this effectively indispensable opening to human achievement, notwithstanding all the corruptions and offences it also bears with it and in it. In saying this I say what St Thomas says with more compression: there is a form of charity, of love of others, which is the love of parents and love of *patria*, and is called *pietas*.[8]

In beginning to speak of a people, our reflections touch upon a central weakness, perhaps ineradicable, of the tradition of legal and political philosophy, namely its scant attention to the question how and by what right any particular state comes into being (and passes away), how far the state should coincide with unities of origin or culture or take, instead, the form of a federation of a more or less inter-national kind. (It is not a weakness peculiar to the central tradition; Jan-Werner Müller's very recent survey and defence of 'constitutional patriotism' admits that none of the versions or theories of this 'post-conventional, post-traditionalist, post-nationalist belonging' goes any way to answering this question of the boundaries and origins of states, and he adds that this is 'a weakness of liberal thought more generally'.[9]) My reflections here will make little or no progress towards filling that lacuna, but will consider some problems and proposals within the traditional sphere of political and legal philosophical discourse, the legal and political system of a community presupposed to be

[7] By 'political community' I mean what I call a state and Maritain calls a body politic; by 'state', Maritain means what I call government and law: *Aquinas* 220; Maritain, *Man & the State*, 8–11.

[8] *ST* II–II q.101 a.1 ad 2: pietas est quaedam *protestatio caritatis* quam quis habet ad parentes et ad patriam—the showing (not feigning) of your love for your parents and your own country.

[9] Müller, *Constitutional Patriotism*, 67–8.

rightfully a state, a particular political community amongst other states or communities of similar rank in the Aristotelian ascent.

The government of such a political community is responsible for shaping and applying its law so as to uphold, where need be coercively, the public good. The public good does not comprise all elements of the common good of that community or its constituent communities. Public good is only that dimension of the common good which involves interpersonal dealings or communications—that is to say, involves justice and injustice, not precisely as virtuous or vicious states of persons' dispositions and character but as states of affairs and forms of conduct which (a) involve or relate to persons *other* than the acting person and (b) would be judged by persons of just character to be just or, as the case may be, unjust. It is desirable to make these elementary clarifications here because the theses of Ronald Dworkin that I am about to discuss emerge in an intellectual context, or cultural *status quaestionis*, in which the distinction between public good and the full common good in all its elements was not—indeed, is not—clearly understood or even present to the minds of the participants in the cultural-political and legal-philosophical debate to which his theses were intended to contribute.

III

Dworkin's first published statement of his thesis took the form of offering a sounder foundation for John Rawls's proposition that government and law must as a matter of justice be neutral between competing conceptions of good and bad in human existence. In Rawls's *A Theory of Justice* that proposition had nothing but fragile foundations in arguments which were not from justice but from self-interested caution lest one, in choosing principles of justice behind a veil of ignorance, then find one's own preferences condemned and outlawed.[10] Dworkin offered Rawls a better foundation, in the thesis that to base political arrangements and laws on judgments about human good is to deny to persons the equal concern and respect which is their 'abstract right' (Dworkin's name for universal or human rights, rights that everyone has, abstracted from particular circumstances and arrangements):

> political arrangements that do not display equal concern and respect are those that are established and administered by powerful men and women who, whether they recognize it or not, have more concern and respect for members of a particular class, or people with particular talents *or ideals*, than they have for others.[11]

[10] See essay III.2, sec. II (1987c at 434–7).

[11] Dworkin, *Taking Rights Seriously* (hereafter *TRS*), 181 (emphasis added) (first published 1973).

A little later Dworkin put the thesis more precisely, using the term 'government' to include law:

> Government must not only treat people with concern and respect, but with equal concern and respect.... It must not constrain liberty on the ground that one citizen's conception of the good life of one group is nobler or superior to another's.[12]

The key term here is *respect*, and the implicit argument is this. If one judges that some form of human activity is wrongful and/or harmful and unreasonable, one manifests one's disrespect for anyone who wishes to engage in such activity—at least if one gives effect to one's judgment by forbidding the action itself or actions or omissions intended or likely to promote such activity. 'Disrespect' is synonymous with 'contempt', so I will call this Dworkin's 'argument from contempt'.

Clearly the argument fails. To judge that a form of life ('lifestyle') or conduct is bad for those who engage in it or those who emulate them, and on the basis of that judgment to coercively deter them from engaging in it, can be a form of charity, uninfected by any self-preference, arrogance, or disdain, or contempt for those whose judgment is contradicted (if indeed it is a judgment, and not a mere succumbing in bad conscience to temptation) and whose actions are coercively regulated.[13] The regulation may be motivated by concern for the good of these individuals, which is indeed a part of the common good even in those kinds of case in which the regulation is unjust because it crosses the line between public and non-public good and so is outside the proper coercive jurisdiction of state government and law. Call such kinds of case pure paternalism. Pure paternalism denies, and plausibly denies, that the argument from contempt is sound in treating restriction of a person's activities as proof, or per se evidence, of hostility to or contempt for the person. So: policies which, unlike pure paternalism, respect the limit of the law's proper jurisdiction to *public* good can even more securely be judged to be free from contempt for the persons whose activities these policies restrict in order to protect the vulnerable from, for example, seduction, corruption, or infection.

[12] *TRS* 272–3 (first published 1977). He adds: 'These postulates, taken together, state what might be called the liberal conception of equality; but it is a conception of equality, not of liberty as license, that they state.'

[13] [As Hart rightly says:

> The majority imposing such external preferences [and denying a liberty] may regard the minority's views as mistaken or sinful; but overriding them, for those reasons (however objectionable on other grounds), seems quite compatible with recognizing the equal worth of the holders of such views and may even be inspired by concern for them. ('Between Utility and Rights' at 844; see likewise 843.)]

As if anticipating this objection—that 'moralistic' policies need not be contemptuous of those on whom they impact negatively or even coercively (since they may well be charitable in intent)—Dworkin in the same period advanced an indirect, astonishing, scorched-earth outer defence. He claimed that the very concept of constitutional or human rights rests upon the requirement that utilitarian counting and summing of preferences, even though it be egalitarian in counting everyone's personal preferences, must be curtailed so as to exclude from the counting every preference a person has about *other* people and their fate (well-being or benefit; harm or loss).[14] To count such 'external' preferences would be to upset equality by introducing double-counting, that is, multiple weighting of some people's preferences, to the disadvantage of other people's. His arguments and illustrations, in support of this exclusion of external preferences, mostly concerned the risk that the external preferences in question would be 'moralistic' or racist preferences expressive of hatred, disdain, or '[adverse] prejudice'. But quite explicitly he asserted that even 'altruistic' preferences, in favour of the well-being of others, must be excluded too.[15] That is why I call this outer defence a scorched-earth strategy. Within five years, in response to criticism by H.L.A. Hart, Dworkin drastically modified it so as to allow the counting of 'altruistic' preferences (or as we would say, charitable and/or disinterestedly [impartially] fair preferences) about the welfare of others.[16] The outer defence of the argument from contempt is, correspondingly (and in the same work), reassigned to a new[17] argument whose importance—that is, social influence—I would like to emphasize. Dworkin articulates this new argument by saying that what he is condemning is 'a political process that assumes that *the fact that people have such reasons* is itself part of the case in political morality for what they favor'.[18] Elsewhere, in the same period, he put it like this: legislative decisions are denials of equality (and thus contemptuous of those whose equality is denied) when they 'count the majority's convictions about how other people should live' as the ground, or indeed as a ground, for 'legislation that can be justified only by appealing to the majority's preferences about which of their fellow citizens are worthy of concern and respect', which Dworkin immediately treats as identical to legislation that 'can be justified only on the ground

[14] My presentation and discussion of this argument owes much to Yowell, 'A Critical Examination of Dworkin's Theory of Rights'.

[15] See *TRS* 235, 238 (first published 1976); 277 (first published 1977).

[16] 'Do We Have a Right to Pornography?'(1981), 177, republished in Dworkin, *A Matter of Principle* (hereafter *MoP*): see 368.

[17] But it was foreshadowed in Dworkin, 'Political Judges and the Rule of Law' (1978: republished in *MoP*). For my critique see essay III.1 at nn. 19–23 (1985a at 309–11).

[18] *MoP* 368.

that the majority finds [the conduct restricted by the legislation] distasteful, or disapproves the culture it generates'.[19]

The key move in this new argument is its assumption that when the legislators or majority enact a restrictive law, their *reason* and *justification* for the enactment relies upon the sheer fact that they hold the moral opinion they do. This is our opinion, and because it is ours we can ignore your contrary opinion and restrict your liberty. The new argument provides, I believe, a significant part of the context in which a majority of the US Supreme Court now willingly declares that certain laws can be set aside because they manifest the legislative majority's 'animus against' the persons whose conduct is restrained by the law which the Court invalidates. Such declarations are made without any significant evidence in the case record of such 'animus' (sc. emotional, prejudiced hostility), and the finding of animus is treated as exempting the Court from examining the moral, cultural, or other substantive arguments which the legislators actually did use, or could reasonably have used, to justify their legislation. The fallacy in this procedure, and in Dworkin's argument, consists in its implicit denial of *transparency* to the legislators' or citizen-majority's pronouncements.

For we do not understand the vital distinction between *propositions* and the statements or utterances which articulate them unless we understand the transparency of first-person singular affirmative statements (assertions, etc.). The statement 'I think that it is true that X is bad' is transparent for 'It is true that X is bad', which is transparent for 'X is bad', which is the proposition that I assert by uttering the statement. That is to say: except in special contexts, the 'I think', like the 'it is true that', drops away, leaving still the *whole content of what was asserted* by the original statement, the whole proposition in question. And this has its counterpart in the logic of argumentation. The fact that *I believe that* X is bad, or that P is true, is for me no argument in favour of my belief; the belief, like the fact that I have it, adds nothing to, indeed is no part of, the justification I may have, or could offer, for that belief.

The same holds when many particular individuals find that they each share the same belief. They may find some comfort or reassurance in the fact that the belief is widely held, or is the belief of the majority. But they cannot reasonably propose that fact as justification for the belief. And very often legislation is proposed, defended, and enacted by majorities without the majority seeking to rely for justification upon the fact that their opinion is more widely held than contrary opinions. The fact that

[19] *MoP* 68.

theirs is the majority opinion may well be essential to the legal validity of their legislative activity, but it is no part of the justification for that legislation. They are guiltless of the form of self-preference that is alleged in Dworkin's 'new' (but now aging) defence of his core claim that legislation restricting freedom to promote activity judged bad manifests disrespect for persons who wish to engage in or promote such activity. The defence is, in fact, a plain fallacy or sophism, and its cultural success is a deplorable testimony to decay in standards of public argumentation. Indeed, it is a form of refined incivility. And its nullity as an argument leaves the core claim undefended and indefensible.

Joseph Raz shared the position on which much of our law relies, that legislation which seeks to promote the good and discourage the bad is not per se disrespectful of those whose conduct it restrains.[20] But in more recent work, much though not all of it on the less traditional topic of multiculturalism, he has adopted a position which involves him, I believe, in a confusion which is like Dworkin's both in its content and in its likely cultural impact.

Raz frames his reflections on multiculturalism in a way we should find congenial, saying:

> I see the universal and the particular to be complementary rather than antagonistic, and the point has always been clear in the best philosophical tradition, that is the one descending from Aristotle. The universal must find expression in the particular and the particular can only get its meaning from the fact that it is subsumed under the universal.... universal values are realized in a variety of different ways in different cultures....[21]

What does he have in mind when he speaks of *cultures* and thus of multi*culturalism*? This is not very clear. He speaks of 'cultural groups' or 'cultural communities', but examples given prominently include 'gays... Christians... black people',[22] none of which would count as viable communities in any but the most extended sense (in which persons who have *some* common characteristic of interest to themselves or others can be called a community). But *multiculturalism* is said by Raz to concern

> those societies in which there are several stable cultural communities both wishing and able to perpetuate themselves. It does not apply, for example, to a

[20] Raz's acceptance of a Mill-like 'Harm Principle' distinguishes his 'perfectionist' position from pure paternalism, and approximates it to the position that coercive legislation must be for *public* good.

[21] 18 Raz, *Ethics in the Public Domain* (hereafter *EPD*), 120, 179; see also his *The Morality of Freedom*, 265. The quoted passage ends: 'and... they [the world's different cultures] are all worthy of respect'.

[22] Raz, 'Multiculturalism' at 204.

country which receives many immigrants from diverse cultures, but where those from each culture are few in number...[23]

A society of the first kind, he says, can be called multicultural(ist) in a purely descriptive sense. Multiculturalism as a 'normative principle' or 'evaluative approach' 'is a policy of saying yes to this situation'. Then '[M]ulticulturalism requires a political society to recognize the equal standing of all the stable and viable cultural communities existing in that society', the equal standing of, for example, Raz says, 'Turks in the Netherlands and Bangladeshis in Britain'.[24] He might have added here (but did not) that it is the officially acknowledged experience in both the Netherlands and Britain that the children or grandchildren of those who came to these countries as Turks or Bangladeshis frequently lose much sense of being members of a Turkish or Bangladeshi community, and regard themselves instead as members of a religious community and culture in which such national distinctions are strenuously subordinated to an identity which is not the less 'political' for being 'religious', since it holds that devotion to *this* divine revelation should be the organizing principle of a single, universal, that is worldwide political community, pending the emergence of which, with a universal government and law, all believers should consider themselves members of a universal 'nation' (that word being one of the reasonable and common translations of *Ummah*).

I return to Raz. He is as conscious as we all should be of political (and therefore legal) philosophy's dependence upon *factual* as well as evaluative premises. To give an example (mine not his) of such dependence, consider the justification of regimes of private property in Aristotelian and Thomist theory (a justification which I think remains valid and central to this day). It rests on a 'rule' of human experience: natural resources, and the capital resources and consumer durables derivable from them, are more productively exploited and more carefully maintained by private enterprise, management, husbandry, and housekeeping than by either individuals using common resources on their own initiative or the 'officials' (including all employees) of public enterprises. At least for the times and places and the classes of resources for which this factual rule of experience holds true,

[23] *EPD* 173. Immediately preceding Raz's essay 'Multiculturalism' in *EPD* is his essay 'Free Expression and Personal Identification', where the term used for cultures is 'styles of life', 'ways of life', or 'forms of life', explicitly synonymous with 'cultures' (e.g. *EPD* 155). And in the latter essay, *multiculturalism* is called instead *pluralism*, or *strong pluralism*, and the primary referent of 'cultures' is what Americans refer to when they talk of 'culture wars'. That names a set of arguments within a linguistically, ethnically, educationally homogeneous culture about abortion, embryo use or abuse, marriage, euthanasia, pornography and censorship, sexual promiscuity or repression, recreational drugs, patriotism, and so forth—the list might in principle include architecture, music, literary criticism, philosophy, and much else.

[24] *EPD* 189, 174, 173, 175.

a régime of private ownership will be a requirement of justice, provided that the increased stock of goods yielded by such a regime is not hoarded by a class of successful private owners but is made available by appropriate mechanisms (for example profit-sharing; trade under competitive market conditions; redistributive taxation; full employment through productive investment; etc.) to all members of the community, in due measure.[25] Here then is Raz's comparable summary of rules of experience concerning the existence and well-being of another kind of social institution, political communities, a summary articulated in an address to an audience in Germany:

The need for [a common bond of political society] cannot be doubted. Political societies are characterized by the fact that they claim authority over individuals, and in the name of that authority they not infrequently require individuals to make sacrifices for the benefit of other members... Redistributive taxation... and all the institutions of the welfare state are examples of state institutions imposing sacrifices on some for the sake of others. The willingness to share is not purchased easily. Without it political society soon disintegrates, or has to rely on extensive force and coercion.

How is this willingness to share maintained?... members of a modern political society need to share a common culture.... Willingness to share depends on capacity for empathy... on the ability of people to feel for others and that depends on their ability to understand and empathise with other people's experiences, aspirations and anxieties.

... Ultimately political unity depends on people's free and willing identification with the political society they belong to: on the fact that they feel German, that their sense of their own identity as German is totally instinctive and unproblematic. And it depends on the fact that they are proud to be German.[26]

[25] I am quoting *NLNR* 170–1, where I go on:

Of course, *if* the active members of the community were more detached from considerations of private advantage, from love of 'their own', etc., then common ownership and enterprise *would* be more productive of benefits for all. But a theory of justice is to establish what is due to persons in the circumstances in which they are, not in the circumstances of some other, 'ideal' world. And those many members of the community who reasonably depend for their livelihood upon the productive efforts and good husbandry of other members can rightly complain of injustice if a regime of property (exploitation, production, management of resources) is adopted, on the basis that it *would* enhance their well-being if the non-dependent members of the community had characters different from those that in fact they have, but which *actually* yields them (and everyone else) a lower standard of living than they would enjoy under a different regime of property operated by the non-dependent members as they *actually* are.

[26] Raz, 'Multiculturalism' at 202–3. The last sentences must not be misunderstood. They must be taken in such a sense that they are compatible with the proposition that multiculturalism rightly 'rejects common nationality as a common bond' (*ibid.* at 201) and 'aims to replace nationalism as the common bond of political society' (*ibid.*, 202). So 'German' must here be understood not as member of a nation (at least *stricto sensu*), but as member of the political society, perhaps as citizen or perhaps as persons who might well be citizens though not eligible under actual German law because of its ethnic basis for citizenship.

In the light of this powerful statement of the preconditions for the Rule of Law and decent government, we are bound to ask why multiculturalism should not be judged a public harm. Raz's thesis that it is a public good, or net public good, relies upon some further factual premises or presuppositions.

The most important of these is: absence of a common language is merely a 'nuisance', not really a public harm, still less a very great public harm.[27] I cannot share that factual judgment. I agree with him that 'our understanding of the bonds which keep a political society together is very tenuous'.[28] But I think wide historical experience supports the presumption that in the absence of a common language in which people can really understand each other, there is little reason to expect that a 'totally instinctive and unproblematic sense of common identity' as members of the same political community will emerge or, if it exists, survive, unless perhaps in face of some urgent common threat (enemy). Is there not instead strong reason to expect tension, bitterness, and disintegration—at worst (but it is not very uncommon) Balkanization with the accompanying atrocities, expropriations, and forced displacements of populations, at best such spectacles as the 1968 division of the library of the Catholic University of Flemish-speaking Leuven to create the French-speaking Catholic University of Louvain-la-Neuve (all that could be agreed upon was that Leuven should keep volumes 1, 3, 5, 7...of encyclopedias, and sets of collected works), and in between best and worst the intermediate conditions of political paralysis, discord, and intermittent dictatorship now endemic in, say, Fiji?

What then is Raz's reason for holding that multiculturalism is an 'ideal', a public good, rather than a considerable evil as a state of affairs and a serious mistake as a policy or precept? Notice, as he says, that

> liberal multiculturalism is not opposed in principle to the assimilation of one cultural group by others.... So long as [i] the process is not coerced, [ii] does not arise out of *lack of respect* for people and their communities, and [iii] is gradual, there is nothing wrong with it.[29]

Of these three conditions, condition [ii] must be decisive. Coerciveness alone and as such could not be a sufficient objection to assimilative programmes,

[27] *Ibid.* at 202:

> We know that a common culture [such as modern political society needs] does not mean a common religion, and it does not mean membership of a common ethnic or racial group. It does not even mean a common language, though the absence of a common language can be a nuisance.... They certainly help when they are present. But they are not necessary, and this is just as well, for the thought that political societies must be based on a common religion or race is not much more appealing than the suggestion that they must be based on a common enemy.

[28] *Ibid.* at 201. [29] *EPD* 182. That multiculturalism is an ideal: 'Multiculturalism' at 196.

any more than it is to programmes of compulsory education or vaccination or, *mutatis mutandis*, town-planning or zoning regulations, or examination regulations. Moreover, the mere requirement of assimilation—for example that your children must attend a school which teaches only in the country's official language—is not as such a manifestation of disrespect, since (as we recall him saying) 'multiculturalism [as a precept]... does not apply, for example, to a country which receives many immigrants from diverse cultures, but where those from each culture are few in number'.[30] In relation to all such scattered, isolated, and not numerous immigrants, it is reasonable to impose, and for them to accept, the set of losses and impairments of their cultural interests that is involved in assimilation. The immersion of these immigrants and their children in the official language and dominant culture, with the consequent weakening of the children's membership in their parents' culture, is—in the case in question—no more than an acceptable *side effect*, that is, an unintended effect, of the requirement that children be educated combined with the practical non-availability of education in the parents' language and culture. So, being a side effect, that is, an unintended effect, the requiring of educational assimilation need involve no 'slighting' of, or other disrespect for, that culture whatever, or of its value. There need here be no offence to anyone's dignity, and Raz accepts that there is none.

But now we reach the climax of the argument. Where the situation is different from that just mentioned, and the immigrants of a particular culture are sufficiently numerous to provide education in their own language and culture, then Raz proposes the normative multiculturalist theses, especially that government and law must permit and subsidize their education in their immigrant languages and cultures to the same extent as the government and law permit and subsidize the schools of the (hitherto) dominant culture. For, he says:

> [1]... the demand for a forced retraining and adaptation is [2] liable to undermine people's dignity and self-respect. It [3] shows that the state, their state, has no respect for their culture, finds it inferior and plots its elimination.[31]

But [1] the 'force' here is nothing but the compulsory education which Raz was happy to see applied to *scattered* and isolated immigrants, and [2] the supposed undermining of dignity and self-respect is no more than a side effect which he was happy to accept in the case of scattered and isolated immigrant parents. So his case rests entirely on [3] the claim

[30] *EPD* 173. [31] 'Multiculturalism' at 200, referring to *EPD* 178.

that assimilative education of children of substantial minority immigrant cultures 'shows that the state, their state, has no respect for their culture, finds it inferior and plots its elimination'.

Is this what it shows? Suppose that those who determine the law and policies of this political community believe just what Raz articulates in his powerful statement of the preconditions of a stable Rule of Law and decent government. Then there is no reason whatever to suppose that their demand that immigrants assimilate manifests disrespect for the immigrants' culture, or that they find that culture inferior or plot its elimination. The rationale of their policy of, say, assimilative education may well be *purely* to maintain the conditions for political survival and flourishing convincingly outlined by Raz. (Perhaps that rationale's factual premises would need to include the judgment, which should and can be sober and impartial—that lack of a common language is no mere 'nuisance'.)

So, since a policy of assimilation can reasonably be intended solely to avert the great social evils outlined by Raz, especially the replacement of the Rule of Law and decent government by regimes of force, such a policy cannot reasonably be presumed to be motivated by judgments of disrespect for persons or their cultures, or to have a purpose of eliminating those cultures, even if the withering away of those cultures in this country is expected to be a side effect of assimilation. Correspondingly, it will in such cases be unreasonable for members of the immigrant cultures to feel slighted, disrespected, offended, or contemned by the adoption of the relevant laws and policies. And wrong for philosophers like Raz or Dworkin to hold otherwise by loosely extending the categories of 'disrespect' and 'offensiveness'.

Now suppose a different case. A particular immigrant culture may define itself, or many members of ethnically diverse immigrant groups may come in one or two generations to define themselves, as members of a religious-political culture of a kind such as I outlined earlier. These inhabitants of our country and subjects of our legal system may use, or come to use, the term 'our country' and 'our legal system' to refer to something substantially transformed so as to make normative for us, here and now, or here and soon enough, *their* culture's beliefs and norms. May we not—indeed, must we not—now *consider and judge* whether the changes they envisage and promote will be changes we are morally bound to accept as improvements on our laws and way of life? And might we not judge, rightly, that such changes would not merely be not morally required of us, but would rather be harmful, evils of the kind we are morally entitled and perhaps bound to resist out of that form of charity which I discussed before? Might we not conclude that their culture is indeed *inferior* in ways which present a challenge to both our common good and our public good? Indeed, we can suppose—or, more frankly, recognize—a challenge of that kind, which might become a threat and then a war. That charity, to recall, included an element of 'universal' judgment about what is good or bad for any human being, and included also an element of *pietas* for one's particular *patria*.[32] Even when it repudiates the religion or politics or marital culture of the immigrants as, in part, morally evil, that does not entail, and need not psychologically involve, any contempt for the persons as such. Even when considering those members of that group who have freely and cognisantly chosen, by self-determining acts of belief and commitment, to devote themselves to purposes which we must judge unjust, uncharitable, and so forth, we need have no *unjust* disrespect for them.

A decision to exclude the (further) immigration of members of such cultures can, therefore, be fully consistent with the reasonable and probably intended and authentic meaning of Vatican II's two statements: on the one hand, since all are children of God and brothers:

No foundation therefore remains for any theory or practice that leads to discrimination between man and man or people and people, so far as their human dignity and the rights flowing from it are concerned.[33]

And on the other hand:

Christians belong to the nation in which they were born. They have begun to share in its cultural treasures by means of their education. They are joined in its life by manifold social ties... They feel its problems as their very own... They must give expression to this [Christian] newness of life in the social and cultural framework of their own homeland [*patriae*], according to the traditions of their own nation, a culture which they should get to know, heal, preserve, develop in accordance with contemporary conditions, and finally perfect in Christ.[34]

[32] See Wright, *National Patriotism in Papal Teaching*, 3–6 and passim; Grisez, *Living a Christian Life*, 836–44.

[33] Declaration *Nostra Aetate* (1965) s. 5. Cf. Pastoral Constitution *Gaudium et Spes* (1965) s. 29:

Nevertheless, with respect to the fundamental rights of the person, every type of discrimination, whether social or cultural, whether based on sex, race, color, social condition, language or religion, is to be overcome and eradicated as contrary to God's intent.

There is here no reference to nationality or citizenship. (Note, incidentally, that the section goes on: 'For in truth it must still be regretted that fundamental personal rights are still not being universally honored. Such is the case of a woman who is denied the right to choose a husband freely, to embrace a state of life or to acquire an education or cultural benefits equal to those recognized for men.') When all the references in *Gaudium et Spes* are compared it is clear that the term 'discrimination' is used to mean unjust discrimination and there is no assertion that differentiations in treatment are always unjust.

[34] Decree *Ad Gentes* (1965) s. 21.

Such a decision would be legitimately subsumable under the norms implicit in Pope Benedict XVI's statement that:

> Single believers are called to open their arms and their hearts to every person, from whatever nation they come, allowing the Authorities responsible for public life to enforce the relevant laws held to be appropriate for a healthy co-existence.[35]

And such an exclusionary decision, in respect of the kind(s) of culture I described, would be in accordance with sound political theory.

This remains true, I think, even if we or some of us have to take into account the fact that the politically dominant ethos of *our own* culture has come to embrace moral evils with at least as much complacency as Roman jurists preserved when contemplating slavery.

IV

I have touched upon a grave question for contemporary political and legal theory, one that loose doctrines of offensiveness threaten to make it unsafe to discuss, and still more unsafe to *deliberate* about publicly together. But is there a more grave and searching question for a contemporary political and legal theory than this related but distinct one: Do people (perhaps *the* people, the whole population) of some areas of the world have a right, in justice, to choose to emigrate from those areas and immigrate into another country of their preference—a right such that it would be an injustice for the authorities or people of that other country to refuse to accept them into the territory as at least potential citizens? That question is not settled by the demonstration that arguments like those of Dworkin and Raz are invalid and erroneous in claiming to identify types of political or legislative action which they say necessarily, regardless of the intentions of those who engage in them, involve a constructive or irrebuttably presumptive disrespect for persons, disrespect of a kind that would be (as they say) 'wrong in itself'.[36]

The question is not altogether unlike the question that has always faced the Church in relation to the rich: Does Dives have an obligation in justice to let the poor satisfy their needs or desires by taking from his property

[35] Benedict XVI, Address to the Pontifical Council for Pastoral Care of Migrants and Itinerant People, 15 May 2006.

[36] In relation to censorship of opinions, Raz says (*EPD* 162–3):

> Given that that is the social significance of such acts of censorship, that they are perceived as condemning the way of life as a whole, such censorship constitutes condemnation. The defence 'we did not intend to condemn' is of no avail. What counts is what the government did, not what it intended to do.... Such measures cannot be justified. They are wrong in themselves.

It is clear that he would say the same of other forms of (what he considers) disrespect *for persons* along with way of life.

as they select?[37] Does he have rather an obligation to distribute to the poor, on his own initiative and preferences as owner, all the resources he holds in excess of what he needs to maintain himself, his family, and close dependants? Or is he entitled to devote the excess, so defined, to pursuing his professional or skilled vocation, educating his children, supporting the institutions and arrangements appropriate to maintaining the Rule of Law, the advancement of knowledge, architectural and other glories of God, and so forth? Dire emergency and famine aside, may he not treat as *superflua*, dedicated to relief of the poor, *only* what is left after contributing reasonably to these 'vocational' good works? Saintly philosophers such as St Thomas, like the universal church's most authorized pastors and teachers, have favoured the last of these possible answers.[38]

The right of a particular political community's members, acting through its government and law, to exclude from entry or residence all non-members whose residing would directly or indirectly pose a risk to that community's common good[39] is a right similar in ground and structure to the rights of exclusion and exclusionary use which are central to *dominium* and other analogous rights of property or ownership. Both kinds of right must be understood and exercised compatibly with the truths, first (1) that the Earth belongs to all, and second (2) that it can be and almost universally is reasonable, indeed required by justice, to divide it up and appropriate its material resources and its territories to some for their exclusionary use. For, as to resources: their cultivation and management will be more fruitful in economic and moral goods than if they were tended as common or as publicly owned. And, as to the territories of states: the culture, law, and politics carried forward on them will be more human, adequate, and just than if carried on (a) in a context of deep disharmony among their inhabitants and/or (b) where those preconditions for law (and much else) which Raz identified for us are not in place or would be negated by the entry of many and different peoples. For, in turn, immigration of such a scale or kind can overwhelm or outrun assimilation, dissipate the general (near unanimous) 'sense' (including intelligently willed disposition) of identification with the country, nation, state, government, and law that our forebears built upon this land, and thereby bring about the elimination or non-fulfilment of the preconditions for peace, welfare, and good government. So, (1) since the Earth belongs to all, the right of exclusion must be subject to override by the kind of real necessity that in our tradition's teaching, as articulated by St Thomas, makes property revert to common availability to the extent required to relieve such necessity. That kind of override

[37] Luke 6: 19–31. [38] *Aquinas* 188–96. [39] See essay III.9 (2007a) sec. III.

is found in the Convention relating to the Status of Refugees 1951 as extended temporally and geographically by Protocol of 1967. But (2) as that Convention shows in its *determinationes* of the universal right of refuge, the exercise of even this fundamental right is by no means unconditional, and requires, among other things, that the refugee conform to our (just) laws and regulations as well as to (just) measures taken for the maintenance of our public order. I have been meditating in this essay—scarcely arguing—about some aspects of the common good of political communities that bear at least indirectly on their public good and even on their public order, and so are fit matter for law and legislative deliberation.

7

COSMOPOLIS, NATION STATES, AND FAMILIES*

I

If practical reason finds its master moral principle in the ideal of integral or universal human fulfilment, and if revelation identifies and is transmitted in a universal (that is, 'catholic') human society ('the new and universal Israel')[1] whose teachings include the proposition that all created subpersonal goods or resources have a 'universal destination';[2] and if both reason and this religion endorse the contemporary moral-political consensus articulated in the Universal Declaration of Human Rights (1948), the question fairly arises: What should we think about 'universalism' in political theory, and about 'cosmopolitan' duties of justice? Those are labels for the thesis that whatever duties of and rights to assistance we owe to our neighbours (say, our fellow citizens) must be owed in equal measure to all persons everywhere. How might that thesis be applied? Take just one of the many ways in which that question might be posed: Is it ever right to discriminate (distinguish in treatment) between persons, at our borders, on the ground that this person is a national, a citizen, and therefore may certainly enter, and that person is not and therefore may perhaps not?[3]

* 2008a, secs IV–V. For secs I–II see essay I.5; for sec. III see essay V.8.

[1] Wojtyla (John Paul II), *Memory and Identity*, 81.

[2] *Catechism of the Catholic Church* (1997), under the heading 'The universal destination and the private ownership of goods', says:

> 2402 In the beginning God entrusted the earth and its resources to the common stewardship of mankind to take care of them, master them by labor, and enjoy their fruits. The goods of creation are destined for the whole human race. However, the earth is divided up among men to assure the security of their lives, endangered by poverty and threatened by violence. The appropriation of property is legitimate for guaranteeing the freedom and dignity of persons and for helping each of them to meet his basic needs and the needs of those in his charge. It should allow for a natural solidarity to develop between men.
>
> 2403 The right to private property, acquired by work or received from others by inheritance or gift, does not do away with the original gift of the earth to the whole of mankind. The universal destination of goods remains primordial, even if the promotion of the common good requires respect for private property, for the right to it and for its exercise.

[3] See essay III.9 (2007a), sec. V; 2008f; and essay 6, sec. IV (on the perhaps most grave and searching question for contemporary political theory).

That question was approached independently and with varying explicitness addressed, in 1993, by two persons, Karol Wojtyla and John Rawls, who had each reflected long on inter-personal ethics; and each later wrote up and published his response. In his *Memory and Identity*, appearing within two weeks of his death in 2005, Wojtyla says:

> The term 'nation' designates a community based in a given territory and distinguished from other nations by its culture. Catholic social doctrine holds that the family and the nation are both natural societies, not the product of mere convention. *Therefore, in human history, they cannot be replaced by anything else.*[4]

The right way of avoiding unhealthy nationalism is, he says,

> through patriotism. Whereas nationalism involves recognizing and pursuing the good of one's own nation alone, without regard to the rights of others, patriotism ... is a love of one's native land that accords rights to all other nations equal to those claimed for one's own.[5]

And

> the native land (or fatherland [*patria*]) is in some ways to be identified with patrimony, that is, the *totality of goods bequeathed to us by our forefathers.* In this context ... one frequently hears the expression 'motherland'. Through personal experience we all know to what extent the transmission of our spiritual patrimony takes place through our mothers. Our native land is thus our heritage and it is also the whole patrimony derived from that heritage ... the land, the territory, but more importantly ... the values and the spiritual content that go to make up the culture of a given nation.[6]

[4] *Memory & Identity*, 77–8 (emphasis added); likewise 75. See also Vatican II, Decree *Ad Gentes* (1965), sec. 21:

> Christians belong to the nation in which they were born. They have begun to share in its cultural treasures by means of their education. They are joined in its life by manifold social ties ... They feel its problems as their very own ... They must give expression to this [Christian] newness of life in the social and cultural framework of their own homeland [*patriae*], according to the traditions of their own nation, a culture which they should get to know, heal, preserve, develop in accordance with contemporary conditions, and finally perfect in Christ.

[5] *Memory & Identity*, 75. For the background in earlier forceful papal teaching on patriotism, see Wright, *National Patriotism in Papal Teaching*. Wright (later a cardinal) shows how, in this extended body of teachings, strongly supportive of a not unconditional patriotism, the elements constitutive of the *patria* and the nation are primarily 'cultural, historical and religious traditions', with shared language given a certain priority in Wright's exposition, and the shared [love of] 'this our native land' firmly included, and the upshot being a certain shared *mentalité*: 56–66. Wright's arguments (28–51) for discounting certain other factors, not least what Rawls (quoting Mill) will list as 'race, descent' (see at n. 9 below), are in some tension with his (Wright's) general account.

[6] *Memory & Identity*, 66 (emphasis added). Here and elsewhere Wojtyla refers to and quotes (96–7) from his papal address of 2 June 1980 to UNESCO, especially

> concerning the right of the nation to the foundation of its culture and its future ... a stable element of human experience and of the humanistic perspective of man's development ... a fundamental sovereignty of society which is manifested in the culture of the nation ... through which, at the same time, man is supremely sovereign.

John Rawls's far-reaching theory of universal justice denies that a justice universal in its reach is cosmopolitan in its content, that all persons everywhere have equal basic rights, entitlements, and liberties.[7] Instead it speaks of justice—equal rights, etc.—between peoples, and within each people, but not directly as between all the individuals in the world as if the world were one people.

Rawls uses 'a people' to refer to what John Paul II and John Stuart Mill and most people call a nation.[8] Like John Paul II and Mill, he takes shared culture to be central to the reality of a particular people. He analyses this cultural reality into (a) first, and primarily, the members of this people being 'united among themselves by common sympathies which do not exist between them and others', which (b) 'make them cooperate with each other more willingly than with other people...', and (c) may result from various causes, such as commonality of race, descent, language, and religion but 'strongest of all is identity of political antecedents... of national history, and consequent community of recollections, collective pride and humiliation, pleasure and regret, connected with the same incidents in the past'.[9] Then he articulates the legitimate fundamental interests of peoples: their political independence and their free culture; the security, territory and well-being of their citizens; and 'their proper self-respect of themselves as a people,

This was taken up again by Pope Benedict XVI in his address to the bishops of France on 14 September 2008:

> I am convinced, in fact, that nations must never allow what gives them their particular identity to disappear. The fact that different members of the same family have the same father and mother does not mean that they are undifferentiated subjects: they are actually persons with their own individuality. The same is true for countries, which must take care to preserve and develop their particular culture, without ever allowing it to be absorbed by others or swamped in a dull uniformity. 'The Nation is in fact'—to take up the words of Pope John Paul II—'the great community of men who are united by various ties, but above all, precisely by culture. The Nation exists "through" culture and "for" culture, and it is therefore the great educator of men in order that they may "be more" in the community'. (Address to UNESCO, 2 June 1980, no. 14).

[7] See *Law of Peoples*, 82–5. The present essay's discussion of Rawls does not touch directly on the question whether he was justified in refusing to extend from the internal arrangements of political communities to the worldwide community of all persons that principle of justice most distinctive of his *A Theory of Justice*, namely the 'difference principle', that all social decisions (at least about the basic structure of society) should improve as far as possible the well-being of the worst-off group in the state. Forbidding immigration would be (in principle, and on certain conditions) compatible with accepting the very demanding requirements of a 'global difference principle'. But in practice the application of the principle would require world government, which again *might* not abolish boundaries—but would certainly relativize boundaries as it dissolved all conceptions of nationality as for some purposes decisive. [For critique of the Rawlsian difference principle, see essay III.3 (1973a); for reasons to agree with Rawls's refusal to extend it to the world considered as a single cosmopolis, see the penultimate paragraph of, and second endnote to, essay III.7 (1992b); and the addition to n. 45 in essay III.13.]

[8] See *Law of Peoples*, v, 23–5.

[9] *Ibid.*, 23 n. 17 quoting J.S. Mill, *Considerations on Representative Government* (1862), ch. 16. For Rawls's tentative speculation about how far all these elements are necessary for a just constitutional regime, see *Law of Peoples*, 24–5.

resting on their common awareness of their trials during their history and of their culture with its accomplishments'.[10]

Does not the ethical legitimacy of these fundamental interests suffice to legitimate the maintenance of boundaries and the concomitant limitation of (or right to limit) immigration? Rawls does not consider that question. Instead he grounds the right to limit immigration on the Aristotelian argument for the justice of the institution of property, whereby parts of the world's resources including land are appropriated to a particular person or group of persons: the argument that an asset tends to deteriorate 'unless a definite agent is given responsibility for maintaining [it] and bears the loss for not doing so'.[11]

Rawls is right, I think, to link the justice of boundaries with the justice of property.[12] Property rights—at whose core is the right to exclude others from free use of one's property—are well understood in the main tradition to be qualified both by their purpose of benefiting not merely the owners or other holders but in one way or another the whole community, and by their liability to being overridden in situations of real necessity. But Rawls uses a particularly thin version of Aristotle's argument about the purpose of property systems, an argument made even thinner by Rawls's focus on maintaining the territory 'and its environmental integrity',[13] as if for their own sake rather than for the sustenance and flourishing of those who cultivate it and those within and without who consume its fruits.[14] Only in a footnote does he observe that 'another reason for limiting immigration is to protect a people's political culture and its constitutional principles'.[15] He might very appropriately have brought to bear, right here, his own judgment that a good political culture will itself be dependent on what he calls 'common sympathies', shared by this people because of its shared memories and identity. Such shared sympathies, and the willingness to cooperate that they encourage, he might well have called, with Aristotle, civic friendship, or, with John Paul II, solidarity within the framework

[10] *Ibid.*, 34. For the implications of this kind of reality for a 'multiculturalist' politics, see my critical engagement with Joseph Raz's essays on multiculturalism (e.g. his 'Multiculturalism'), in essay 6, sec. III.

[11] *Law of Peoples*, 39; also 8.

[12] This is not to say that national territory *is* best understood as a form of property: see Freeman, 'Distributive Justice and the Law of Peoples' at 247–8.

[13] *Law of Peoples*, 38–9.

[14] Cf. essay 6, sec. IV:

> Is there a more grave and searching question for a contemporary political and legal theory than this...: Do people (perhaps *the* people, the whole population) of some areas of the world have a right, in justice, to choose to emigrate from those areas and immigrate into another country of their preference—a right such that it would be an injustice for the authorities or people of that other country to refuse to accept them into the territory as at least potential citizens?...

[15] *Law of Peoples*, 39 n. 48.

of patriotism. Modern political experience and reflection suggests that without a real and fairly pervasive sharing of sympathies, nothing short of massive state coercion[16] will suffice to ensure that people's loyalties to their family and its wealth and other interests are transcended *sufficiently to sustain what we call a welfare state*.[17] Since the maintenance of a welfare state within the framework of the rule of law is a major component of the common good and a strong requirement of justice, it will be a rather strong requirement of justice—in conditions favourable to mass movement—that immigration be regulated by discriminating among some kinds of non-nationals and other kinds, with a view to preserving one's people from the destruction or corrosion of these various cultural and dispositional preconditions for a just and stable common good.[18]

Two additional points about Rawls's defence of the ethics of maintaining strong, secure nations. They are points of special importance, I think, in the face of the ever more indiscriminate use by courts and activists of an anti-discrimination principle, which functions rather like a new communism. The first point to be made is that Rawls's defence of nations, which is significant because it cuts against what many assumed were the implications of his original theory of justice, depends not only on factual assumptions, that is, judgments, about the conditions under which the common good can be maintained but also on strongly (albeit highly plausible) substantive and positive evaluations. Think particularly of his thesis that it is right, or at least often right, for a people to be united in judging that their historic culture has been and is, at least substantially, a good one—that it has 'accomplishments' on which they can look with legitimate '*amour propre*'.[19] So, secondly, Rawls's affirmation of the necessity and legitimacy of this particular, substantive evaluation by the people (or the dominant portion of them) significantly limits—if not eliminates—the application

[16] 'Extensive force and coercion': Raz, 'Multiculturalism' at 202.

[17] And, to recall Mill's point, such sympathies are particular to the members of this people; as sympathies, they 'do *not* exist between them and others'. Plato was so impressed by the problem of overcoming exclusive family and/or tribal loyalties that, with due hesitations, but repeatedly, he postulated an ideal of a community-wide sharing of women and children, so that (as a penetrating modern interpreter puts it) 'the profound sentiments arising from sex relations, as well as the parent-child relations, will no longer be contained in the small family but will be communized' (Plato's word: *koinōneō*). See Voegelin, *Plato and Aristotle*, 118. Plato himself was aware of the extremism of this communist (or excessively universalist) proposal, and Aristotle's criticisms of it (see *ibid.*, 319–22; *Pol.* II.1–2: 1260b37–1264b3; *NLNR* 144–7, 158) enhance the efficiency argument for private property with elements relating to independence, autonomy, and generosity. These elements are not included in the efficiency argument later deployed by Aquinas and, though thinly, as we have seen, by Rawls. But they are present in mutated form in one part of Leo XIII's defence of property in *Rerum Novarum*, Encyclical 15 May 1891, secs 13–15.

[18] See essay 6; essay III.9, sec. V; and 2009e. Neither that set of essays nor this essay provides a sufficiently comprehensive consideration of the questions of justice and charity at stake in large-scale immigration by disparate peoples.

[19] *Law of Peoples*, 34 ('what Rousseau calls *amour propre*').

of two of the more famous theses that together are central to his account of 'public reason'. The first is that a liberal society (the main one of only two legitimate forms of nation) has *no* 'comprehensive conception of the good';[20] and the second is that his own theory of 'political liberalism' is not put forward as true but as an exercise in 'constructivism'.[21] His willingness to affirm what amounts to the necessity of patriotic evaluations makes yet more visible how much his programmatic constructivist deflation of such affirmations shares with the sceptical 'postmodern' deniers of truth, whose self-refuting approach to philosophy is nicely caught by Bernard Williams, paraphrasing Alisdair MacIntyre's genial remark about

> the awkwardness that inevitably catches up with the writer...who holds up before the reader's lens a sign saying that something is true or plausible or worth considering [or, we may add, legitimate], and then tries to vacate the spot before the shutter clicks.[22]

II

In what I have just been saying about the pre-conditions for the degree of unity (as opposed to diversity) necessary for the rule of law and a welfare state, the family figured as source, or at least locus, of an acute, standing threat to the common good of the polity. So it is necessary to add that it seems equally clear that those same pre-conditions include appropriate sound nurturing of children within families flourishing as families. Family as threat to the political common good is only the perversion of family as foundation of that common good. This foundational significance doubtless includes various elements, biological, psychological, and cultural. So, for example: if the shared culture so important to a state's stability and fruitfulness for good is to be maintained, it must be transmitted in the first instance by the nurturing of children within their families. Neither political nor legal theory can neglect, or pass over as if embarrassed by, the thesis given a declaratory articulation by the Universal Declaration of Human Rights, art. 16(3): 'The family is the natural and fundamental group unit

[20] *Ibid.* But this is no more than a summary recall of the elaborate constructivist theory of 'public reason' articulated by Rawls in his *Political Liberalism*, where concern for the truth of moral and political principles is replaced by a *postulated* obligation to make one's political judgments and decisions within the confines of a supposed overlapping and stable consensus of 'all reasonable people' or at least of 'a sizable body of adherents in a more or less just constitutional regime' (15).

[21] 'Constructivism' here signifies a proposal to replace the question of a proposition's truth or falsity with the question whether the proposition has been arrived at by an appropriate 'procedure of construction' (*ibid.*, 90) such as, in the context of Rawls's *A Theory of Justice* (i.e. of justice *within* political communities) a (postulated) agreement within an 'original position', or, in the same context as reconceived in *Political Liberalism*, within the 'overlapping consensus'.

[22] Williams, *Truth and Truthfulness*, 19.

of society and is entitled to protection by society and the State.' To call the family (or with Wojtyla, the state) 'natural' is not, primarily, to say that it exists by necessity, or by instinct or sub-rational inclination. Rather it is to say, above all, that the possibility of establishing, maintaining, and living in a family can easily be understood to be an object of choices that is desirable because fulfilling, not only as a means to other ends but in itself, inherently[23]—and fulfilling not only for the choosers but for many others, especially those whose very existence is an effect of such choices.

Despite Plato's dalliance with a communism of wives and children as solution to the problem created for political communities by family loyalty, both he and the critic of that communism, Aristotle, thought their way through to an understanding, real albeit not flawless, that family is essential to the soundness of the *polis*, marriage is essential to the family, and sex acts are meaningful and ethically sound only in the context of marriage. One measure of the perhaps surprising extent of Plato's clarity on these matters: the leading scholarly study of love and friendship in Plato and Aristotle in the last thirty years concluded, with manifest reluctance, that the sex ethics of Plato, Pope Paul VI, and Pope John Paul II were essentially identical.[24] (As for Aristotle, his prime example of the category of acts always wrong in themselves is adultery.[25]) Four centuries later, around the end of the first century AD but independently of Jewish and Christian influences, we find the Roman Stoic philosopher Musonius Rufus and the Greek polymath Plutarch articulating with clarity the two essential elements of the basic human good of marriage: procreation/parenthood and friendship between husband and wife, who act as equals in the acts of bodily union by which they experience, actualize, and express both those elements together.[26] Does it not once again appear that revelation was needed for nothing more (or less) than this: that its teachings—here its teachings on marriage[27]—make more widely and stably available some

[23] As Aquinas never tires of saying, X's nature is understood by understanding its capacities, which are understood by their act(uation)s, which are understood by reference to their *objects*. See *Aquinas* 29–32.

[24] Price, *Love and Friendship in Plato and Aristotle*, 229–35, esp. 233, 235; Finnis, 1994b at 1060, and see 1057–63 for Plato's views as a whole. For brief replies to some responses to that article, see the 1995 version at 18–26. What the predicate 'is natural' means in relation to the family is equally what the predicate 'is unnatural' asserts is opposed or violated, in Plato's repeated description of homosexual acts as *para physin*, contrary to nature, unnatural: e.g. *Phaedrus* 251a; *Laws* 636c, 836, 838, 841. [In all cases, as Aquinas will make clear, the claim about nature/natural is about what is reasonable, in view of the goods at stake: see essay III.22 (1997d) at n. 4.]

[25] *NE* II.6: 1107a9–17; also *Eudemian Eth.* II.3: 1221b20–2; for the questionableness of the common opinion that these passages merely make a linguistic and thus tautologous point about the pejorative word 'adultery', see *MA* 31–2.

[26] See 1994b at 1062–5 (24–30).

[27] John Paul II, *Familiaris Consortio*, Apostolic Exhortation, 22 November 1981; see esp. sec. 29.

important truths which were always *accessible* to natural reason and had in fact been affirmed by philosophical reflection and even, to some extent, by some cultures which had not been informed by that revelation?

To answer that question with appropriate generality, one should go back to what the reflections of Bernard Williams, Hume, Kant, and so many other philosophers missed: the first principles of practical reason which direct us towards the basic intelligible human goods, goods that are in countless ways both the source of all intelligibility and reasonableness in our choices, and the outline of human flourishing—of human nature in its full actuation. Each of these first principles is, so to speak, *transparent for* the human persons in whom such good can be actualized, so transparent that it is, in truth, those persons for whose sake we are responding when we respond at all to the summons and direction of those principles.[28] But this actualization of universals does not exhaust the reality of what is present in such flourishing. Specificity and particularity always *add* to what is more universal or generic.[29] Love responds to all that is there in the beloved; it responds to the passing stranger in the desert,[30] but makes its necessarily exclusive commitments, and has its necessarily discriminatory loyalty to this my people or my friend. But to say this is still to speak too generally. Human nature, as the child can see in its parents, is not quite complete (whether in capacities, dispositions, or fulfilments) in either male or female. That is why one of the basic human goods is marriage. It is also why—since marriage has the specific kind of act in which it can be actualized, experienced, and expressed—there is a part of ethics which particularly concerns the conditions under which choosing behaviour that is or might be of that kind respects that universal good sufficiently to be judged reasonable and right.[31] The conditions, as everyone knows, are demanding enough for revelation to be needed to confirm, and in some lesser measure to clarify, deepen, and extend, what the most careful thinkers of Greece and Rome could recognize and teach, even in the midst of a culture devoted, in ways paralleled and surpassed in our day, to shadows in the Cave.

[28] See essay I.1, last page (= 2005a at 131).

[29] *ScG* II cc. 26 and 42.

[30] See Anscombe, *Faith in a Hard Ground*, 234:

> ...there are lesser friendships: there are friendships of advantage or pleasure, the friendships of fellows in an association, of fellow workers and of fellow citizens—and also of fellow men, as would make its appearance if fear did not when two humans alone find one another in the desert.

[31] See essays III.20 (= 2008c) and III.22 (= 1997d); *Aquinas* 143–54.

Part Three

Acts and Intentions

8

HUMAN ACTS*

I

A position characteristic of a certain moral theology contrasts a 'morality of acts' with a 'morality of persons', commends the latter, and may even claim that for the moralist there are no human acts but only acting persons.[1] A position characteristic of secular thought asserts that one is responsible for what one does and causes, but not for what one is.[2] According to the position implicit in scripture and the tradition, these contrasts are misplaced. One's character as an acting person is known in the acts one freely chooses to do; that character is, indeed, decisively formed and settled by those choices and their carrying through; and though not responsible for all one causes, one is responsible for what by one's choices one causes oneself to be.

A preliminary clarification. I shall use the term 'act of the person' to refer to acts which Aquinas called *actiones humanae* [human acts] as distinct from *actiones hominis* [acts of a human being].[3] But just as Aquinas signalled that his terminology was a mere scholarly convenience, neither capturing nor dependent upon the ordinary connotation of the terms *humana* and *hominis*,[4] so too my use of the phrase 'act of the person' does

* 1987b ('The Act of the Person').

[1] e.g. O'Connell, *Principles for a Catholic Morality*, 79:

> ... if one is discussing objective morality, then motive is not at all germane. For actions, as such, do not have motives; they only have ends or results. Agents have motives; human persons, human subjects, have motives. Thus, if one really wants to include the element of motive, then one must talk of subjective morality, about the sinfulness or virtuousness of an action.... then it is clear that the motive is the primary determinant of the morality. Indeed, motive is the *only* determinant of the morality. For morality, in this subjective sense in which we have understood it in these pages, is not a quality of deeds but a quality of persons.

Mahoney, *Seeking the Spirit*, 206: 'strictly speaking, there are no such things as moral acts. There are only men and women acting morally'.

[2] Cf. Hart and Honoré, *Causation in the Law*, lxxx–lxxxi.

[3] *ST* I–II q.1 a.1c.

[4] This is signalled by Aquinas's rapid and frequent departure from his own terminological distinction between *actio humana* and *actio hominis*: see e.g. the *ad* 3m of the same article, I–II q.1 a.1, where he uses the two phrases interchangeably.

not imply that acts done by a human being without (or with diminished) voluntariness are not done by a person—are not acts (behaviour) of a person. The human person is essentially bodily, and every division between the human being and the human person must be rejected as an inadmissible dualism. Nonetheless, acts (behaviour) done without (or with diminished) voluntariness are in one sense not 'of' the person, for either or both of two aspects of the person are not (or not fully) engaged by such acts: the ability to *envisage* something *as* a good, and to know what one is doing in pursuing it; and the initiation of one's own activity in setting out upon, and carrying through, that pursuit. As we shall see, if what one does is done otherwise than by that supremely or paradigmatically voluntary voluntariness, free choice, there is another aspect of the person that is not engaged: self-determination, the ability to form and settle 'what sort of person' one is to be, what character and personality one is to have.

II

Theologians today often deny that one can know oneself in, and by reflection upon, one's choices and actions. They propose an account of the person, and of knowledge, according to which the self is a reality radically unaffected by many fully free choices and actions, a reality which, unlike choice and action, remains inaccessible both to consciousness and even to reflective knowledge. Timothy E. O'Connell offers a clear version:

> people... are comprised of myriad layers... None of these layers can stand by itself, and yet each has its own identity. At the outermost layer, as it were, we find their environment, their world, the things they own. Moving inward we find their actions, their behaviour, the things they do. And then the body, that which is the 'belonging' of a person and yet also *is* the person. Going deeper still we discover moods, emotions, feelings. Deeper still are the convictions by which they define themselves. And at the center, in the dimensionless pinpoint around which everything else revolves, is the person himself or herself—the I.
>
> ... personhood is the one thing about human beings which we cannot actually see.... Repeatedly I attempt to gaze upon the very center of myself. But I always fail. For the real person that I am always remains the viewer, and can never become the viewed. As a person I am a subject. And I cannot become an object, even to myself.[5]

[5] *Principles for a Catholic Morality*, 59. Likewise e.g. Fuchs, *Human Values and Christian Morality*, 98:

> As soon as the self, as subject, grasps at the self as object, the subjective self that acts is no longer to be found within the self confronting it as object.... The spiritual person... emerges from his spiritual unity into the physically conditioned diversity of his development in space and time, to which his personal freedom of choice is directed.

On this view, even freely chosen actions are only a superficial manifestation of the person, whose reality remains far beneath them, and hidden from view. Indeed, they are more superficial even than 'moods, emotions, feelings', and than the 'convictions by which one defines oneself' (and a 'conviction', a judgement that such-and-such is the case, is something one can acquire without choice and without commitment). Notice: choices (acts of choosing) do not figure in this listing of 'layers' of the human person; nor in the parallel passages which list the categories of personal reality.[6]

This rather common view rests upon simplistic and superficial conceptions of knowledge, of free choice, and of the knowledge one has of one's free choices.

Knowledge cannot be adequately understood on the model of looking (O'Connell's 'gaze'), for understanding, reasoning, and judgment are not comprehensible on that simple model.[7] Self-knowledge differs from knowledge of objects other than the self (the subject), not because it is like trying to see oneself out of the corner of one's eye or to peer inwards with an eye that looks only outwards, but because the consciousness (conscious experience) one has in one's activities such as questioning, considering, reasoning, judging, and choosing, is an experience different from the experience (perception) one has of objects other than oneself. It is experience precisely of oneself as a subject, and this experience is not the perception of another *object* somehow additional to the objects of one's questioning, considering, reasoning, judging, or (*mutatis mutandis*) choosing. One *encounters* (or, as in choosing, *envisages*) those objects in these activities; but one does not *encounter* or confront (or envisage) one's activities in doing them, but rather *does* them, consciously.[8]

Yet, this consciousness *in* one's activities (such as choosing) makes it possible for those activities, and their subject (the one[self] who carries them out), to become objects of knowledge. This knowledge—knowledge in the strict sense, the understanding assent to true propositions—is acquired by reflective questioning, hypothesizing, considering, reasoning, and judging about intelligent activities such as questioning, hypothesizing, considering, reasoning, judging, choosing, and carrying out one's

Ibid., 105:

> objective reflection on the self can never take in the whole self as subject; the subjective 'I' which reflects and acts on this reflection remains, precisely as such, outside the 'I' that is the object of reflection.

[6] e.g. *Principles for a Christian Morality*, 62: 'The central core of myself, the "I" which is my personhood, is confronted with... the reality of my world, my situation, my body, my feelings, my attitudes and prejudices'.

[7] See Lonergan, *Insight*, ch. XI, esp. 321–3.

[8] See Lonergan, *Collection*, 173–92.

intentions. It is knowledge, then, of those activities precisely as activities of this subject, oneself, and is knowledge of oneself precisely as the subject who has carried them out.

There is no reason to accept the claim that one knows oneself better by what happens to one or in one (one's 'moods, emotions, feelings'), or by what one acquires (for example, 'convictions'), than by what one freely chooses to do. The greater self-disclosing significance of one's choices is particularly evident when one considers choices which relate to—choices to do something about—oneself, as when one chooses to ignore one's feelings, or to reject such-and-such a mood as a motive, or to trust another person and to believe and act on what he proposes... But each of one's free choices is intelligible only as the choice *of* a subject whose character is thereby more or less disclosed—more or less, but certainly more by this *response* which one as subject is thus making to what one experiences, undergoes, or acquires, than by those experiences, happenings, or acquisitions themselves.

Equally, we should reject as self-refuting the claim that the self or person is a dimensionless pinpoint of which nothing can be known because subject can never be object and everything that is known is known as object. Such claims, and the many associated claims of theologians who purport to know about the self-disposition of whole selves or persons in fundamental options, offer to convey knowledge of the very object said to be unknowable. We can reject their denial of knowability, and then assess with serenity the evidence they advance for their (not too consistent) hypotheses about self-disposition in those 'fundamental' or 'transcendental' 'acts' or 'options' which are not, they say, free choices.

By thus rejecting an epistemology dominated by the image of taking a look, or gazing, or confronting, we rejoin the perennial methodology: whatever is known is known insofar as it is in act; the character of soul is known by the soul's capacities, but those capacities are known by and in their actuations. And, more specifically,

> action constitutes the specific moment whereby the person is revealed. Action gives us the best insight into the inherent essence of the person and allows us to understand the person most fully.[9]

Still, getting rid of distractions is only the beginning of providing an account, and there are many difficulties in the way of understanding the acts of a person. Some difficulties are epistemic, and concern the confusing conditions under which actions have to be experienced and considered if

[9] Wojtyla, *The Acting Person*, 11.

they are to be understood. Other difficulties relate to the complexity of personal life, extended in time and multiform in activities, experiences, and undergoings. In the next section, I advert to some of these complexities, in giving a somewhat more specific account of the way in which the acts of the person can reveal the person because they go to constitute that person's personality.

III

As performances, that is, as items of behaviour available to sensory perception, actions come and go. But as the carrying out of choices, actions, like the choices which they carry out, *persist.* They *last* in the self to whose self-determination (self-constitution) they contribute. They last unless and until they are repudiated by a subsequent choice to repent of them.

Thus the transitive effects of choice and action—the states of affairs constituted by the chosen behaviour and its further results—are transitory. But the intransitive effect of free choice—the becoming the sort of person who chooses *thus*—is a spiritual reality which is lasting, though not, as such, irrevocably permanent. People express their awareness of this 'persistence'[10] of choice in various ways. One way is a certain use of the idiom of 'being committed to ...' (not a commitment in the sense of an undertaking or a promise): 'I chose to do X, and so I'm now committed to doing XA'—which does not mean merely that XA is a means to X.

This sort of commitment is the counterpart in one's will (that is, in one's identity as a chooser between radically open alternatives) of the 'logic' of universalization in practical reasoning. For the alternatives between which one chooses are attractive, and choosable, as offering *intelligible* goods, that is, under descriptions which, however specific, are universal. What appears good in this situation here and now could appear good in any *like* situation. Free choice is not of bare particulars. So the principles, categories, and methods of evaluation one uses in identifying X as a desirable option here and now are principles, categories, and methods applicable in like fashion, to future situations. Nothing short of repentance, that is, a subsequent new and incompatible choice, will free one from the implications of one's former decision to *adopt* the proposal which those principles, categories, and methods made seem attractive. For those implications were not merely the logical implications of the logic of universalization; they were

[10] This is the term used *ibid.* at 160, to summarize the lasting intransitive effects of (chosen) action, powerfully expounded at 149–52. On the relation between this analysis and some themes of Vatican Council II, *Gaudium et Spes* sec. 35, see 1983d at 20–5.

also a tracing of the shape of what one willy-nilly, by one's earlier choice, determined oneself to be.

Thus it is seriously mistaken to suppose, with O'Connell and others, that there are

> two sorts of freedom...the categorical freedom of human-as-agent, the freedom associated with human action...[and] transcendental freedom, the freedom of human-as-person, the freedom associated with perduring being.[11]

The human agent is the human person, and his free choices perdure† in the person whom, in those choices, he constitutes himself to be. For persons, the contrast between being and doing is fallacious. Even in one's small choices, as I have said, one is choosing to *be* the sort of person who does that sort of thing.

And one's largest choices, to enter upon a whole form of life by becoming a spouse or a priest or a scholar or a pirate or a Christian, are choices to *do* something. (I call such overarching and open-ended choices 'commitments', in a sense of 'commitment' rather more specific than that mentioned earlier in this section.) The initial doing, in pursuance of one's commitment, may be something small and symbolic, but the choice of commitment organizes the countless and often unforeseeable choices that will be required to live it out, as well as pervading the countless activities one does, voluntarily but perhaps without any further choice (*stricto sensu*), in order to carry out one's commitment in the way one has chosen.

What I am here recalling, in broad outlines, are but some of the complexities of the act of the person: the distinction between act as behaviour and act as carrying out of choice; the distinction between (a) choices which seek to organize the whole or much of one's life, (b) choices which do not, but which do create or maintain an aspect of one's perduring being, and (c) voluntary acts which, while often spoken of as choices or decisions, are best regarded as rather the spontaneous adoption of a means of carrying out a choice; and the distinction between choices to do or omit something, and choices to repent of those former choices, acts, and omissions. In relation not only to choices of this last sort but to choices of every kind, there is a particular complexity to be noted.

All free choices go to constitute and determine, creatively, the self, the character, the personality, of the one who chooses and carries them out. And in that sense the self is the primary, certainly the nearest, 'object of the action'. Nonetheless this intransitive effect and significance of choice is normally accomplished without the self, or self-determination, being

[11] *Principles for a Catholic Morality*, 63.

the *object* of choice, whether 'object' in the sense of the proposal which, in choosing, one does adopt, or 'object' in the sense of one's reason for adopting that proposal. Typically, the self-determining effect of choice is matter rather for reflection than for motivation (though, of course, the reflections may, on occasion, provide grounds and motives for another choice, for example to repent . . .).

IV

The self-shaping, self-constituting, and in those senses self-determining, effect of moral choice is the very centre of moral life. As I have just noted, it is not the sole or even the typical *point* of moral choices, for these have in view some human good (for example the life or death of a human person) distinct from the moral character of the chooser. In treating this character, this self-shaping, rather than simply the states of affairs involved in and caused by behaviour, as the centre of moral life, Christian moral teaching and reflection makes no fetish of 'moral purity'. Rather, it insists that the moral way is the only fully reasonable way to be concerned about the human goods which may be affected by chosen behaviour (or omissions); other ways involve arbitrary restrictions and biases in their conceptions of human fulfilment. Concern for rightness of choice is not a form of concern for self such as is suggested by the jibe, 'keeping one's hands clean'. Rather, it is a concern to avoid, for example, the arbitrary self- or group-preference latent in amoral 'realism' (and its consequentialist rationalizations), or the incoherent assumption of universal responsibility proposed by certain forms of consequentialism.[12]

This essay is not, of course, the place to expound an understanding of the basic human goods, and the fundamental requirements of practical reasonableness (or modes of responsibility in choosing), which delineate the moral life. But reflection on the act of the person would be radically incomplete if it omitted or marginalized a reflection upon the significance of choice and action as the human person's responses—adequate or inadequate, virtuous or vicious—to the appeal of human goods, some external to the person of the choosing subject, but others intrinsic to the self which the subject *constitutes* in choosing and acting. Reflection on the ways in which human choices effect, so to speak, a synthesis between the acting subject and human goods will, moreover, require and enable us to refine our understanding of what I have, thus far, referred to without differentiation as human action.

[12] See e.g. *FoE* ch. IV and 110–11.

Many people, including even some philosophers and theologians, unreflectively assume a rather simple model of human action, with three elements: (1) a possible state of affairs which a potential agent wants to realize; (2) a plan to realize it by causal factors in the agent's power; and (3) the carrying out of the more or less complex set of performances to bring about the desired result.

This model of action is inadequate, yet it does refer to something: to what Aristotle called *making* as distinct from *doing*. Human goods are conceived as definite goals, and rightness of action as efficiency in obtaining results. Here we have the conception of action implicit in consequentialism.

The model fails to account for people's living their own lives as something more than a series of more or less well-planned attempts to produce certain results. Reflection on one's own experience as an agent will verify a more complex model of action. Common language makes this evident, though common language hinders as well as advances a clear account of the structure of choices and actions. For common language reflects, not a disciplined moral concern about the relation of a particular type of choice to integral human fulfilment, but a diversity of largely conventional and emotional concerns with choices, actions, and behaviour.

Acts are understood by understanding their objects, and the objects of human acts are goods—anything a person can in any way desire.[13]

Some goods are definite objectives, desired states of affairs—for example getting an enemy to surrender unconditionally, fulfilling the goals of the current five-year plan, or successfully completing a research project. But the basic human goods, in themselves, are not definite objectives. Interest in peace and justice, for example, goes beyond any particular objective sought for their sake, for they transcend any particular state of affairs which can instantiate them; those dedicated to such goods never finish doing what can be done to serve them. Peace and justice are more than things one wants, or goals one hopes to accomplish. Acting alone and in various forms of community with other persons, one can contribute to the realization of such goods and share in them, but can never become wholly identified with them.

But if the basic human goods are thus not definite objectives, not goals to be achieved, how do they guide action? By providing the reasons to consider some possibilities as choiceworthy opportunities. Thus the

[13] People desire many things—e.g. pleasure, wealth, and power—which when made principles of action seem to empty a person and divide persons from one another. There are, however, other goods—e.g. knowledge of truth, and living in friendship—the pursuit of which of itself seems to promote persons and bring them together. Goods like these are intrinsic aspects—that is, real parts—of the integral fulfilment of persons. I call these intrinsic aspects of personal full-being 'basic human goods': basic not to survival but to human full-being.

enemy's unconditional surrender becomes an objective to be pursued for its supposed contribution to lasting peace; the fulfilment of the five-year plan's goals is sought as a step towards a dreamed-of, just world order; particular projects of theoretical research are carried on in the hope that their results will add to knowledge. These reasons for choosing and acting provided by basic human goods require no prior reasons. Prospects of human fulfilment—a fulfilment not restricted, of course, to the agent's own self-fulfilment—are held out by peace, justice, knowledge, and so on. These prospects naturally arouse corresponding interests in human persons as potential agents.

Thus, human practical reflection and deliberation, with a view to choice and action, begins from the basic human goods—expanding fields of possibility which underlie all the reasons one has for choosing, all the desires one has to realize any particular goal. This is what gives human life both its constant and universal features, and diversity and open-endedness. The basic human goods explain the creativity characteristic, in our experience, only of human beings. One's interest in these goods underlies one's desire to realize any particular goal.

In human action, the acting person shares in and makes actual some part of what belongs to the full being of persons. Actions have their primary moral significance as a voluntary synthesis with (participation in) human goods. But there are at least three ways in which one's actions have this moral significance. These constitute three senses of 'doing'; from the moral point of view these are irreducibly diverse and must be carefully distinguished if acts are to be described adequately for moral evaluation.

First, one acts when one *chooses and does something for its intrinsic value*, something by which one immediately participates in a good. For example, when one gives a gift as an act of friendship, one chooses to realize a certain state of affairs—giving the gift—as a way of serving the good of friendship, the very fulfilment of self and other in this form of harmony, which is instantiated by giving and receiving the gift.

Secondly, one acts in a different way when one *chooses and does something* not for itself but *as a means* to some ulterior end. What is chosen is willed not as an instantiation of a basic good, but as something through which one expects to bring about an instantiation of a good. For example, one takes bitter medicine for the sake of one's health; one may fight a war for the sake of peace; many people work only to get their pay. The chosen means need not be such that it would never be chosen for its intrinsic value: for business purposes one sometimes makes a trip one might take as a vacation. The first two sorts of doing can be present together, as when one mixes business with pleasure.[§]

Thirdly, one is 'doing something' in a still different way in as much as one *voluntarily accepts side effects* incidental to acting in either of the two prior ways. Here one is aware that executing one's choice will affect, for good or ill, instances of goods other than the instances on which one's interest directly bears. Although one does not choose this impact on other goods, one foresees and accepts it—sometimes gladly (for example when one accepts the bonus of making new friends when one decides to go on a course of training), sometimes reluctantly (for example when one accepts the loss of the diseased organ to save one's life, or the leading of some listeners or readers into errors or confusions when one tries to communicate something complicated).

Because these three sorts of willing relate acting persons to goods in different ways, they ground three distinct meanings of 'doing'. A professional's playing a game only to make money is not playing the game in the same sense—it is not the same *doing*—as the amateur's playing of the game for the sake of doing as well as he can in the performance itself. One who unwillingly benefits another by incidental effects of some action is not doing the other a favour.

The significance of these differences is clearest in negative cases. A woman may choose to have her womb removed out of hatred of human procreation, or as a means (perhaps reluctantly adopted) to enjoying sex without fear of a pregnancy which would prevent the acquisition of a holiday house; or she may have it removed to avert the spread of a cancer. In each case, she can be said to be 'getting herself sterilized'. Physically identical, these are, however, different as human acts; only in different senses are the first two and the third 'sterilization'. And corresponding to the ambiguity of 'action' (and action-words) are diverse meanings of other words important in moral evaluation: 'responsible', 'deliberate', 'intentional', and so on.

In formulating moral norms, it is especially important to distinguish the meanings of 'intentional', in relation to what one tries to bring about as an instantiation of a good, what one chooses as a means to something ulterior, and what one accepts as a side effect. In a loose common idiom, side effects which are foreseen and accepted (and thus voluntarily caused), will on the one hand be described as unintended and unintentional if the question is whether they were part of the agent's plan, but on the other hand be described as intentional or intentionally caused, if the question is whether they were caused inadvertently or 'accidentally'.

Moral analysis, rightly employed, uses a more precise and stable conception of intention. This conception is tightly linked to the moral significance of choice. To choose is essentially to *adopt a plan or proposal* which one has devised and put to oneself in one's practical reasoning and deliberation on the merits of alternative options, that is, plans or proposals.[14] Whatever, then, is included within one's chosen plan or proposal, whether as its end or as a means to that end, is *intended*, that is, is included within one's intention(s). What one does is done 'with intent to X' if X is a part of one's plan either as its end (or a part of its end, or one of its ends) or as a means. And one's will bears upon X in a morally equivalent way if one chooses *not* to do something, precisely in order to bring about X (whether as an end one considers worthwhile itself or as a means to bringing about some further state of affairs). That is to say, there can be omissions which correspond to the action which carries out a proposal adopted by choice.

On the other hand, states of affairs which one foresees will result from carrying out one's plan or proposal, but which one does not need or want as part of one's way of bringing about what one plans or proposes to bring about, are side effects, *accepted* ('permitted') but not intended. One is responsible for causing these side effects, and one's willingness to accept them (and to adopt a plan or proposal which results in them) may be culpable, for instance as unfair, or unfaithful, or as a violation of some other moral requirement. But one's responsibility for side effects is not like one's responsibility for what one chooses and intends to bring about.

V

Evil may not be done that good may come[15] is a principle which applies only to the choice of a means to an ulterior end. It does not apply to the accepting of side effects. Whenever one chooses to destroy, damage, or impede one instantiation of a basic good for the sake of some other instantiation of that or another basic good, the second instantiation is preferred to the first. Since the goods immanent in possibilities available for choice cannot be commensurated, this preference provides no rational ground for judging the choice to be other than what it directly and immediately is: a choice of evil. Such a choice is at odds with openness to integral human fulfilment, and its wrongness is thus settled, whatever other factors may mitigate or aggravate its wrongness. But to accept the destruction, damaging, or impeding of a basic good as the unwanted and unchosen (side) effect of one's choice need not be a choice of evil.

[14] 'Objectum voluntatis est id quod *proponitur* a ratione' ['one's will's object is what is proposed', reasonably or unreasonably, rightly or wrongly, 'by one's reason']: *ST* I–II q.19 a.5c; 'actus dicuntur humani, inquantum procedunt a voluntate deliberata': q.1 a.3c. ['proponitur' = is proposed; 'propositum' = that which has been proposed—a proposal.]

[15] See *FoE* 109–12.

Consequentialists or proportionalists, of course, deny this difference between what one intends as end or means and what one merely accepts as a side effect of one's choice. It is instructive to observe the process by which a theologian loses his grip on the distinction and surrenders to consequentialist unconcern with the structure of choice. Consider a representative example. By 1973, Richard McCormick SJ had accepted the consequentialist or proportionalist notion that in situations of morally significant choice, goods can be adequately commensurated by reason, so that alternative options can be assessed as offering greater good or lesser evil overall. But he clung to the Christian conviction that, in his words,

> the will relates differently to what it intends and what it permits... the intending will (hence the person) is more closely associated with the evil than is a permitting will. This bespeaks [sc. indicates or manifests] (in some admittedly obscure way) a greater willingness that it occur.[16]

Now, as he recounted in 1978, McCormick sent the lecture containing this passage to Bruno Schüller SJ,[17] who replied:

> the person who is prepared to realize the good even by intending the evil is more willing that the evil exist, but only because he is more willing that the good exist.[18]

And equally:

> If someone is ready to bring the good into existence only by permitting the evil, it has been suggested [by McCormick] that he is less willing that the evil exist. Yet it must also be said that he is less willing that the good exist.[19]

From those two propositions, Schüller himself immediately concluded:

> Therefore, I am strongly inclined to believe that in point of fact 'intend as a means' and 'permit', when referring to a non-moral evil, denote exactly the same mental attitude.[20]

McCormick did not draw that conclusion, which is indeed quite unsupported by its premises. But the premises themselves did so impress McCormick that, when publishing his argument about the intending will being more closely associated with the evil than is the permitting will, he described that argument as 'somewhat circular and considerably less than

[16] McCormick, 'Ambiguity in Moral Choice', in *Doing Evil to Achieve Good* at 30–1, 40–2; see also 35–6. Being already a consequentialist, McCormick added to the sentence last quoted: 'Now such a willingness is morally acceptable only to the extent that such an intention represents a choice of what is the lesser evil.'

[17] See *ibid.*, 241.

[18] *Ibid.*; also 43, and in Schüller's own text 'The Double Effect in Catholic Thought: A Reevaluation', *ibid.*, 191.

[19] *Ibid.*, 241, 243.

[20] *Ibid.*, 191 (Schüller's emphasis).

satisfying',[21] and in 1978 he abandoned it altogether, saying that Schüller's objection was 'fatal'.[22]

The strategy of Schüller's objection is clear enough. It accepts McCormick's original observation that A, who intends evils, more closely associates his will with those *evils* than does B, who only permits them; but then it seeks to neutralize the observation by bringing into play the goods which A hopes to achieve by intending evil, and which B is willing to forgo rather than intend such an evil. (Throughout this discussion, 'evil' refers to the destruction, damaging, or impeding of some instantiation of some basic human good.) If B (says Schüller) is willing to achieve a good by means that involve permitting but not intending an evil, and A is willing to achieve the same good by means that involve intending that evil, then B is less willing than A that that evil exist, but only because B is less willing that that good exist; and A is more willing that the evil exist but only because he is more willing that the good exist.

Schüller's argument is fallacious, and an object-lesson in the perils of common language's ambiguities, ambiguities which require moralists to stabilize their own use of terms on the basis of a clear analysis of choice and intention—for example, in terms such as I have proposed in the preceding section of this essay. For Schüller's argument rests on one or both of two equivocations.

Perhaps he conflates 'more willing that the good exist' with 'willing that more good exist'. That would, of course, be a startling confusion, and a mere repetition of the consequentialist or proportionalist claim that, in a situation of morally significant choice, one can and should discern the option promising an overall net greater amount of good ('more good') and can *thus* identify that option as morally right and indeed obligatory. As I have said, and as I and others have extensively argued elsewhere,[23] this contention should be rejected as incoherent with the conditions of rational deliberation for free choice. 'More', 'less', 'most'... good can rationally be predicated of options as one way (not the clearest) of expressing the application to those options of *moral* or *conventional* or *aesthetic* or *emotional* or *technical* or many other perfectly legitimate criteria of evaluation and commensuration; but those terms cannot be predicated of options *for choice*, and on the basis of the assessment which consequentialism needs, an assessment of 'overall' amounts of 'non-moral' good. Since consequentialism (or proportionalism)

[21] *Ibid.*, 43. [22] *Ibid.*, 241.

[23] See e.g. *FoE* 86–90; Grisez, *Christian Moral Principles*, 152–4; *NDMR* 251–60; [and 1990f.] [On the terms 'consequentialist', 'proportionalist', 'utilitarian', 'teleological ethics', etc., see *FoE* 80–6.]

has been refuted independently of the analyses of action, we can in any case reject analyses of action which presuppose it.

More probably, however, Schüller was equivocating on the term 'willing', which can signify at least the following three quite distinct realities.

(1) Choosing to (try to) bring about X, in the sense that if X does not result, one's choice and efforts have failed. In this sense, there is no question of being 'more' or 'less' willing; either one is choosing ('willing') X or one is not. Tightly connected with this sense is the 'willingness' of one who has made a conditional choice, to bring about X if situation S arises; this willingness, too, is not in itself a matter of degree: either one is willing to do or bring about X if S; or one is decided not to do so; or one is uncertain what one would do if S, because one has made neither the conditional choice to do X nor the conditional choice not to.[24]

(2) Accepting (permitting) X as a foreseen side effect of what one is choosing and trying to do and bring about. In this sense, one is willing for the side effect to occur, though one will be glad or at least content if it does not occur, since it is no part of the proposal one adopts by one's choice. And in this sense, like sense (1), there is no question of more or less. If one adopts the proposal, one is willing that the foreseen side effect occur, whether one cares much or little about that side effect, and whether or not one does anything to reduce the likelihood of its occurring.

(3) 'Willing' in a third sense has to do with dispositions such as those just mentioned: wanting, hoping, welcoming, resenting, regretting. All these are indeed matters of 'more' or 'less', of choosing, doing, permitting, or accepting X 'willingly' or 'unwillingly', 'very willingly', 'rather unwillingly', and so on.

Schüller's argument was framed in terms of 'more' and 'less', so we may test it in relation to the third, dispositional sense of 'willing'. Its implausibility is then apparent. It is mere fallacy to assert that because A's willingness in sense (1) to bring about some good, unlike B's, is unregulated by any moral principle about the means chosen to bring it about, therefore A has the 'greater willingness' to bring about that good.

Consider two communities facing an evil aggressor. Community A is prepared to deter the aggressor by capturing 10,000 of his children and old people, and killing them one by one until the aggressor withdraws. Community B will accept anything rather than choose to kill non-combatants, but is prepared to spend its blood and treasure on arduous military campaigns to defend the just peace of its people. Who will believe

[24] Both the last two states of mind are covered by the ambiguous negative: 'I am not now willing to X if S'.

Schüller's claim that, simply because community B is not willing to choose to kill non-combatants as a deterrent, it must be 'less willing' than A that the good of a just peace exist?

Or consider two couples confronted with bringing up a severely handicapped child. Must we say that couple A who kill the child to save it pain and 'preserve their marriage' have a 'more willing' love of the good of the child and of their marriage than couple B who resolve to, and do, devote themselves for years to the arduous upbringing of the child rather than destroy the good which, in that child's life, has been entrusted to them?

The fact is that the emotional dispositions or attitudes which enable us to speak of degrees of willingness and unwillingness do not control, and are often scarcely or in no way correlated with, the choices one makes. One's enthusiasm, one's reluctance, one's repugnance, and so forth, are not the ground of one's choice. Nor do such attitudes remain constant, even when one is showing one's constancy or vicious obduracy by persisting in one's choice and in the activity which carries it out. The moral life is in large measure a struggle to *integrate* one's feelings and attitudes, one's 'willingnesses and unwillingnesses', with intelligent commitments, projects, and other choices for understood goods.

Schüller's equivocation between willing as intelligent choosing (and trying to carry out one's choices), and willing as emotional attitude, had a further manifestation: an equivocal conception of 'approval'. This conception now dominates the moral analyses of certain theologians, most notably McCormick, who adopted it from Schüller when adopting the 'willingness' equivocation. When one chooses to kill as a means to some ulterior end, one need no more (they say) 'approve' the evil (the destruction of the basic human good of life) than when one accepts death freely as a side effect; hence, again, they deny the moral significance of the distinction between killing directly (intending to kill) and killing indirectly (merely accepting death as a side effect of one's chosen action).[25] As McCormick admitted, this makes it difficult to understand why the same direct-indirect distinction is vital in a case where both he and Schüller wished to retain it: the case of causing another's *sin*.[26] Nonetheless, McCormick now makes the presence or absence of approval quite central to his analysis of moral problems. For example: a legislator who votes specifically to fund and thus procure abortions, in order that poor women be allowed fair access to the abortive relief available to wealthy women, does not (says McCormick)

[25] McCormick and Ramsey, *Doing Evil*, 254–62; Schüller in *ibid.* at 190–1; McCormick, 'Notes on Moral Theology: 1984' at 59–60.

[26] *Doing Evil*, 258–9.

formally cooperate in abortion *if he does not approve of abortions* but only procures them reluctantly, regretfully, etc.[27]

As a matter of choice and action, of course, we can readily see that such a legislator precisely does *approve* abortions; his vote of approval is intended to, and does, bring them about. His choice to approve them, however reluctant, shapes him just as it shapes the community in which he helps to bring about such killing for convenience and equality of convenience.

We are left, then, with the position from which the earlier McCormick was dislodged by Schüller's fallacy or fallacies, the classic position (so reminiscent of an essential thesis in the Christian treatise *de Deo creante*)[28] that 'the will relates differently to what it intends and what it permits ... the intending will (hence the person) is more closely associated with the evil than is a permitting will'. We can refine this formulation to express the true position more exactly, by eliminating the inappropriate metaphor of proximity ('more closely associated'). Then we can say, better, that persons who intend to destroy, damage, or impede a basic human good embrace and integrate into their will (that is, into themselves as subjects) the evil which, precisely by thus choosing and adopting it, they treat as if it were a good. The destruction, damaging, or impeding of the basic good is something which, by choosing, they *set themselves* (however reluctantly) to bring about; their choice is frustrated, and *they themselves* (pro tanto, as exerting themselves transitively) *fail*, if the destruction, damaging, or impeding is prevented by some other factor. But those who merely permit such evil—not intending it as an end, not choosing it as a means, and not acting in any other way immorally in accepting it—in no way treat evil as a good, or embrace or constitute their will (themselves) around that evil. They never set themselves to bring it about, and do not fail if some other factor prevents it.

VI

Suppose, finally, that we inquire after the deepest intelligibility of the doctrine which, as *Reconciliatio et Paenitentia* declares, is

> based on the Decalogue and on the preaching of the Old Testament, and assimilated into the *kerygma* of the Apostles and belonging to the earliest teaching of the Church, and constantly reaffirmed by her to this day ...

[27] McCormick, 'Medicaid and Abortion' at 716–17; and see Grisez, 'Public Funding of Abortion' at 32 and 45–51. See also 'Notes on Moral Theology: 1984' at 59, where McCormick claims that an 'attitude of approval' can be 'justifiably inferr[ed]' when someone has chosen e.g. an abortion 'without a truly justifying reason'!

[28] See *DS* 1556 (Trent, Decree on Justification [1547], canon 6). [See essay 8, n. 37.]

namely, that

there exist acts which, *per se* and in themselves, independently of circumstances, are always seriously wrong by reason of their object.[29]

Here the decisive concept is of the 'object' which can settle the moral character of an act as wrong whatever the circumstances. It must be admitted that the term 'object' is not used with satisfying clarity in the tradition.[30] But one thing is wholly clear: in choosing to act to bring about some state of affairs as a means, whatever one thus envisages doing and bringing about as that means, together with whatever state of affairs one envisages as the end to which that means is a means, together constitute the 'object of the act' so chosen.[31] Now I have been explaining choice as the adoption of a proposal, viz. a proposal for action (or omission) in order to bring about a state of affairs either as an end in itself or as means to some such end. Hence, my account of choice is equivalently an account of the 'object' of the acts so chosen.[32]

In choice, then, the human person integrates himself around, and in a certain sense synthesizes himself with, the object of his choice, which is the shape his reason takes in directing the performance of the action carrying out the choice. As a transitive performance, the action may be wholly frustrated by circumstances. The goods he sought in action may remain wholly unrealized. Yet unless and until he repents of it, the acting subject retains the character specified, in part, by that object of his choice, that proposal he once freely adopted.

By choosing and acting in the world, and in both the transitive and intransitive efficacy of his choosing and acting, the person obviously participates in the work of creation. But Christian faith teaches that participation in creation can become, by virtue of the efficacy of the Cross and Resurrection, a participation in the Redemption *peracta* by Christ.[33]

[29] *Reconciliatio et Paenitentia*, 2 December 1984, n. 17, text at n. 96. Cf. McCormick, 'Notes on Moral Theology 1977' at 103: 'Many theologians are arguing that one cannot isolate the object of an act and say that it is *always* wrong in *any* conceivable circumstances.'

[30] See Belmans, *Le sens objectif de l'agir humain*.

[31] For although, 'considered as a certain state of affairs [*res*], the end is an object of the will different from the means', nonetheless, 'considered as the reason for willing, it and the means are one and the same *object*' ('Finis, inquantum est res quaedam, est aliud voluntatis objectum quam id quod est ad finem, sed inquantum est ratio volendi id quod est ad finem est *unum et idem objectum*'): *ST* I–II q.12 a.4 ad 2. In short, end and means, as envisaged in the proposal adopted by choice, constitute the object.‡

[32] There are, of course, legitimate vocabularies, more specialized than the one I have adopted, which reserve 'intention' for the willing of the end and 'choice' for the willing of the means, as Aquinas explains in the *ad* 3m of the same article and in art. 13 and elsewhere. But nothing relevant to our present reflections requires such a differentiation, which, in any case, Aquinas himself quite often sets aside: see the analysis of texts in Boyle, '*Praeter Intentionem* in Aquinas' at 651–3.‡

[33] *Laborem Exercens*, AAS 73 (1981), 577, nn. 2, 24.

Thus in human action, even when directed as 'work' on instrumental goods,

> we find always a glimmer of new life, of the new good (*bonorum novorum*), as if it were an announcement of 'the new heavens and the new earth' in which man and the world participate precisely through the toil [of] work... Is not this new good—the fruit of human work—already a small part of that 'new earth' where justice dwells?[34]

Starkly and insistently, we are warned by the scriptures that all the terrestrial products of human activity may end in ruin. Each of John Paul II's first three encyclicals reminds us of the shadow of a catastrophe in which evil would prevail over and sweep away good as in a new flood.[35] The transitive effects of our choices, though the primary point of our choices as we make them, may all be brought to nothing. Yet Vatican II, in concordance with sacred scripture and liturgy, teaches that

> when, in the Spirit of the Lord and in conformity with his commandment, we have cultivated in this world the goods of human dignity, brotherly community and liberty—i.e. all the good fruits of our nature and our activity—we will find all those goods again, cleansed from sin, illuminated and transfigured, when Christ returns to the Father the eternal and universal kingdom of truth and life, of holiness and grace, of justice, love and peace.[36]

How can this be? The outlines of an answer are given in the teachings which the Council there re-expressed. While the figure of this world deformed by sin is passing away, charity and its fruits will endure, and among those fruits are the 'works' that may survive the testing by fire of Judgement (1 Corinthians 3:14; 13:8). These 'works' which can survive the passing away of this world are, we must conclude, the actions by which persons shape and constitute themselves, the choices which persist until repented of or, if the time for repentance has passed, for ever.

NOTES

† *Free choices perdure in the person*...(at n. 11). Neither O'Connell nor I was using 'perdure' in the sense stipulated by Derek Parfit, which connotes his theory that there is no enduring or subsistent personal or personal identity, but only a 'perduring' sequence of persons or personal identities which we call me (or Derek Parfit).

§ *Mixing business with pleasure*...(p. 139). This sentence, like the previous one, might be misunderstood as suggesting that business is or is to be engaged in solely as a means, and has no intrinsic value—does not instantiate a basic human good. But that is not so, and working merely for pay is either a vice

[34] *Ibid.*, n. 27.

[35] See *Laborem Exercens*, nn. 2, 12; *Redemptor Hominis*, AAS 71 (1979), pp. 257–324 at 271, 286 (nn. 8, 15); *Dives in Misericordia*, AAS 72 (1980), pp. 1177–232 at 1212, 1229 (nn. 11, 15).

[36] *Gaudium et Spes*, n. 39.

or a misfortune (depending on the nature of the work and one's circumstances). Excellence (within one's capacities) in one's work is an aspect of a basic good inadequately identified in *NLNR* as 'play'.

‡ *'end and means, as envisaged in the proposal adopted by choice, constitute the object'*... (n. 31). But, as n. 32 partly points out and the next essay, essay 9, elaborates on, there can be reason to distinguish between end and means, and to appropriate the words 'intended end' to the (or a relevant) end and 'chosen object' to the (or a relevant) means. This is done, for example, in the encyclical *Veritatis Splendor* (1993) no. 78, where the purpose is to teach that there can be means ('objects') which can never be rightly chosen, however good the end ('intention'). But if one uses the more specialized vocabulary (as Aquinas sometimes does), one will say, e.g. that 'external acts are called good or bad by reference to the state of will [that they manifest]—not, however, by reference to the will simply as *intending* but [also] as *choosing*... [for] an action's being good requires not only that its ultimate purpose (with which one's will is concerned as intending) be good but also that any proximate purpose (with which one's will is concerned as choosing) be good' ['secundum voluntatem dicitur actus exterior bonus vel malus, sed non secundum voluntatem intendentem solum, sed secundum voluntatem eligentem.... ad bonitatem rei non solum exigitur bonitas finis ultimi quem respicit voluntas intendens, sed etiam bonitas finis proximi, quem respicit voluntatem eligens'] (*Sent.* II d.40 q.1 a.2 ad 2 and 3). And then one may appropriately express the thought of *Reconciliatio et Paenitentia*, n. 17 [and *Veritatis Splendor* n. 78] as Aquinas does with those sentences, plus this:

> Non... bonitas voluntatis intendentis sufficit ad bonitatem actus: quia actus potest esse de se malus, qui nullo modo bene fieri potest. Si autem consideretur voluntas secundum quod est eligens, sic universaliter verum est quod a bonitate voluntatis dicitur actus bonus, et a malitia malus. (*Sent.* II d.40 q.1 a.2c.)
>
> [Goodness in the intending will does not suffice to make the act good, for an act may be bad in itself, in that it can in no way be done well. But if we are considering the will as *choosing*, then it is universally true that acts are good by reason of the will's goodness and bad by reason of badness in the will.]

9

INTENTIONS AND OBJECTS*

Intention is of end, choice is of means. A human act is specified by (and so is correctly described in terms of) its end. A human act is specified by (and so is correctly described in terms of) its object. An act which is bad by reason of its object cannot be justified by its end (its good intention). A human act is specified by (and so is correctly described in terms of) its intention....

Such a sequence of statements of Aquinas ought to leave an impression of confusion. That impression would be heightened by the traditional representation of his analysis of acting in a schema of twelve terms signifying a sequence of psychological acts involved in willing and doing something. For in this analysis, intention seems to precede deliberating, judging, and choosing, and so, as deliberating, judging, and choosing often present themselves to consciousness distinctly, intention is presented in this analysis as if it were a distinct content of consciousness. When intention is so conceived, it becomes possible to imagine that one can, so to speak, choose to direct (an) intention to, or withhold it from, the various aspects of one's chosen behaviour, for example those consequences which one foresees and welcomes or those one chooses to bring about but only with regret.

To some contemporary moralists, such approving or regretting of consequences is precisely what engages or disengages one's will and thus one's responsibility; what Christians or Jews used to regard as immoral can be uprightly done if done merely as a means to good ends and only with reluctance, regret, disapproval, that is, if in no way approved or adopted as an end, that is, if not really *intended*.[1] Other modern moralists deny that one's responsibility for consequences of deliberate behaviour can be so dependent on an inner act of intending (as distinct from the choosing

* 1991a.

[1] Cf. e.g. McCormick, 'Medicaid and Abortion' at 716–17.

and doing); they judge one responsible for everything one deliberately and with foresight causes.[2] So they, too, reject the 'doctrine' of double effect which Christian moralists had articulated as a development or codification of the elements of St Thomas's discussion of self-defence, a discussion the first premise of which is that a human act is specified (that is, identified for the purposes of moral assessment) by its intention. Today there are other moralists again who combine the two foregoing lines of thought: they reject the doctrine of double effect as giving exaggerated importance to choice (means) over intention (end); they say one should take into account all foreseeable consequences of one's choice and ensure that it is likely to have a greater proportion of good than of bad consequences, and one must never approve (intend) any bad consequences—one may never deliberately cause them as ends but only as means, means which one deliberately causes, not for their own sake, but only for the sake of those proportionately greater good (or less bad) consequences which one does intend.[3]

All these influential contemporary positions are deeply confused and mistaken. Though the mistakes go wider than the theme of this essay, the confusions (and equally that impression of confusion which I mentioned at the outset) could be overcome by attention to the controlling elements of St Thomas's thought on intention and choice.

I shall focus on two of those controlling elements: (1) in choosing, one not only intends as one's end some intelligible[4] benefit, but also *prefers* one proposal offering such benefit to one or more alternative available proposals offering the same or some other intelligible benefit; (2) in choosing means (adopting one proposal for the sake of its intelligible benefit), one not only *constitutes that means as the (proximate) end* for any technique, procedure, or performance one may use to do or carry out one's choice but also *settles the end (the benefit) one intends.*

[2] Cf. Schüller, 'The Double Effect in Catholic Thought: A Reevaluation' at 191: '... "intend as a means" and "permit", when referring to a non-moral evil, denote exactly the same mental attitude'. Schüller, 'La moralité des moyens' at 211 (*causing* moral evil is never justified, *causing* non-moral evils is justified in pursuit of non-moral good of corresponding importance); 221–2: 'pour tous les biens dont la possession contribue au bien-être de l'homme... [q]uoi que l'on choisisse... les conséquences négatives qui résultent du choix sont un pur moyen en vue des conséquences positives qui en résultent.'

[3] Cf. Peschke, 'Tragfähigkeit und Grenzen des Prinzips der Doppelwirkung' at 110–12, where Peschke states the 'principle of double effect' (which he ascribes to Catholic theology and attacks) in terms not of what is directly or indirectly willed or intended or chosen or done, but in terms of what is directly/indirectly 'caused'.

[4] i.e. what it seems intelligent to seek and secure. Of course, one's capacity to seek and secure such benefit can certainly be harnessed by sensory, sub-rational desires, emotions, and feelings. I shall not further consider this aspect of the matter, on which see 1987f at 122–5.

I

The neo-scholastic schema proposed as a representation of St Thomas's analyses of deliberate human acts conveys both the truth that any such act has its primary intelligibility as means to end and the truth that will is always response to reason's envisaging an intelligibly good objective. But these two virtues of the schema are overwhelmed by its defects as an interpretation of St Thomas and an analysis of action.

A standard version:[5]

	Intelligence	Will
Concerning the end		
	1. Simple understanding	2. Simple volition
	3. Judgment: end is attainable	4. Intention
Concerning the means		
	5. Deliberation (*consilium*)	6. Consent (*consensus*)
	7. Judgment on means (*sententia/iudicium*)	8. Choice (*electio*)
Executing the choice		
	9. Direction (*imperium/praeceptum*)	10. Application (*usus*)
	11. Application of intelligence in executing choice	12. Enjoyment (*fruitio*)

That nothing in St Thomas's discussions clearly corresponds to phases 3 and 11 need not concern us. What should concern us is that, in discussing the *consensus*, here placed as phase 6, Aquinas himself always and unambiguously locates it after a *sententia* or *iudicium* concerning means: it is one's more or less welcoming response to the practical judgment that some action is an eligible and appropriate way of achieving some end which seems to one to be desirable.[6] But in the neo-scholastic schema, the *iudicium* concerning means appears only as phase 7, after *consensus*.

[5] The schema is found thus (in all essentials) in e.g. the notes by Pinckaers in *Somme Théologique: Les Actes Humaines*, i, 414–37; the notes by Gilby in *Summa Theologiae*, vol. 17, 211; and the introduction to *La Somma Teologica*, vol. 8 (1958) 168 (with reservations by the editor, T. Centi OP, 169–70). [For the schema as I believe is accurate, both in reality and as an understanding of Aquinas's presentation of it, see *Aquinas* 71, which provides also full citation of his texts, and surrounding discussion using realistic examples.]

[6] See *ST* I–II q.15 a.3c (potest…esse consensus, inquantum motus appetitivus applicatur ad id quod ex consilio *iudicatum est*); q.74 a.7 ad 1.

Why this apparent defiance of Aquinas's account, this reversal of the order of consent and judgment? In order, I think, to preserve the alternating sequence in which will responds to intelligible good; if consent is a response of will to practical judgment, there would be no room for a distinction between *consensus* and the choice itself, which the commentators rightly[7] make the response precisely to judgment. But here their most fundamental oversight becomes evident. In drawing up their schema, they have forgotten something to which the sounder of them often, if elsewhere, attend: the fact that, by definition, choice is *between* eligible options, between mutually (here and now) exclusive practical alternatives (proposals[8] for action).

Indeed, the whole neo-scholastic schema or diagram hides what St Thomas makes central to his account of choice: that choice is between alternatives, is an *alteram alteri praeoptare*[9] or *praeeligere*,[10] an *unum alteri praeferre*,[11] *praeacceptatio unius respectu alterius*,[12] the decisive preferring of one alternative to another or others. So, where practical reasoning is followed by choice, that reasoning must have 'left something open' to choice. More precisely: choice, being an act of *will*, and one which could have gone the other way, must be between alternatives each of which is *shaped* by reason. (Option B need be no more than: not to choose option A, for a reason.) Any deliberation which ends in *choice* must have yielded, not one judgment affirming the choiceworthiness of an option awaiting adoption by the will, but (at least) *two* judgments. (One of these judgments may be no more than: there is reason not to act on the other.) And there is need for choice because one responds to the attraction—the different attractions—of the respective alternative options which one judges to be, each in its own way, a suitable way of doing or getting or carrying on something one is interested in. Each of those options, those *eligibilia*, arouses in one that form of willingness which St Thomas calls *consensus*.

[7] See *ST* I–II q.13 a.1 ad 2; 3c; *de Ver.* q.17 a.1 ad 4. Note: I am not suggesting that *iudicium* should be removed from its place immediately 'prior to' *electio*. I in no way deny the thesis articulated as no. 21 of the 24 Theses promulgated by the Congregatio Studiorum on 27 July 1914, as interpreted by e.g. Garrigou-Lagrange, *De Beatitudine*, 253–4 (see also 222, 247, 260, 265). There is an 'ultimate practical judgment' that this (the option being chosen) is preferable (at least for me, here and now); but the option thus being chosen is an option shaped by the prior deliberation which yielded more than one eligible option, each shaped by deliberation and affirmed as choiceworthy by a practical judgment; and that it is *this* option, rather than the other(s), that the *ultimate* practical judgment declares preferable is settled by the choice (the will's *electio*). Such seems to be the gist of the last, anti-Leibnizian sentence of Thesis 21, and I agree with it: 'sequitur... electio judicium practicum ultimum; at quod sit ultimum, voluntas efficit'.

[8] 'Obiectum... voluntatis *proponitur* ei per rationem': *ST* I–II q.19 a.3c; 'obiectum voluntatis est id quod *proponitur* a ratione...': q.19 a.5c.

[9] 'eligere est alteram alteri praeoptare': *Sent.* II q.24 a.1 ad 2c.

[10] *ST* I–II q.13 a.4 ad 3; q.15 a.3 ad 3.

[11] *de Ver.* q.22 a.15c.

[12] *ST* I–II q.13 a.2c; discretio unius ab altero (ad 1); *de Ver.* q.22 a.15c.

The point I am making against the schema is made clearly enough in the heart of St Thomas's discussion of *consensus*:

electio addit supra consensum quamdam relationem respectu eius cui aliquid praeeligitur; et ideo *post consensum adhuc remanet electio.* Potest *enim* contingere quod *per consilium inveniantur plura ducentia ad finem,* quorum dum quodlibet placet in quodlibet eorum consentitur; sed *ex multis quae placent praeaccipimus unum eligendo.*[13]

choice adds to *consent* a certain relationship to that over which something else is chosen; and so one who consents to something has not yet chosen it. For it can happen that in deliberating one sees that to the end one desires there are a number of means, each of which seems satisfactory and to each of which one therefore consents; yet out of this set of acceptable means one gives preference to one, by choosing it.

The body of the same article makes it clear that consent (and therefore choice) is a movement of appetite *ad id quod ex consilio iudicatum est,* towards what deliberation *has judged* to be a suitable means to a desired end: *appetitus eorum quae sunt ad finem praesupponit determinationem consilii,* the consent to these means presupposes that deliberation, about one at least of a range of possible means, has concluded.[14] Those who set out the commentators' schema designed it as if deliberation must conclude to only *one* acceptable means, that is, as if the role of choice were really played by practical reasoning and judgment.

Wherever there is a choice to be made—that is, in the standard case of morally significant self-determination in action—neither practical judgment nor the willingness St Thomas calls *consensus* settles anything. There is a practical judgment or judgments affirming the suitability of an option or options eventually rejected. And there is an interest in (*consensus* to) an option or options which one does *not* adopt, make one's own, act upon.

Should we, then, say that one also *intended* those suitable and attractive but ultimately rejected options for action, and/or at least *intended* the benefits (ends) for the sake of which such options might have been chosen? After all,

[13] *ST* I–II q.15 a.3 ad 3; he adds:

Sed si inveniatur unum solum quod placeat, non differunt re consensus et electio, sed ratione tantum; ut consensus dicatur secundum quod placet ad agendum; electio autem, secundum quod praefertur his quae non placent [ie in the case where only one option is at all attractive]. [See 232 n.38]

If one bears in mind that there is only one final integrating end, integrating a limited number of ends for their own sake—such as life, knowledge, friendship—one will see that the case in which deliberation 'happens' to find '*plura* ducentia ad finem', *many* ways leading to something desirable, is the standard case of the morally significant situation; the case where only one possible course of action is attractive is perhaps rather rare, except insofar as prior choices have effectively and closely shaped one's commitments and dispositions.

[14] I–II q.15 a.3c.

in the schema, intention is phase 4, as if it were something which arises and has its role prior to any deliberation about alternatives, just as deliberation is prior to choice. But if we said that one's intentions include options which one not only never carries out but never even adopted, or benefits which one never made the point of any choice, we would defy not only our common speech but also a primary element in St Thomas's account of intention. In that account, intention is of end(s), and there can of course be real interest in an end prior to and without there ever ensuing any choice of means.[15] But even when we have an interest in an end in view, we have as yet no relevant intention (but only a [*simplex*] *voluntas*, whether of a *bonum universale* such as human life or of some more specified object of interest such as the life and health of such-and-such a set of people). There is intention only when and insofar as one settles on *something* as a means of achieving an end. What is thus adopted may be only a procedural (rather than substantive) means: in this case, one chooses (or perhaps spontaneously decides, by *consensus* without need for choice) *to deliberate* with a view to deciding upon means of substantively realizing the end or some end in which one is interested. But whether it is such a procedural proposal one adopts, or a substantive proposal to act, it is then (and only then) that one can say that one has formed an intention—that is, has adopted such-and-such a means with the intention of... In short:

intentio est actus voluntatis respectu finis. Sed... non... *solum ex hoc intendere dicimus* sanitatem quia volumus eam, sed *quia volumus ad eam per aliquid aliud pervenire.*[16]

intention is an act of the will bearing on an end. But we do not say that we *intend* health simply because we are interested in it as a desirable end, but only when and because we will to get it *through something else.*

Or again:

intendere in hoc differt a velle, quod velle tendit in fine absolute; sed *intendere dicit ordinem in finem* secundum quod finis est *in quem ordinantur ea quae sunt ad finem.*[17]

intending differs from willing, in that willing is directed towards an end unconditionally, whereas *intending signifies a relationship to end* just insofar as there is an end *to which means are referred.*

[15] I–II q.8 a.3.

[16] q.12 a.1 ad 4, which is repeatedly referred back to throughout the *quaestio*. In the passages the omission of which is indicated by ellipses, Aquinas refers to the simple *voluntas* by which we will health in a completely general way (*absolute volumus sanitatem*), and the *voluntas* by which we appreciate (*fruitio*) having/getting it. See also *ibid.*, ad 3: 'hoc nomen, intentio, nominat actum voluntatis, praesupposita ordinatione rationis *ordinantis in finem*'. Also *de Ver.* q.22 a.14c.

[17] *De Ver.* q.22 a.13c; see also ad 16: 'intentio est actus voluntatis in ordine ad rationem ordinantem ea quae sunt ad finem in finem ipsum'; and 14c: 'intentio dicitur inclinatio voluntatis in finem secundum quod ad finem terminantur ea quae sunt in finem'; and the summary on *velle, intendere*, and *eligere* at the end of 15c.

So: there is no intending until there is adoption of means, typically by choice.[18] And then, when there is choosing there is intending, an only formally distinguishable aspect of what is (as St Thomas devotes a whole article to stressing) *one and the same act of will*: 'unus et idem subiecto motus voluntatis est tendens in finem et in id quod est ad finem'.[19] As a state of affairs (*res*), the end is something distinct from the means (as my being healthy is a state of affairs distinct from my taking medicine); but insofar as it is the intelligible benefit for which I choose the means, the point of my choosing and doing, the end is simply an aspect of *one and the same object* of volition:

finis, inquantum est res quaedam, est aliud voluntatis obiectum quam id quod est ad finem. Sed *inquantum est ratio volendi id quod est ad finem, est unum et idem obiectum.*[20]

Insofar as it is a certain state of affairs, an end is not the same object of will as the means to it. But insofar *as* it is *the reason for willing the means to it, it is one and the same object.*

[18] This may seem to be bluntly contradicted by the last words of *ST* I–II q.12 a.4 ad 3:

> intentio finis esse potest, etiam nondum determinatis his quae sunt ad finem, quorum est electio; there can be intention of an end even when the means, which are what is chosen, are not yet determinate.

But the whole sense of the ad 3 is in the opposite direction; it is a reply to an argument that as movement(s) of the will, choice, and intention differ as willing the means and willing the end differ; and the reply is:

> motus qui est unus subiecto potest ratione differe secundum principium et finem, ut ascensio et descensio.... Sic igitur inquantum motus voluntatis fertur in id quod est ad finem, prout ordinatur ad finem, est electio; *motus autem voluntatis qui fertur in finem, secundum quod acquiritur per ea quae sunt ad finem, vocatur intentio*; cujus signum est quod intentio finis esse potest, etiam nondum determinatis his quae sunt ad finem, quorum est electio.

On any view, it is difficult to see how the possibility referred to in the last words is a *sign* of that unity of intention and choice which it is the purpose of the reply, of the whole article, and of the immediately preceding phrase to defend. To be consistent with the immediately preceding words, and with the passages quoted above at nn. 16 and 17, the phrase in question must be understood as saying, not that there can be intention without choice, but that there can be intention while many of the means necessary to put it into effect remain undetermined. Thus, I can *decide* (choose) to do something about my toothache—what I call in the text a procedural decision—before setting about finding a painkiller or a dentist, selecting a dentist, and fixing an appointment...

Note also that the statement in I–II q.19 a.7c that 'intentio... se potest habere ad voluntatem... ut praecedens' does not contradict what I have said; the sense of *praecedens* meant here, as the whole of the corpus of a.7 shows, does not involve the notion of an intention existing without any *voluntas* (in the sense of *electio*).

[19] I–II q.12 a.4c.

[20] I–II q.12 a.4 ad 2: note that this is the reply to the objection that *intentio* and *electio* are distinct, and *electio* is the willing of means, therefore intending an end cannot be the same movement of will as choosing the means. The discussion in *Sent.* II d.38 q.1 a.4c and ad 1 adds refinements: it is in relation to means which have nothing desirable about them in their own right that *idem est motus voluntatis qui est in finem et in illud quod est ad finem* (and in such a case, which is the one considered in *ST* I–II q.12 a.4 ad 2, the end, as *ratio volendi* [reason for willing something] stands to the means as form to matter, or as light to colour: *Sent.* II d.38 q.1 a.4 ad 1); but where some means to an end is itself desirable, i.e. is also itself an end in its own right, then there *can* be two objects of will and two distinguishable acts of willing.

One's willing of the end *in* adopting (and carrying out) the means—paradigmatically by choice—is what intention is.[21]

II

In another way, the unity of ends and means is emphasized by St Thomas in his repeated but widely neglected teaching that in choosing means one constitutes that means as the (proximate) end for any technique, procedure, or performance used to do or carry out that choice.[22]

'Means' is, of course, the standard but free translation of *id quod eat ad finem*, that which is for, or towards, an end. In discussing intention and choice, Aquinas makes clear that the means referred to when we say that choice is of means are *human actions*: 'electio semper est humanorum actuum'.[23] Technical 'means', viz. implements, instruments, devices, systems, and 'procedures' as such (that is, just insofar as they could in principle be replicated by machines or other devices), are not means in the sense intended when we say that choice is of means. Rather, technical means are means in a derivative, participative sense, insofar as they are used in the acting which is the (carrying out of) the means properly so called.[24]

This is articulated in St Thomas's commentaries on the *Metaphysics* and the *Physics*, in which he carefully shows both why 'means' is a good translation of *id quod est ad finem* and, more importantly, why human means (actions) are themselves characteristically also ends:

Non solum autem ultimum, propter quod efficiens operatur, dicitur finis respectu praecedentium, sed etiam *omnia intermedia quae sunt inter primum agens et ultimum finem, dicuntur finis* respectu praecedentium.[25]

It is not only the ultimate end, for the sake of which the agent acts, that is called *end* in relation to what precedes it; *each* of the intermediate means which are between the primary agent and the ultimate end is called an end in relation to what precedes it.

[21] If one were confronted with an end so satisfactory that no alternative could have any intelligible attraction, then one could intend and adhere to it without any *praeeligere*. But that is not our situation.

[22] This is richly illustrated in Anscombe, *Intention*. See also, on this and other main aspects of this essay, Boyle, '*Praeter intentionem* in Aquinas', esp. at 652–3. See also n. 24 below.

[23] *ST* I–II q.13 a.4c.

[24] *Ibid.*, and ad 1. A more exact account than any articulated by St Thomas would, I think, apply to the account which I am here tracing a further distinction adumbrated by him in his distinction between the four orders in the prologue to his *Commentary on the Nicomachean Ethics* (ed. Leonine, p. 4, lines 15–54), in particular the distinction between the third order (of human acts precisely as chosen) and the fourth (of things used or made). For insofar as they are not chosen, but simply decided upon and carried out in the execution of a choice but without need for further *choice*, human performances themselves may pertain rather to the fourth order than the third and should be distinguished from means *stricto sensu*, i.e. from the precise object of choice. I shall not pursue the implications of this here.

[25] *In V Meta.* lect. 2: ad 1013a35–b3.

Or again:

Et ulterius [Aristoteles] addit quod *omnia quae sunt intermedia inter primum movens et ultimum finem*, omnia *sunt quodammodo fines*: sicut medicus ad sanitatem inducendam extenuat corpus, et sic sanitas est finis maciei; maciem autem operatur per purgationem; purgationem per potionem; potionem autem praeparat per aliqua instrumenta. Unde *haec omnia sunt quodammodo finis*: nam macies est finis purgationis, et purgatio potionis, et potio organorum, et organa sunt fines in operatione vel inquisitione organorum.[26]

Aristotle adds, moreover, that all those factors which are intermediate between the primary agent and the ultimate end are in one way or another *ends*: thus the doctor, for the sake of improving health, shrinks a distended body, and health is thus the end of slimming; but slimming is brought about by purging, and purging by some potion, and the potion is prepared by him with certain implements. So *each of these is in a way one of the doctor's ends*, since slimming is the purpose of purging, and purging the purpose of the potion, and the potion the purpose of the implements, and the implements are his goal when he is hunting for them or setting about using them.

Using the same medical example, the commentary on the *Metaphysics* adds the necessary clarification:[27]

Huiusmodi... omnia sunt propter finem; *et tamen unum eorum est finis alterius.* Nam attentuatio est finis purgationis, et purgatio pharmaciae. *Haec autem intermedia posita differunt adinvicem* in hoc, *quaedam eorum sunt organa*, sicut instrumenta quibus medicina praeparatur et ministratur, et ipsa medicina ministrata qua natura utitur ut instrumento; *quaedam vero sunt opera*, idest, operationes sive actiones, ut purgatio et attenuatio.[27]

In this way, *all these factors are means-to-an end*, yet *each of them stands to another as end stands to means.* For slimming is the end of purging, and purging of the medicines. But these various intermediate factors differ from one another in this respect: some of them are instruments, like the implements with which the medicine is prepared and administered, and indeed the medicine itself which, once administered, is used by nature as an instrument; but others are deeds, performances, actions, like purging and slimming.

[26] *In II Phys.* lect. 5: ad 194b35.

[27] *In V Meta.*, loc. cit., closely echoed in *ST* I–II q.1 a.3 ad 3: 'idem actus numero... non ordinatur nisi ad unum finem proximum, a quo habet speciem: sed potest ordinari ad plures fines remotos, quorum unus est finis alterius'.

And it is the latter, the operations, actions, performances, deeds, that are means in the strict sense, just insofar as they are within the precise object of choice, the willing of means. To which we can now add that just to the extent that some prior activity empowers one to carry out one of these means, that means stands to that prior action as end stands to means; the reason for (point of) the prior activity is to get into a position to be able to carry out the means to... the ultimate benefit of health. And this in turn explains why 'intention', albeit that it is defined to be 'of end', can be applied directly or by some close analogy all the way down to the most basic performance or omission, that is, that performance or omission the success of which is not the reason for any prior performance or omission.[28] Here we find the reason, too, why

> in relation to the act of will (unlike the acts of other powers), to say it is good by reason of its object is no different from saying it is good by reason of its end—except perhaps incidentally, in as much as one end depends upon another end, and one willing on another.[29]

As that remark of St Thomas indicates, 'object' is a term no more narrowly fixed in its reference than 'end' and 'means'. Just as a means to an end can be an end relative to some prior means, so one can say that the whole nested set of means/ends is one object, or one can equally say that each means within that set is itself an object being pursued with some further end in view, an object chosen with the intention of.... Then, in the latter, more specialized use of the term 'object', one will say with St Thomas that object and intention are distinguished from each other by this, that 'object' signifies the proximate end and 'intention' the further or more remote[30]—remembering always that what is proximate, and what further, depends upon where in the chain or nested set of ends the speaker's present focus of interest lies.[31] But as 'object', 'end', and 'means' are all in this way

[28] 'Omission' here is meant, of course, in a popular sense: a non-performance chosen as a means of obtaining some benefit, e.g. starving a child to death in order to be relieved of the burdens of supporting it in later years. Such omissions, as objects of choice, are morally significant actions. On omissions or forbearances in a stricter sense, in which they are properly contrasted with actions *in genere moris*, see n. 54 below.

[29] finis est obiectum voluntatis, non autem aliarum virium. Unde quantum ad actum voluntatis, non differt bonitas quae est ex obiecto a bonitate quae est ex fine, sicut in actibus aliarum virium: nisi forte per accidens, prout finis dependet ex fine, et voluntas ex voluntate. (*ST* I–II q.19 a.2 ad 1.)

Note also: 'actus exterior est obiectum voluntatis ...': q.20 a.1 ad 1.

[30] e.g. *de Malo* q.2 a.4 ad 9: 'finis proximus actus idem est quod obiectum'; q.2 a.6 ad 9: 'actus moralis non habet speciem a fine remoto, sed a fine proximo, qui est obiectum'. Also *In Sent.* II d.36 q. un. a.5 ad 5: 'actus aliquis habet duplicem finem, scilicet proximum finem, qui est obiectum eius, et remotum, quem agens intendit'.

[31] Thus, the *obiectum* is sometimes spoken of as including end as well as chosen means (e.g. *Sent.* II d.38 q.1 a.4 ad 1; *ST* I–II q.12 a.4 ad 2); and, conversely, the *obiectum* in the sense of 'means'

relative, so 'intention' takes on the same flexibility—a flexibility not urged by loose thinking but by the very analysis of action. Thus, as St Thomas notes in one of his last works, by 'intention' one can mean not only the intending of end but also the willing of deeds, 'and then it is true that, in good and evil alike, what one does is what one intends—*quantum aliquis intendit tantum facit*'.[32] Intention in this broader sense, then, is the measure (*quantum* ... *tantum*) of precisely what is chosen and done.

III

Few if any methodological principles are more fundamental to St Thomas's entire work than the principle that acts are specified by their objects, and that to understand an act for what it is is to understand it in terms of its object: *per obiecta cognosc[i]mus actus.*[33] Equally fundamental to his methodology: things are to be understood and described primarily in terms of what they are *per se*, not by what they are *per accidens.*[34] In relation to acts done for a reason, these principles are specified by a principle less all-pervasive in St Thomas's writings but clearly fundamental to his thought: what end-directed things are per se is to be described in terms of their intention—is what their author(s) intend them to be:

operatio ... recipit speciem et nomen a per se obiecto, non autem ab obiecto per accidens. In his autem quae sunt propter finem, per se dicitur aliquid quod est intentum: per accidens autem quod est praeter intentionem.[35]

action has its type and its name from what is per se its object, not from what is only incidentally its object. But in things which are on account of an end, whatever is intended is said to be per se, and what is *praeter intentionem*, outside the intention, is said to be incidental.

and 'proximate end' is often said to be 'chosen', not 'intended' (e.g. *Sent.* II d.40 q. un. a.2c), but is often spoken of as *intended*: e.g. *ST* I–II q.12 a.3c; q.73 a.3 ad 1 and a.8, ad 3; II–II q.43 a.3c; q.64 a.7c.

[32] *De Malo* q.2 a.2 ad 8; quoted at n. 48 below. Likewise, *ST* I–II q.72 a.8c: species peccati attenditur ... ex parte actus ipsius, secundum quod terminatur ad obiectum in quod fertur intentio peccantis.

[33] 'per obiecta cognosc[i]mus actus, et per actus potentias, et per potentias essentiam': in *II de Anima* lect. 6 (n. 308); 'obiecta sunt priora operationibus in via definiendi' (*ibid.*, n. 305); 'obiecta praecognoscuntur actibus et actus potentiis': *ST* I q.87 a.3c; see also e.g. I q.77 a.3c; I–II q.18 a.5; q.72 a.1c; *in IX Meta.* lect. 7. See also *FoE* 20–1, 25.

[34] 'Nihil autem specificatur per illud quod est per accidens, sed solum per illud quod est per se': *in Eth.* V lect. 13 (n. 1036) ad 1135a18.

[35] *ST* II–II q. 59 a.2c. [And p. 248 n. 29 below.]

Or again:

sicut enim in rebus naturalibus id quod est per accidens non constituit speciem, ita etiam nec in rebus moralibus. In quibus quod est intentum est per se: quod autem sequitur praeter intentionem est quasi per accidens.[36]

For just as in natural things what is incidental does not go to constitute their type, so too in moral matters. In moral matters, what is intended is per se, but what follows *praeter intentionem* is, so to speak, incidental.

It is important not to confuse the distinction between the *per se* and the *per accidens* with that between the *propter se* and the *propter aliud*.[37] What is willed *propter se* is willed as an end in itself, as an (not necessarily *the*) ultimate end, an end considered desirable for its own sake, intrinsically, and not as a means to some further end: some end like life or health, knowledge, friendship, or practical reasonableness itself.[38] But what is willed per se is what is intended, and what is intended, as we have seen, extends down through the whole nested set of means which are also ends of the agent's choosing and doing. This implication of our earlier analyses is confirmed by a number of the passages in which St Thomas is distinguishing between the *per se* and the *per accidens*: the *intentum*, which defines the act per se, extends to even quite proximate means, means which are, moreover, desired in no way for their own sake.[39]

[36] *ST* II–II q.39 a.lc. This is undoubtedly the sense in which the Council of Trent used the term 'per se' in its canon on Justification, in the course of defending the reality of free choice:

> If anyone says that it is not in man's power to make his ways evil, but that God performs the evil works just as he performs the good, not only permissively but also properly and *per se* ...: anathema sit. (Sess. 6 [1547 AD], can. 6; *DS* 1556.)

Neither as end nor as means does God in any way intend human evil (the canon gives an instance: Judas's treachery); God merely permits it. The defined dogma of faith pertains to God's permission of moral evil, human sin—a foreseen and permitted side effect of his creation of human free choice. But the proportionalist willingness to intend pre-moral human evil (the destruction or damaging or impeding of human persons in basic aspects of their reality and fulfilment) jars against the massive tradition of theological reflection on the divine will and providence, expounded by Aquinas and before him by St John Damascene, insisting that for God to will per se (i.e. intend) *anything* which intelligence would call an evil is inconsistent with his holiness: see John of Damascus, *De Fide Orthodoxa* II, 29; Aquinas, *ST* I q.19 a.9; Lee, 'Permanence of the Ten Commandments ...' at 435–6. Especially illuminating is Aquinas, *de Ver.* q.5 a.4 obj. 10 and ad 10, arguing that doing evil/causing harm (*facere malum*) is wholly foreign to good persons, whether human or divine, but that 'ordering' evil/harm, by permitting it for the sake of eliciting some good, is consistent with divine goodness. See further *MA* 74–7.

[37] For an example of this confusion, see Walter, 'Response to John Finnis' at 186–7.

[38] Such ends are the basic human goods, the first principles of the practical reasoning that shapes proposals for choice, and the ends of the virtues and the moral precepts: see *ST* I–II q.10 a.lc; q.94 a.2c; q.100 a.11c; II–II q.47 a.6c and ad 3; q.56 a.lc; *Sent.* I d.48 q.1 a.4c; etc.

[39] e.g. *ST* I–II q.76 a.4c; II–II q.37 a.1c; q.39 a.lc; q.43 a.3c; q.64 a.7c. See likewise Cajetan on the last-cited text. Note that Aquinas sometimes links together *directe et per se*, as opposed to *indirecte vel per accidens*, the distinction being precisely that what is willed *directe et per se* is willed as a means: I–II q.76 a.4 (choosing to remain ignorant of something, so as to remain undisturbed in some sinful course of conduct, is choosing ignorance *directe et per se*; choosing to neglect one's studies in favour of some other activity, aware that the upshot will be ignorance, is choosing ignorance only *indirecte et per accidens*).

It is also important to see that the distinction between what is intended and what is *praeter intentionem* is not got up for the purpose of justifying some pre-ordained moral judgment. It is part and parcel of St Thomas's fundamental understanding of reality: the basic texts are in his commentaries on the *Physics* and the *Metaphysics*.[40] Moral judgments must take account of this aspect of reality; moral norms must be understood as directing action precisely as it is to be understood in the light of this real distinction.

The distinction between what is intended and what is outside the (intention and object of the) act is a distinction to be drawn in identifying just what act is being chosen and done in *genere moris*. For, as St Thomas often says (though never explains with satisfying precision), in conscience (prudent practical deliberation and judgment) actions are to be assessed not as they are *in genere naturae*, that is, as physical behaviour, but as they are *in genere moris*, that is, under the description which is morally relevant, which is the description they have *as* willed (and therefore *as* intended and chosen).[41]

The distinction between behaviour *in genere naturae* and acts *in genere moris* is readily misunderstood;[42] people treat it as conveying simply that behaviour understood *in genere naturae* is assessed by comparison with moral norms and consequently judged and described *in genere moris*, that is, with the peculiarly moral predicates such as 'just', 'unjust', 'virtuous', 'vicious', and so forth.[43] A number of Aquinas's illustrations of the distinction are worded in ways which encourage this misunderstanding. This is no mere accident, but results from the fact that St Thomas's interest in how behaviour of one and the same 'natural' or physical type can constitute morally significant acts of different types is an interest focused on the moral payoff. That is to say, it is an interest in the cases where the difference of type entails a difference between right and wrong, virtue and vice, moral goodness and moral evil. Still, the importance St Thomas attributes to the distinction between acts *in genere naturae* and *in genere moris* is quite unintelligible unless we understand that talking of acts *in genere moris* is

[40] See *in II Phy.* lect. 8 (no. 214); *in VII Meta.* lect. 6 (no. 1382); *in XI Meta.* lect. 8 (nos. 2269, 2284).

[41] e.g. *de Malo* q.2 a.2 ad 13:

actus exteriores non pertinent ad genus moris nisi secundum quod sunt voluntarii; acts external [to the will's own acts] have a moral character only according as they are willed.

[42] Notice that by thus distinguishing between 'behaviour' and 'acts', in line with the distinction between *in genere naturae* and *in genere moris*, I (like Grisez and others) use a terminological distinction which has no clear parallel in Aquinas (other than the latter distinction to the extent that it is clear!).

[43] See the critique of this misunderstanding in Rhonheimer, *Natur als Grundlage der Moral*, 327 n. 25. But we should not fail to note that St Thomas is willing to identify or specify acts by reference to morally relevant circumstances which are *praeter intentionem* and thus in a sense is willing to treat good and bad, right and wrong, virtue and vice, as if they were somehow categories *specifying* acts within the moral order (see e.g. *ST* I–II q.18 aa.4 and 10), and that this is a source of confusion.

no more and no less than talking of them under the descriptions which *enable* the peculiarly moral predicates to be accurately applied to them.

More particularly: acts are morally significant and are morally assessed in terms of their type, their intrinsic character, just insofar as they are willed, are expressions of the agent's free self-determination in choice. More precisely: for moral assessment and judgment, the act is what it is just as it is per se, that is, just as it is intended, under the description it has in the proposal which the agent adopts by choice—not under some self-deceiving description offered by conscience to conscience to rationalize evil, but under the description it has in the practical reasoning which makes the option (the proposal) seem to the chooser intelligent, eligible, 'the thing for me to do', Thus, we have the core of successive articles in the *Commentary on the Sentences*, discussing Peter Lombard's rejection of the Abelardian 'ethics of intention',[44] a rejection which Aquinas regards as fundamentally correct but excessive:[45]

actiones differunt specie secundum diversitatem formarum, quae sunt principia actionum, quamvis etiam agentia specie non differant... Forma autem voluntatis est finis et bonum, quod est obiectum et volitum; et ideo oportet quod in actibus voluntatis inveniatur differentia specifica secundum rationem finis. Et *quia actus sunt in genere moris ex hoc quod sunt voluntarii, ideo in genere moris est diversitas speciei secundum diversitatem finis.*[45]	actions differ in type, according to the diversity of their forms (which are the principles of actions), even when what is acting does not differ in type... Now: the will's form is the end and the good which is the will's willed object. And so there must be differences of type in acts of will, in accordance with difference of end. And because acts have moral significance from the fact that they are acts of will, so there is morally significant difference of type insofar as those acts have diverse ends.

But ends are more and less ultimate or proximate, and the more ultimate can be said to be the intention with which the more proximate, chosen

[44] See Peter Lombard, *Sentences* II d.40. Lombard says here that, in relation to something wrongful (*malum*) per se, we should deny that its wrongfulness comes from purpose or will (*ex fine et voluntate*, or *secundum intentionem et causam*). With this denial Aquinas disagrees. His disagreement is not with the judgment that there are acts which, as he states, are wrong in themselves and cannot in any way be rightly done (*de se malus, qui nullo modo bene fieri potest*). It is with Lombard's denial that such acts are wrong by reason of will, intention, purpose (*finis*). Such acts, says Aquinas, *are* wrongful by reason of the acting person's will. There need be nothing wrong with his *intentio* or *voluntas intendens*, his ultimate motivating purpose (*finis ultimus*), e.g. to give money to the poor. What is wrongful is, rather, his choice, his *electio* or *voluntas eligens*, his immediate purpose (*obiectus proximus* or *finis proximus*) e.g. to forge this testament: *Sent.* II d.40 q.2.

[45] *Sent.* II d.40 q.1 a.1c.

object—most proximately, the outward action itself, or the action's *materia circa quam*[46]—is chosen. So:

...voluntas dupliciter potest considerari: vel secundum quod est intendens, prout in ultimum finem fertur; vel secundum quod est eligens, prout fertur in obiectum proximum, quod in finem ultimum ordinatur. Si consideretur primo modo, sic malitia voluntatis sufficit ad hoc quod actus malus esse dicatur: quia quod malo fine agitur malum est. Non autem bonitas voluntatis intendentis sufficit ad bonitatem actus: quia actus potest esse de se malus, qui nullo modo bene fieri potest. *Si autem consideretur voluntas secundum quod est eligens, sic universaliter verum est quod a bonitate voluntatis dicitur actus bonus, et a malitia malus.*[47]

Willing can be considered under two aspects, (i) as intention, insofar as it bears on an ultimate end, (ii) as choice, insofar as it bears on a proximate object ordered towards that ultimate end. Then: (i) When we take willing as intending, we can say that the will's badness suffices to make the act bad, since whatever is done for a bad end is bad. Yet the goodness of the intending will is not sufficient to make the act good, for the act may be bad in itself, an act which in no way can it be good to do. But (ii) if we take the will as choosing, then it is universally the case that the will's goodness makes the act good, and the will's badness makes the act bad.

[46] 'actus aliquis habet duplicem finem: scilicet proximum finem, qui est objectum eius, et remotum, quem agens intendit': *Sent.* II d.36 q.5 ad 5; in the ad 4m, Aquinas says that the *materia circa quam* (as apposed to the *materia ex* [or *in*] *qua*) 'est idem cum fine, quia objectum finis actus est', and he will repeat this quite straightforwardly in *ST* I–II q.72 a.3 ad 2 and q.73 a.3 ad 1. See also *Sent.* II d.40 q.1 a.3c: 'quia actus exterior comparatur ad voluntatem sicut obiectum'; later he will say that 'actus exterior est obiectum voluntatis, *inquantum proponitur voluntati a ratione ut quoddam bonum apprehensum et ordinatur per rationem*: et *sic* est prius quam actus voluntatis': I–II q.20 a.1 ad 1; 'quia actus exterior constituitur in genere moris inquantum est voluntarius, oportet quod formaliter consideretur species moralis actus secundum obiectum interioris actus; nam species actus consideratur secundum obiectum': *de Malo* q.7 a.3c. See further Rhonheimer, *Natur als Grundlage der Moral*, 94–7, 318–43.

[47] *Sent.* II d.40 q.1 a. 2c. (The question of circumstances is left aside in Aquinas's implicit assessment of the Lombard's position.) Likewise *ST* III q.20 a.2c:

> Si igitur voluntas sit bona et ex obiecto proprio et ex fine, consequens est actum exteriorem esse bonum. Sed non sufficit, ad hoc quod actus exterior sit bonus, bonitas voluntatis quae est ex intentione finis: sed si voluntas sit mala sive ex intentione finis sive ex actu volito, consequens est actum exteriorem esse malum.

But I–II q.20 a.1c adds a refinement to the thought that *a bonitate voluntatis dicitur actus bonus*:

> Bonitas autem vel malitia quam habet actus exterior secundum se, propter debitam materiam et debitas circumstantias, non derivatur a voluntate sed magis a ratione. Unde si consideretur bonitas exterioris actus secundum quod est in ordinatione et apprehensione rationis, prior est quam bonitas actus voluntatis.

This, of course, in no way qualifies but rather confirms the general strategy of judging the moral goodness and badness of behaviour by judging it as it is *in genere moris*, i.e. as willed, i.e. *in ordinatione et apprehensione rationis*.

And, ten to fifteen years later, St Thomas will say the same in the *De Malo*:[48]

Si... sub intentione comprehendatur non solum intentio finis sed voluntas operis, sic verum est, in bono et in malo, quod *quantum aliquis intendit tantum facit.*[48]

If by 'intention' one understands not only the intending of end but also the willing of means, then it is true to say that, in good deeds and bad alike, *what one does is what one intends.*

Before illustrating this, I should forestall a possible misgiving or misunderstanding. Does all this amount to saying that one's moral responsibilities are exhausted by one's responsibilities to choose or to exclude actions of certain types described *in genere moris*? By no means. *Bonum ex integra causa, malum autem ex quocumque defectu.*[†] One has important responsibilities to avoid or prevent certain states of affairs which are not included within the description *in genere moris* of one's own or perhaps any one else's acts. Some of these states of affairs may be picked out as being within one's moral responsibility (that is, as being morally relevant circumstances) precisely by being foreseen *effects*, though side effects (effects *praeter intentionem*), of *one's own action*. Still, consequences (foreseen or unforeseen) which follow *praeter intentionem* from what one does are not part of what one does; they are within one's moral responsibility by virtue of moral principles and norms quite distinct from those reasons (those moral principles and norms) which require or exclude doing certain types of things.

I return to the theme of intention's role in the characterizing, the very identification, of actions. St Thomas's clearest example of the distinction between behaviour *in genere naturae* and the same behaviour considered precisely as morally significant, as an act *in genere moris*, is: sexual intercourse with someone not one's spouse and sexual intercourse with one's spouse:

cum recipiat speciem ab obiecto, secundum aliquam rationem obiecti specificabitur actus comparatus ad unum activum principium, secundum quam rationem non specificabitur comparatus ad aliud.... Si ergo obiecta humanorum actuum considerentur quae habeant differentias secundum aliquid per se ad rationem pertinentes,

Since acts have their character by reason of their object, one aspect of its object may give an act a specific character in relation to one active principle when the same aspect of its object does not give the act a specific character in relation to another active principle.... So, considering human acts' objects as they differ in accordance with a factor per se

[48] *De Malo* q.2 a.2 ad 8.

erunt actus specie differentes secundum quod sunt actus rationis, licet non sint species differentes secundum quod sunt actus alicuius alterius potentiae; sicut *cognoscere mulierem suam et cognoscere mulierem non suam sunt actus habentes obiecta differentia secundum aliquid ad rationem pertinens*; nam suum et non suum determinantur secundum regulam rationis; quae tamen differentiae per accidens se habent si comparentur ad vim generativam vel etiam ad vim concupiscibilem. Et *ideo cognoscere suam et cognoscere non suam specie differunt secundum quod sunt actus rationis, non autem secundum quod sunt actus generativae aut concupiscibilis.* In tantum autem sunt actus humani in quantum sunt [NB!] actus rationis. Sic *ergo* patet quod *differunt specie in quantum sunt actus humani.* Patet ergo quod actus humani ex specie sua habent quod sint boni vel mali.[49]

pertaining to reason, there are acts which differ in character insofar as they are acts of reason even though they do not differ in character insofar as they are the acts of some other capacity. Thus, *intercourse with one's own wife and intercourse with a woman not one's wife are acts which have different objects* in accordance with a factor pertaining to reason—for being or not being one's own is a matter settled by a criterion of reason; but such differences are incidental in relation to the generative capacity or even to the sensory appetite. *And so intercourse with one's wife and intercourse with another differ in type insofar as they are* [NB!] *acts of reason, but not insofar as they are acts of the reproductive capacity or of bodily desire.* But they are human acts just insofar as they are [NB!] acts of reason. *So* it is clear that *they differ in type precisely as human acts.* Thus it is clear that human acts by their type have something which makes them good or bad.

For there seems no reason to doubt that intercourse with someone not one's spouse can feel just the same as marital intercourse, involves the same psychosomatic dynamisms and performances, can be reproductive in just the same biological way—will regularly, therefore, be the same sort of act *in genere naturae.* But though non-marital intercourse can be very human, can intend various sorts of benefits, even mutual benefits, it cannot have the object, the intention, of expressing a permanent and exclusive commitment to cooperation for the all-round good of one's spouse and of children present and future—cannot be the same sort of act *in genere moris.*

[49] *De Malo* q.2 a.4c; also *Sent.* IV d.26 q.1 a. 3 ad 5; *ST* I–II q.18 a.5 ad 3. This difference is a difference in object, i.e., in intention; that the one with whom one has intercourse is also someone else's spouse is a difference in circumstance rather than in object, though a circumstance which is so important that it too changes the moral type (from fornication to adultery): *De Malo* q.7 a.4c. Notice, too, that the morally bad (unreasonable) act is judged as it is, i.e. as an act of reason, i.e. of adopting by choice a proposal shaped by intelligence (though an intelligence partially mastered by passions):

> bonum per rationem repraesentatur voluntati ut obiectum: et inquantum cadit sub ordine rationis, pertinet ad genus moris, et causat bonitatem moralem [or *malitiam moralem*, insofar as the *bonum* is merely apparent: ad 1] in actu voluntatis. (*ST* I–II q.19 a.1 ad 3.)

Likewise, the physical behaviour and causality and outcome, and even in some cases the emotional and imaginative accompaniments and sequelae, can be *exactly the same* in (a) a case of shooting, foreseen *as* lethal but chosen as the only available means of self-defence, as in (b) a case of shooting to kill, chosen to take advantage of circumstances which will support the legal defence/excuse called 'self-defence'; but lethal self-defence and intending to kill in the course of self-defence are quite different acts *in genere moris*, even though some acts of lethal self-defence are immoral because unfairly careless about the availability of non-lethal means of self-defence. Self-defence is, of course, a case carefully analysed in this way by Aquinas;[50] other cases which illustrate the relevant distinctions may readily be added. For example: hysterectomy to deal with a uterine disease is *in genere naturae* identical with, but *in genere moris* quite different from, hysterectomy of the same uterus to prevent a possible future pregnancy; administering pain-killing drugs to relieve pain, with awareness that they will also shorten life, involves the same behaviour but is not the same act as administering the same drugs to hasten death and thereby eliminate pain; washing out the uterus with a spermicidal solution to repulse a rapist's invasion of a woman's body involves the same behaviour but is not the same act as washing out the same uterus with the same spermicide to prevent pregnancy as a result of intercourse to which the woman consented. And so forth.[51]

This section's theme, confirming the preceding section's conclusion, has been that what a human act is *per se* is what it is *intended* as—what it therefore *is*, *in genere moris*. This thesis has an implication already touched upon. The *actus exterior* which St Thomas's later writings, more

[50] *ST* II–II q.64 a.7.

[51] I entirely accept the contention of Hallett, *Christian Moral Reasoning*, 23, that the appropriate perspective for discussing all these matters is the perspective of the antecedent conscience (i.e. of practical reasoning in response to the question what shall I do). But his inference that in this perspective intention 'drops from consideration' and one considers 'sheer behavior such as aborting a fetus, pre-marital intercourse, sending arms to El Salvador, legalizing marijuana, divorcing and remarrying, fixing prices, registering for the draft' (loc. cit.) is entirely mistaken; no behaviour can be identified as constituting one of these actions without reference to the intentions of the parties, and in most if not all of these cases there could be instances in which a person *deliberately behaving* in the way Hallett has in mind would not be doing the act described *in genere moris* by one or other of the terms used by Hallett: e.g. one who removes a cancerous pregnant womb which he knows to be pregnant need not be adopting the proposal to *abort a fetus*; an air traffic controller who orders an aircraft loaded with arms to divert to El Salvador to save the crew from a hurricane is not adopting the proposal to send arms to El Salvador; a legislator who votes for an omnibus bill simply because it outlaws abortion, and who has tried to excise its provisions legalizing marijuana, is not adopting the proposal to legalize marijuana, i.e. is not legalizing marijuana [though what he is doing contributes to the legalizing of marijuana, an effect which he has the moral responsibility to accept only if he judges doing so fair to those who will suffer from the effects of this effect].

prominently and systematically than his earlier writings,[52] distinguish from the *actus voluntatis* is the outward act considered not as a piece of behaviour *in genere naturae* but precisely as the doing of what was chosen, that is, as the carrying out of the proposal shaped by intelligence and adopted by choice—that is, considered under the description which it had in the practical reasoning which made it seem the thing to be doing.[53]

IV

I return to the confused and mistaken positions which I outlined at the outset.

Intention is a matter of what one chooses to do, not a matter of the emotions with which one makes or carries out the choice. Many things people choose to do they choose and do with great repugnance and reluctance, 'regretting' the steps they take ('regrettable necessities'). So 'no one approves of abortion', but many people choose it 'as the lesser of two evils'. The young surgeon who with a great reluctance performs half-a-dozen 'social indication' abortions, solely because otherwise he would not be allowed to become an obstetrician and help babies endangered in pregnancy and birth, fully intends to abort and destroy the fetuses he aborts and destroys. Their destruction is for him not an end in itself, but is something he needs in order to show his competence and willingness to participate in the healthcare system; it is a means his choosing of which constitutes an end for (and in) the carrying out of his technical performance in the operation.

In considering oneself (or others) morally responsible for what one intends—in that central sense of responsibility which is the only sense relevant to the specific negative moral absolutes, such as do not blaspheme, commit suicide, commit adultery, kill the innocent—one is not attributing any significance to some supposed inner act somehow supplementing or

[52] The distinction is present in his early works: see n. 46 above and *Sent.* II d.40 q.1 a.2c; art. 1c of that *quaestio* had just stated the proposition I am now advancing in the text, in this way:

> hoc modo aliquid ad genus moris pertinet quo voluntarium est; ideo ipsi actus voluntatis qui per se et immediate ad voluntatem pertinent, per se in genere moris sunt;...actus autem imperati a voluntate, eliciti per alias potentias, [these are the acts which the *Summa* will call exterior] pertinent ad genus moris per accidens, scilicet *secundum quod sunt a voluntate imperati*....

[53] The refinements and terminological adjustments in *ST* I–II q.20 aa.1–3 do not affect the fundamental position reached in *Sent.* II d.40 q.2: Si...consideretur voluntas secundum quod est eligens [as distinct from *intendens* in the narrow sense of intending a relatively *ultimum finem*], sic universaliter verum est quod a bonitate voluntatis dicitur actus bonus, et a malitia malus. For, as Aquinas goes on to point out then and there, the goodness or badness of the choice depends on the goodness or badness of the deliberation to which the choice is a kind of conclusion, and so the choice will be bad if deliberation has (e.g.) proposed some bad object, even with a good intentions (i.e. as means to some further and good object in view). [See essay 8, final endnote.]

reinforcing one's act of deliberately doing (namely, of choosing to do...). There is no such preliminary or in any other way supplementary inner act. Choosing to do something is what intending something is; to acknowledge that reference to intention can add something to talk of choice is simply to acknowledge that whatever one chooses to do has some point, is chosen for some reason, with a view to some benefit; talk of intention in the narrow sense simply picks out that point, that reason, that supposed benefit.

What consequences, results, outcomes of one's choosing and doing are to be judged intended and what are to be judged side effects (*praeter intentionem*) is not to be determined by considering which consequences were foreseen or foreseeable and which not, which were physically immediate ('directly caused') and which not, which were humanly important or emotionally impressive and which not, which are treated by convention and common speech as part of the action and which not. It is settled simply by considering why one is doing what one is doing, counting as within the proposal one has adopted by choice everything which one wants for its own sake or for the sake of what one wants for its own sake, and describing each and every aspect of the behaviour just as, and to the extent that, it is described in the practical reasoning which identifies its point.[54] 'The innocent may not be *directly* killed' does not mean: You must not take steps which result immediately in killing innocents. Nor does it mean: You may take steps for the sake of killing innocents so long as the killing is neither desired for its own sake nor factually inseparable from what you do desire. Still less does it mean: You may not kill the innocent unless doing so is a proportionate means to some greater good such as saving more lives. It simply means: You may not make the killing of an innocent either your end (as in revenge) or a means (as in funding abortions for the sake of securing equality between rich and poor women).[55] Intention cannot be explained, and intentions cannot be identified, by reference to what one 'knowingly gives rise to' or 'deliberately causes' or 'immediately and necessarily causes' but only by attending to the course of practical reasoning in the deliberation which ends in choice.

[54] Omissions and forbearances, in the morally precise (contrast n. 28 above) sense of decisions *not to* do something, to avoid the bad side effects of doing it, require special attention: see the analyses of non-contraceptive periodic abstinence in 1988e.

[55] Thus 'direct' killing of the innocent is explained as killing either as an end or as a means, by Pius XII (12 November 1944: *Disc. & Radiomess.* VI, 191–2), by Paul VI (*Humanae Vitae* (1968), n. 14), and by the Congregation for the Doctrine of the Faith (*de Abortu Procurato*, 18 November 1974, para. 7; *Donum Vitae*, 22 February 1987, n. 20). For similar explanations of 'direct' in terms of 'as an end or as a means', see Pius XII, *AAS* 43 (1951): 838 (killing), 843–4 (sterilization); *AAS* 49 (1957): 146 (euthanasia); *AAS* 50 (1958): 734–5 (sterilization). On the question of craniotomy, see essay 10 at n. 37; Grisez, *Christian Moral Principles*, 309, n. 5; and essay 13, sec. III.

In sum: St Thomas's account of intention, properly understood, yields much of the clarification essential to moral analysis. Fuller clarification will attend more thoroughly to the distinctions which St Thomas himself identified as fundamental but did not systematically elaborate, between the four orders: of nature, of reasonings, of choices, of techniques.[56] What is *per se* and what *per accidens* in one order does not settle what is *per se* and *per accidens* in another; what is naturally or technically intermediate between agent and end does not settle what is means and what side effect in the moral order of choices made for reasons. There is much in St Thomas's vocabulary, as in the idiom of our own culture, which obscures such distinctions and thus impedes the appropriation of moral truth, including certain truths which Aquinas himself willingly affirmed.

NOTE

† *Bonum ex integra causa, malum ex quocumque defectu*...(text after n. 48): '[a choice or act is] good when all the contributing factors or aspects are good, and bad from any defect in them'. This is an old tag which Aquinas often quotes, and attributes to the writer (probably late fifth- or early sixth-century Syrian) known to Aquinas as Dionysius : see e.g. *ST* I–II q.18 a.4 ad 3; q.19 a.6 ad 1; q.71 a.5 ad 1; II–II q.79 a.3 ad 4; see *Aquinas* 148 at n. 73.

[56] See n. 24 above.

10

INTENTION AND SIDE EFFECTS*

The distinction between what is intended and what is not intended but brought about as a side effect is at the basis of the vast modern law of tortious liability in negligence; it is the focus, too, of the criminal law's long-accepted distinction between murder and manslaughter. As those facts suggest, it is not the esoteric preserve of some sectarian moral teaching, but a morally significant distinction which is intrinsic to practical reasonableness.

But accounts of it, judicial, legal-academic, and philosophical, remain deeply confused. The confusion can be traced to two main sources: (1) failure to distinguish free choice from spontaneity, and rational from sub-rational motivation; and (2) lack of an ethical theory clear enough to identify the variety of different moral norms which human conduct is required to satisfy, some norms bearing only on what one intends (and does) but others bearing, in other ways, on what one foresees and thus somehow controls as the side effect(s) of what one intends (and does).

It would be good to show how several philosophical accounts of modern tort law—notably those inspired by economic analysis—overlook the significance of the intention/side effect distinction for the entire structure of tort.† But in this essay I shall attend only to criminal law. In that restricted context, I shall try to advance a clarification of issues by discussing a newly, though not wholly, clarified judicial understanding of intention and side effect. One can summarize this understanding in two propositions:

(1) one may intend to achieve a certain result without desiring it to come about; and
(2) one's foresight of a certain result as likely (or even, perhaps, as certain) to follow from one's action(s) does not entail that one intends that result.

So, given that juries can convict of murder only if they find that the accused intended to kill (or to cause grievous bodily harm), this English

* 1991b.

judicial doctrine holds that they should be directed that he can intend to kill without desiring to kill, and that they are legally free to find he foresaw death as certain but did not intend it. Though they may consider his foresight that his actions would cause death a sufficient and compelling ground for inferring intent to kill, the inference is entirely for them to make or not make, on a consideration of all the evidence about what the accused said and did.[1]

In sec. I, then, I discuss intention and 'desire', and in sec. II, intention and foreseen consequences. In sec. III, I sketch some abstract but fundamental grounds for accepting the human and moral importance of the distinction between intending ends and means and accepting the side effects which one knowingly causes.

I. INTENTION AND DESIRE

The first element of the newly clarified English judicial doctrine is its distinction between intention and desire: one may intend to achieve a certain result without desiring it to come about.[2]

This salutary assertion contradicts the principal academic criminal lawyers and legal theorists of the mid-twentieth century. Almost unanimously, they have adopted *desire* as the middle or fundamental term of their explanation of intention: to intend a consequence is to desire it, whether as end or as means; so, for example, consequences which are merely foreseen as probable, but are not desired, are not intended.[3]

Now the same writers, equally unanimously, go on to assert that the 'legal concept of intention' includes among intended consequences all results which are foreseen as *certain*, even results which are in no way desired by the agent. This aspect of academic legal doctrine is the theme of sec. II below. Here I wish only to make a concession: that *one* reason why some judges have distinguished sharply between intention and desire seems to have been their acceptance of the same notion, viz. that

[1] Williams, *The Mental Element in Crime*, 10, reports that (to his regret) 'no English judgment defines intention as involving desire'. What is new is the explicit rejection of invitations to use such a definition, and the insistence that juries be warned against such an account of intention.

[2] See *R v Nedrick* [1986] 3 All ER 1 at 3–4 (CA per Lord Lane CJ); *R v Hancock* [1986] 1 All ER 641 at 645e (CA per Lord Lane CJ); 649, 651b (HL per Lord Scarman); *R v Moloney* [1985] 1 All ER 1025 at 1027f (Lord Hailsham), 1037c, 1038c–h (HL per Lord Bridge); *A-G v Newspaper Publishing plc* [1987] 3 All ER 276 at 304c (CA per Donaldson MR). Likewise Goff, 'The Mental Element in the Crime of Murder' at 42–3.

[3] See the analysis of texts in White, *Grounds of Liability*, 72–3; also Williams, *Textbook of Criminal Law*, 74. This account of intention has been disputed, rightly, by virtually all the recent philosophers who have interested themselves in the law: for helpful discussions: see White, *Grounds of Liability*, 75–82; Kenny, *Will, Freedom and Power*, 46–69; Duff, 'The Obscure Intentions of the House of Lords' at 772–3; also Michael Moore, 'Intentions and *Mens Rea*' at 246.

consequences foreseen as certain are, or count as, intended.[4] That said, however, it seems clear that usually the judicial purpose in distinguishing intention from desire has been much wider: not merely to deal with the special case of consequences undesired but foreseen as certain, but to insist quite generally that 'intention is something quite distinct from motive or desire'.[5]

In the confused conflict between the judges and the legal academics, both sides are in important ways right. But the truth asserted by the judges is the more important for an understanding of intention. The academics are right insofar as 'desire' (like 'want') is indeed equivocal—as they fail, however, to make clear—between (a) one's response to an intelligible good *qua* intelligible and understood to be good (whether or not morally good), that is, *qua* rationally motivating, and (b) one's response to what, as a concrete and experienced or otherwise imaginable possibility, appeals to one's feelings; and one cannot intend without in some way desiring in at least one of these senses. The judges are right insofar as 'intention', 'intend', and 'with intent' unequivocally belong with sense (a) of 'desire'; these terms refer to what is *freely chosen* just insofar as it is *chosen* as an intelligent and rationally appealing option, desirable in sense (a), whether it is also desired in sense (b) *or not*. One can choose and intend to do what is utterly repugnant to one's dominant feelings—that is the important reality (or the most important of the realities) which judges recall when they state, at large, that one can intend what one does not desire.

(I shall be relying upon these sharp distinctions—between intelligible factors and factors contributed by sense and imagination, and correspondingly between volitions including choices, and feelings. This may give the impression that I hold a dualistic view of human personality and action. But I do not. All the distinctions are made, for analytic purposes,

[4] Thus *DPP v Smith* [1961] AC 290 at 302 (CCA per Byrne J): 'intent and desire are different things and... once it is proved that an accused man knows that a result is certain the fact that he does not desire that result is irrelevant'. The judgment of the Court of Criminal Appeal in *Smith* was approved, but particularly insofar as it denies that foresight of *probable* consequences amounts to intention, in the Court of Appeal in *Hancock* [1986] 1 All ER at 645a, per Lane LCJ. But in stating later (at 645e) that 'desire and intent are two different things', Lane LCJ does not reassert that to foresee consequences as certain is to intend them; rather, he insists that the jury must be left to find intention with no more explanation of the meaning of 'intention' than the negative clarification that 'if you are sure [that the accused intended to cause death or really serious bodily injury,] the fact that he may not have desired that result is irrelevant'. The House of Lords (651g) deprecated even this degree of 'generalization' in directing juries as to intention, and did not repeat Lane LCJ's approval of the dicta in *Smith*. Williams, 'Oblique Intention' at 430 n. 49, concedes that it is 'still unclear' that the judicial understanding of intention extends (as he would wish it) to 'known certainties'. See also n. 17 below.

[5] *Moloney* [1985] 1 All ER at 1037c, per Lord Bridge; see also *Lynch v Director of Public Prosecutions* [1975] 1 All ER 913 at 934e, per Lord Simon (dissenting; but the majority decision was overruled in *R v Howe* [1987] 1 All ER 771 [HL]).

among the dynamic aspects of one reality, the acting person, who alone is properly said to imagine, understand, feel, and will. It may be helpful, however, to note that 'feeling' and 'emotion' have some unwelcome connotations of conscious experience and intensity. The motivations consequent on sensory cognition, and generically common to human beings and brute animals, are in fact normally effective without one's being aware of them. But for want of better words, I use 'feeling' and 'emotion'; the unwelcome connotations are in any case, perhaps, less troublesome in the more or less dramatic context of criminal offences, in which these not-specifically-human motivations do usually, even in the heat of 'unselfconscious' action, become more or less intense and rise to consciousness.)

The conception of intention used in moral and legal reasoning, properly understood, is tightly linked to sense (a) of 'desire' precisely because it is tightly linked to the moral significance of *choice*. To choose, in the relevantly rich sense of 'choice', is essentially to *adopt a plan or proposal* which one has put to oneself in one's practical reasoning and deliberation on the merits of alternative options, that is, of alternative plans or proposals which one sees some reason to adopt, that is, understands as desirable. Whatever, then, is included within one's chosen plan or proposal, whether as its end or as a means to that end, is *intended*, that is, is included within one's intention(s).[6] What one does is done 'with intent to X' (or: 'with intent that X') if X is a state of affairs which is *part of one's plan* either as its end (or a part of its end, or one of its ends) or as a means.[7]

(It goes without saying that 'plan' and 'proposal' must not be understood as connoting some ponderous or formal process of deliberation. One can form and act on an intention in a moment. But if the choice so to act was intelligent and free, one will always be able to identify the plan or proposal thus instantly and informally conceived and opted for, and that plan or proposal will always be analysable in terms of ends and means. It

[6] What I call 'proposal' is called by some 'goal' or 'purpose'—the context making it clear that they do not mean end as distinct from means, but rather everything one is trying to do (considered not as being done but as being envisaged). Thus, e.g. Fletcher, *Rethinking Criminal Law*, 442, rightly says:

> The basic cleavage in the states of mind used in criminal legislation is between those that focus on the actor's goal (willfulness, intention, purposefulness) and those that focus on the risk that the actor creates in acting (recklessness and negligence).

Similarly, the Model Penal Code's 'conscious object': MPC 2.02(2)(a):

> A person acts purposely with respect to a material element of an offense when: (i) if the element involves the nature of his conduct or a result thereof, it is his conscious object to engage in conduct of that nature or to cause such a result...

[7] And one's will bears upon X in a morally equivalent way if one chooses *not* to do something, precisely in order to bring about X (whether as an end one considers worthwhile in itself or as a means to bringing about some further state of affairs). That is to say, there are omissions which correspond to the action which carries out a proposal adopted by choice.

should also be understood that means are not always materially distinct from ends—for example, when one chooses something for its intrinsic value, for instance to give a gift as an act of friendship, with no ulterior purpose.)

In sense (a) of 'desire'—what I call volitionally desiring—it is analytically true that what one intends one desires. But it remains true that one often chooses, intends, and does what one does not desire, that is, what one's dominant desire—one's strong or strongest emotional desire—is *not* to do or *not* to bring about. The Hobbesian or Spinozist conception—adopted with more or less philosophical consciousness by legal theorists such as John Austin and Glanville Williams—according to which action necessarily manifests one's dominant desire,[8] is equivalently a denial of the reality of free choice: choice between rationally appealing, incompatible alternative practical proposals such that there is *no factor* save the choosing itself which settles which alternative is chosen. But free choice (the reality of which I shall not defend here)[9] is a central presupposition of the importance attributed to intention in the moral theory which the criminal law as we know it more or less steadily embodies and enforces. Still, even those philosophers who deny that choice can be free can recognize the reality, and something of the importance, of distinguishing between desire and intention, provided that they have a fairly clear concept of *reasons for acting* and *acting for a reason.*[10]

The distinction between desire and intention—that is, between what is desired emotionally and what is desired volitionally—is not to be understood as expressing some rationalistic conception of human motivation. The central case of action done with intention is rationally motivated action, but even rationally motivated actions are never done—or even deliberated about—without emotional motives as well. In a full account of human action, it is therefore important to distinguish between two aspects of one's *purpose* in acting, that is, of that for the sake of which, and in the hope of realizing which, one acts. Though such an account is not necessary for the purposes of this essay, it may be of interest for me to digress for four

[8] Hobbes, *Human Nature* (1651), ch. 12.2; *Leviathan* (1651), ch. 6, s.v. Deliberation (a passage reproduced in Austin, *Lectures on Jurisprudence* [1869], addenda to lect. 18); Spinoza, *Ethics* (1677), Part III, note to prop. ii; Williams, *Criminal Law: The General Part*, 36: 'Intention is, by definition, the desire that prevails and issues in action'. See also Glanville Williams, 'The *Mens Rea* of Murder: Leave It Alone' at 390. (But cf. his more cautious formulation in *Textbook of Criminal Law* [1983], 74: '*if I decide to try to* achieve my desire... the desire becomes the intention with which I act' [emphasis added].) [And see essay II.12 at p. 228]

[9] It is defended adequately in Boyle, Grisez, and Tollefsen, *Free Choice: A Self-Referential Argument*; see also *FoE* 137; [and sec. I of the Introduction to this volume].

[10] Thus Moore, 'Intentions and *Mens Rea*' at 245–6.

or five paragraphs to sketch my understanding of the relation between (rational) volition and (emotional) desiring in purposive action.[11]

Rational and sub-rational motivation in purposive action

By 'purpose' I mean a state of affairs—something concrete which can exist or not exist in reality. What it is about one's purpose that makes one *rationally* interested in it is some intelligible good, whether instrumental or basic. Achieving the purpose will instantiate the good which is the reason for which one acts for that purpose. Thus, in going to the doctor, one's purpose is to regain one's health; regaining one's health is a state of affairs instantiating the intelligible good of health, an intelligible good which doctors hope all their patients will participate in, and which is not exhausted by its instantiation in any concrete state of affairs which it could be one's purpose to realize. In short, one's purpose is in one aspect desired, volitionally, by reason of an intelligible good. In this aspect the purpose, while remaining a concrete state of affairs, is proposed by intellectual, propositional knowledge which commends acting for the purpose by reason of that intelligible good (and ultimately by reason of a basic good, some basic aspect of human flourishing which the agent hopes to share in or to help another or others to share in).

But in another aspect, every purpose is desired, emotionally, as concrete and imaginable. In this aspect, the purpose is just the particular objective, a state of affairs envisaging which arouses the feelings the agent needs to act for it. (Sometimes these feelings are aroused by something linked by psychological association with the objective.) Whereas rational motives motivate toward some fulfilment of some person as a whole, emotional motives motivate toward some fulfilment of the agent's sentience. But though they are distinct from one another, emotional and rational motives are dynamically united—so much so that it is easy to confuse emotional motives with reasons for acting. (*Common talk about 'reasons' for action often manifests this confusion*, or want of differentiation.) The goal of some emotional motivation—say, eating a particular meal—can be understood and generalized; one thinks of eating in general as a good, in which one is interested. But as a reason for acting, such an intelligible good can never be more than instrumental, since a fulfilment of sentient nature just as such is not yet a fulfilment of the person as a whole. So eating can be *deliberately chosen* only insofar as it is instrumental to basic goods such as life and fellowship, goods one's anticipation of which renders one's choice not merely instrumental to the satisfaction of feelings but rational in its ultimate motivation.

[11] The account follows that in 1987f (with Grisez and Boyle) at 102–6.

There are, moreover, intelligently ordered performances the only ultimate motives of which are feelings—that is, the motivation of which is not specifically human. For example, a traveller spontaneously responding to nature's call may follow signs towards a toilet. Common speech, attending to the fact that he is pursuing an intelligently guided causal process, will say he is acting intentionally (and 'rationally'). But his actions, insofar as they are spontaneous (rather than deliberately chosen by him for a reason, in preference to some rationally appealing alternative such as catching his plane), do not instantiate choice and intention in their focal senses and should not be confused with rationally motivated action; he is not acting for a reason, in the strict sense used here and in sec. III below.

Common speech will also say that the signs which our traveller is following are 'means' he is using or employing to reach his 'end' or destination. But technical 'means' (objects), such as signs or other tools, are not to be confused with means in the sense relevant to the analysis of the central cases of intention. Means, in the latter sense, are states of affairs—one's actions and, often, certain resulting states of affairs—which one chooses to bring about for the sake of some further purpose (one's end), and which figure accordingly in the plan or proposal one adopts by choice. Means, then, are purposes. But they are instrumental purposes, adopted for their intelligible appeal as promising to bring about the further purposes. In the paradigm cases of intention, means are instrumental to purposes adopted for the human fulfilment they are taken to instantiate—that is, purposes adopted, like the means, for their appeal to reason.

The law may have to allow uses of its terms which go beyond their paradigm senses. It would be futile to object to a judge or jury finding that our traveller *intended* to find a toilet. But if there is to be any *explanation* offered to guide the judge's or jury's deliberations (and wherever there is a question whether someone's intention was *this rather than* that), it must respect the distinctions which are important to understanding the paradigms that give the law its shape, even if they are lost in some of the peripheral extensions of terms.

Intention and side effects: some interim payoffs

I have distinguished intention from desire by suggesting that intention includes all that is *chosen* whether as end or as means, and noting that what is chosen as means is often strongly repugnant to desire in the sense of feelings and emotion. I conceded that there is no action without some emotional motivation, some appeal to feeling. But the appeal to feeling may often come entirely from the end; in such a case, the means—perhaps deeply repugnant to one's feelings—have nothing motivating about them but their bare appeal to reason, that is, their bare promise of bringing about the end. And even the end may, and in cases of fully intentional action will, have been adopted not *for* its appeal to feeling but for its appeal to reason. For choice, in the full sense, is of proposals which link (a) the intelligible benefit(s) that make more or less ultimate purposes (ends) appealing to reason with (b) the intelligible empowerments (instrumental goods) that make immediate purposes (means) appealing to reason.

The analysis so far yields several payoffs in relation to 'side effects'.

First payoff There are states of affairs which stand to some *technique* or technical process as side effects, but which those who choose the technical process adopt as means (or even, sometimes, as end) and thus intend.

A simple example: a commander orders the instant destruction of a city by nuclear bombing, in order to shock the adversary out of the war or to deter escalation by the adversary. The targeters select some purely military installation in the city as their aim-point, and tell themselves that what they intend is the destruction of that target; 'all else is side effect'. But they merely deceive themselves. For side effects, in the sense relevant to morals (and law), are effects which are not intended as end or means, that is, which figure neither as end nor as means in the plan adopted by choice. And the plan in the execution of which the targeters choose to participate is a plan which includes the destroying of the entire city and very many of its inhabitants, as a means adopted precisely for the sake of achieving the desired further effects (on the adversary's willingness to continue and/or to escalate the war). Intent is determined not by the technical processes of targeting (aiming a bomb, and delivering it onto its aim-point—its 'Desired Ground Zero'), but by the more or less strategic plan which directs that those techniques (technical means) be employed to effect the means and thus, it is hoped, the end. The objective of the targeters and bomb-aimers is the target; but the tactical/strategic objective is the destruction of the city; the more ultimate strategic objective is the hoped-for change in the adversary's will and operations; and both tactical and strategic objectives are fully intended and in no morally relevant sense are side effects.[12]

A slightly more complex example: on 30 October 1940, RAF Bomber Command was ordered to adopt a new bombing policy, in which objectives such as 'centres of communication' would be selected precisely because they were 'suitably placed in the centres of towns or populated districts', and incendiary bombs were to be used with the aim of causing fires 'either on or in the vicinity of the targets'. On 9 July 1941, Bomber Command

[12] See *NDMR* 92–6, 102–3, 165.

was ordered to carry out its night attacks with the double aim of economic dislocation and reduction of civilian morale, by attacking targets described as 'suitably located for obtaining incidental effect on the morale of the industrial population'.[13] Thus, even at this early stage of the city-bombing campaign, the policy was one which included the destruction of civilians and civilian housing among its *intended* effects, notwithstanding that both the *targets* and the *primary objects* of attack still remained military (that is, non-civilian) in a fairly strict sense. A secondary and in that sense 'incidental' effect can be a fully intended effect; a secondary or supplementary means is still a means.

Second payoff What states of affairs are means and what are side effects depends on the description which they have in the proposal or plan adopted in the choice which brings them about, that is, in the clear-headed practical reasoning which makes that plan seem a rationally attractive option.

For example: suppose that Minsk is attacked by British nuclear missiles in retaliation for a Soviet attack on Birmingham, and in order both to dissuade the Soviets from carrying out any more attacks on British cities and to manifest British resolve not to surrender. The British attack may be targeted on military installations and personnel in Minsk (because the targeters have conceptions of decency and like to 'direct their intention' in that way) and it may well have some significant impact on Soviet military operations. History might (or might not) relate that that particular effect—on Soviet military targets and operations—turned out to be decisive in subsequent military campaigns. But if that effect did not enter into the practical reasoning of those who ordered the attack, then it was a mere side effect, and those Soviet military personnel killed in the attack were killed not *as*—that is, under the description of—combatants but simply *as* inhabitants of a city which, with its inhabitants, is intended to be destroyed in a terrific act of threatening (and perhaps of 'punishment'): that is to say,

[13] See *ibid.*, 40–1. In 1942, the orders were changed again, authorizing Bomber Command to employ its forces 'without restriction'; their 'primary object' was to be 'focused on the morale of the enemy civil population'; commanders were specifically instructed that, because the policy now included attack on enemy morale, the rule applicable to enemy-*occupied* territory (e.g. occupied France), forbidding 'the intentional bombardment of civilian populations, as such', did not apply to the bombing of enemy territory (e.g. Germany itself). It would be very naïve to think that those who gave and received these orders supposed that the desired effects on morale would be achieved simply by moving the destruction of military-industrial targets into close proximity with civilians who would thus be more shocked and depressed by that destruction than if they saw it on the horizon or read about it in the newspaper; or by an impressive and frightening fireworks display. Fireworks displays become frightening and thus morale-depressing only when they are carried out in such a way as to make all who see them fear for the destruction of themselves, their friends, and their most treasured possessions. There is no way to make people develop a lasting fear for themselves, their friends, or their possessions other than by destroying some of the people and possessions in question. *That* was therefore the relevant though secondary objective and intention.

these Soviet combatants were killed *as* non-combatants. The intention was to kill them as non-combatants.

Third payoff Any who welcome and rejoice in an effect of their actions, but who in *no* way adapt their practical reasoning (and thus the plan they adopt and execute) with a view to bringing about that effect, do not intend it.

This payoff follows from the distinction between intention and the emotions which, in one form or another, always accompany it. But, since such bonus side effects can be genuinely side effects even when foreseen (if they are in no way provided for in the chosen proposal), a full understanding and acceptance of this payoff must depend upon the issue to which I now turn: intention and foresight.

II. INTENTION AND FORESIGHT

The second element in the new English judicial understanding of intention is its sharp distinction between intention and foresight: the fact that one foresees a certain result as likely or even certain to follow from one's action(s) does not entail that one intends that result.

As I noted in sec. I, legal academic writers have virtually unanimously asserted that the 'legal concept of intention' includes among intended consequences all results which are foreseen as *certain*, even results in no way desired by the agent.[14] I have also noted that it remains rather uncertain quite how far the judges have confronted and rejected this view. Certainly they have rejected the view—to be found 'in legal systems across the Western world'[15]—that an agent who foresees consequences as *probable*, or at least as highly probable, intends those consequences.[16] But that was a view long campaigned against by Glanville Williams, yet he

[14] And not merely the legal academics: see e.g. Sidgwick, *The Methods of Ethics*, 202; Chisholm, 'The Structure of Intention'.

[15] Fletcher, *Rethinking Criminal Law*, 443; but cf. 445 on the important doctrinal difference between German and Soviet law, on the one hand, and Anglo-American (and possibly French) law on the other. The former systems draw the distinction between intentional and negligent conduct by including *dolus eventualis* within the contours of intending a particular result.

[16] See esp. *R v Hancock* [1986] 1 All ER 641 at 649g–j; likewise, Lord Goff, 'The Mental Element' at 43–7. Thus they have clearly, if implicitly, overruled the direction in *R v Desmond & Barrett, The Times*, 28 April 1868 (that it is murder 'if a man did [an] act not with the purpose of taking life but with the knowledge or belief that life was *likely* to be sacrificed by it'), on which H.L.A. Hart founded his view that 'for the law, a foreseen outcome is enough... the law does not require in such cases that the outcome should have been something intended in the sense that the accused set out to achieve it, either as a means or an end': Hart, *Punishment and Responsibility*, 119–20. Equally clearly, the judges have rejected Sidgwick's claim that 'for purposes of exact moral or *jural discussion*, it is best to include under the term "intention" all the consequences of an act that are foreseen as certain *or probable*': *The Methods of Ethics*, 202 (emphasis added).

simultaneously campaigned for the view that to foresee consequences of one's act as certain, or 'morally certain', or 'virtually certain' or 'practically certain', *is* to intend them ('obliquely'). Still, it seems to me that the English judges, at the highest level, have decided not to encumber the understanding of 'intention' with a distinction as tenuous and artificial as that thus drawn between 'highly probable' (and so *not* necessarily intended) and 'virtually certain' (and so *necessarily* intended) consequences.[17‡]

The essence of the new judicial doctrine is that intent is a commonsense concept which must be left to the jury without any attempt to give directions imposing or even suggesting some special legal meaning of 'intend', 'intention', 'with intent', etc. This being so, it is well to recall how foreign to the commonsense concept of intention is the academics' notion that what is foreseen as certain is intended.

One who hangs curtains knowing that the sunlight will make them fade does not thereby intend that they shall fade. Those who wear shoes don't intend them to wear out. Those who fly the Atlantic foreseeing certain jetlag don't do so with the intention to get jetlag; those who drink too heavily rarely intend the hangover they know is certain. Those who habitually stutter foresee with certainty that their speech will create annoyance or anxiety, but do not intend those side effects.[18] Indeed, we might well call the academics' extended notion of intent the Pseudo-Masochist Theory of Intention—for it holds that those who foresee that their actions will have painful effects upon themselves *intend* those effects.

Moreover, common morality attributes considerable importance to the distinction between what is intended and what is foreseen as certain. Throughout the Second World War, the British Government felt constrained by this morality to preserve for public consumption the wholly false pretence that its bombing policy did not include attacks intended to kill and injure civilians as such; ministers consistently deceived Parliament by insisting that the bombing of dwellings located near factories was no more than a side effect, though *admittedly certain*, of night bombing of the factories and other 'military objectives'. When the commander of Bomber Command secretly protested to the Air Ministry about this sort of deception, and asked the Ministry to stop its public denials that the intention of the bombing campaign was 'the obliteration of German cities

[17] The House of Lords' approval, in *Moloney* at 1039d, of the judgment of the Court of Criminal Appeal in *R v Steane* [1947] KB 997 at 1004, entails (as Glanville Williams implicitly concedes, 'Oblique Intention' at 428) a rejection of the doctrine that consequences if certain are intended.

[18] See further Boyle and Sullivan, 'The Diffusiveness of Intention Principle: A Counter-Example' (giving citations to other counter-examples advanced by Anscombe, Austin, Kenny, Fleming, and Pitcher. Boyle and Sullivan's own counter-example: stuttering as a vividly foreseen and struggled-against side effect of trying to defend one's father's reputation).

and their inhabitants as such' and to cease claiming that the wiping out of German cities was only an 'inevitable accompaniment of all-out attack on the enemy's means and capacity to wage war', the Ministry refused, and insisted that 'this distinction is in fact one of great importance in the presentation to the public of the aims and achievements of the bomber offensive'.[19] The distinction in question was, of course, simply that between effects foreseen as certain and effects intended.

Against all this, the theorists of 'oblique intention' offer a very restricted diet of unanalysed examples. The pièce de résistance, invented by Glanville Williams and everywhere repeated,[20] is the blowing up of an aircraft in flight in order to collect the cargo or hull insurance, thereby killing the pilot; this, it is said, is a clear case of (obliquely) intending to kill. What should be said?

It is in no sense a case of intending to kill, intention to kill, or intent to kill—and adding the qualifier 'oblique' is to no effect, save in a jargon driven not by the insights *reflected* in common speech but by a theory which, as an analysis of intention, has nothing to be said for it. One must immediately add, however, that by a nuance of our language, it *is* a case in which the accused cannot be said to have killed *unintentionally*—for 'unintentionally' connotes accident or mistake or lack of foresight.[21] By another nuance of our language, it is also a case, I think, of 'wilfully' killing—for 'wilfully', to my ear, means not unintentionally. But the bomb's effects on the pilot, though not unintentional, are not intended, for they are no part of the accused's end or means as these figure in the proposal he adopted by choosing to blow up the plane. They are side effects, in the morally relevant sense.

Compare another aircraft case. Terrorists hijack a plane. One of them is carrying a timing device primed to detonate a bomb in a city; the instrument can be destroyed only by free-fall from a great height. The terrorists call for a parachute to be prepared, so that the woman among them can exit during the flight. The steward selects two parachutes and cuts off the ripcord of one of them, planning (a) to give over the dud parachute if the

[19] See *NDMR* 42–4. It must be borne in mind that the distinction was preserved only for public consumption: the secret standing orders to Bomber Command made it unambiguously clear, from at latest 14 February 1942, that attacks were to be made against civilian dwelling houses *in preference to* war-related factories; accordingly, e.g., the massive and repeated attacks in 1943 on Hamburg included in the planned bombing area *none* of Hamburg's war-related facilities and *only* its residential districts; and the operational orders began 'Intention: To destroy Hamburg': *ibid.*, 41.

[20] Williams, *Mental Element in Crime*, 34–5; [English] Law Commission, 'Imputed Criminal Intent', Law Com. No. 10 (HMSO, 1967), para. 18; *Hyam* [1975] AC at 77C, per Lord Hailsham; Law Reform Commission of Canada, *Report on Recodifying Criminal Law*, vol. 1 (1986), 20. Cf. Law Reform Commission of Canada, Working Paper 29, *Criminal Law: The General Part: Liability and Defences* (1982), 181–2; Williams, 'The *Mens Rea* of Murder' at 388.

[21] It is thus a killing which is both intentional and not intentional, for 'intentional(ly)' is equivocal between 'intended' and 'not unintentionally'.

exiting terrorist is carrying the timing device, but (b) *to give over the good parachute if she is not;* the steward's sole concern is that the timing device be destroyed. In the event, the terrorist who asks for the parachute is carrying the device, so she is given the dud chute and falls to her death. Glanville Williams, the 'theorist of oblique intention', says (of any case in which a flight steward deliberately gives an exiting criminal a dud parachute):

> it seems clear that, as a matter of law, the steward must be credited with an intention to kill the criminal. He foresees the certainty of the criminal's death if the events happen as he sees they may, even though he does not desire that death.[22]

To me it seems clear that my story's steward (whose practical reasoning has a content overlooked by Glanville Williams) manifestly did not intend to kill the terrorist, though he foresaw and accepted that his own choice would certainly bring about her death. Her free-fall and death are side effects of the steward's plan to destroy the timing device.

Of course, the steward does the terrorist no injustice; one going about to kill others is not treated unfairly by lethal countermeasures. The pilot killed by the cargo bomber, on the other hand, is treated with gross injustice; his life is simply treated as if it were of less value than the insurance moneys gained by the bomber; the bomber violates the Golden Rule since he would not wish his own life to be thus wilfully destroyed by others acting not pursuant to any moral responsibility (for example, of defence of self or others) but to desire for gain.

In a legal system which divides all criminal homicide into two sharply distinguished categories—murder and manslaughter—ranked in gravity, it is easy to sympathize with the pressure to assign the cargo bomber to the more serious category, notwithstanding that the categorization centres on the distinction between the intended and the non-intended but reckless or culpably negligent causing of death, and that the cargo bomber's killing is not a case of intending to cause death. But the clear-headed way of acceding to this pressure is, I suggest, to broaden the definition of murder to include not only (a) killing with intent to kill but also (b) doing without lawful justification or excuse an act which one is sure will kill.[23]

[22] Williams, *Mental Element in Crime*, 52–3.

[23] Doesn't this reintroduce a distinction (between certainty and awareness of high probability) which I said the judges seem to have rejected as tenuous and artificial? Yes. But here it is employed not in the explication of the key *explanans* of murder (intent) but in an independent definition of a distinction which is inevitably artificial (that between murder and manslaughter, as exhaustive and exclusive categories of criminal homicide). For the conceptually chaotic travails of legal systems which attempt to expand 'intention' artificially to include *dolus eventualis*, see Fletcher, *Rethinking Criminal Law*, 325–6, 445–9. For other techniques for defining a class of murders without intent to kill, see *ibid.*, 264–7.

Such a definition would have the same reach as those proposed by the Law Reform Commissioners of England and Canada in 1985 and 1986. But each of these proposals involves imposing an artificial legal meaning on the deceptively common-language terms 'intention' and 'purpose', used to pick out the mental element in their definitions of murder. The English Commissioners define murder (in its main limb) as intending to kill, and they define *intending* an element of an offence as (a) wanting it to exist or occur, or (b) being aware that it exists, or (c) being almost certain that it exists or will exist or occur.[24] They distinguish acting 'intentionally' (that is, with intention) from acting 'purposely', which is that subclass of acting intentionally (in their artificially extended sense) where one *wants* the relevant element of the offence to exist or occur. The Canadians, however, select 'purposely' as the term to be artificially extended. They define murder as purposely killing, and define acting 'purposely', as to a consequence, as acting 'in order to effect either that consequence or another consequence' which one 'knows involves that consequence'.[25]

The strains imposed by these special definitions of common-language terms show up even before the proposed Codes are applied to particular cases. The Canadians, when giving the extended definition of purpose, say that 'oblique or indirect intent' extends to consequences which, to one's knowledge, are 'entailed by' the consequences which are one's aim. But when recalling this extension of 'purposely', on the occasion of defining murder, their only illustration of 'oblique or indirect purpose' is of causing death, which one does not desire, 'as a *necessary step to* some other objective', which one does desire. They thus give unwitting testimony to the pull of intention's (or purposive action's) true analysis in terms of means to ends, steps to objectives. Meantime, the English Commissioners have equipped themselves with a similarly factitious definition of 'intention(ally)', an artefact constructed simply by tacking the whole of their definition of 'knowingly' onto the whole of their definition of 'purposely'. Hence my modest proposal: to define the mental element in murder disjunctively, as either intention in its ordinary sense or certainty ('knowledge') that death would be brought about by an act which one does without lawful justification or excuse.

The last-mentioned qualification is needed to accommodate not merely my perhaps fanciful case of the steward and the parachute, but the most elementary and commonplace example of the vital distinction between

[24] Law Commission, *Codification of the Criminal Law*, HC 270 (London, 1985), 202 (draft Code s. 56), 183 (draft Code s. 22).

[25] Law Reform Commission of Canada, *Recodifying Criminal Law*, vol. 1 (1986), 54 (murder), 20 ('purposely').

intention and foresight of certainty: the administration of drugs in order to suppress the pain of the dying with the knowledge that the painkillers will hasten death. It is in relation to *this* case, and in explicit contradiction of 'the Roman Church's doctrine of "double effect"', that Glanville Williams in 1956 first said: 'When a result is foreseen as certain, it is the same as if it were desired or intended.'[26]

The contrary view, he claimed, involved the artificiality and/or hypocrisy of distinguishing between a doctor who has 'in the forefront of his mind the aim of ending his patient's existence' and a doctor who gives the same dose *in order to relieve pain* and who 'keeps his mind steadily off the consequence which his professional training teaches him is inevitable' and who does not 'welcome his patient's death as a merciful release'.[27] Thus Williams manifested the most thoroughgoing misunderstanding of the so-called doctrine of double effect, which in the aspects here relevant is nothing more than an analysis of intention in terms of chosen means and ends. Such an analysis of intention has nothing to do with 'keeping one's mind off' the unintended but foreseen consequences, or with whether one emotionally welcomes that consequence. It is entirely concerned with what figures in the rational proposal (moral or immoral) which one adopts by choice and which thus constitutes one's immediate reason for acting as one does. On Williams' own account it is clear that the second doctor is acting 'in order to relieve pain' by giving a dose which is 'the minimum necessary to deaden pain';[28] all that figures in this doctor's proposal is his responsibility to relieve pain, and the fulfilling of that responsibility by administering a dose calculated not so as to bring relief *by* bringing death but so as to relieve pain. Such a doctor can realistically and resolutely resolve never to intend to kill, or intentionally bring about death, and yet welcome the patient's death just insofar as it is a relief from suffering. This is not a 'direction of intention', artificial, hypocritical, or at all.

Difficult moral questions do, however, appear at the margins of this clarity. What if the person carrying the timing device, whom the steward therefore treats to the dud parachute, is an innocent passenger? What if the person suffering agonizing pain which could be relieved only by *de facto* lethal doses has years more expectation of fairly normal life? That which is done 'for a lawful purpose' may yet be in some respects unreasonable. The law could mark this by means analogous to the category of manslaughter by 'excessive self-defence'.

[26] Williams, *The Sanctity of Life and the Criminal Law*, 286. [27] *Ibid.*, 286, 288.
[28] *Ibid.*, 285, 286.

That was a category invented by the Australian courts in the late 1950s and proposed by the English Law Commissioners for adoption in England and by the Canadians for Canada. But the Australian High Court has now rejected its own progeny, denouncing the intermediate category as a practically unworkable source of excessive refinements in directing juries who should be left to make a broad judgment, facing only the alternatives of convicting of murder and acquitting outright.[29] No one will imagine that these arguments about the workability and consequent procedural fairness of directions to juries are arguments which helpfully trace the relevant *moral* boundaries, that is, the boundaries relevant to the deliberations of the upright conscience.

Private defence and intent to kill

The common law of private defence, as recently stated by the High Court of Australia, departs from morality in another important respect. For, according to the High Court, those who act reasonably in private defence are not guilty of murder even if they acted with intent to kill.[30] But the classic moral doctrine, stated by Aquinas in the passage which is the principal historical source of the so-called doctrine of double effect, is that while private defence justifies *behaviour known to be death-dealing* (provided that it does not go beyond what is needed to protect from serious assault), it does not justify *acting to* kill, that is, the same behaviour executed with the intent to kill.[31]

Nor is the latter a theologian's refinement foreign to the conscience of practical people; on the contrary, it finds a place in moral thought wherever that is not corrupted by feelings of antipathy or of discriminatory superiority (or by bad philosophy). Let me illustrate popular moral thought in its uncorrupt and corrupt forms, by two examples from the British colonial empire.

In 1854, the legislature of Western Australia enacted an ordinance 'for the suppression of violent crimes committed by Convicts illegally at large'—the said convicts being, of course, of the same stock as the legislators. Having recited that 'the lives of officers of justice and their assistants, while in the execution of their duty in endeavouring to apprehend such offenders, have been periled by resistance with deadly weapons', the ordinance provided that when an armed convict is challenged to surrender himself but refuses to do so and instead

[29] *Zecevic v Director of Public Prosecutions* (1987) 162 CLR 645, overruling *R v Howe* (1958) 100 CLR 448 and *Viro v R* (1978) 141 CLR 88.

[30] *Zecevic* at 662.

[31] *ST* II–II q.64 a.7.

give[s] reasonable cause to believe that he is about to use [his weapon] for the purpose of preventing his apprehension, then, and in such case, it shall be lawful for such Justice, policeman, constable, or officer... or for any free person acting in aid... by the discharge of any loaded firearms... *to disable and over-power such convict, with a view to his apprehension,* without bodily injury to his captor; and in case the death of such convict shall be thereby caused, the same shall be deemed an act of justifiable homicide.[32]

Less than three years later, the legislature of Hong Kong under Governor Sir John Bowring LLD,—the editor of Bentham's *Works*—enacted an ordinance 'for better securing the Peace of the Colony'. A key provision:

Every person lawfully acting as a sentry or patrol at any time between the hour of eight in the evening and sunrise is hereby authorized, whilst so acting, to fire upon, *with intent* or effect *to kill,* any *Chinaman* whom he shall meet with or discover abroad and whom he shall have reasonable ground to suspect of being so abroad for an improper purpose, and who being challenged by him shall neglect or refuse to make proper answer to his challenge.[33]

There is, I think, no need to comment on these two lucid provisions.

'But doing X just is doing Y!'

Some will be impatient with the distinction drawn by Aquinas. Some acts, they will say, just *are* killing, whether done in self-defence or not; one who chooses to do such an act just is, willy-nilly, intending to kill. Intentionally firing a shotgun at close range directly at robbers just is acting with intent to kill them, even if done as the only way of stopping their violent assault. And this sort of claim is made, or at least conceded, by many who otherwise acknowledge that one's intention is defined by one's practical reason, in terms of the desirability characterization under which one wills the end and the description under which one judges one's chosen means appropriate to that end.[34]

Thus Anscombe, in relation to the fat man blocking the escape of potholers (cave explorers) threatened by rising waters, speaks of a proposal

[32] No. 7 of 1854 (WA), preamble and s. 5 (emphasis added). Section 6 similarly provided that convicts attempting to escape might be shot by sentries or guards 'for the purpose of preventing such escape'.

[33] No. 2 of 1857 (Hong Kong), s. 11. After being in force for seven months, this Ordinance was suspended (evidently on the instructions of the Colonial Office in London) and was replaced on the same date (15 July 1857) by an Ordinance (No. 9 of 1857) substantially identical but omitting the provision I have quoted. Ordinance No. 2 remained in suspense until repealed by a Statute Law Revision Ordinance in 1887.

[34] e.g. Kenny, 'Intention and *Mens Rea* in Murder' at 165, 173 (but contrast 165); Duff, 'Obscure Intentions' at 774, 778.

to make an exit by moving a rock, the moving of which will crush the fat man's head:

> At this point the Doctrine of Double Effect helps itself to an absurd device, of choosing a description under which the action is intentional, and giving the action under that description as *the* intentional act. 'I am moving what blocks that egress', or 'I am removing a rock which is in the way'. The suggestion is that that is *all* I am doing as a means to my end.[35]

I interject. *First:* the description under which what is done is intended is not 'chosen' as a 'device', or 'given' as some kind of defence devised to satisfy an examining tribunal. It is settled by one's practical reasoning as an agent, by the intelligible benefit one seeks and the means one chooses under the description which promises to yield that benefit. *Second:* to speak of 'the suggestion ... that that is *all* I am doing as a means to my end' is equivocal, since 'doing', like every other term in this area, is equivocal as between the action *qua* intentional (intended) and the behaviour *qua* humanly interesting pattern of movements and results. The 'suggestion' is true in the sense that that is all one is *doing intentionally* (reading 'intentionally' as the strict cognate of 'intention' and 'intend', not as the contrary of the colloquial 'unintentionally', that is, accidentally). The suggestion is false if it is taken to deny that one has moral responsibility for what one knowingly causes as the fully foreseen and inevitable side effect of one's chosen means. But the 'doctrine of double effect', properly understood, makes no such denial.

Anscombe continues:

> This is as if one could say 'I am merely moving a knife through such-and-such a region of space' regardless of the fact that that space is manifestly occupied by a human neck, or by a rope supporting a climber.

I interject: the doctrine of double effect in no way suggests that one can choose 'regardless' of the certain side effects. One's acceptance of the side effects must satisfy all moral requirements (must 'be proportionate', as it was often vaguely put). That something is a side effect rather than an intended means entails the satisfaction of one, important, but only one, moral requirement: that one never *choose*—intend—to destroy, damage, or impede any instantiation of a basic human good.

> 'Nonsense', we want to say, 'doing that is doing this, and so closely that you can't pretend only the first gives you a description under which the act is intentional.' For an act does not merely have many descriptions, under some of which it is indeed not intentional: it has several under which it is intentional. So you cannot just choose one of these, and claim to have excluded others by that.

[35] Anscombe, 'Action, Intention and "Double Effect"' at 23.

I interject again. *First:* it is true that an act will have several descriptions under which it is intentional, even recalling the ambiguity of 'intentional' to which Anscombe does not attend—that is, several descriptions under which it is intended, corresponding to the several parts of one's plan.[36] Thus, one who is moving a rock to clear an egress from a cave is, in the strong sense identified above, intentionally (a) moving a rock, (b) cooperating in a team effort, (c) clearing an escape route, and so forth. One cannot choose just one of these and claim to have excluded the others. But *second:* the 'doctrine' of double effect is not about choosing descriptions, let alone just one description. It holds rather that what is *being done* is not settled simply by looking at behaviour, to see what movements are being made, with what awareness and what results. Rather, that is settled by what one chose, under the description which made it attractive to choice (not: the description which makes it acceptable to onlookers, or to 'conscience'). And this is not some 'doctrine' got up for a special, evasive purpose. Rather, it is the implication of a quite general conception that the one factor which cannot but settle what kind of act, morally speaking, a human act is is the intention with which what is done is done.[37]

Anscombe continues:

Nor can you simply bring it about that you intend *this* and not *that* by an inner act of 'directing your intention.

I agree.

Circumstances, and the immediate facts about the means you are choosing to your ends, dictate what descriptions of your intention you must admit...Suppose for example that you want to train people in habits of supporting the Church with

[36] As Anscombe says, *Intention*, 46 (para. 26):

So there is one action with four descriptions, each dependent on wider circumstances, and *each related to the next as description of means to end*...(Emphasis added.)

[37] See e.g. *ST* I–II q.18, aa. 2, 4, 5, 6, 7, 10 (acts are morally specified by their 'objects'); q.12 a.4 ad 2, and q.19 a.5c (the 'object' of will is the end and the means taken together in the agent's reason's proposal); q.72 a.3 ad 1 and 2 (means as objects of effort are ends and thus intended); also II–II q.64 a.7c; see Boyle, '*Praeter Intentionem* in Aquinas' at 653–4, 663–5; Foot, 'The Problem of Abortion and the Doctrine of Double Effect', in her *Virtues and Vices* at 21; and Moore, 'Intentions and *Mens Rea*' at 261, consider that to analyse intention in the way I do here would (in Foot's words) 'make nonsense of [the doctrine of double effect] from the beginning'. On the contrary, the doctrine in its origins *(ST* II–II q.64 a.7) and in many of its plausible and important applications depends on drawing distinctions as fine-grained as this. What Foot and Moore may have in mind is that such distinctions yield the result that a certain type of abortion condemned by common Catholic teaching is not an intended killing—and they may assume (a) that sustaining this condemnation is the main point of the doctrine, and (b) that the condemnation depends on the killing being intended. The first assumption is wholly mistaken, and the second quite questionable (see essay III 18 at 298–302 (= 1973b at 138–41), though my discussion on these and nearby pages fails to distinguish adequately between the means v side effect issue and the justified v unjustified side effect issue). [And see now essay 13, esp. sec. III.]

money. If you exact money from them as a condition of baptism you cannot say that you are not making them pay for it.

I interject: what is said about this example is right, but cannot support Anscombe's argument against the account of intention which I have proposed. For 'exacting money from people as a condition of baptism' and 'making people pay money for baptism' express one and the same proposition. So, since intention is propositional, there here cannot but be an intention to make people pay for baptism (as a means to training them in supporting the Church financially).

All this is relevant to our pot-holer only where the crushing of his head is an immediate effect of moving the rock... if you do know [that in moving the rock you would crush his head], then where the crushing is immediate you cannot pretend not to intend it if you are willing to move the rock... [But] consider the case where the result is not so immediate—the rock you are moving has to take a path after your immediate moving of it, and in the path it will take it will crush his head. Here there is indeed room for saying that you did not intend that result, even though you could foresee it.

I think this attempt to distinguish the intended from the unintended by reference to sheer physical 'immediacy' of cause and effect is unsound, a confusion of categories, an elision of human behaviour with human action. I know of no *argument* that Anscombe has brought against her own analysis, twenty-five years earlier in her book *Intention*, of the intentions of the man who pumps poisoned water into a house. In one variant of the situation, 'the man's intention might not be to poison [the inhabitants] but only to earn his pay' by doing his usual job:

In that case, although he knows concerning an intentional act of his—for it, namely replenishing the house water-supply, is intentional by our criteria—that it is *also* an act of replenishing the house water-supply with *poisoned* water, it would be incorrect, by our criteria, to say that his act of replenishing the house supply with poisoned water was intentional. And I do not doubt the correctness of the conclusion; it seems to shew that our criteria are rather good.[38]

Notice how fine-grained is the analysis which Anscombe accepted as correct: not merely that the poisoning of the inhabitants—which is not physically 'immediate'—is not intentional, but that the *replenishing of the house water-supply with poisoned water* is not intentional (because that the water be poisoned is not part of the pumper's proposal, viz. to do his usual job of replenishing the water supply). Nothing could be more 'immediate' than the known presence of the poison in the water supply: as *behaviour*,

[38] Anscombe, *Intention*, 42 (para. 25).

replenishing the supply with water *just is*, in this case, replenishing it with poisoned water. Yet the criteria for a sound analysis of intention(ality) and thus of *action* require that we distinguish knowingly pumping in poisoned water from intentionally pumping in poisoned water (or: pumping water with intent to contaminate the water supply). That the water supply be poisoned was, for this man on this occasion, a side effect.

Anscombe, in 1957, had a final reflection:

> The question arises: what can be the interest of the intention of the man we have described, who was only doing his usual job, etc.? It is certainly not an ethical or legal interest; if what he said was true, *that* will not absolve him from guilt of murder! We just *are* interested in what is true about a man in this kind of way.[39]

But how can we be so sure that law and ethics are indifferent to an admittedly interesting truth about human persons? Anscombe has not, I think, offered an ethical theory which would show that ethics must be indifferent to such true and interesting distinctions. And the fact that the water-pumper would, in all readily imaginable circumstances, be found guilty of murder in English law only goes to show that murder in law extends beyond its main limb, killing with intent to kill (or to do grievous bodily harm), and includes also, in effect, a secondary limb: doing without lawful justification or excuse an act which one knows will kill.

But surely this is all unrealistic! Surely there are cases where the known physical character of one's behaviour just does define what one is intending and doing! Glanville Williams reverts to this case:

> If an eccentric surgeon, while operating on an appendix, removed his patient's heart for the purpose of a later experiment, we should not listen with much sympathy to the surgeon's argument that he did not intend to cause the patient's death, but was quite happy that the patient should go on living if he could do so without a heart.[40]

In an earlier version of the 'eccentric surgeon' paradigm, Glanville Williams concluded that 'such a case would clearly be murder'.[41] Indeed it would. But not because D intends to kill P. As Anscombe has elsewhere remarked, such killings may be more callous and heinous than some that are intentional.[42]

[39] *Ibid.*, 45 (para. 25). [40] Williams, *Mental Element in Crime*, 13.

[41] Williams, *Criminal Law: The General Part*, 39.

[42] As Anscombe and I have joined in observing:

> intention and foresight are distinct, and...the intention (i.e. the purpose) of harm or danger to the victim is not a necessary part of the mental element in murder. Even without such intent, unlawful acts can be murderous. 'Unlawful' is closer in sense to 'wrongful' than to 'illegal', and the unlawfulness of an act may reside in its endangering someone's life without excuse.

Linacre Centre, *Euthanasia and Clinical Practice*, 26 [ed. Gormally, *Euthanasia, Clinical Practice and the Law*, 39].

The surgeon intends to and does deal with the body, that is, the very person of the patient, as his own to dispose of. Though his choice is not precisely, to kill or even, perhaps, to impair the functioning of the patient/victim—that is, though death and impairment of functioning are side effects—the surgeon's choice *is* precisely to treat the bodily substance and reality of that other human person as if that person were a mere subhuman object. The moral wrong, on a precise analysis of the surgeon's intent, is a form of *knowingly death-dealing enslavement*; one who inflicts death, even as a side effect, in order to effect such an instrumentalization of another has, in the fullest sense, 'no excuse' for thus knowingly causing death. We should not complain if both law and common moral thought treat this as murder. But nor should we distort our understanding of intention so as to bring this within the category of murder supposed, too casually, to be limited to *intent* to kill (or seriously harm).[§]

III. WHY INTENTION MATTERS

The distinction between what one intends (and does) and what one accepts as foreseen side effect(s) is significant because free choice matters.[43] For there is a free choice (in the sense that matters morally) only when one is rationally motivated towards incompatible alternative possible purposes (X and Y, or X and not-X) which one considers desirable by reason of the intelligible goods (instrumental and basic) which they offer—and when nothing but one's choosing itself *settles* which alternative is chosen. Now, in choosing, one adopts a proposal to bring about certain states of affairs. And the states of affairs which one commits oneself to bringing about—one's instrumental and basic purposes—are precisely those identified under the intelligible description which made them seem rationally appealing and choosable. And what one thus adopts is, so to speak, synthesized with one's will, that is, with oneself as an acting subject; one *becomes* what one saw reason to do and chose to set oneself to do—in short, what one intended. Nothing but contrary free choice(s) can reverse this manifold self-constitution.

And no form of voluntariness other than intention—for example, the voluntariness involved in knowingly causing the side effects one could have avoided causing by not choosing what one chose—can accomplish the self-constitution effected by the very fact of really forming an intention. Forming an intention, in choosing freely, is not a matter of having an

[43] For a more detailed account of the issues touched on in this section, see Boyle, 'Toward Understanding the Principle of Double Effect'; also *NDMR* 288–94.

internal feeling or impression; it is a matter of *setting oneself* to do something. Thus, for example, if one fails to do what one set oneself to do, *one has failed.* (Of course, one is not committed to the means in the same way that one is committed to the end. If an alternative and less repugnant means became available, one might change one's choice and adopt the new means without any vivid sense of changing one's project. But many ends are also means, and even ends valued for their own sake can be set aside without a strong *sense* of having changed one's personality. The significance of willing is not determined by one's 'sense', that is, one's feelings.)

The distinction between the intended and the side effect is *morally* significant. For, one who chooses (intends) to destroy, damage, or impede some instantiation of a basic human good chooses and acts contrary to the reason constituted by that basic human good. It can never be reasonable—and hence it can never be morally acceptable—to choose contrary to a reason, unless one has a reason to do so which is rationally preferable to the reason not to do so. But where the reason *not* to act is a *basic* human good, there cannot be a rationally preferable reason to choose so to act. (For the basic goods are aspects of the human persons who can participate in them, and their instantiations in particular persons cannot, as reasons for action, be rationally commensurated with one another. If they could be—that is, if there were a rational method of ranking such reasons for action—the reason ranked lower and thus identified as rationally less preferable would, by that very fact, cease to be a *reason;* the higher ranked reason would be rationally unopposed, and the situation would cease to be a situation of rationally motivated free choice between rationally appealing alternatives.) Thus one who *intends* to destroy, damage, or impede some instantiation of a basic human good necessarily acts contrary to reason, that is, immorally.

But every choice and action has some more or less immediate or remote negative impact on—in some way tends to damage or impede, or blocks the impeding of the damaging or impeding of—some instantiation(s) of basic human good(s). So, while one can refrain from the *choice* to harm an instance of a good, one *cannot* avoid *harming* some instances of human goods; that there will be some such harm is inevitable, and so cannot be excluded by reason's norms of action. For, moral norms exclude irrationality over which we have some control; they do not exclude accepting the inevitable limits we face as rational agents. Accepting—knowingly causing—harms caused to basic human goods as side effects will be contrary to reason (immoral) only if doing so is contrary to a reason of another sort, viz. a reason which bears not on choosing precisely as such but rather on knowing acceptance, awareness, and causation. There certainly are reasons of this other sort—particularly reasons of impartiality and fairness (the Golden Rule), and reasons arising from role-responsibilities and prior commitments. These moral norms, while not excluding absolutely actions in virtue of aspects of those actions which are unavoidable if one is to act at all, do recognize that we have some discretion about *which* bad side effects to accept. Save in a relatively few kinds of case,* where the acceptance of the side effect is clearly unfair or wanton, there can be no absolute moral norms here. For in many cases, the side effects of alternatives will be equally harmful to some human goods, or harmful to very important but incommensurable goods.

Very often, then, options should be rejected because bringing about the side effects would be unfair or unfaithful. The only situation in which one can be, so to speak, *a priori* certain that harmful side effects are *not* such as to give reason to reject an option is (a) the situation in which the feasible alternative option(s) involves *intending* to destroy, damage, or impede some instantiation of a basic human good, or (b) the situation (if any) in which any feasible alternative option, while not involving such an intention, is necessarily accompanied by harmful side effects which it could not be reasonable to accept.

NOTES

† *Economic Analysis of Law and its non-recognition of intention in tort*...(p. 173). See now essay 11 ('Intention in Tort Law'), sec. II; earlier and briefer is essay IV.16 ('Allocating Risks and Suffering: Some Hidden Traps') (1990b), sec. IV.

‡ *English judicial doctrine stabilized in 1985–1987 rejects assimilation of foresight of virtual certainty with intention*...(at n. 17). Unfortunately, the House of Lords in *R v Woollin* [1999] 1 AC 82 at 93, purporting to follow *Nedrick* and *Hancock*, cast the law back into confusion by reading 'may' and 'the decision is one for the jury' as meaning 'a result foreseen as virtually certain *is* an intended result' (in the context of a charge of murder where there is no evidence of desire to kill or cause serious injury). This very unsatisfactory ruling forced the Court of Appeal in *Re A (Children) (Conjoined Twins: Medical Treatment)* [2001] Fam 147 to purport to treat as 'murderous' the intentions of the doctors proposing to separate conjoined twins with shared organs (that could not sustain both) in order to save the stronger twin, but at the same time to hold that they were not 'intentionally', i.e. purposely, depriving the weaker twin of her right to life for the purposes of the European Convention on Human Rights, art. 2 and were justified in their operation either by its 'necessity' (the unsatisfactory basis adopted by Ward and Brooke LJJ) or because the weaker twin 'would die, not because she was intentionally killed, but because her own body cannot sustain her life' (Walker LJ at 259). (On the twins case see further the next endnote and the first endnote to essay 13.)

Even before *Woollin*, however, all was not well. The presentation of judicial doctrine in this essay glosses over many infelicities in the cases cited. For an example, see the passage from *Moloney* discussed in essay 14 n. 10.

§ *Eccentric surgeon and intent to impair functions*...(pp. 193–4). My discussion fails to consider sufficiently whether the surgeon's intent, which does not include death, does include mutilation—violation of bodily integrity as a means. In the postulated case the removal of the heart is a means to advance medical knowledge; in routine cases of exceptionlessly wrongful mutilation the impairment of function and violation of integrity is a means, e.g. to facilitation of begging, or an end, e.g. when done out of grudge. The issue arose in relation to the separation of conjoined twins (see previous endnote) and is considered at the end of the first endnote to essay 13. What is decisive for the intention- and act-analysis in such cases is whether the bodily position or activity of person V is itself a threat to the well-being of another or other persons and the cutting into or dismemberment of V is a means of mitigating that threat. That is why war-like acts in legitimate defence of self, others, or common good can be brought under Aquinas's analysis of defensive intent, in respect not only of the good of life (which is the aspect considered in *ST* II–II q.64 a.7, and in *CCC* 2263, 2267; essay 13 at n. 66) but also of the good of bodily integrity. Conversely, where there is no threat from V, as in the eccentric surgeon case, V's bodily impairment—at least as an irruption into V's bodily integrity—is intended, albeit only as a means. As a matter of means considered as means, surgical interventions on V, from cutting to amputation, are not violations of V's bodily integrity or impairments of V's functioning when done for the sake of preserving V's bodily integrity and functioning. (As always, the effects on V considered as side effects are subject to a second moral analysis, in terms of the norms, especially of fairness, which govern the incurring and accepting of side effects.)

* *Unfair or wanton acceptance of side effects*...(p. 196). In later writing, focused on moral absolutes, I do not allow this exception, and restrict the term 'moral absolute' to norms which exceptionlessly exclude a kind of act specified by its object, that is its intention.

11

INTENTION IN TORT LAW*

Need liability in tort be based on anything other than negligence? Is it necessary, indeed is it right, to treat *intent to harm* as a distinct basis for liability, independent of issues about reasonable foresight and the appropriate range and standards of care? Should the early twentieth-century bifurcation of torts into the intentional and the negligent be abandoned? Questions such as these cannot sensibly be answered without a clear understanding of intention as a real element in human conduct. They are questions which this essay does not undertake to settle. Its purpose is rather to indicate how academic writings as widely different as economic analysis of law and the *Restatement (Second) of Torts* have obscured the reality of intentions, and how that reality is clarified in the judicial development of doctrines as widely different as battery and conspiracy to injure in trade and labour relations.

I. INTENTION: ENDS AND MEANS, OR HOPES AND DESIRES?

Intention is a tough, sophisticated, and serviceable concept, well worthy of its central role in moral and legal assessment, because it picks out the central realities of deliberation and choice: the linking of means and ends in a plan or proposal for action *adopted* by *choice* in preference to alternative proposals (including to do nothing). What one intends is what one chooses, whether as end or as means. Included in one's intention is everything which is part of one's plan (proposal), whether as purpose or as way of effecting one's purpose(s)—everything which is part of one's reason for behaving as one does. In reading the words 'plan', 'proposal', 'deliberation', and 'choice', one should ignore all connotations of formality and 'deliberateness'; in the relevant sense there is a plan or proposal wherever there is *trying*, or doing (or refraining from doing) something *in order to* bring about something

* 1995a; secs I and II are a later version of essay IV.16 (1990b), secs III–VI.

or *as a way of* accomplishing something. And there is deliberation and what I am calling adoption of a proposal by choice wherever one course of conduct is preferred to an alternative which had attraction. On all these matters there is a substantial and well-grounded measure of agreement among philosophers.[1]

Accordingly, common speech has many ways of referring to intentions and the intentional. It deploys not only the cognates of 'intend', but also such phrases as 'trying to', 'with the objective of', 'in order to', 'with a view to', 'so as to', and, often enough, plain 'to', and many other terms.

Consider, for example, Holmes's phrase 'prepared an injury' in dictum in *United Zinc & Chemical Co. v Britt*:[2]

> The liability for spring guns and mantraps arises from the fact that the defendant has not rested on [the] assumption [that trespassers would obey the law and not trespass], but on the contrary has expected the trespasser and *prepared an injury* that is no more justified than if he had held the gun and fired it.[3]

Nearly thirty years earlier, Holmes had put the same point in the language of intent: a landowner who sets mantraps

> has contemplated expressly what he would have had a right to assume would not happen [that is, the trespass], and the harm done stands just as if he had been on the spot and had done it in person. His *intent* may be said to make him the last wrong-doer.[4]

The argument had been brilliantly spelled out in Sydney Smith's famous critiques of *Ilott v Wilkes*, the decision of the King's Bench in 1820 that a landowner who gave notice of his spring-guns and mantraps[5] was not liable to trespassers injured by them. Here is one of Smith's sallies:

> I do not say that the setter of the trap or gun allures the trespasser into it; but I say that the punishment *he intends* for the man who trespasses after notice is death. He covers his spring gun with furze and heath, and gives it the most natural appearance he can; and in that gun he places the slugs by which *he means* to kill the trespasser. This killing of an unchallenged, unresisting person, I really cannot help considering to be as much murder as if the proprietor had shot the trespasser with his gun.... Does it [matter] whose hand or whose foot pulls the string which

[1] Among recent writings, see e.g. Duff, *Intention, Agency and Criminal Liability*, chs 2 and 3; Kenny, *The Metaphysics of Mind*; Moya, *The Philosophy of Action*; White, *Grounds of Liability*, ch. 6; White, *Misleading Cases*.

[2] 258 US 268 (1922).

[3] *Britt* 258 US at 275, per Holmes J for the Court (emphasis added).

[4] Holmes, 'Privilege, Malice, and Intent' at 11 (emphasis added). Holmes adds (*ibid.* at 12) that the intent in question is 'actual intention', not the 'external standard' form of 'intent' which, in his view (*ibid.* at 1), the law finds where there is manifest and great probability of harm.

[5] The typical mantrap was in fact a spring-gun: a heavily loaded shotgun, its trigger attached to springs and wires arranged in hidden lines along which the blast of shot would travel when anybody tripped them. Typically, such guns were set in woods and gardens to deter, disable, and punish poachers, who under the law of the day were no more than trespassers.

moves the trigger?—the real murderer is he who *prepares* the instrument of death, and places it in a position that such hand or foot may touch it, *for the purposes of destruction*.[6]

Or as Smith puts it in the first of his two *Edinburgh Review* articles:

[W]hat is the difference between the act of firing yourself, and placing an engine which does the same thing?...There is the same *intention* of slaying in both cases—there is precisely the same human agency in both cases; only the steps are rather more numerous in the latter case.[7]

Thus both Holmes and Smith make manifest the synonymity of 'intention' with many alternative terms and phrases. Put strictly in the language of intent, their thesis is that, just as personally shooting a trespasser engaged in no act or threat of violence is simply killing or wounding with intent to kill or wound, so too setting a spring-gun involves intending (conditionally but really) to do the same 'without personally firing the shot'.[8] And what one cannot lawfully, with intent, accomplish 'directly' (in person) one cannot, with the same intent, accomplish 'indirectly' (mechanically).

Now this argument was in fact put squarely by the plaintiff's counsel in *Ilott v Wilkes*, and unanimously rejected by four well-regarded judges of the Court of King's Bench.[9] The judges' arguments to distinguish shooting by machine from shooting in person are weak. Of greater interest is the preliminary argumentation employed in two of the four judgments, argumentation to which Justice Holmes's dictum in *Britt* is a response. Chief Justice Abbott puts it thus:

I believe that many persons who cause engines of this description to be placed on their grounds do not do so with the intention of injuring any one, but really believe that the notices they give of such engines being there, will prevent any injury from occurring, and that no person who sees the notice will be weak and foolish enough to expose himself to the perilous consequence likely to ensue from his trespass.[10]

And Bayley J like this:

Such instruments may be undoubtedly placed without any intention of doing injury, and for the mere purpose of protecting property by means of terror; and

[6] Smith, 'Man Traps and Spring Guns', in his *Works* at 345–6 (Smith italicized only the words 'to kill'). The passage is put on the mouth of an imaginary fifth judge in *Ilott v Wilkes* and hence is deliberately more ponderous than Smith's own usual style.

[7] Smith, 'Spring Guns' in his *Works* at 324.

[8] *Robert Addie & Sons v Dumbreck* [1929] AC 358, 376, per Lord Dunedin. On conditional intentions, see *NDMR* 81–6, 99–100, 111–12, 124; and essay 12 below.

[9] *Ilott v Wilkes*, 3 B & Ald 304, 106 ER 674 (KB, 1820); see the opening sentences of the argument of counsel for the plaintiff respondent, 3 B & Ald at 307, 106 ER at 676.

[10] *Ibid.* at 307, 106 ER at 676.

it is extremely probable that the defendant in this case will feel as much regret as any man for the injury which the plaintiff has sustained.[11]

The fallacies about intention are in each case clear enough. Chief Justice Abbott, unless he was supposing a high degree of ignorance or self-deception about the frequent[12] 'accidents' involving spring-guns, clearly confuses intending with *hoping*. Landowners of the kind he envisages may well both desire and hope that no one will trespass and thus that no one will be shot, yet they clearly do intend that those (if any) who do trespass will be shot. As Sydney Smith puts the point:

> But if this be the real belief of the engineer—if he think the mere notice will keep people away—then he must think it a mere inutility that the guns should be placed at all: if he think that many will be deterred, and a few come, then he must *mean* to shoot those few. He who believes his gun will never be called upon to do its duty, need set no gun, and trust to rumour of their being set, or being loaded, for his protection.... He who sets a *loaded* gun *means* it should go off if it is touched.[13]

'Means to' is another synonym for 'intends to'.

As for Bayley J's arguments, the first fails to recall that one intends not only one's ultimate ends (say, protecting one's property) but also all the means one has chosen to further those ends (say, injuring or killing poachers as a punishment, and as a deterrent to and disablement from future poaching). One's chosen means are indeed one's *proximate ends*,[14] some more and some less proximate. ('Why are you carrying that gun and wire?' 'In order to lay a man trap.' 'Why do that?' 'In order to punish, deter, and disable poachers.' 'Why do that?' 'To have game for hunting.' 'Why hunt?' 'For the opportunity to show my skill and meet my friends and associates.') And Bayley J's second argument simply confuses one's forming and having an intention with one's having emotions, such as enthusiasm or vindictiveness as opposed to *ex ante* reluctance and *ex post* regret. Many crimes (and therefore batteries and other torts) of the most deliberate intent are committed with great regret, if only because of the risk of detection.

Sydney Smith's articles orchestrated the movement for reform which culminated in an Act of 1827 outlawing in England all laying of outdoor

[11] *Ibid.* at 307, 106 ER at 677.

[12] See Hansard, 17 Parl. Deb. (series 2) col. 19 (23 March 1827); see also col. 26, where the Home Secretary, Robert Peel, speaks of the 'daily accidents and misfortunes arising from the use of [spring guns as man traps]', In *Ilott*, the victim was gathering nuts; in *Bird v Holbrook*, 4 Bing 628, 130 ER 911 (CP, 1828), he was retrieving a neighbour's wandering peahen.

[13] Smith, 'Spring Guns' in *Works*, 325 (Smith italicized only 'loaded').

[14] For the explanation of this important feature of intention by Aristotle (who lacked the word, but scarcely an understanding of the reality) and Aquinas, see essay 9, pp. 161–3.

spring-guns. The last and most brutally frank of the parliamentary speeches in defence of spring-guns was given by Lord Ellenborough, the rising young politician son of the late Lord Chief Justice Ellenborough. But even he felt the need to veil the proximate intention of mantrappers by confusing it with their motive (further end, further intention):

> The *object* of setting Spring-guns [is] not personal injury to any one, but to deter from the commission of theft; and that object [is] as completely obtained by hitting an innocent man as a guilty one. [T]he bill [is] contrary to that principle of the English law, which [gives] a man protection for his property, in proportion to the difficulty with which it would be protected by the ordinary means.[15]

The veil is here truly diaphanous, for the argument tacitly concedes that the deterrent 'object' (intent) will be attained only by the infliction of injury or death on at least a few trespassers, culpable or innocent; such injury or death is thus intended as a means to achieving the deterrent object. And in the fundamental structure of the common law, as of sound jurisprudence, one private person's killing or injuring another with such an intent is simply a commutative injustice, whatever the person's further purposes, objects, motives.[16] It is the sort of conduct, the sort of transaction between persons, which cannot be justified by alleged assumption of risk or by appeal to the maxim *volenti non fit injuria*,[17] fear of future greater harm, or any considerations of distributive or allocative justice as between landowners, game consumers, and poachers, whether game-seeking or (like the unlucky Ilott) nut-gathering.

When young Lord Ellenborough frankly identified a common purpose of laying spring-guns as being precisely to *do harm*, as a deterrent *means* of stopping poaching, he was not inaccurate. His point is illustrated by the facts in *Bird v Holbrook*.[18] The defendant tulip gardener testified that his reason for not posting notices was: he wanted to catch the tulip thieves, *by injuring them*. Instead, of course, he mutilated only young Bird, who was

[15] Hansard, 17 Parl. Deb. (series 2) col. 296 (9 April 1827) (substituting direct for indirect speech).

[16] See below, pp. 211–15.

[17] The maxim (meaning: someone who is willing to run a risk is not wronged if the risk materializes) was a primary ground for the judgment of Bayley and Holroyd JJ in *Ilott v Wilkes*; their thesis was that provided (or: since) there is no *intent* to injure, warning negates liability (since the person warned is *volens*—willing to run the risk of being shot).

[18] (1828) 4 Bing 628, 130 ER 911. The facts arose before the Act of 1827, and the case was accordingly decided on the basis of the unreformed common law, which the Court of Common Pleas, per Best CJ (who had been the junior justice of the King's Bench in *Ilott v Wilkes*), determined had always been in line with the Act of 1827 so far as concerned spring-guns laid *without warning notice(s)*. This ruling is foreshadowed by the explanation which Best J made from the bench on 3 June 1821, in response to the excoriating attack upon him in Sydney Smith's first article against *Ilott v Wilkes*. See Smith, 'Man Traps' at 341–2.

trying, in broad daylight, to help a neighbour by recapturing a peahen which had strayed into Holbrook's booby-trapped garden.

II. INTENTION MISUNDERSTOOD AND REJECTED

Richard Posner made *Bird v Holbrook* the centrepiece of his earliest published exposition of the implications of economic analysis for the common law.[19] Indeed, this is the one case which Posner cites in his textbook treatment of the category of intentional torts.[20] Disclaiming (at that point) any normative purpose, and offering only to 'explain' the law's 'pattern',[21] Posner says that the issue in the case 'was the proper accommodation of two legitimate activities, growing tulips and raising peacocks'.[22] Spring-guns may be the most cost-effective means of protecting tulips in an era of negligible police protection; but they discourage the owners of domestic animals from pursuing them onto other people's property 'and so increase the costs (enclosure costs or straying costs) of keeping animals'.[23] The challenge for the common law judges accordingly was, in Posner's view, to design 'a rule of liability that maximized the (joint) value of both activities, net of any protective or other costs (including personal injuries)'.[24]

So with a stroke the whole question of intention to injure is swept from view; not only are the 'personal injuries' homogenized into the other costs of keeping peacocks, but the fact that *these* injuries were done by one who *intended* to injure a human being (albeit not anticipated to be a mere peacock-pursuer) is treated as wholly irrelevant. The argument which had prevailed in Parliament in 1827 and subsequently in common law courts all over the United States[25] is treated as of no consequence. And explicitly so: 'intentionality is neither here nor there', according to Posner.[26] Why not? The answer is a paradigm of the *non sequitur*.

[I]t is surely not correct to say that society never permits the sacrifice of human lives on behalf of substantial economic values. Automobile driving is an example of the many deadly activities that cannot be justified as saving more lives than they take. Nor can the motoring example be distinguished from the spring-gun

[19] Posner, 'Killing or Wounding to Protect a Property Interest' at 209 et seq.

[20] Posner, *Economic Analysis of Law*, 206–11.

[21] 'Killing or Wounding' at 211.

[22] *Economic Analysis of Law*, 207 (7th edn, 2007, p. 205).

[23] *Ibid.*

[24] 'Killing or Wounding' at 210.

[25] See e.g. *State v Childers* 14 NE 2d 767, 770 (Ohio 1938):

By the overwhelming weight of authority, a person is not justified in taking human life or inflicting bodily harm upon the person of another by means of traps... unless, as a matter of law, he would have been justified had he been personally present and had taken the life or inflicted the bodily harm.

[26] 'Killing or Wounding' at 206.

case on the ground that the one who sets a spring-gun intends to kill or wound. In both cases, a risk of death is created that could be avoided by substituting other methods of achieving one's ends (walking instead of driving); in both cases the actor normally hopes the risk will not materialize.[27]

In short, intending death and carelessly risking causing death are equivalent because both involve creating the risk of death; A is equivalent to B if A includes something important about B. And there are other equivocations in the passage.

First, an equivocation on 'sacrifice'. Posner's use of the phrase 'sacrifice of human lives' treats as equivalent the decision to build a skyscraper, expecting that about three construction workers will fall off and be killed, and the decision to kill three construction workers to encourage the others to meet their performance targets. Secondly, an equivocation on 'hopes'. Posner's claim that, both in carelessly and in intentionally killing, 'the actor normally hopes the risk will not materialize' merely synthesizes and repeats the confusions of Chief Justice Abbott and Bayley J in *Ilott v Wilkes*. Careless drivers hope there will be no collision *and*, that if there is, no one will be killed. Mantrappers hope that no one will invade their property but that anyone who does *will* be shot. And in confusing emotion with will, Posner fails to observe the emotional reluctance with which many or even most murders are committed.

Posner's writings on intention are replete with fallacies and oversights. For example: to prove that the distinction between intentional and unintentional torts is 'confusing and unnecessary', his textbook begins:

Most accidental injuries are intentional in the sense that the injurer knew that he could have reduced the probability of the accident by taking additional precautions. The element of intention is unmistakable when the tortfeasor is an enterprise that can predict from past experience that it will inflict a certain number of accidental injuries every year.[28]

It is tempting to dwell on the corrupting potential of this conception of intention. For example, one can foresee that lecturing and writing on difficult topics, unless extended beyond one's allotted measure, is certain to confuse some of one's audience. One therefore, on Posner's account, has the intention of confusing. Well then, why not throw in a few deliberate falsehoods, with (real) intent to confuse and deceive, when convenient for attaining one's legitimate educative or persuasive goals?

[27] *Ibid.*
[28] *Economic Analysis of Law*, 119 (similarly, 7th edn, 2007, p. 204, where, however, the conclusion that the distinction between intentional and unintentional torts is unnecessary is no longer drawn explicitly).

But the more direct objection is that Posner's conception of intention is a fiction, a faulty understanding of human action. The central reality of action in those intentional torts which Posner mentions at the outset of his subsequent treatment of them is, as he says, that 'the defendant [was] *trying* to harm the plaintiff'.[29]

In this later treatment by Posner (with Landes), however, that glimpse of reality is soon obscured and lost to sight, as the facts about intention and action get thoroughly confused with normative considerations and conclusions. Landes and Posner's first move is the right one: a rejection (albeit tacit) of Posner's earlier claim that those who conduct an enterprise knowing that injuries are highly probable must intend the injuries. But they make this move on the basis of an economic argument whose conclusion—that no economic purpose is served by classifying the injuries from risky enterprises as intentional—is reached only with the aid of two assumptions: (1) that the risk run by the enterprise is justifiable, and (2) that the injuries are neither desired by nor beneficial to those conducting it.[30] The economic argument is thus question-begging and redundant. And the conception of intention suggested by the second assumption is unsound.

For 'desire' is never the mark of intention (unless 'desired' is given a narrow sense precisely equivalent to 'intended'). The mantrapping landowner may strongly desire that no one will trespass and be shot, yet intend that anyone who *does* trespass *will* be shot. Conversely, side effects (effects which one is not trying/intending to bring about) may be welcome, and in that straightforward sense desired—and yet are not intended. One may choose to join the army (as conscript or as volunteer) only because it is one's legal or patriotic duty, yet welcome and thus desire, without intending, the bonus side effects of gaining exposure to a diversity of personalities. The commanders of a bombing force may regard civilian casualties and consequent demoralization and highway-obstructing civilian refugee columns as a welcome bonus, and yet not intend them. This is possible, provided that (a) they do not regard civilian casualties and their welcome effects as even a secondary aim, and (b) they select only military targets, calibrate the bombs and plan the bombing runs *exclusively* for the purpose of destroying those targets, and desist from bombing areas containing civilians as soon as the military targets are removed.

Having declared that the operators of a *reasonably* risky railroad do not intend the deaths which they foresee as certain to be incurred by its operations over time, Landes and Posner's next move is simply to relapse

[29] Landes and Posner, *The Economic Structure of Tort Law*, 149 (referring to assault, battery, and false imprisonment).

[30] *Ibid.*, 150, 151.

into what they call 'the probability theory of intent', oddly described as a sub-category of 'deliberately inflicting an injury whether or not the injurer believes he is acting wrongfully'.[31] 'When someone does something that is overwhelmingly likely to produce a specific result, we are properly skeptical when he denies that the result was intended.'[32] But in many cases such scepticism would be wholly misplaced. Think again of lecturers who know that they will leave some of their audience confused; or stutterers who know that they will annoy some of their listeners; or people who wear shoes knowing that they will wear out, or who fly the Pacific knowing that they will get jetlag. All these undesired effects are not merely foreseeable but certain.[33]

One should return to the thought which Landes and Posner put first, and affirmed, but then (as we have just seen) rendered nonsensical. Those who intend a result, whether for its own sake or as a means to something else, are trying (however reluctantly) to bring it about. Persons so intending a result are not trying to create a risk of a result but trying to create that result. Not content to leave things to chance (to hazard, to risk), such persons are instead intervening to achieve a result they intend. As regards that result, the risk which they are concerned about is not the risk of it happening but the risk of it *not* happening. And, since we lack the capacity of making something be the case simply by willing it, the risk that the results one intends will not happen is just an inevitable side effect or incidental concomitant of one's intention, choice, and action.

III. INTENTION: ENDS AND MEANS, OR FORESEEN CONSEQUENCES?

English law takes the position that intent to harm does not render tortious conduct which but for such intent would be lawful. But the House of Lords

[31] *Ibid.*, 151.

[32] *Ibid.*, 153. Landes and Posner add that, to accommodate cases where a result is wanted but improbable (e.g. B's trying to destroy a speeding car by dropping a boulder from a bridge),

> intent can also be inferred from any combination of probability, severity, and cost of avoidance that shows that the injury was not merely a by-product of lawful activity. B will not be heard to deny that he wanted to damage the car; there is no other plausible interpretation of his motives.... The critical factor is that the costs of avoidance to the injurer are low relative to the social benefits of the activity. (*Ibid.*)

Here questions of overall justification have completely swamped the purported discussion of intention. A realistic interpretation of motives does not depend either on knowing the costs of 'avoiding' behaviour or on the behaviour's (un)lawfulness. 'By-product', however, is a concept dependent on the distinction between intention (what is intended, because an end or means within a proposal adopted by choice) and side effect. The confusion of normative with anthropological considerations could scarcely be more complete.

[33] One is almost tempted to call the 'probability theory' of intention, classifying such painful side effects as intended, a pseudo-masochistic theory of intention.

decisions which adopted this position—*Mayor of Bradford v Pickles*[34] and *Allen v Flood*[35]—were marred by confusion between physical behaviour and human action, between intention and feeling, and between what is intended and what is side effect. Their broad denial of the relevance of motive was promptly, generally, and persuasively rejected in American law. Moreover, their impact has been greatly reduced by the development of a doctrine of tortious conspiracy to harm, a development which reflects a generally sounder understanding of the real character of intentions, their role in identifying what act is being done, and their distinction from motivating feelings and from knowingly causing side effects.†

Pickles's intention, in drawing off water which would otherwise have percolated into the land of the local public water-supply company, was to force the company to buy him out. The pleader's claim[36] that this involved an intent to harm the company could well have been, and to some extent was, rejected as a mere misdescription. For the proposal which Pickles adopted—the idea he had in mind—was not to cause harm to the company, whether as end or means, but make his land (and/or the flow of water from it) valuable.[37] Of course, that purpose *might* have been motivated by the further purpose of damaging the company's finances—an ulterior motive which might have been an end in itself (a case of spite) or a means to some yet more ulterior purpose. But the pleadings made no suggestion that it was.[38] So the case might have rested there. The wide dicta[39] in the House of Lords, to the effect that acts otherwise lawful cannot be made tortious by malice or other motive or intention, were gratuitous. And the accompanying dicta appealing to a symmetry between right-making and wrong-making factors—the claim that, as good motives cannot legitimate unlawful means, so bad motives cannot delegitimate lawful means[40]—sophistically ignore one of morality's most elementary principles and moral philosophy's most

[34] [1895] AC 587. [35] [1898] AC 1.

[36] The statement of claim included an allegation paraphrased in *Pickles* [1895] AC at 589 thus:

> [He] had not a *bona fide* intention to work his minerals, and…his intention was to injure the appellants and so to endeavour to induce them either to purchase his land or to give him some other compensation.

[37] See above n. 36, below n. 38, and *Pickles* [1895] AC at 595, per Lord Halsbury LC and 600, per Lord Macnaghten.

[38] In the secondary literature, Pickles is often said to have been motivated by spite but the trial judge, North J, made no such finding and held that he had acted out of economic self-interest. North J's finding that Pickles was in 'bad faith' meant no more than that Pickles's claims to be digging shafts for the purpose of commercial mining were insincere. See *Corporation of Bradford v Pickles* [1894] 3 Ch 53, 68:

> his operations are intended for the drainage of his stone, not in order that he may be enabled to work it, but in order that the Plaintiffs may be driven to pay him not to work it.

[39] See *Pickles* [1895] AC at 594, per Lord Halsbury LC, 598, per Lord Watson, 598, per Lord Ashbourne, and 601, per Lord Macnaghten.

[40] See *ibid.* at 594, per Lord Halsbury LC and 599, per Lord Ashbourne.

strategic themes. There is no such symmetry. One's conduct will be right only if *both* one's means *and* one's end(s) are right; therefore, *one* wrong-making factor will make one's choice and action wrong, and *all* the aspects of one's act must be rightful for the act to be right. The acting person's intentions must be acceptable all the way down (or up).

In *Allen v Flood*,[41] the defendant, an official of an ironworkers' union, was sued for threatening to call his union members out, thereby 'maliciously' inducing employers to dismiss (lawfully) the plaintiffs, members of a shipwrights' union. There was evidence that the threat was issued to punish the shipwrights for having, in the past and for other employers, done ironworkers' work. Having been directed that 'maliciously' meant 'with the intention and for the purpose of doing an injury to the plaintiffs in their business', the jury found that the defendant had maliciously induced the employers to terminate the plaintiffs' contracts. The House of Lords, by a narrow majority, overturned this verdict, and their conclusion is not incompatible with an appropriately fine-grained understanding of the defendant's intentions. But the understanding of intention actually displayed in the opinions is deeply confused. In the leading judgment, for example, Lord Watson (author of the loosest dictum in *Mayor of Bradford v Pickles*) openly assimilates 'motive' with 'internal feelings' as opposed to 'outward acts'.[42] This approach betrays the common unsound assumption that human acts can be identified, for purposes of moral or legal assessment, independently of the acting person's intention(s). To be sure, outward *behaviour* can be so identified. But countless *acts* cannot be truly identified for what they are (*prior* to assessment as right or wrong, lawful or unlawful) unless and until the outward behaviour which they involve is understood as *the carrying out of such-and-such an intention.* Should this pat on the back be deemed a greeting, a warning, an encouragement, a condescension, a code sign to waiting police officers, or something else?

Forming and carrying out these formative and act-defining intentions is a matter of having not 'internal feelings' but a practical idea, a plan, a proposal—however instantaneous and informal—which one adopts by choice. Such a plan includes end(s) and means, perhaps very closely related (as in giving a greeting). Carrying out any plan, engaging in any conduct, has side effects, caused and perhaps knowingly caused and fully foreseen by the acting person, yet not intended.

41 [1898] AC 1.

42 [I]n any legal question, malice depends, not upon evil motive which influenced the mind of the actor, but upon the illegal character of the act which he contemplated and committed.... [W]hen the act done is, apart from the feelings which prompted it, legal, the civil law ought to take no cognizance of its motive. (*Allen* [1898] AC 1 at 94, per Lord Watson.)

I am altogether unable to appreciate the loose logic which confounds internal feelings with outward acts, and treats the motive of the actor as one of the means employed by him. (*Ibid.* at 98, per Lord Watson.)

Inept handling of the concept of intention (under whatever name) marks most of the judgments in *Allen v Flood*, most notably in their failure to identify the equivocation in the conception of 'malice'[43] with which the legal sources and professional discourse then current, and the trial judge's direction to the jury, confronted them. On that conception, malice includes having a purpose to 'benefit oneself at the expense of one's neighbour'. But 'at the expense of' extends equivocally to two very different cases: (1) where loss to the neighbour is the ultimate *or intermediate* object/purpose/intent (and benefit to oneself is not more than a welcome side effect), and (2) where benefit to self is the object (and loss to the neighbour is only a foreseen, perhaps even a welcome, side effect).[44] To be sure, the House of Lords rejected the conception of malice which involves this confusion; the judges discerned its incompatibility with the lawfulness of any winner-takes-all commercial competition.[45] Yet they did not identify the confusion's source: failure to distinguish the intention to secure all the available trade (and in this sense 'win') from the certain side effect of such trading success—causing loss to the loser.[46]

That distinction, implicit in the competition cases from *Mogul Steamship Co. v McGregor, Gow & Co.*[47] onwards, finally becomes an explicit and

[43] See *ibid.* at 118–21, per Lord Herschell. Note the sentiments of Holmes in his letter to Pollock of 21 October 1895 in relation to *Allen v Flood* in the Court of Appeal: 'how little importance I attach to the discussions of the run of judges, whether English or American, on matters involving general theory—beyond the *fact* that in a given jurisdiction they do so and so'; and of Pollock in his letter to Holmes of 30 March 1898 in relation to the same case in the House of Lords: 'that decision I think is the only safe one for a world of people who mostly get muddled over subtle distinctions and think them unjust whenever they can't understand': Howe, *Holmes-Pollock Letters* i, 65, 84–5.

[44] I do not assume that wherever loss or harm to the neighbour is intended there is or should be liability. Ames, 'How Far an Act May be a Tort Because of the Wrongful Motive of the Actor', which is still perhaps the most helpful and illuminating treatment of the issues around *Allen v Flood*, identifies a wide group of cases in which even a defendant with the most reprehensible motives (further intentions) escapes liability because, e.g. what he was requiring the plaintiff to do or abstain from doing was already the plaintiff's legal duty to do or not do: *ibid.* at 412–13, or because the defendant enjoyed legal privilege: *ibid.* at 413–14, or because the defendant's malevolence extended only to non-feasance in a situation where he had no duty to act: *ibid.* at 416 n. 1.

[45] See *Allen* [1898] AC at 164, per Lord Shand and 179, per Lord James.

[46] Indeed, Lord Herschell, in rejecting the concept of malice, stated that lawful competitive practices include cases where

> the very object of the defendants was to induce shippers to contract with them, and not to contract with the plaintiffs, and thus to benefit themselves at the expense of the plaintiffs, and *to injure them* by preventing them from getting a share of the carrying trade. Its express object was *to molest and interfere* with the plaintiffs in the exercise of their trade. (*Ibid.* at 140 (emphasis added).)

Intention and side effect are here completely confused with each other.

[47] [1892] AC 25. The uncertainty with which the Lords handle intention and side effect in this case can be exemplified by one quotation:

> there is nothing indicating an intention to injure the plaintiffs, except in so far as such injury would be the result of the defendants obtaining for themselves the benefits of the carrying trade, by giving better terms to customers than their rivals, the plaintiffs, were willing to offer. (*Ibid.* at 60, per Lord Hannen.)

Similarly, see *ibid.* at 36, per Lord Halsbury LC.

central theme when Viscount Simon LC's leading judgment in *Crofter Hand Woven Harris Tweed Co. v Veitch*[48] identifies the true question at issue:

> The question to be answered... is not 'did the combiners appreciate, or should they be taken as appreciating, that others would suffer from their action,' but... 'what is the real purpose of the combination?' The test is not what is the natural result to the plaintiffs of such combined action, or what is the resulting damage which the defendants realize or should realize will follow, but what is in truth the object in the minds of the combiners when they acted as they did. It is not the consequence that matters, but purpose.[49]

Lord Simon thus avoids the term 'intention', preferring the language of 'object' or 'purpose'; but later cases and discussions often adopt his analysis while speaking synonymously of intent(ion).[50]

For English and Scots law, the *Allen v Flood* rule that motive or intention is irrelevant is definitively confined by *Crofter Harris Tweed* to situations where there is no combination (conspiracy).[51‡] Wherever there is combination, intention to harm is of decisive significance, albeit in somewhat various ways depending on whether the means employed to effect the combiners' purpose are themselves actionable or not.[52] For, even when the conspirators' chosen means are per se actionable without proof of intent to harm, the presence of such intent establishes that the conduct of the conspirators will not be capable of justification.[53] And where intent to harm is a prerequisite for establishing liability (because the means are not otherwise actionable), such intent is also *sufficient* to establish liability,

[48] [1942] AC 435. [49] *Ibid.* at 444–5.

[50] See e.g. *Lonrho plc v Fayed* [1992] 1 AC 448, 463–8. In *Lonrho Ltd v Shell Petroleum Co.* [1982] AC 173, 189, Lord Diplock treats 'intent' and 'purpose' as synonymous in this context, passing in silence over his own view that in law, or at least in criminal law, foreseen results are intended (see e.g. *Hyam v Director of Public Prosecutions* [1975] AC 55, 86). Clerk and Lindsell, *Torts*, 886 n. 13, 888 n. 34, having commended the word 'object', moves easily into speaking of paramount intention and predominant intent to injure.

[51] This tort of conspiracy to injure has recently been much described as 'anomalous' (see e.g. *Lonrho plc v Fayed* [1992] 1 AC at 463, 467), but on a larger view it is the wide doctrine of the irrelevance of intention (motive), i.e. of *Bradford Corporation v Pickles* and *Allen v Flood*, which is anomalous in the face not only of American and civil law but even of aspects of English common law including not only the tort of conspiracy to injure but also of malicious prosecution and the type of nuisance instantiated in *Christie v Davey* [1893] 1 Ch 316 (1892) and *Hollywood Silver Fox Farm Ltd v Emmett* [1936] 2 KB 468.

[52] If the means are unlawful, any intent to harm the plaintiff will suffice; if they are in themselves lawful, the intent to harm must be the combiners' predominant purpose: *Lonrho plc v Fayed* [1992] 1 AC at 463, 468.

[53]
> Insofar as the cases talk of a need for 'just excuse' or 'justification' those words seem to be no more than a description of the need for evidence (as to his trade or other legitimate interests) which a defendant can put in to meet the plaintiff's case when the latter has adduced evidence of *apparent intention* to injure on the defendant's part.

Clerk and Lindsell, *Torts*, 890–1 (citations omitted) (emphasis added).

except where that intent is merely a secondary accompaniment[54] to another predominant and legitimate purpose and is not accompanied by any unlawful act.

American tort law in this area has developed along different lines. On the one hand, the doctrine that motive cannot render tortious a lawful act has met general disfavour.[55] Even Holmes rejected it, distinguishing the relevance of motive in this context from his strong support for the 'external standard' in general negligence law.[56] And Ames's nuanced yet powerful attack upon the irrelevance-of-motive doctrine was adopted almost verbatim in what became the leading case, *Tuttle v Buck*.[57] The opinion in *Tuttle v Buck* sets out one of Lord Watson's wide dicta in *Allen v Flood*, goes on to demonstrate its overbreadth and implausibility, and concludes with an unacknowledged transcription of Ames's clinching scenario:

> To divert to one's self the customers of a business rival by the offer of goods at lower prices is in general a legitimate mode of serving one's own interest, and justifiable as fair competition. But when a man starts an opposition place of business, not for the sake of profit to himself, but regardless of loss to himself, and for the sole purpose of driving his competitor out of business, and with the intention of himself retiring upon the accomplishment of his malevolent purpose, he is guilty of a wanton wrong and an actionable tort.[58]

On the other hand, Holmes, Ames, and the American courts failed to adopt the English position that intent to harm negatives justifiability. Instead, the relevant American tort doctrine (as Holmes desired)[59] generally embraced a position which at least in its formulation is congenial to utilitarian moral thought and far less congenial to traditional common morality: the

[54] Fleming, *The Law of Torts*, 669–70 states that the combiners may lawfully intend harm as a means to advancing a purpose which is really or predominantly constructive. But his authority is a dissenting judgment at first instance on a motion to strike out in a 1900 case.

[55] This falls short of full-blooded repudiation. See e.g. *Restatement (Second) of Torts* (1977), § 870 comment i.

[56] 'It has been considered that, *prima facie*, the intentional infliction of temporal damage is a cause of action, which...requires a justification if the defendant is to escape....It is no sufficient answer to this line of thought that motives are not actionable and that the standards of the law are external. That is true in determining what a man is bound to foresee, but not necessarily in determining the extent to which he can justify harm which he has foreseen.' (*Aikens v Wisconsin* 195 US 194, 204 (1904) (citations omitted), per Holmes J for the Court.) This is foreshadowed in Holmes, 'Privilege, Malice, and Intent' at 2–3.

[57] 119 NW 946 (Minn. 1909).

[58] *Ibid.* at 948. Cf. Ames, 'Wrongful Motive' at 420:

> If, however, a man should start an opposition shop, not for the sake of profit for himself, but, regardless of loss to himself, for the sole purpose of driving the plaintiff out of business and with the intention of retiring himself immediately upon the accomplishment of his malevolent purpose, would not this wanton causing of damage be altogether indefensible and a tort?

[59] See e.g. Holmes, 'Privilege, Malice, and Intent' at 3: 'the intentional infliction of temporal damage...is actionable *if done without just cause*' (emphasis added). See generally Kelley, 'A Critical Analysis of Holmes's Theory of Torts' at 705–7.

intentional infliction of harm is actionable, whether or not there is conspiracy, if and *only if* imposing liability would be in line with the 'balance' of the conflicting interests of the litigants with the social and economic interests of society in general.[60]

IV. CONSTRUCTIVE INTENTION, REAL INTENTION, AND JUSTICE TO PERSONS

The common law of torts and crimes has for at least two centuries been working itself free from the artificialities of objective form which were exemplified by such doctrines as felony-murder and trespassory liability for all direct injury. The process of introducing the morally relevant 'subjective' distinctions into legal doctrine has been complicated by utilitarianism. Utilitarianism had no patience with the old fictions, but it also had an agenda of its own, in which—since only 'outcomes' matter—the distinction between intention and foresight or even foreseeability has no fundamental or generally important role. So the reshaping of legal doctrine has been conducted under the shadow of the thought which Henry Sidgwick, master of the late nineteenth century's mature utilitarianism, expressed with characteristic directness: 'For purposes of exact moral or juristic discussion, it is best to include under the term "intention" all the consequences of an act that are foreseen as certain or probable.'[61]

This assimilation of what even Holmes called 'actual intention' with a merely deemed, fictitious intention has been repudiated with increasing force and clarity in English,[62] if not in American[63] criminal law. But it is installed (not without some significant modification) at the heart of American tort doctrine by the definition of intent in the *Restatement (Second) of Torts*:

> The word 'intent' is used throughout the Restatement of this Subject to denote that the actor desires to cause consequences of his act, or that he believes that the consequences are substantially certain to result from it.[64]

[60] See *Restatement (Second) of Torts* (1977), § 870 comments c, e.

[61] Sidgwick, *The Methods of Ethics*, 202.

[62] See Goff, 'The Mental Element in the Crime of Murder' at 42–3; and essay 10 at nn. 2–5, 16–17 .

[63] See e.g. *United States v United States Gypsum Co.* 438 US 422, 445 (1978); *Sandstrom v Montana* 442 US 510, 525–6 (1979):

> The element of intent in the criminal law has traditionally been viewed as a bifurcated concept embracing either the specific requirement of purpose or the more general one of knowledge or awareness.

This is the position increasingly repudiated in England. [And see now essay III.16 (1998b), n.22.]

[64] *Restatement (Second) of Torts* (1963) § 8A. Comment b adds: 'As the probability that the consequences will follow decreases, and becomes less than substantial certainty, the actor's conduct

Thus the golfer whose only hope of winning at the last hole is to take a very long drive across water 'intends'—according to the *Restatement*—to lose the ball in the pond.

The case for imposing this fiction upon the law is that outcomes do indeed matter, and people have moral responsibilities in respect of outcomes which they foresee (as highly probable) and can avoid. The case against the fiction is partly that it is indeed fiction, and partly that in common morality, as opposed to utilitarianism, those moral responsibilities are assessed by standards which—for reasons sketched in the remainder of this section—are distinct from the standards governing what one intends. The basic distinction between murder and manslaughter, as understood in modern criminal law, is only the most obvious monument to this broad distinction between types of standard.[65]

In drawing this distinction, common morality is not indifferent to outcomes. But it includes among the significant outcomes the impact of choosing and intending upon the character of the chooser. It attends to the fact that *choices last.* The proposal which one adopts by choice in forming an intention, together with the reasoning which in one's deliberation made that proposal intelligently attractive, *remains,* persists, in one's will, one's disposition to act. The proposal (and thus the intention) is, so to speak, synthesized into one's will, one's practical orientation and stance in the world. And this is a real, empirical (though spiritual), and inbuilt effect of one's adopting a proposal. Whatever consequences lie *outside* one's proposal, because neither wanted for their own sake nor needed as a means, are *not* synthesized into one's will. Though one may foresee these results and accept that one will be causing them, or the risk of them, one is not adopting them. They are side effects, incidentals. One may well be culpable in accepting them. But the ground of culpability will not be that one intended them, but that one wrongly, for example unfairly, accepted them as incidents of what one did intend. The effect on one's character of accepting them is not like the dynamic, shaping effect that forming an intention (even a reluctant intention) has.

When one intends some harm to (an)other human person or persons—when one's proposal includes, however reluctantly, some damage to (for example) their bodily integrity, or to their participation in knowledge

loses the character of intent.' This notion of *degrees of intent* dramatizes the difference between the American Law Institute's conception of 'intent' and intention as understood in common sense and philosophy.

[65] Not every detail of the definition of murder is, or perhaps need be, derived from intent to kill or cause grievous bodily harm: see essay 10 at n. 23.

of reality, or to their means of sustenance[66]—one is shaping oneself as one who, in the most straightforward way, exploits others. And this is so, whether one intends that harm for its own sake, as in revenge or spite, or as a means, as in killing or maiming *pour encourager les autres*, deception for the sake of fraud, perjury for the sake of justice, or the engineering of financial ruin for political purposes. In each case, one is radically subjecting the reality and the fulfilment of those other persons to one's own reality and fulfilment, or to the reality and fulfilment of some other group of persons. In *intending* harm, one precisely makes their loss one's gain, or the gain of some others; one to that extent uses them up, treats them as material, as a resource for a good that no longer includes their own.

Common, non-utilitarian morality's principle that one must never choose (intend) harm to the person of any human individual both expresses and preserves the understanding that each human individual is more than just a locus of utility or wealth (to be measured at some arbitrarily chosen future moment), or a channel or conduit for maximizing that wealth or utility (again, a maximum as measured at some *chosen* future moment). It expresses and preserves each individual person's *density*, so to speak, or *dignity*, if you will, as an equal of *everyone* else in basic rights. To choose harm to the person is the paradigmatic wrong, the exemplary instance of denial of right.

A primordial and always primary (though not the only primary) function of government and law is to rectify this denial of right, this commutative injustice, by ensuring that the injurer does the injured the commutative justice of reparation.[67] No doubt there is a distributive, allocative aspect to this activity of government and the legal system. From a common stock of possible activities to be undertaken, costs incurred, and individual responsibilities to be drawn upon and distributed, the law assigns some part to this task of underwriting and guaranteeing commutative justice. Doing so is an act of distributive justice, but is ancillary to the prior, identifiable relationship of commutative injustice and potential commutative, reparative justice between the individuals. In this way, again, the dignity of the individuals, each ends in themselves (and in each basic aspect of

[66] The moral significance of intent to damage property or to harm persons in their wealth can be different from the moral significance of intent to harm persons as such, in as much as property and wealth are instrumental rather than basic goods intrinsic to the person, and in as much as in time of necessity the subpersonal resources of the world, including items of property, become common to the extent necessary to meet the emergency. Cf. *Vincent v Lake Erie Transp. Co.* 124 NW 221 (Minn. 1910). The obligation to pay compensation (not damages) seems to have been founded not on intent to harm but on an intentional act directly causing harm, i.e. on some sort of tacit analogy with intentional trespass to land or chattels.

[67] Aquinas's term 'commutative justice' better embraces the variety of relevant considerations than does Aristotle's not dissimilar notion of 'corrective justice'. See generally *NLNR* 178–9.

their reality and potentiality as persons), is again expressed and preserved. So, for judges to try to decide a case like *Bird v Holbrook* by the method commended by Posner—comparing costs (and benefits) of tulip growing with costs (and benefits) of peacock rearing—would be a denial of right.

In acts of reparative justice, government and law can be seen to have a role quite distinct from achieving any future 'end-state' state of affairs. The political community, unlike a one-project firm which must account to its shareholders at the end of the project, has no *goal*. Its success in fulfilling its responsibilities cannot be measured by any technique comparable to accounting. Success and failure are measured by quite other norms, among which the rule proscribing and rectifying intentional harm to the person is fundamental.

Moral responsibility and consequent legal liability for intentional infliction of harm are paradigmatic, exemplary. Avoiding such wrongs is only a necessary, not a sufficient, condition of acting justly. But the same respect for each individual whom one might have harmed as a means to an end carries over into, and informs, the quite different principle of fairness. Here one encounters the quite different principles of commutative injustice involved in the imposing of harmful foreseen side effects by persons who in their actions or omissions fail to comply with rational principles such as the Golden Rule, in contravention of truths such as that no one has an a priori superior claim on the earth's resources and no one, therefore, has unqualified dominion over any part of them. The Golden Rule in its application involves, first, a discernment of one's feelings and then, secondly, a dispassionate rational adherence to the standard of care established by one's feelings.[68]

Without confusing the norms of fairness with the norms outlawing certain intentions, legal thought can and does reasonably find criteria of fairness and unfairness in *analogies to the intentional*. So the wrongfulness of laying spring-guns with intent to wound affords an analogue, a paradigm, for identifying as unjust the omissions of those who inherit already laid spring-guns and retain them without such intent to wound; or who allow similarly lethal and concealed conditions to persist on their land when they know that what disguises the lethality also exercises a fatal attraction or allurement to innocent strangers, including trespassers. But the range of the analogy must be controlled not by verbal or 'conceptual' considerations—wordplays on 'trap', 'entrapment', etc.—but by considerations of fairness: how one wishes others to behave towards oneself and one's friends; how

[68] See essay I.14, sec. VII (= 1992a at 149).

one would behave, and would want others to behave, when one's friends or children strayed from the straight and narrow.

This conception of the fairness which is a shaping principle of commutative justice recognizes the proper role of sentiments in giving content and application to a moral principle which itself is simply rational. The normal way in which these sentiments make their presence felt in jurisprudence and legal reasoning is in the form of conventions and customs and in the far from bloodless life of the 'reasonable person' in our community here and now.[69]

And reasonable people never act (or refrain from acting) with intent to harm their neighbours. To the extent that the law continues on its centuries-long trajectory of convergence with morality, and is not deflected into the broad and easy utilitarian way (which offers to commensurate incommensurables and so can never succeed in doing more than provide rationalizations for what powerful people want),[70] judges and jurists will become less and less content with the easy-going assumption that harm done to a person by a forcible act of justified self-defence (including a private person's defence of others) is *intended*. Instead, they will become more and more interested in, and attracted to, the analysis of private defence of self or others proposed by the philosophical thinker who gave common morality and the reality of intention alike their perhaps most profound and influential discussion.[71] When defending oneself, it may of course be the case that one is intending to harm one's assailant as an end (satisfying one's hatred, spite, resentment, desire to get one's own back) or as a means (of deterring the assailant or potential assailants, or of disablement from some future revenge attack). But if one has none of those intentions, then one's *intent* can and should be simply to *stop this attack* by whatever means of stopping it are at hand. All the harm to the assailant, including the harm one foresees as certain, can be a side effect, unintended. And therefore, out of respect for persons, such a side effect should be unintended—and so too should be no tort, provided one acts fairly by choosing the least harmful of the efficacious means one knew or ought to have known were safely and readily available.[72]

V. CONCLUSION

My discussion has hinted at answers to the questions with which this essay began, questions about the very foundations and structure of tortious

[69] See generally Kelley, 'Who Decides? Community Safety Conventions at the Heart of Tort Liability'.

[70] See essay I.15 (1997b). [71] *ST* II–II q.64 a.7. [72] See essay 10 at nn. 31–3.

liability. But the argument of the essay has focused on three preliminary issues: what intention is, independently of artificial conceptual extensions; why intention, so understood, is morally significant; and how an intent to harm is a per se wrong-making factor in any conduct, independently of other wrong-making factors such as negligence. The key to all these preliminary issues is the set of related distinctions between intention and desire, between behaviour and action, and between intended upshot and foreseen (and even welcome) side effect. These distinctions become clear when the forming of an intention is understood for what it is: the adoption of a proposal which, however rapidly and unselfconsciously, one has shaped in deliberation and preferred to any alternative option available for one's choice.

NOTES

† *Reduced impact of the doctrine that intent to harm does not make tortious otherwise lawful conduct*...(text after n. 35). The impact is further reduced by the revival and clarification, in *OBG v Allan* [2007] UKHL 21, of two further distinct economic torts each predicated precisely on intention (and unconnected with conspiracy): (i) D's use of otherwise lawful means with intent to induce T's breach of a contract with P; (ii) D's use of unlawful means with intent to cause harm to P (whether via lawful decisions by T or via other causality). The explanations of intent(ion) given in the two leading judgments by Lord Hoffmann and Lord Nicholls are relatively perspicuous. Lord Hoffmann's explanations each included remarks about both torts, because 'the concept of intention is in both cases the same'. I insert notation indicating the parties on the P, D, T schema used above:

> 42. The next question is what counts as an intention to procure a breach of contract. It is necessary for this purpose to distinguish between ends, means and consequences. If someone knowingly causes a breach of contract, it does not normally matter that it is the means by which he intends to achieve some further end or even that he would rather have been able to achieve that end without causing a breach. Mr Gye [D] would very likely have preferred to be able to obtain Miss Wagner's [T's] services without her having to break her contract [with Mr Lumley, P]. But that did not matter. Again, people seldom knowingly cause loss by unlawful means out of simple disinterested malice. It is usually to achieve the further end of securing an economic advantage to themselves....
>
> 43. On the other hand, if the breach of contract is neither an end in itself nor a means to an end, but merely a foreseeable consequence, then in my opinion it cannot for this purpose be said to have been intended. That, I think, is what judges and writers mean when they say that the claimant must have been 'targeted' or 'aimed at'. In my opinion the majority of the Court of Appeal was wrong to have allowed the action in *Millar v Bassey* [1994] EMLR 44 to proceed. Miss Bassey [D] had broken her contract to perform for the recording company [T] and it was a foreseeable consequence that the recording company would have to break its contracts with the accompanying musicians [P], but those breaches of contract were neither an end desired by Miss Bassey nor a means of achieving that end.
>
> 62.... In the *Lumley v Gye* tort, there must be an intention to procure a breach of contract. In the unlawful means tort, there must be an intention to cause loss. The ends which must have been intended are different.... [O]ne may intend to procure a breach of contract without intending to cause loss. Likewise, one may intend to cause loss without intending to procure a breach of contract. But the concept of intention is in both cases the same. In both cases it is necessary to distinguish between ends, means and consequences. One intends to cause loss even though it is the means by which one achieved the end of enriching oneself. On the other hand, one is not liable for loss which is neither a desired end nor a means of attaining it but merely a foreseeable consequence of one's actions.

63. The master of the *Othello* [D] in *Tarleton v M'Gawley* may have had nothing against the other trader [P, whose customers were intimidated by D's gunfire]. If he [P] had gone off to make his fortune in other waters, he [D] would have wished him well. He simply wanted a monopoly of the local trade for himself. But he nevertheless intended to cause him loss. This, I think, is all that Woolf LJ was intending to say in a passage in *Lonrho plc v Fayed* [1990] 2 QB 479, 494 which has proved controversial:

'Albeit that he may have no desire to bring about that consequence in order to achieve what he regards as his ultimate ends, from the point of view of the plaintiff, whatever the motive of the defendant, the damage which he suffers will be the same.'

64. On the other hand, I think that Henry J was right in *Barretts & Baird (Wholesale) Ltd v Institution of Professional Civil Servants* [1987] IRLR 3 when he decided a strike by civil servants in the Ministry of Agriculture in support of a pay claim was not intended to cause damage to an abattoir which was unable to obtain the certificates necessary for exporting meat and claiming subsidies. The damage to the abattoir was neither the purpose of the strike nor the means of achieving that purpose, which was to put pressure on the government.

(Lord Hoffmann's explanation in para. 63 of Woolf LJ's dictum is very charitable; on its face the dictum seems to express the characteristic consequentialist indifference to intention. 'What does it matter whether you get killed by intention (as a means or an end) or as a side-effect? You're just as dead either way!')

Lord Nicholls's explanation of intention in *OBG v Allan* equally relies on the distinction between ends or means and side effects, but makes explicit that the use of unlawful means deprives D of the kind of fine-grained distinction between means and side effects (see text and nn. 44 and 58 above) which is employed in the American doctrine rejected by English law in *Allen v Flood*. Speaking of the second (unlawful means) tort, Lord Nicholls said:

164.... the other key ingredient of this tort [is] the defendant's intention to harm the claimant. A defendant may intend to harm the claimant's [P's] business either as an end in itself or as a means to an end. A defendant may intend to harm the claimant as an end in itself where, for instance, he has a grudge against the claimant. More usually a defendant intentionally inflicts harm on a claimant's business as a means to an end. He inflicts damage as the means whereby to protect or promote his own economic interests.

165. Intentional harm inflicted against a claimant in either of these circumstances satisfies the mental ingredient of this tort. This is so even if the defendant does not wish to harm the claimant, in the sense that he would prefer that the claimant were not standing in his way.

166. Lesser states of mind do not suffice. A high degree of blameworthiness is called for, because intention serves as the factor which justifies imposing liability on the defendant for loss caused by a wrong otherwise not actionable by the claimant against the defendant. The defendant's conduct in relation to the loss must be deliberate. In particular, a defendant's foresight that his unlawful conduct may or will probably damage the claimant cannot be equated with intention for this purpose. The defendant must *intend* to injure *the claimant*. This intent must be a cause of the defendant's conduct... The majority of the Court of Appeal fell into error on this point in the interlocutory case of *Miller v Bassey* [1994] EMLR 44. Miss Bassey did not breach her recording contract with the intention of thereby injuring any of the plaintiffs.

167. I add one explanatory gloss to the above. Take a case where a defendant seeks to advance his own business by pursuing a course of conduct which he knows will, in the very nature of things, necessarily be injurious to the claimant. In other words, a case where loss to the claimant is the obverse side of the coin from gain to the defendant. The defendant's gain and the claimant's loss are, to the defendant's knowledge, inseparably linked. The defendant cannot obtain the one without bringing about the other. If the defendant goes ahead in such a case in order to obtain the gain he seeks, his state of mind will satisfy the mental ingredient of the unlawful interference tort. This accords with the approach adopted by Lord Sumner in *Sorrell v Smith* [1925] AC 700, 742:

'When the whole object of the defendants' action is to capture the plaintiff's business, their gain must be his loss. How stands the matter then? The difference disappears. The defendant's success is the plaintiff's extinction, and they cannot seek the one without ensuing the other.'

(Lord Hoffmann at para. 134 quotes the same passage of Lord Sumner's, to the same effect. Neither he nor Lord Nicholls notes that this paragraph of Lord Sumner's is concerned with combinations or conspiracies, and is scarcely consistent with the developed doctrine of tortious conspiracy to harm, in *Crofter v Veitch* [1942] AC 435, because Lord Sumner's rhetoric is intended to persuade us that malice, even in conspiracy, does not render conduct tortious, whereas Lords Hoffmann and Nicholls quote the very same words for the more or less opposite purpose of persuading us that a purely self-interested purpose of gain does not negative that 'intent to cause loss' which is requisite for liability for use of unlawful means.)

‡ *Is the intent-based tort of conspiracy to harm anomalous?...* (n. 51). In *OBG v Allan* [2007] UKHL 21, which reaffirms the doctrine in *Allen v Flood*, Lord Hoffmann remarks (para. 15) that in conspiracy 'a bad motive can, exceptionally, found liability'. Lord Nicholls at paras 145–8, while reaffirming that, absent conspiracy, 'intentionally causing damage without using unlawful means is not of itself actionable', accepts that the criticisms of this requirement of unlawful means have force, and that the doctrine is not so much rational or principled as 'pragmatic' (147). There is force in Lord Hoffmann's point (15) that the American doctrine creates 'a good deal of uncertainty'—doubtless because the distinctions it requires to be drawn between what is and is not intended, and the qualifications needed to make its impact fair (see n. 44 above), call for a lot of precision and, therefore, complexity.

On the restricted importance of doctrines of abuse of right(s) in legal systems that articulate them, see e.g. Reid, 'The Doctrine of Abuse of Rights: Perspective from a Mixed Jurisdiction' (2004) Electronic J Comparative L 8: 3.

12

CONDITIONAL AND PREPARATORY INTENTIONS*

I. ON CONDITIONAL INTENTIONS

Putting an end to an inglorious legal muddle, the Court of Appeal in June 1979 denounced the concept of conditional intention, calling it 'pseudo-philosophical'.[1] But the muddle was home-grown by lawyers, and scarcely nurtured by philosophy, true or counterfeit.

In December 1977 the same court had declared: 'it cannot be said that one who has it in mind to steal only if what he finds is worth stealing has a present intention to steal'.[2] Now, many who go stealing know not what they will find, and few of these are resolved to take and carry away whatever they come across. And for a year or so, the Court of Appeal's words were treated by lower courts[3] as a charter for thieves and burglars.[4] Then, on a reference of the issue by the Attorney General, the Court of Appeal explained[5] that its words had been elliptical for: those who intend to steal only if they find something worth stealing, but who do not yet know what they will find, cannot be said to have the intention to *steal a specific* item, and so must be acquitted of attempting to steal that item. The problem was henceforth to be avoided by making charges less specific: those who took a holdall containing equipment which they abandoned on discovering it should be charged not with attempting to steal certain equipment [specified in the

* 1994a.

[1] *Re Attorney-General's References (Nos 1 & 2 of 1979)* [1980] QB 180 at 186, per Roskill LJ.

[2] *R v Husseyn* (1977) 67 Cr App R 131 at 132, per Lord Scarman.

[3] e.g. *R v Bozickovic* [1978] Crim L Rev 686: one who enters a flat as a trespasser with intent to steal anything worth stealing cannot (in the light of *Husseyn*) be held to have entered the flat with intent to steal. This ruling in the Nottingham Crown Court was implicitly disapproved by the Court of Appeal decision of 1979.

[4] See Law Commission Report No. 102 (1980), appendix E ('"Conditional Intention" and *R* v. *Husseyn*'), para. 6:

> within a few months of the decision in *R v Husseyn*, submissions that 'conditional intent is not enough' were being accepted by magistrates and Crown Court judges in all these theft and related offences, causing frustration and perplexity to prosecuting authorities and bringing the criminal law into disrepute.

[5] Loc. cit., n. 2 above.

charge] contained in a holdall, but with attempting to steal (some or all of) the contents of a holdall.[6]

Of more lasting interest is the fact that the judges whose imprecision in 1977 caused the fuss had deprecated talk of 'conditional intention' with as much vehemence as the court which put the matter to rest.[7] Likewise counsel and the Law Commission.[8] Why? The lawyers scarcely elaborate the grounds of their objection. But what they say suggests the following.

The conditions referred to in calling an intention 'conditional' do not condition the adopting of a plan or purpose, the making of a decision, the forming of the intention. Rather, they condition only the carrying out of the plan, decision, or intention. Those who rifle through another's property, looking to see whether there is anything there worth stealing, may be undecided whether or not to steal at all. But more commonly they have *decided to steal* anything which they may, on inspection, judge profitable and safe to steal. What needs to be determined by the jury is: Had that basic decision been made, or did the person remain, at the time of the alleged offence, in two minds about stealing anything?[9] In a case where the decision to steal had been made, it matters not—provided the charge is prudently unspecific—that the intention, fully stated, included a condition:...if I find something worth stealing (for example, money). And the reason it does not matter can be stated as above: the condition is a condition limiting the object[10] of the intention (what is intended), not the subject, the agent who has really formed (and in this case has begun to act upon) a culpable intention and is wrongfully intending...When we say 'has really formed', we might equally say 'has unconditionally formed', meaning that the formation of the intention, having actually occurred, is no longer conditional on anything. So we can quite understand the anxiety of judges lest juries be invited to puzzle about the conditionality

[6] [1979] 3 All ER at 153. See also *Scudder v Barrett* [1980] QB 195, (1979) 69 Cr App R 277; and *R v Bayley & Easterbrook* [1980] Crim L Rev 503 (*Appeal No. 4903/B/79*, Lexis transcript) where in each case the charge was of 'attempting to steal the contents of a box belonging to...' and the purpose of the unsuccessful appellants was only to take such items, if any, as they might fancy.

[7] See [1979] Crim L Rev 444, [1979] 3 All ER at 145.

[8] [1978] Crim L Rev 444–5, [1980] QB 180 at 186; Law Com. Rep. No. 102 (1980), appendix E.

[9] See *R v Walkington* [1979] 2 All ER 716 at 724, approved in *Re A-G's References (Nos 1 & 2 of 1979)* [1980] QB 180 at 194. Thus:

> the distinction that has to be drawn in any case of intention in this field is between the man who has decided to steal and the man who has not yet decided whether or not to steal. (Letter to the Editor [1978] Crim L Rev 444.)

[10] Throughout, 'object' refers not to one's (the subject/agent's) ultimate objective(s) (i.e. motives, e.g. to please one's spouse) nor to a physical object involved in one's action (e.g. the thing which one intends to steal) but to *the action which one intends*, conditionally or unconditionally, *to carry out* (e.g. to steal (that thing, or something in there) in order to please one's spouse).

of intentions which, though conditional in their object or content, have really—unconditionally—been formed.[11]

Or we could state the peril thus: forensic talk of conditional intentions would invite adept counsel to shift (unimpeachably) from 'I shall do X if C' to 'If C, I shall do X' and then to claim (sophistically) that in merely conditional intentions the real decision and resulting intention to do X *follows* occurrence of C in time as in the latter locution's surface grammar.[12]

II. DOES AN INTENTION'S CONDITIONALITY REALLY MATTER?

A wide philosophical consensus accepts that there is a distinct class or type of intention which may properly be called conditional intentions.[13] This consensus goes along with another: that even where an intention is *not* one of these conditional intentions, the subject's forming of it will, nonetheless, rarely if ever have been unconditioned, that is, formed 'regardless of the circumstances';[14] and that few if any subsisting intentions (intendings) are unconditional in the strong sense of indefeasible or 'irrevocable' ('I intend to do it come what may'). Not forgetting these two further points of agreement, it seems convenient to call intentions which are not conditional 'unconditional'.

[11] The anxiety is not far-fetched. A number of the leading American appellate decisions on the nature of the intent required for an assault with intent to kill display a good deal of confusion. Some courts hold that where A assaults (menaces) B with intent to kill B if B does not comply with the demands accompanying the menaces, A commits the offence: *People v Connors* 97 NE 643 (1912) (Supreme Ct of Illinois). Other courts hold that the offence is not committed unless A intends to kill B *by means of* the assault: *State v Irwin* 285 SE 2d 345 at 349 (1982) (North Carolina Ct of Appeals). So far so good; either doctrine is a defensible reading of the statute. But a number of leading cases which reach the same result as *Irwin* do so, not by requiring that the assault be intended as a means of killing, but by declaring that a conditional intent accompanying the threat is not a 'real intent to kill': 'in such a case there can be no actual or present intent to kill, and may never be, since the intent is conditioned upon some other event which may not happen': *Stroud v State* 95 So 738 (1923) (Mississippi Supreme Ct).

[12] Note: in such schematic representations of conditional intention ('to do X if C'), the 'if' is to be read as normally signifying 'if and only if'. I will use the form 'I shall...' as equivalent to 'I intend to...', using this now obsolescent auxiliary form to distinguish between expressions of intention and predictions.

[13] See e.g. Meiland, *The Nature of Intention*, 15–25; Castañeda, 'Conditional Intentions, Intentional Action and Aristotelian Practical Syllogisms' at 248–9; Wilfrid Sellars, 'Conditional Promises and Conditional Intentions (Including a Reply to Castañeda)' at 202–3, 207–8, 212–14; Castañeda, 'Reply to Wilfrid Sellars: Intending and the Logic of Intentions' at 423, 427–33; Cartwright, 'Conditional Intention' and literature there cited.

[14] Cartwright, *ibid.* at 236, says:

> ... all intentions are formed against the background of a complex web of beliefs, some of which are conditions of the formation of the intent.... Indeed the formation of any intention is subject to such conditions. All intentions are thus externally conditional.

Conditional and unconditional intentions, it is said, differ irreducibly in type because they 'have different types of object', that is to say 'the type of thing that the agent intends is different in each case'.[15] Specifically,

> the condition—... 'If Jones is there'—is not a condition of the agent intending to... That is, [such] conditions are not conditions of his having these intentions.... The object of the intention contains a condition; the condition is in some way *part of what is intended or part of what the intention is about.*[16]

This difference of types of object can be seen, Meiland says, in three criterial differences; of these, two seem to me plausible.[17] (1) Where C is a circumstance or condition specified in the object of one's intention ('to do X if C obtains'), and one comes to believe that C will *certainly* not obtain, one cannot *change one's mind* about doing X just on the ground that C will certainly not obtain; but where one has an intention which is unconditional (at least as to C), and learns that C will not obtain, one can change one's mind about doing X (and change it precisely on the ground that C, which one had thought would obtain, will not obtain).[18] (2) Where one has the conditional intention to do X if C, one need have no belief that C will ever obtain, and so need have no belief that one will ever try to do X; but one cannot have an *unconditional* intention to do X and at the same time not have the belief that one will try to do X.[19]

But both these criterial differences have more to do with the dispositions of the subject than with the content of the object. Moreover, what is

[15] Meiland, 16, 26.

[16] *Ibid.*, 15, 16–17 (Meiland's emphasis). Cartwright, 'Conditional Intention' at 235, puts the point in terms of a distinction between internal conditions (which are part of the content of the intent) and external conditions (which are conditions of the formation of the intent).

[17] Meiland, 17–18. Meiland points to a third difference, which seems unsound: (a) where C is part of the object of an intention (which will thus be a conditional intention), the fact that C obtains (if and when it does) will be then a reason for doing X, but the reasons for having the intention need not include any belief that C will obtain; (b) if the belief that C will obtain is part of the agent's reasons for having the unconditional intention to do X, then the fact that C obtains will be a reason for then doing X. Here Meiland's logic seems awry, for what is said in (b) of unconditional intentions is also true of even those conditional intentions which the agent forms without any belief that C will in fact obtain.

[18] Meiland, 18.

[19] Meiland's exposition is confused because he says:

> unless he changes his mind about doing X, comes to believe that it is not possible for him to do X, or is prevented from trying to do X, the agent cannot have an *unconditional* intention to do X and at the same time not have the belief that he will try to do X.

But if one has changed one's mind about doing X, one no longer has the intention to do X; and if one comes to believe that one's doing X is and will remain impossible, one cannot retain the intention to do X (though one might still intend to try, vainly, to do it—to exert every muscle to push a 100-ton block); and if one knows that one will always be prevented from even trying to do X, one can, similarly, no longer intend to do it. So I ignore the proviso.

asserted in difference (1), though real,[20] seems unimportant. What does it matter that on the non-obtaining of C, an intention of the one sort can be terminated by change of mind whereas an intention of the other sort simply ceases to 'be operative' and withers away? Ulrich enters a house intending to go to the dining room and steal the silver cutlery he once saw there—an intention which on the consensus/Meiland view is not conditional but unconditional. Clarrie enters the house intending to steal silver cutlery if any there be therein, and provided that he see no internal burglar alarms—a conditional intention. On entering, each finds the house empty of everything except burglar alarms. Ulrich changes his mind about his project, and retreats. Clarrie retreats 'according to plan'. *This* difference between unconditional and conditional intentions seems to ground no distinction between Ulrich's and Clarrie's moral or legal responsibility, nor between the terms in which and force with which each might appropriately repent of his purpose if his conscience worked effectively as he approached the house.

What of Meiland's difference (2)? In considering whether there is a significant difference between 'I shall do X if C' and 'I shall do X when C', how important is the fact that the latter, unconditional intent is accompanied by a belief that C will obtain? Meiland's point is that the latter belief is accompanied by, and grounds, a further belief: that 'I will try to do X when C'.[21] But he does not deny that a conditional intent, 'I shall do X if C', is accompanied by the belief that 'I *would* try to do X if C'. Nor does he

[20] ... for the intention was never meant to be executed in these circumstances... there is no change of mind if the person believes the condition is not fulfilled and his reason for abandoning the intention and its execution is this supposed non-fulfilment. (Cartwright, 'Conditional Intention', at 250.)

Yes, but to be more precise, one should also speak of the case where there was no particular time at which the condition was expected to obtain, and the change of belief is simply from the belief that C might sometime occur to the belief that C cannot occur (or cannot occur during any period of time in respect of which the agent had decided to do X if C). Meiland's statement, '... comes to believe that C will in fact not obtain', refers primarily to such a belief in X's impossibility. (The relevant 'impossibility' is, I think, practical impossibility. Broderick, 'Conditional Objectives of Conspiracies' at 903, criticizes the Model Penal Code's acceptance of conditional purposes as satisfying the requirement of purpose in crimes involving purpose; he argues that this would result in absurdities such as the conviction of people who agree to blow up the Capitol if the Nazi Party wins a majority at the next congressional election. But such an agreement does not manifest an intention or common purpose to blow up the Capitol unless at the time of the agreement the parties to it regard a Nazi victory as a practical possibility. Broderick's further thesis that a common purpose to do X if C should be punishable only if the conspirators consider C *likely* is defensible, but not well defended by his claim (at 906) that where conspirators consider C unlikely, they 'never genuinely expect to fulfill their agreement'.)

[21] Scheer, 'Conditional Intentions', argues that 'I intend to try to do X' is equivalent to the conditional 'I shall do X if I can', and is thus the appropriate formula for a paradigmatic *conditional* intention. His principal purpose is to contest Davidson's view that one can *intend to do* what one is unsure one can do; in such cases, according to Scheer, one can only intend to *try*—any other statement of intention to do X refers, in a such a case, only to 'intention' in the distinct sense of a goal, something one has in mind but has not yet *decided* to do. I neither contest nor adopt Scheer's thesis.

deny that the predictive beliefs accompanying an unconditional intention may be subject to express or tacit provisos or defeating conditions which in many cases would render the predictive 'I will (unless ...)' scarcely distinguishable from the 'I would, if ...'. Some of the many ways in which intentions can be subject in their subsisting and/or execution to such conditions and provisos can be indicated by the following incomplete set (sequence?):

'I shall not do X unless ...'
'I shall not do X until ...'
'I would do X if ...'
'I shall do X if ...'
'I shall do X when ...'
'I shall do X, provided that....'
'I shall do X unless ...'
'I shall do X whenever ...'
'I am going to do X.'

The last formula is included because, as already mentioned, such an unqualified statement is usually not an expression of irrevocable and indefeasible intent ('come what may', 'no matter what'), any more than a report or other assertion unqualified by 'Unless I'm mistaken' is or involves a claim to infallibility.[22] Presuppositions (such as that the world will continue in much the same shape as it is today) condition every or virtually every formation of an intention, and every intending, but many of them come to one's attention only in unusual circumstances, and most of them ordinarily go without saying.[23] And if all these tacit presuppositions and

[22] Analogously, Anscombe, *Intention*, 92, says:

> In the small activities of everyday life, to say 'I am going to, unless I am prevented' would be absurd, like putting 'unless my memory deceives me' after every report one gave of what had happened.

[23] Davidson, 'Intending' at 94:

> ... there can be no finite list of things we think might prevent us from doing what we intend or of circumstances that might cause us to stay our hand.... We can be clear what it is we intend to do while being in the dark as to the details, and therefore the pitfalls.

These observations seem independent of Davidson's contentions: (a) that intentions are 'all-out' desirability judgments or evaluative attitudes; (b) that *all* the conditions in conditional intentions are reasons for action contemporary with the intention (at 94); and (c) that one may intend to do something even though one is not sure one will be able to do it (92). Moya, *The Philosophy of Action*, 156, shows how Davidson is compelled to adopt contention (b) by his acceptance of the widely and effectively criticized contention (a) (a contention which omits the *decision* to do what is desirable); Moya further suggests (150–8) reasons for qualifying contention (b) by recognizing that the conditions in a conditional intention may include, besides conditions which are now reasons for action, also conditions as to the *availability* of means or, indeed, of the end (the intended benefit). Scheer, 'Conditional Intentions' argues that (c) is misleading, and that if one is unsure whether one can do X one's intention will be 'to do X if I can' (equivalent to 'to try to do X'), e.g. 'to go to Law School if I can pass the exam' or 'to *try to* go to Law School'.

provisos qualify the intention articulated by the last formula, so too they will qualify 'I shall do X when C'. Once again, Ulrich's 'I shall steal the silver when I get into the dining room' seems to differ little in significance from Clarrie's 'I shall steal the silver if I find any there' or 'I hope to find drugs, but if I found any silver I'd steal it.'

The subject/agent-related criterial differences Meiland offered should not make us forget his principal thesis: unconditional and conditional intentions differ just in their respective objects, and a conditional intention's conditions are not conditions of the subject's having (forming) that intention. That thesis seems right. Intentions of each type are alike formed in the making of some choice (decision),[24] and are equally capable of being stable or unstable, equally subject to unstated provisos, equally coherent or incoherent with the agent's other intentions, equally accompanied by eager anticipation or feelings of reluctance, and so forth. Differences between conditional and unconditional are insignificant compared with the difference between one who has and one who has not formed an intention—between those who have made up their minds and those who are still in two minds. (As we will see, even the latter distinction is of limited importance when the hesitation is between options, one of which is unconditionally immoral or illegal.)[25]

To see the ultimate unimportance of distinguishing between conditional and unconditional intentions, consider the spring-gun mantrap (which brought disgrace to the common law in the early nineteenth century, and in the mid-twentieth century gave Richard Posner occasion for manifesting how an untempered Economic Analysis of Law will flout requirements of elementary morality).[26] Those who, to deter poachers, arrange for shotguns to be pointed along trip wires may well hope that poachers will

[24] Not all intentions are the content of a choice or 'decision'. E.g. one may form the intention to catch the last train, the 11.10, and then, on being told that the 11.10 is cancelled, form the intention to catch the 10.45, without needing to make any fresh decision or choice or even to make a recommitment to catching the last train. And this is common in the execution of choices; one carries forward the chosen course of action, adapting intelligently to circumstances as they arise and forming intentions spontaneously. But this is not the paradigm of intending or, certainly, of forming intentions, which is the adopting of proposals by choice. (Is this one of the cases Anscombe had in mind when stating that intention need not be started off by a forming of intention? See her 'Events in the Mind' at 63.) As to intentions in the sense of goals one has in mind, see n. 21 above and text of sec. III below.

[25] And for some purposes, the conditionality of a fully formed intention may weaken its significance. Thus in *R v Immigration Appeal Tribunal, ex parte Masood* [1991] Imm App R 283 (High Court, 22 January 1991, Lexis transcript), Simon Brown J held that, where the legal issue is whether the *primary purpose* of marrying is to live together or to gain entry to the United Kingdom, the fact that the parties' real intention to live together was 'a conditional intention', viz. contingent on being able to live in England, so 'diluted the weight that would otherwise attach to the accepted intention' that the intent to live together could reasonably be judged not primary.

[26] See essay 11, secs I and II, commenting inter alia on Posner, 'Killing or Wounding to Protect a Property Interest' at 209–11; Posner, *Economic Analysis of Law*, 119–32.

be so effectively deterred (for example, by notices warning of spring-guns) that no one will ever be shot. But if they load the guns with real shot, they manifest their belief that someone *may* come poaching. And, assuming that they are at all clear-headed, their intention must be that, if poachers come, they will be shot. Is that intention conditional or unconditional? The question relates to the object, and seems to have no clear answer. ('If C, X will automatically happen, because I've made sure it will' is not identical to 'If C, I shall certainly do X', but perhaps is practically equivalent.) What is clear, in such a case, is that on the side of the subjects (those who arrange for the guns to be set and loaded in this fashion) there really is an intention to shoot any outsider who intrudes into their woods or gardens.[27]

Yet: it remains important for philosophical reflection on intention to keep conditional intentions firmly on stage. If Alan Donagan, for example, had recalled the reality of conditional intentions, he could hardly have denounced St Thomas's categories of *usus* and *imperium* as muddled and misplaced.[28] For Donagan knew better than most that one identifies the components of human action not by introspection but by reflecting on the various kinds of cases where one's movement towards deliberately doing something begins but is not completed.[29] But Donagan's list of such kinds of cases simply omits the cases where one has chosen one's course of action but the occasion for carrying out one's choice has not yet arisen. So he joined the long line of philosophers and theologians who have hastily treated as mere fiction the *imperium* by which, long after deliberation has been terminated by judgment and choice, one exercises rational dominion over what one does, in the twists and turns of circumstance.[30]

III. ON PREPARATORY INTENTIONS

The object of some intentions is certain possible future deliberations and intentions of the subject, and the conditions under which they might be engaged in and carried through to action. If there are 'goals', things one 'has in mind', which are intentions rather than mere hopes even though one has not yet decided to go for them, that is because one has decided to take them seriously by, not just daydreaming, but really *deliberating* about

[27] Thus Criminal Code (Revised Statutes of Canada 1985, C–34), s. 247(1):

> Every one who, *with intent to* cause death or bodily harm to persons, whether ascertained or not, sets or places or causes to be set or placed a trap, device or other thing whatever that is likely to cause death or bodily harm to persons is guilty of an indictable offence ...

This is a clarified and superior version of the Offences Against the Person Act 1861, s. 31 (UK), originally enacted as a special statute in 1827.

[28] Donagan, 'Thomas Aquinas on Human Action' at 649–52.

[29] *Ibid.* at 654.

[30] See *NLNR* 337–42.

how to attain or do them or how to get into a position to be able to attain or do them.

In his mock natural-scientific way, Hobbes considered deliberation to be nothing but alternating imaginations of good and evil consequences 'or (which is the same thing) alternate hope and fear, or alternate appetite to do or quit the action' under consideration. Each of these 'appetites to do, and to quit, that come upon a man during his deliberations, are called', said Hobbes, '*intentions*, and *inclinations*, but not wills, there being but *one* will, which also in this case may be called the *last* will, though the *intentions* change often'.[31] But these claims jar with more than mere idiom. Deliberating on the attractions of alternative options is not a matter of swinging between intentions, of chopping and changing, of successive changes of heart.

Take the leading English case on the relation between intention and deliberation. A landlord who intends to demolish the premises on the expiry of a lease cannot (a statute, as interpreted, provides) claim from the departing tenant compensation for dilapidations; but a landlord who instructs professional advisers to make plans for demolition and redevelopment, and to submit them to the authorities so as to discover the costs and conditions involved, may be merely

> reserving his decision until he shall be in possession of financial data sufficient to determine whether the project will be commercially worth while. A purpose so qualified and suspended does not... amount to an 'intention' or 'decision' within the principle. It is mere contemplation until the materials necessary to a decision on the commercial merits are available and have resulted in such a decision.[32]

Taken at face value, such talk of 'contemplation', though less obfuscating than lawyers' talk of steps 'calculated to...', is almost as extravagant as Hobbes's opposite claim that one's conflicting inclinations when deliberating

[31] Thomas Hobbes, *Of Liberty and Necessity* (1654), in Raphael, *British Moralists 1650–1800*, para. 96 (Hobbes's emphases). John Austin seems to have gone along with this: *Lectures on Jurisprudence* (1869) 1, 429. Glanville Williams certainly did: *Criminal Law: The General Part*, 36. See generally essay 10 at n. 8.

[32] *Cunliffe v Goodman* [1950] 2 KB 237 at 254, per Asquith LJ. Note that the so-called 'principle' was simply that where an intention to demolish exists the premises can, by judicial interpretation and ruling, be treated as coming within the statutory concept of premises which 'would at or shortly after the termination of the tenancy have been or be pulled down ...' (Landlord and Tenant Act 1927, s. 18(1)). The judicial interpretation looks to the fact that s. 1 of the 1927 Act refers to an 'intention to demolish', but the different language of s. 18(1) invites the use of a concept of intention clearly distinct from any state of indecision. Later statutes, which coexist with the 1927 Act, speak explicitly of what the landlord intends or, in other provisions (and apparently synonymously), proposes to do: Landlord and Tenant Act 1954, s. 3(1)(f); Opencast Coal Act 1958, s. 30(3)(c); Housing Act 1985, s. 556 and Sch. 2, Part 2; Housing Act 1988, Sch. 2, Part 1 ('intends' or 'intention' to demolish); Landlord and Tenant Act 1954, s. 12(1)(a); Leasehold Reform Act 1967, s. 17(1); Local Government and Housing Act 1989, Sch. 10 ('proposes to demolish').

between alternative options are oscillating intentions. But Lord Justice Asquith hardly meant by 'contemplation' something contemplative! He meant a process of active consideration, exploration of options: 'I'm thinking of pulling down the building'. According to Lords Justices Asquith and Cohen this might involve a 'provisional' intention, not to be confused, they stressed, with a 'settled' but 'revocable' intention.

Were they right to speak of provisional intention, here? The case they were considering could, I think, be understood on one or other of two models:

(1) I decide to demolish if the net predicted costs are below £1 m, yet I have no idea whether they will turn out on investigation to be more or less than that sum; here I might equally say *either* that I have provisionally decided (have the provisional intention) to demolish *or* that I have as yet made no decision (formed no intention) *to demolish.*

Or the case could be understood, as its actual facts and some of the judges' remarks rather suggest, on another model:

(2) I decide to investigate the pros and cons of demolition, and such an investigation may (as in the post-war conditions considered in *Cunliffe v Goodman*) require that I take many of the steps I would have taken were I acting on a settled intention to demolish; but my purpose in taking those steps is simply to get into a position to make a well-informed decision whether or not to demolish.

To the extent that Lords Justices Cohen and Asquith understood the facts on model (2), their willingness to speak of an intention *to demolish*, even a merely 'provisional' intention, seems to go too far.[33]

Still, even on model (2)—and *a fortiori* on (1)—there is an intention; there has been a decision; things have gone beyond mere interest in and openness to the possibility. The intention is, I shall say, *procedural* or *preparatory*. It is (formed by) the adoption of a proposal or purpose: to do what is needed (a) *to make an informed decision* whether or not to demolish, and further, in many cases, to do at the same time what is needed (b) *to be in a position* such that, if one does decide to demolish, one will be well placed to do it. And intentions of this procedural or preparatory kind are themselves, of course, unconditional.

[33] Of course, there are contexts in which 'provisional intent(ion)' is the exact description, e.g.: Before imposing a compensation order the sentencing Judge should tell counsel of his provisional intention [to do so] so that a proper inquiry as to the defendant's means can be carried out and submissions made by counsel. (*R v Hewitt* (1990) 155 JP 243 (Court of Appeal, Crim. Div.))

Should we say that, if one makes such a preparatory decision—to get into such a position that one could, if one so chose, do X and do it successfully—one is forming a (very) conditional intention to do X, that is, an intention to do X if on investigation it seems appropriate? That description seems possible.[34] Still, it glosses over the fact that when an option comes to seem to me 'appropriate in all the circumstances' I may yet fail to choose it, that is, to adopt it (and to adopt it would be to form the intention to act accordingly). What is glossed over is the fact that the substantive decision—to do X—remains to be made (and may never be made, even if one at some future time judges the circumstances altogether propitious for doing X and thinks no alternative option so appropriate).

Common idiom can be left to its ambivalence about whether preparatory intentions (which are rather common) are a type of conditional substantive intention. More significant is the fact that those who make such a procedural decision[35]—to deliberate about and/or to get into a position to decide about and 'if need be' carry out X—show themselves *willing to do* X. And if X is something that no one should ever do, such a procedural/preparatory decision participates in the immorality of substantively intending and doing X. (That is not to say that it is 'equally bad' as substantively intending, or that the latter is 'just as bad' as carrying out that intention; it is only to say that it involves the same sort of immorality—say, theft, or murder—as the substantive intention to do X and the deliberate doing of X.)

Two imaginary examples (later I shall point to a real case, close to home). (1) On getting married, someone says to himself that he will be a faithful husband, but decides to keep his address book of good-time girls just in case marriage fails to give him all the satisfactions he expects. By that decision, he is in his heart an adulterer, even though he has made no substantive decision to use the book, telephone a girl, or make a sexual assignation. (2) A woman married to a brutal drunkard considers setting his bed on fire while he sleeps if ever he goes too far, decides to treat that

[34] Cf. Luke 14: 28:

> For which of you, intending (KJV/AV, JB; Gk. *thelon*; Vulgate 'volens'; RSV 'desiring'; Douai and Knox 'ha[ving] a mind'; NAB 'if one of you decides') to build a tower, sitteth not down first, and counteth the cost, whether he have sufficient to finish it?

[35] I do not maintain the thesis proposed by Pink, 'Purposive Intending' at 343–4, that 'intending to do A is...a goal-directed, actionlike state—a state formed and held by an agent *as a means* to his subsequently doing A' (emphasis added); see also 356. Some cases, of procedural intending, may approximate to that state. But the thesis is extravagant. Better balanced, on the whole, is Pears, 'Intentions as Judgements' at 229:

> We certainly can form intentions intentionally, and when they remain with us we regard their firmness as something to which we can make an intentional contribution....[W]e form and maintain our intentions not only in order to attain our deferred goals...but also occasionally for a further reason...the advantage of acquiring in advance, and being able to count on[,] dispositions to perform particular actions.

as a real option which she may some day adopt and, accordingly, to 'keep the option open', buys a can of petrol and puts it in her cupboard. Her decisions make her in her heart a murderer. When one decides to get ready, in this way, one forms an unconditional intention, makes a straightforward though procedural decision: to make preparations now such that, *if* C, one could *either* form the unconditional intention to do X then and there *or, if* one preferred, form the conditional intention to do X *if* C_1. And any such deliberate decision will be a *choice*, the adoption of this (procedural) option in preference to alternative, incompatible options.

In each of the cases just considered, there is a conditional willingness, originating in a decision to treat a possible intention as not merely an 'abstract' possibility but rather as an intention which one might indeed ('might well') form if certain conditions obtained. True, this willingness is, or may be, doubly conditional, for the (substantive) intention which one thus has the (preparatory) intention to be ready to form is an intention which might, if and when formed, be either conditional or unconditional. So the preparatory intention has a perhaps doubled-up conditionality of object. Nonetheless, just insofar as it is itself formed by adopting a proposal, the preparatory intention has, on the side of the subject, the unconditionality and so the self-determining, character-forming significance of all intentions. And it has some unconditionality on the side of the object, too. It is not yet the choice to do X, nor even the choice to *do X if C*. It is the definite intention not to exclude the option of doing X from (further) deliberation,[36] as a mere temptation, but rather to retain that option within one's deliberations as still an *eligibilium*, as choiceworthy (choosable *by me*). In that sense, one gives a real though as yet limited assent of will to that option (while not yet preferring it to others by choosing to adopt it).

IV. TREATING AN OPTION AS ACCEPTABLE: *CONSENSUS*

In his analysis of deliberate action, St Thomas reserved a place for an act of will whereby one assents to a definite proposal for action yet without making a choice; he called this assent *consensus*. It is a sort of willing: one is minded, disposed, willing to treat some means, X, as acceptable. Very often some alternative option, Y, is also acceptable; one has not yet adopted (and may in fact never adopt) either X or Y in preference to the

[36] Cf. Minucius Felix, *Octavius* (c. 190/220 AD), 35, 6:

You forbid adultery, yet you do it. We [Christians], however, are known as men only to our wives. You punish crimes when they have been committed. With us, it is a sin even to consider [*cogitare*] a crime. You fear witnesses. We fear even our own conscience, which we cannot escape.

other.[37] In this common case, *consensus* is distinct *re* [in reality] as well as *ratione* [conceptually] from *electio*, choice.[38] But in any case what makes the *consensus* is not simply the judgment that X (and Y) would be an effective way of securing some benefit in which one is interested, but the treating of X (and/or Y) as an acceptable option, the being interested in an option as one which I will keep in play as a live option notwithstanding that there remain incompatible alternatives in which I remain likewise interested.

As a real disposition, consent can be a mortally sinful acceptance of a possible option even though, not having chosen to do it, one does not intend, even conditionally, to do it. But Aquinas's formal account of consent uses the term *placet* for what I have called 'treating as acceptable',[39] and his later discussion of sinful *consensus* goes off on a particular type of case where one takes a kind of sensory pleasure, *delectatio*, in imagining and savouring some possible action.[40] That is not the issue in considering reluctant but real willingness to commit acts of injustice. Then many neo-scholastics confused matters pretty thoroughly by proposing a schema of action in which *consensus* precedes (rather than, as in St Thomas, follows) reason's judgment that such-and-such an option (specific means) is available and suitable for some end in which one is interested.[41] Thus it became all too easy to lose sight of the fact that one's assent to some option yet unchosen may (like some choices) be accompanied by very strong feelings of repugnance, and may be an assent only to what one supposes is the lesser of great evils—and yet be a wrongdoing (as yet in one's heart)[42] which one must repent of while one can.

[37] *ST* I–II q.15 a.3.

[38] *Ibid.*, a.3 ad 3:

si inveniatur unum solum quod placeat, non differunt *re* consensus et electio, sed *ratione* tantum: ut consensus dicatur secundum quod placet ad agendum; electio autem, secundum quod praefertur his quae non placent. [If only one [proposed course of action] is found acceptable, consensus and choice are not distinct in reality, though they are distinct in concept since here one can say that there is consenting, in that the proposed course of action is [found] acceptable, or that there is choosing, in that this course of action is being preferred to those found unacceptable.]

[39] *Ibid.* [40] I–II q.74 a.7; cf. aa. 6 and 8. [41] See essay 9, sec. I.

[42] Cf. the commentary of Peter de Scala OP (interpolated into Aquinas's *Commentary* [*Reportatio*] *on St Matthew's Gospel* and long ascribed to Aquinas), commenting on Mt 5: 28 ('Anyone who looks on a woman to lust after her has committed adultery with her already in his heart'); de Scala explains that the text says 'to lust after her' (rather than directly 'with a view to committing adultery') so as to teach that not only the bad deed, and *consensus* to the bad deed, are wrong but also the *intentio* or *consensus* to taking pleasure [in the bad deed]. And he notes the explanation offered by Augustine and Jerome, that the phrase is equivalent to 'so that he may look at her in order inwardly to lust after doing it [adultery] *if* the opportunity were to present itself' (*idest ut eam eo fine videat ut faceret si facultas se offeret*). Thus the tradition treats intention and *consensus* as morally in like case, and explains a paradigm of immoral sins of thought on the model of conditional intention.

V. PREPARATORY INTENT IN BRITISH NUCLEAR DETERRENCE

'If a policy is one that it would be wicked to execute, then it is also wicked to counsel it and wicked to make plans for executing it.'[43] Of course, one who counsels intends to be taken as commending the formation of an intention. And the obvious meaning of 'to make plans for executing a policy' is: to take the preliminary steps towards carrying out a present (even if conditional) intention. But, as Geach noted in the same place, some defended the morality of the deterrent on the score that 'the policy' they were 'counselling' was no more than: to give the appearance of having a policy the execution of which would involve mass murder. And others said the policy was no more than: to keep our options open, though without the slightest commitment to the murderous option which we would be in a *position* to choose 'on the day'. So there remained room for debate about the applicability of the premise which Geach had articulated for judging the morality of the nuclear deterrent. Gradually the debate shifted to the question of the (conditional) intentions involved in any credible deterrent policy, and Geach's premise came to be articulated more commonly as the 'wrongful *intentions* principle': what it would be wicked to do it is wicked to intend (even conditionally).

All serious attempts to show reason for rejecting or qualifying the wrongful intentions principle have proved, hitherto, to depend upon consequentialist premises, and thus to be as radically unsound as the consequentialist theory of moral judgment.[44] Equally, any supposition that the nuclear deterrents maintained by modern states are or may be a bluff has been shown to be not merely factually groundless but also, surprising as this may seem, logically impossible.[45] But analysis of actual public policies of deterrence shows that the British policy (unlike those of France or the United States) has involved something short of the straightforward, substantive conditional intention to do X if C—to carry out (inevitably murderous)[46] city swaps or final retaliation if our cities are attacked. Instead, British policy has involved a preparatory intent[47] like the intent in the preparations of the adulterous bridegroom and the murderous abused woman.

The decision made in adopting and/or participating in the policy is no more—and no less—than to treat such deeds as 'open', 'real' options. This is not a matter of 'making plans' in the way a staff college may draw up plans

[43] Geach, 'Conscience in Commission' at 92.

[44] The *locus classicus* is Kavka, 'Some Paradoxes of Deterrence'. For the consequentialist character of Kavka's argument, see *NDMR* 79n, 180–2, 244–6, 251–67.

[45] *NDMR* 113–23, 128–31.

[46] *Ibid.*, chs IV and VI.

[47] *Ibid.*, 6–11, 31–3, 57–8.

as an exercise in practising a technical skill. It is a matter of (in Geach's phrase) making plans *for forming* (*and executing*) an intention which, if it were ever formed, would be to murder. Its multi-layered conditionality of content does distinguish a deterrent policy such as the British from a mantrap or a doomsday machine (a fully automated system for inevitable massive retaliation), and from the (un)conditional intention expressed in classic US or French policies. The British policy nonetheless has involved consenting, however reluctantly, to the two strategically essential but inevitably murderous elements of a coherent deterrent: the carrying out of city swaps (in an effort to cap escalation and deter further attacks on our civilians), and the unleashing of a final retaliation against enemy societies (if ever we 'have nothing more to lose'). The question whether to *call* such assent or willingness (to murder) a *conditional intent* (to murder) is a quite secondary issue to be settled, if you will, by stipulation.[48]

[48] As we do in *ibid.*, 80, 82 ('For in a moral analysis, what matters is not the word "intention", but the reality of the will to act, even if there are conditions to be fulfilled'), 99–100.

13

'DIRECT' AND 'INDIRECT' IN ACTION*

I

The adjectives 'direct' and 'indirect' have been used in some documents of the Catholic Church's teaching authority to qualify nouns referring to certain ways in which one brings about bad outcomes. Those adjectives are used to distinguish cases in which an acting person intends the bad outcome either as an end or as a means[1] from cases in which the moral agent, in doing some other, morally upright action, only accepts the bad outcome as its side effect. Rather than using 'direct' and 'indirect', it seems preferable to speak of what is *intended* and what is *accepted as a side effect*,[2] and we shall usually do so here.

To understand this distinction, one should begin by considering free choices and the actions that carry them out. Those are good or bad—in the first instance good or bad for the human persons who shape themselves by making such choices and carrying them out. Groups of persons also deliberate and act, and their actions affect and shape them too. Of course, each individual who participates in the communal action will in doing so make his or her own free choices.

Moral good and evil are a matter of whether and how fully or deficiently these choices are reasonable, that is to say, in accord with fully reasonable judgments about what is to be done or avoided.[3]

* 2001a (with Germain Grisez and Joseph Boyle).

[1] See e.g. *CCC* 2271; John Paul II, encyclical *Evangelium Vitae*, 25 March 1995, no. 62: 'direct abortion'. A primary source for these and other recent documents, on this point, is the set of statements of Pius XII cited in *Evangelium Vitae* no. 62 at n. 66 [and see essay 9, n. 55].

[2] See Grisez, *Living a Christian Life*, 473–4.

[3] Of course, this statement must be qualified. People's capacities to judge correctly what to do and to exercise their freedom in acting on their judgment can be more or less limited in various ways. So, a person's moral quality depends on his or her self-determination in relation to his or her capacity to act reasonably. Thus a person whose capacity to act reasonably is limited may be a good person even while determining himself or herself to an act of a kind that is wrong and would never be done by a good person free of those limitations. For that reason, Catholic moral theology and pastoral practice have recognized the difference between the 'subjective' good and evil of persons and their choices, on the one hand, and, on the other, the 'objective' good and evil of actions measured

Before children can make free choices, emotional motivations attract them to, or avert them from, certain possibilities, and motivations of this sort are still operative in one's adult life. As one becomes capable of being motivated by reasons, one enters the moral domain by reasoning about what to do, by more or less integrating one's emotional motivations with each other and with reasons, and by more or less reasonably making free choices. But what is it to have a reason for action by which one might thus be motivated and guided towards choice? Essentially, it is to understand the intelligible connection between some benefit by which one, and/or others, could be fulfilled and some action(s) that one anticipates could involve or bring about that benefit.

Choice is between alternatives. Both emotional and rational motives suggest possible purposes that seem to be within one's power to achieve in a certain way or ways. In one's deliberating about what to do, one considers both the proposal to pursue this purpose in this way for the sake of this benefit, and the alternative proposal to pursue the same purpose in a different way, or to pursue an alternative purpose for the same or some other benefit. One has to choose just because there are these alternative proposals—alternative options—including the proposal to do nothing.

The ideas introduced and linked with one another in the preceding three paragraphs make possible the understanding of actions as morally significant. In making that understanding possible, they also make possible a proper understanding of the words, concepts, and realities with which moral and legal analysis is centrally concerned, not only in Judaeo-Christian but also (as will be shown) in widely different cultural contexts: intention, choice, and foresight; ends, means, and side effects.

The most perspicuous way of getting clear about these words, concepts, and realities is to consider some examples of proposals (options), choices adopting them, and actions carrying out those choices.

Case A A boy with money to buy Friday lunch sees a beautiful airplane in a shop window. He thinks about the alternatives: buy lunch to satisfy his

by unqualified practical reasonableness. This distinction can also be marked—though we do not recommend this way of speaking—by reserving the adjectives *good* and *evil* to qualify persons and choices, and the adjectives *right* and *wrong* to qualify choices and actions. Of course, the good and the right, the evil and the wrong, are sometimes distinguished in ways that we regard as inconsistent with sound morality and pastoral practice. For example, Keenan, *Goodness and Rightness in Thomas Aquinas's* Summa Theologiae, 173–4 holds that acts commanded by charity or 'benevolence' 'are good, though not necessarily right'—indeed, are good even if wrong—and that 'the defect in rightness does not affect' the description of the act as morally good. Again, some Christian theologians maintain that practical reasonableness sometimes requires an upright person in this fallen world to commit a sin—i.e., to do what is truly wrong. Such ways of distinguishing good from right and evil from wrong separate right and wrong from the basic human good of practical reasonableness and the moral virtue of *prudentia*—something traditional Catholic moral theology and pastoral practice never allowed.

hunger *versus* buy the plane to play with at the weekend. He foresees that if he buys the plane he will be hungry that afternoon, and that if he buys lunch he will have to do without the weekend fun. He chooses to buy the plane for the sake of the weekend fun; the intended end (purpose) is the weekend fun, the chosen means is buying the plane. Being hungry follows inevitably; it is a foreseen side effect. It is a *side effect* precisely because it was not part of the proposal he adopted, to *buy the plane for the sake of weekend fun*, just as going without the weekend fun was no part of the proposal he did not adopt, to *buy lunch to avoid hunger*.

Case B A man with high blood pressure is offered a drug to lower it. Taking this drug has what everyone calls side effects; some of these are very rare but lethal. He knows about these side effects, but chooses to take the drug, realizing that he is incurring some risk of earlier death; and, as it happens, he dies of one of the drug's rare side effects. In choosing to take the medication, he adopted the proposal of using it to lower his blood pressure for the purpose of living longer, but accepted the side effect: the (low) probability of dying from the effects of the drug. Though he foresaw and brought about the risk he accepted, running that risk was no part of his intention—the purpose he was trying to achieve and the means he chose for achieving it.

Case C A man at a party considers three proposals: to stay over and (uncomfortably) sleep on the sofa, to call a (costly) cab, or to drive (woozily) home. To get home cheaply he drives; risking running someone down is a side effect of his choice, and as it happens he runs someone down. This disaster is a further side effect of his choice. He is responsible for that side effect. That is to say, he should have taken such an effect into account and made the reasonable choice of one or other of the alternatives. But if his hostess has had a heart attack and, to get her to hospital, he accepts the same risk by driving in the same condition, his choice to drive may well be reasonable.

Case D A woman has decided to give testimony at her brother's trial, although she is acutely conscious of her uncontrollable stutter. Her purpose is to help her brother get justice, her means of helping is giving evidence, and a side effect is publicly stuttering. This side effect is an inseparable part of the woman's performance; her speaking is always stuttering. But that side effect is unwanted in itself; indeed, it is a side effect that obstructs her purpose in testifying (because it distracts and perhaps annoys the jury). Stuttering is not included in her intentions. She chooses and tries *to speak* as well as she can. She does not choose *to stutter*; indeed, she does her best not to.

Case E A farmer castrates male calves in order to change their hormonal constitution and thereby make them fat and manageable. He accepts that this will make them sterile, and if he did not find it more profitable to fatten and calm them all he would keep some unsterilized for breeding (instead of hiring bulls for breeding in season). Nothing in the *behaviour* he does perform differentiates *sterilizing the calves by castrating them* from *fattening and calming them by castrating them*. But the proposal to fatten is quite distinct from any proposal to sterilize. So, although the *performance* is sterilizing (as anyone would say who looks just at the performance and its physical effects), any question as to what is included in the farmer's proposal is not settled by reference to his behaviour. Indeed, since sterilizing (achieving a state of infertility) is for the farmer neither end (purpose) nor means, it is not included in the proposal he adopts, is not what he chooses, and for the purposes of an account of human action is not what he is *doing*.

The analysis of choice and action applies, as we have said, to groups' acts as well as individuals' acts. (Indeed, talk of 'proposals' is adapted from the realm of deliberative assemblies.) So the next two cases we shall consider happen to be group acts but could equally have been the acts of a powerful individual.

Case F A majority of the members of a club vote for a motion to commend an outgoing president, unpopular with some. In doing so, they accept the side effect of antagonizing the minority. In voting—choosing to commend the president—they carry out the behaviour that constitutes the act of commending her and achieve their purpose in doing so.

Case G A company's directors deliberate about a proposal to shut down the production line for January and an alternative proposal to shut it down in May. Production must be halted for a month, for retooling. For production purposes, May would be much the best month; for short-term financial purposes, January would be marginally better. But closing in January would also have the effect of nipping unionization in the bud, whereas closing in May would have the effect of giving the unions time to organize and impose unwelcome demands on the company. If the directors choose to *shut down the line in January* with a view to nipping unionization in the bud, their intention is not only to shut down the line and to retool but also to nip unionization in the bud—preventing unionization is no mere side effect. If short-term financial gain was not part of the directors' reasons for their decision, they do not intend it. Though they foresee it and will welcome it, it remains a side effect. That being so, if they learn that this time there will be no short-term financial gain, they will see no reason to reconsider their decision. If the directors choose to *close for retooling in May* for production purposes, the enhanced unionization is an unwelcome side effect.

Case H A spy, horrified that his house guest has become aware of his treason, deliberates about what is necessary to ensure her silence. Though wanting her continuing companionship, he very reluctantly decides to kill her. He takes her to a lovely rural spot and with feelings of great regret pushes her over a cliff. Retching with disgust at himself, he checks to make sure she is dead and then, as planned, reports the 'accident'. While his intention, in the sense of the purpose for the sake of which he acts, is to ensure her silence, that is not all he intends. He also intends precisely what he chooses: to kill his companion. Her death cannot be regarded as a side effect. His repugnance, regret, and remorse do not make it any less the case that he intends to kill her.

Though the preceding examples could be multiplied indefinitely, even these eight alone provide enough data to show that the theory of action discussed in this essay is sound, and is applicable across the whole range of choices and actions quite independently of moral judgments about their goodness or badness, rightness or wrongness.

Case A makes it clear that an action carries out a proposal adopted by choice, and that one intends[4] both to carry out that proposal and to achieve the purpose for the sake of which one adopts it. This case also makes it clear that one's actions have unintended side effects, in as much as some of the foreseen and inevitable consequences of one's intentional behaviour are nevertheless not intended.

Case B reinforces the point that, when one knowingly brings about bad effects in carrying out some choice, one need not intend them. Even though one both foresees and causes them, one does not choose them; one only accepts them—indeed freely accepts them.

Case C makes it clear that when one's action has foreseen but unintended side effects, one has moral responsibility in respect to accepting them. But since not all the moral criteria applicable to intending to do something apply to accepting bad side effects, one can sometimes reasonably accept something that it would be wrong to bring about intentionally.

Case D makes it clear that a side effect need not be causally consequent upon the performance that carries out one's choice. Even an integral part of the behaviour by which one carries out a choice can be a side effect, and such a side effect can even precede the part of the behaviour that constitutes one's intended act, and all the more so can precede the effects for the sake of which one is acting.

Case E makes it clear that, depending on what one proposes to do and what one only accepts as a side effect, one can be doing either of two acts

[4] Common language (like Aquinas: see n. 22 below) talks of 'intention' in two different ways: (1) that for the sake of which one does X; or (2) doing X-for-the-sake-of-that. See e.g. *Aquinas* 166.

different in kind even though everything about one's behaviour and the *observable* context is the same.

Case F makes it clear that the structure of actions articulated by our analysis is found even in a case where one and the same behaviour is at once the choosing of the act, the doing of the act, and the realizing of the purpose for which it is done. Despite the unity of all the analytically distinct factors that constitute it, this moral act has a side effect really distinct from itself.

Case G makes it clear that foreseen and welcome effects of what one is doing, effects that could have been reasons for acting, need not be intended even if one chooses precisely as one would if one did intend them. Foreseen effects of what one does are intended only if they actually are among one's reasons for acting. If they are not, they are part of neither the proposal one adopts in choosing nor the purpose(s) for the sake of which one chooses: they are part of neither the means nor the end(s).

Case H makes it clear that intentions are constituted by acting persons' reasons for making their choices and by precisely what they choose to do, not by what they feel, or would like, or are reluctant or eager to do, or regret the 'necessity' of doing.

The preceding cases also illustrate some of the many ways employed in common speech to refer to intentions and the intentional. These ways include not only the cognates of 'intend', but such phrases as 'for the sake of', 'for the purpose of', 'with the object/purpose/aim/goal of', 'in order to', 'so as to', 'with a view to' (at least as we hear and use that phrase), and often enough plain 'to'—as well as other terms. The fact that in this sort of context people easily and accurately communicate, using so many different expressions synonymously, at least suggests that the concepts of intention and side effects are sound and precise, and that what all these terms signify are indeed realities. Moreover, the many formal and informal words and phrases just listed—like their counterparts in the idioms of other languages—all refer one to the relations we have been outlining, relations whose *terms* are captured in the more static-seeming idiom of philosophy: 'end(s)', 'means', 'intentions', 'choices', and 'unintended effects', or (synonymously) 'side effects'.

Realities, even the human realities of deliberation and action, need not be reflectively understood by those who engage in them. The understanding and analysis of intention, choice, and action has undoubtedly reached its greatest clarity in Christian reflection guided by the firm Judaeo-Christian recognition of free choice. But even cultures not shaped by that recognition have more or less clearly acknowledged the reality of intention, its distinction from certain other realities, and its significance for the moral and therefore the legal assessment of conduct.

During the nineteenth and early twentieth centuries many scholars claimed that the ancients had little or no understanding of, or interest in, the distinctions between the intended and the unintended (whether negligent, truly accidental, or foreseen and reluctantly accepted). This common view about ancient thought exaggerates the distance between the later, Christian clarity and earlier, less differentiated thought. The exaggerated form of this modern view about ancient thought has been plausibly contested, notably by David Daube, the Jewish biblicist and historian of Roman law. A few quotations from Daube's review of the evidence[5] suggest its force:

> There is not a single case in the whole of Greek literature—myth, saga, history—or, for that matter, in the Bible, of a man who killed without intent being put to death, be it in the course of self-help, blood-vengeance, be it by public authority; and this although there are laws that (as I just remarked)[6] objectivize *dolus* [wrongful intent] and impose the death-penalty, say, on killing by a direct blow. Not a single case: let that fact sink in.[7]
>
> I repeat: the sources—Oriental, Greek, Roman—offer not one example of an unintentional killer being killed. I do not, of course, count the cases where the prevalent doctrine says, Ah yes, but he would have been killed were it not for such and such special circumstances. I want to be shown one instance where he is killed: surely a modest request. If the prevalent view is right, there ought to be hundreds...[8]

So ancient thought and practice did attend to intent, and distinguished among actions' effects—for example, death brought about intentionally or not intentionally. The latter, of course, includes death brought about accidentally or carelessly, but also includes death brought about as a foreseen side effect in carrying out a choice to do something else.

A similar understanding can be observed in modern, secular legal thought. Legal thinkers influenced by utilitarianism's characteristic denial

[5] See esp. Daube, *Roman Law*, 157–75.

[6] See *ibid.*, 164:

> It is a dogma that, in dealing with homicide, not only does early law equate the unwitting doer with the witting, but this course is taken from blindness or indifference to what separates the two. In reality, full equation occurs much more rarely than the prevalent view has it, and where it does occur it is a *pis aller*, resorted to because of the insurmountable practical obstacles in the way of determining which side of the line a given case falls: by treating as a murderer, say, anyone who kills by a direct blow or anyone who kills with a piece of iron, justice is done in the vast majority of incidents though, now and then, an innocent person gets trapped. The alternative would be for the law to abdicate altogether. In the *Pentateuch* both stages—death to whoever kills by a direct blow and death to whoever kills with a piece of iron—are preserved [footnote: '*Exodus*, 21.12, *Numbers*, 35.16—in their original setting, as yet unprovided with the reservations which in the text before us modify them.']. The latter statute is part of a legislation avowedly concerned with confining the rigor of the law to those who deserve it. But the former too is designed to get at *dolus* [wrongful intent]—the *dolus* being objectivized, established by the external situation.

[7] *Roman Law*, 165. [8] *Ibid.*, 174.

of free choice often argue that the law's typical concern with externally observable performances and their consequences is justified by the purpose of reducing overall net social harm. A notable element in this outlook is the claim, launched by Bentham and vigorously defended by some recent legal theorists, that consequences foreseen as certain or highly probable are intended. But even the leading proponents of this view have found themselves obliged to accept that intention is a reality quite distinguishable, as a specific kind of fact, from the 'intent' which may, by a legal fiction, be imputed to someone who acts or omits while being aware—or in a position to be aware—that harm will very probably be caused by the action or omission. And there are today important areas of law in which the fiction—that consequences foreseen as very probable are intended—is simply rejected or strictly contained. As the US Supreme Court noted in 1980 and reaffirmed in 1997:

> The...common law of homicide often distinguishes...between a person who *knows* that another person *will be* killed as the result of his conduct and a person who acts with the specific purpose of taking another's life.[9]

To be sure, neither present day law nor Christian teaching and reflection deny or overlook that one is morally responsible for outcomes of one's action that are outside one's intention. The case of the drunk driver (*Case C*) illustrates one way in which *side effects* that are foreseen or should be foreseen and have an impact on human well-being are morally significant and not outside the acting person's responsibility. But that case also indicates how accepting such outcomes, or the risk of such outcomes, precisely as *side effects*, is subject to moral (or legal) norms different from the moral (or legal) norms that bear on intended outcomes. The woozy driver is not responsible for the death in the way he would be if he chose (intended) to kill the victim. His accepting, however knowingly and willingly, of the risk to the victim is assessed under the moral and legal norms of negligence, not the moral and legal norms forbidding intentional homicide.

To say that not all the moral criteria applicable to what one chooses to do are applicable to accepting side effects is not to say that the latter is always less serious or culpable. Where a hospital doctor knows he must give a certain patient medication by midnight or she will die, but chooses to go

[9] *United States v Bailey* 444 US 394 at 405 (1980) (judgment of the Court) (emphasis added); the quoted proposition is reaffirmed in the more extensive review in *Vacco v Quill* 521 US 793 at 802 (1997) (judgment of the Court), which concludes with a quotation from an earlier judicial opinion in a lower federal court: 'When General Eisenhower ordered American soldiers onto the beaches of Normandy, he knew that he was sending many American soldiers to certain death...His purpose, though, was to...liberate Europe from the Nazis.' So he had no intent to kill Allied soldiers. The death of his soldiers was only a foreseen side effect, reasonably accepted in accord with what Catholic theologians have often called the principle of double effect (a 'principle' to which the Supreme Court's judgment in *Vacco v Quill* alludes with apparent assent at 808 n. 11).

out and complete an extremely profitable business deal that must be done by midnight (reasoning that no one will know he gave the medication later provided he gives it before the patient dies), he is guilty of manslaughter by very gross negligence (or 'recklessness'). And that homicide may well be a graver sin than, say, a store-keeper's killing a mobster who is subjecting her to extortion.[10]

II

In describing and analysing the cases set out in the preceding section, we adopted the perspective of the acting person or body. In morally evaluating human actions, one must identify the action to be evaluated from that perspective rather than from the perspective of an observer. Indeed, the perspective of the acting person or body is to be taken even in those contexts (such as *Case C*) where the focus of analysis and assessment is not intention to harm but rather some failure to meet a standard such as the standard of due care or some similar moral requirement.

Many theorists, even when discussing actions in the context of moral assessment, do not adopt and steadily maintain the perspective of the acting person, and many do not adopt it at all. They consider actions, behaviour, and outcomes from, so to speak, the outside—from the perspective of a spectator—in which primary or exclusive attention is given to causal relationships. Such displacement or abandonment of the acting person's deliberative perspective was common among Catholic manualists of moral theology: see sec. III below. The observer's perspective can be adopted in other ways, for instance by trying to understand action by reference to 'a variety of factors',[11] or to various 'contexts of meaning',[12] or to outcomes thought to be assessable by comparing the proportions of human good and bad in them. This last displacement of the perspective of the acting

[10] The moral evaluation of side effects is important and difficult, and not yet sufficiently studied in Catholic moral theology. An effort to do some of the necessary work is made in Grisez, *Difficult Moral Questions*, apps 1 and 2.

[11] See essay III.18 (1973b) at 298: 'A variety of factors are appealed to explicitly or relied on implicitly in making a judgment that the bad effect is to count as intended-as-a-means ...' In that essay, Finnis's understanding of intention and action had not reached the precision of, e.g. essay 8 (1987b). [See now the second endnote to essay III.18.]

[12] See e.g. Porter, '"Direct" and "Indirect" in Grisez's Moral Theory' at 631:

> we think of them [sc. our actions] in terms of wider contexts of meaning, some of which reflect the normal causal relationships among different primitive acts, some of which are cultural constructs, and many of which combine both kinds of considerations.

Porter is right in thinking that societies develop action concepts and language to pick out any human behaviour that is interesting for any of a wide variety of reasons. But those reasons often have little or nothing to do with moral evaluation, and often focus upon observable units of behaviour picked out with little or no regard for the perspective of the acting person.

person is characteristic of moralists referred to as 'proportionalists' in the encyclical *Veritatis Splendor*.[13]

So, it was appropriate for that encyclical, in the course of rejecting proportionalism[14] as incompatible with Catholic faith,[15] to affirm the primacy of the internal perspective in the understanding of action for the purposes of moral assessment. Immediately following its formal statement of 'the thesis, characteristic of...proportionalist theories', that is to be rejected by Catholics, the encyclical says: 'The primary and decisive element for moral judgment is the object of the human act.'[16] This statement recalls what was said in the previous section of the encyclical:

> *The morality of the human act depends primarily and fundamentally on the 'object' rationally chosen by the deliberate will*...In order to be able to grasp the object of

[13] In previous writings we have criticized the accounts of action found among proportionalists. See e.g. Grisez, *Christian Moral Principles*, 240 with 248–9 (nn. 5 and 13); Finnis, *MA* 77:

> Christian reflection on God and his holy will, and Christian reflection on the morality of human choosing and doing...advances decisively beyond the undifferentiated concept of 'cause,' replacing it with the act-analytical distinctions between choosing or intending and permitting or accepting. As one reads through the writings of sophisticated proportionalist moralists of the late twentieth century, one sees with amazement that they everywhere lose their grip on the distinction. They have fallen back into the undifferentiated problematic of 'causing' evils (including, of course, the Enlightenment extension of 'cause' to include whatever one could have prevented but did not, a concept incompatible with Christian understanding of divine holiness).

The footnote to this passage reads:

> See, e.g., Bruno Schüller, S.J., 'La moralité des moyens' at 211 (*causing* moral evil is never justified, *causing* nonmoral evils is justified in pursuit of nonmoral good of corresponding importance), 221–22 ('pour tous les biens dont la possession contribue au bien-être de l'homme... [q]uoi que l'on choisisse...les conséquences négatives qui résultent du choix sont un pur moyen en vue des conséquences positives qui en résultent'); Peschke, 'Tragfähigkeit und grenzen des Prinzips der Doppelwirkung'...at 110–12, where Peschke states the 'principle of double effect' (which he ascribes to Catholic theology and attacks) in terms not of what is directly or indirectly willed or intended or chosen or done but in terms of what is directly/indirectly 'caused'; Fuchs, *Christian Ethics in a Secular Arena*, 85 ('prohibitive moral norms which forbid an act because it causes a pre-moral wrong ...').

[14] The rejection of proportionalism in John Paul II, encyclical *Veritatis Splendor*, 6 August 1993, does not depend upon the encyclical's description of it in nos 74–6, but is found rather in its formal (and repeated) condemnation of

> the thesis, characteristic of teleological and proportionalist theories, which holds that it is impossible to qualify as morally evil according to its species—its 'object'—the deliberate choice of certain kinds of behavior or specific acts, apart from a consideration of the intention for which the choice is made or the totality of the foreseeable consequences of that act for all persons concerned. (No. 79; verbatim in no. 82.)

Notice that in that sentence, 'intention' is used in the sense in which the acting person's end [further or ultimate purpose] is distinguished from his or her chosen means—the act's object, also described (indeed, defined) in no. 78 as the acting person's 'proximate end'. In a wider sense of 'intention', which we generally use, both what one does and all the ends for the sake of which one does it are intended.

[15] See *Veritatis Splendor* no. 29 ('some trends of theological thinking and certain philosophical affirmations are incompatible with revealed truth'). The Pope's grounds for his judgment that the theories dealt with in the encyclical, including proportionalism, are incompatible with Catholic faith are to be found e.g. at the end of no. 52 and in the places where he repeatedly uses Scripture (see nos 48, 78–81 quoting Romans 3: 8 and I Cor. 6: 9–10) to verify teachings with which dissenting theories are incompatible. See also Grisez, 'Revelation versus Dissent'.

[16] *Veritatis Splendor* no. 79; likewise no. 82; see n. 14 above.

an act which specifies that act morally, it is therefore necessary to place oneself *in the perspective of the acting person.*[17]

That last sentence is of decisive importance. It is philosophically sound,[18] even if its roots, for the purposes of its affirmation in an encyclical, are firmly embedded in revelation's confirmation of the centrality of conscience, of the heart, the 'within'[19] from which come forth actions good and bad.

The importance of the perspective of the acting person was vividly emphasized in Aquinas's refutation, in one telling paragraph, of two twelfth-century currents in moral theology that, in different ways, failed to recognize the proper significance of the object of the act understood from the perspective of the acting person. The issues are so clearly framed in that debate that it is worth summarizing.[20]

In the second quarter of the twelfth century, Peter Abelard had argued, ambiguously, that behaviour is morally indifferent and the morality of acts depends entirely on *intention.* He was widely understood as denying that there are exceptionless, non-tautologous negative norms. So representatives of the tradition responded. Within a decade or two, Peter Lombard's *Sentences* attacked Abelard's position by contrasting it with passages from Augustine's treatises against lying, interpreted by Lombard as teaching that the acts specified in the exceptionless negative norms of Jewish and Christian tradition are called wrong 'in themselves' (*mala in se*) precisely because—Lombard contended—their wrongfulness does *not* come from the purpose, will, intention, or motivation of the person who does them.

In a single paragraph Aquinas refutes both Abelard (as widely understood) and Peter Lombard. There are indeed, he says, acts each of which is wrong in itself and cannot in any way be rightly done (*de se malus,*

[17] *Veritatis Splendor* no. 78 (emphasis in original). The phrases omitted in this quotation refer to the 'insightful analysis, still valid' in *ST* I–II q.18 a.6.

[18] See *NDMR* 292–3; Boyle, 'Who Is Entitled to Double Effect?' at 486–92; and essays 10 (1991b) and 11 (1995a). Note: some people say that the authors of the present essay, or two or one of them, are significantly responsible for the content of *Veritatis Splendor* (see e.g. McCormick, 'Some Early Reactions to *Veritatis Splendor*' at 486: 'I (along with others) see [Finnis's] hands at work in Chapter 2 [of the encyclical] ...'). So we take the opportunity to say: (a) none of us was at any stage asked to draft anything for the document; (b) Grisez (but not Finnis) was among those asked for suggestions in November 1987, and was asked to comment on the whole first draft in April 1989 and on the second draft of Part II in January 1990, and Finnis assisted him in preparing his comments, but after his response dated 6 February 1990 Grisez was not asked to do anything more, and (like Finnis) had no communication about the work with anyone involved in it during the subsequent 42 months before its signing on 6 August 1993; (c) in making suggestions and comments, we very firmly adhered to our view that nothing peculiar to our thought should appear in an encyclical; (d) Grisez did propose language on a number of points, but virtually none of this language and few of his substantive suggestions—and of these none involved in our disputes with dissenting Catholic moralists—appear in the encyclical; (e) while there are some important points in the encyclical that more or less coincide with views defended by Grisez (notably the treatment of faith as the fundamental option) or by all of us (notably the teaching about fundamental goods), we did not propose that the encyclical make these points and were pleasantly surprised to find them when the encyclical appeared.

[19] See Mark 7: 20–3. [20] See also *MA* 65–7; *Aquinas* 165–6.

qui nullo modo bene fieri potest). But such acts are wrongful precisely by reason of the acting person's will, intention, purpose. When I do such an act, there may be nothing wrong with my further intentions, my *voluntas intendens*, my ultimate purpose (*finis ultimus*), for example to give money to the poor. What is wrongful (and what is picked out for exclusion by the relevant negative norm) is, rather, my choice, my *electio* or *voluntas eligens*, my immediate purpose (*obiectum proximum*; *finis proximus*), for example to forge this document. The goodness or badness, rightness or wrongness, of my 'exterior act' (that is, everything I do to carry out my choice) depends on the goodness or badness, rightness or wrongness, of all my relevant willing: intending ends, choosing means, and accepting side effects.[21]

Aquinas's references to 'proximate' and 'further' objects clarify the issue, both substantially and terminologically (and are echoed in *Veritatis Splendor*). Terminologically one can—and Aquinas not rarely does—call both proximate and remote objects *intended* or *the intention(s)*.[22] But equally one can mark—and Aquinas more often does mark—the distinction between proximate and further objects by calling the former the 'chosen object' (or simply the 'object') and the latter the 'intended end' (or simply the 'intention'). The reason why both the broader and the narrower senses of 'intention' are appropriate is that the distinction between proximate and further objectives is highly relative. *Every* means one adopts in the pursuit of some end will also be an end whenever there is a prior means—one closer in to the agent. Take Aquinas's standard example: in the sequence going to the cupboard, to get herbs, to mix a potion, to slim, to stay healthy..., each element is both an end relative to any preceding element and a means relative to any further element.[23] Speaking of 'intention' in a broader sense, one can say that each element or phase in the sequence is intended (or an intention of the acting person). Or one can speak of 'intention' in a narrower sense, and distinguish closer-in from further-out ends, reserving the term

[21] *Sent.* II d.40 a.2c and ad 2 and ad 3; and see *De Malo* q.2 a.2 ad 8. Note Aquinas's thesis (*Sent.* II d.40 a.3c) that

> because the exterior act stands to the will as *object*, the interior act of will has its goodness from the exterior—though not, of course, from the exterior act as a performance but from the exterior act precisely as intended and willed [quia actus exterior comparatur ad voluntatem sicut objectum, inde est quod hanc bonitatem voluntatis actus interior ab exteriori habet, non quidem ex eo secundum quod est exercitus sed secundum quod est intentus et volitus...]

[22] e.g. *ST* II–II q.64 a.7c; *In Matt.* 7 ad v. 17 [no. 661]. The distinction between the two senses of 'intention' is clearly articulated in *De Malo* q.2 a.2 ad 8, as is the applicability of the broader sense in which means *qua* chosen are included, along with end(s), in 'my intention'. [See p. 167 above.]

> [23] It is not only the ultimate end, for the sake of which the agent acts, that is called *end* in relation to what precedes it: *each* of the intermediate means which are between the primary agent and the ultimate end is called an end in relation to what precedes it (*omnia intermedia quae sunt inter primum agens et ultimum finem dicuntur finis respectu praecedentium*).

(*In Meta.* V.2 n.9 [no. 771]; also *In Phys.* II.5 n.6 [no. 181]; *ST* I–II, q.1 a.3 ad 3; essay 9, sec. II.)

'intention' for the latter. *Veritatis Splendor* uses 'intention' in the narrower way to signify purposes *beyond* that object which 'is the proximate end of a deliberate act of willing on the part of the acting person'.[24]

And in a brief passage (not unlike that in which Aquinas deals at once with Abelard and Lombard), the encyclical rejects both proportionalist overlooking of the specifying significance of object *and* a misunderstanding rather like Lombard's of the actions prohibited by the tradition's exceptionless moral norms:

By the object of a given moral act, then, one cannot mean a process or an event of the merely physical order, to be assessed on the basis of its ability to bring about a given state of affairs in the outside world. Rather, that object is the proximate end of a deliberate decision which determines the act of willing on the part of the acting person.[25]

Employing the contrast between a 'proximate' end (object) and a further end (intention)—the same contrast Aquinas employs in his critique of Abelard and Lombard—the encyclical then articulates its central affirmation: it is possible, as revelation and tradition teach,

to qualify as morally evil according to its species—its 'object'—the deliberate choice of certain kinds of behavior or specific acts, apart from a consideration of the intention for which the choice is made or the totality of the foreseeable consequences of that act for all persons concerned.[26]

Here, as we said, the encyclical uses the term 'intention' in its narrower sense, as contrasted with 'object' (as *end* is contrasted with *means*). But since almost every means can be at the same time an end relative to means still more proximate to the acting person's behaviour, the broader use of 'intention' to include both means and end is also well established in the tradition. This broader sense is particularly common, and apposite, when the issue for moral analysis is not whether something good is being done for bad motives (or, as in *Veritatis Splendor* no. 79, something bad for good motives), but whether an outcome is intended—is part of the chosen (adopted) proposal—or rather is a side effect. Since that is the main issue in questions about the permissibility of using force, even lethal force, to defend oneself or others, it is not surprising to find Aquinas framing his solution to that problem in terms of 'intention' rather than 'object':

Nothing prevents a single act having two effects, only one of which is intended (*in intentione*) while the other is a side effect (*praeter intentionem*: outside the intention). Now: morally significant acts get their species (*recipiunt speciem*) according to what is intended, not what is a side effect (since the latter is incidental/collateral

[24] *Veritatis Splendor* no. 78. [25] *Ibid.* [26] *Ibid.*, no. 79; verbatim in no. 82.

(*per accidens*)) ...[27] So, from the act of one who is engaged in self-defence there can follow two effects: one, the preservation of the person's own life, and the other the killing of the attacker.[28]

But the point is in no way limited to questions of defence of self or others. Quite generally: 'morally significant acts get their species (*species*) not from what happens as a side effect (*praeter intentionem*), but from precisely what it is that one intends (*per se intentum*)'.[29]

III

Moral theologians in recent centuries intensively discussed the legitimacy of bringing about effects that it would be wrong to intend. They tried to identify conditions under which an act's bad effects would not be part of the act considered as a chosen means. But in trying to do this, they unfortunately failed to adopt and consistently maintain the perspective of the acting person. Rather than focusing on the precise object of the acting person's choice, they focused on cause-effect relationships identifiable by outside observers. So, in trying to explicate the requirement that one's chosen means include nothing bad, they reduced means to cause and said that any bad effect of an act must not be a cause of the good effect(s) for the sake of which it is done. For example, in his treatment of double effect, Henry Davis SJ, at the outset of his manual, says:

> It is permissible to set a cause in motion, in spite of its foreseen evil effect, provided...secondly...that a good effect also issues from the act, at least as immediately and directly as the evil effect, that is to say, provided that the evil effect does not first arise, and from it, the good effect.[30]

This was a mistake. That a bad effect issues from an act more immediately and directly than a good effect, or precedes and causes a good effect, does not by itself make the bad effect a means to the good. A heroic soldier who throws himself on a grenade chooses to use his body as a shield so that the

[27] Here there is a back reference, apparently to *ST* I–II q.72 a.1 and II–II q.43 a.3. Universally: 'morally significant acts (*moralia*) get their species (*species*) not from what happens as a side effect (*per accidens*), outside one's intention (*praeter intentionem*), but from precisely what it is that one intends (*per se intentum*)': II–II q.150 a.2c. Even more generally: 'what is *per se* in human acts and conduct is what is *intended* (*secundum intentionem*)', and what is incidental (*per accidens*) is what is a side effect (*praeter intentionem*): II–II q.37 a.1c; q.38 a.1c.

[28] *ST* II–II q.64 a.7c. The fundamental importance of this article of *ST* is suggested by *CCC* 2263: see further n. 66 below.

[29] *ST* II–II q.150 a.2c. Even more generally, 'what is *per se* in human acts and conduct is what is *intended* (*secundum intentionem*)', and what is incidental (*per accidens*) is what is a side effect (*praeter intentionem*): II–II q.37 a.1c; q.39 a.1c; cf. I–II q.73 a.8c.

[30] Davis, *Moral and Pastoral Theology*, i 13–14.

shrapnel will not kill his fellows. Yet he does not choose his own destruction as a means, even though the effect of throwing himself on the grenade—his body's being destroyed as it absorbs or slows down the shrapnel—is more immediate and direct than, and indeed causes, the good effect of the grenade's doing little or no injury to his fellows. More humdrum examples of the distinction between what one intends (and chooses as a means) and what one causes but only accepts as a side effect are given above, as *Cases A* and *B*, with further refinements in *Cases C* to *G*. The contemporary magisterium relies upon the distinction in a number of its teachings. In *Evangelium Vitae*, for example, it is the basis for distinguishing euthanasia from (a) refusal or forgoing of extraordinary or disproportionate means of treatment, and (b) the use of painkillers 'even when the result is...a shortening of life', on the basis that 'in such a case, death is not willed or sought'.[31]

It will be helpful, we think, to consider closely the emergency obstetrical procedure usually referred to as craniotomy. Taken by itself, the word 'craniotomy' strictly means cutting the cranium.[32] But the procedure in question is an operation that, at least at some times in the past, was thought to be medically indicated when a baby's head was too large to allow normal delivery; and instruments could be used to crush the baby's head (perhaps after emptying its skull) so as to allow the child's removal from the birth canal and the survival of the mother who would otherwise perish in childbirth along with her child. In 1884, the Holy Office stated with papal approval that one cannot safely teach in Catholic educational institutions that this procedure is morally permissible; in 1889 it restated this, adding that one cannot safely teach that 'any surgical operation directly lethal to the fetus or to the pregnant mother' is morally permissible.[33]

[31] *Evangelium Vitae*, no. 65, citing inter alia Pius XII, Address to an International Group of Physicians (24 February 1957) III, *AAS* 49 (1957) 147. Likewise *CCC* 2279. Similarly *Vacco v Quill* 521 US 793 at 808 n. 11 (1997), approving New York State Task Force on Life and the Law, *When Death is Sought: Assisted Suicide and Euthanasia in the Medical Context* (1994) at 163:

> It is widely recognized that the provision of pain medication is ethically and professionally acceptable even when the treatment may hasten the patient's death, if the medication is intended to alleviate pain and severe discomfort, not to cause death.

[32] 'Craniotomy' can refer to very different kinds of act. At least since 1945, in medically advanced environments, the only obstetrical craniotomies are those commonly called 'partial birth abortion', where the operation's purpose is precisely to kill the unborn or partially born child. Those are not the operations discussed as problem cases for Catholic moral theology or doctrine, though reflection on the differences between partial birth abortion and the obstetrical crises discussed in Catholic theology would shed some light on the proper description, understanding, and moral assessment of the crisis cases under discussion here.

[33] *DS* 3258/1889–90. In 1895 the Holy Office stated, with the Pope's approval, that 'in accordance with the rulings of 1884 and 1889' one 'cannot safely undertake' procedures which, to save the life of the mother, seek the premature expulsion of the fetus even if the intention is that the fetus be delivered if possible alive although too premature to survive: *DS* 3298/1890a.

That craniotomy is often thought to be direct killing, and to be morally unacceptable, is readily understandable. A number of points can be made to express or reinforce this thought. (a) Doing a craniotomy surely *just is* killing the baby. Anyone can see what is going on: the baby's destruction and death is observed, not merely foreseen. And (b) killing the baby by crushing its skull does not, itself, help the mother. Saving her depends on the further procedure of removing the baby's corpse from the birth canal. Nor (c) can the killing be said to be unintentional. If someone says to the surgeon 'You're killing the baby', the surgeon cannot credibly reply 'I don't mean to be doing that' or 'I'm not doing it on purpose', as the surgeon can say credibly if removing a gravid cancerous uterus. Moreover (d) in any other context than this obstetrical crisis, the same kind of behaviour would be intentionally killing the baby—what is nowadays called 'partial birth abortion'. (e) This kind of behaviour *never* is done to help the baby. (f) It is repugnant, horrible, and (g) contrary to Church teaching.

Though plausible, these arguments are not sound, and each of them can be refuted.

(a) Considering the behaviour and its results as an event, or sequence of events, or set of causes and effects in the natural world, observers can readily see craniotomy to be killing the baby and rightly describe it as doing so directly. But *Veritatis Splendor* teaches that it is wrong to consider behaviour and its results in that way when carrying out moral reflection and seeking to determine what kind of human act is or was being deliberated about, chosen, and done.

> By the object of a given moral act, one cannot mean a process or an event of the merely physical order, to be assessed on the basis of its ability to bring about a given state of affairs in the outside world.[34]

As Aquinas regularly puts it, the species of a human act, which (when measured by reason's requirements) settles the moral character of the act as good or bad, right or wrong, is not its species *in genere naturae* (in the order

[34] *Veritatis Splendor* no. 78. As no. 79 makes clear, the morally relevant species of the act is determined by—indeed, is essentially equivalent to—its object. There is no *morally relevant* 'nature' of the act other than the species so determined. So May, 'The Management of Ectopic Pregnancies: A Moral Analysis' at 141, is mistaken in thinking that *an act*—as distinct from a piece of behaviour considered as a physical event—can be 'one which of its very nature kills a person' if killing is not included within the proposal adopted by the acting person and so within that person's object. May's assertion, *ibid.*, that 'if I adopt by choice the proposal *to crush the skull and brain of an infant* I simply can not... *not intend the baby's death*' is simply unsupported by argument and, in context, a mere *petitio principii*. His equivalent assertion (*ibid.*) that when my proposal is to blow out someone's brains 'I can not reasonably claim that I did not intend, i.e., choose, to kill that person... [or] that I was adopting by choice a proposal to *stop an unprovoked attack*, i.e. to defend myself by an act of measured force' is contrary to the clear sense of *ST* II–II, q.64, a.7 and to the implications of *Veritatis Splendor* nos 78 and 79, as well as of *CCC* 2263–7 (see n. 66 below).

of nature) but its species *in genere moris* (in the order of human deliberating and choosing).[35] To be faithful to the tradition and to the contemporary magisterium, it is necessary to get beyond one-sided 'commonsense' accounts of 'what is being done'—accounts in which what can be seen, and factors such as causal sequences, are given an unreflective priority over the realities illustrated in sec. I above, realities also, as we saw there, recognizable by commonsense viewing matters from the perspective of the acting person. In the wider secular debate, one-sided appeals to 'common sense' are regularly made to deride the position, affirmed by Pius XII, Paul VI, and John Paul II, that distinguishes between administering analgesics in order to suppress pain while accepting the hastening of death as a side effect, and administering perhaps the very same dose to suppress pain *by* terminating life. The rejection of this and other similar intention-focused distinctions frequently appears in arguments for euthanasia and assisting suicide.

(b) It is true that crushing the baby's skull does not of itself help the mother, and that to help her the surgeon must carry out additional further procedures (remove the baby's body from the birth canal). But many surgical procedures provide no immediate benefit and by themselves are simply destructive: removing the top of someone's skull, stopping someone's heart, and so forth. Proportionalist critics of the tradition frequently claim that all these are cases in which *doing evil* is obviously justifiable as the means to a good end. But when any such surgical procedure, including the obstetrical-crisis craniotomy, is considered not as a mere sequence of movements but as a human act formed by the adoption of a proposal, its moral species becomes clear. More is said about this in sec. IV below.

(c) It is true that a surgeon removing a gravid cancerous uterus might credibly say 'I don't mean to be killing the baby' or 'I'm not killing the baby on purpose'. And, because craniotomy immediately causes the destruction of the baby with impressive physical directness, a surgeon performing a craniotomy would not be likely to say the same things. Still, a surgeon who performed a craniotomy and could soundly analyse the action, resisting the undue influence of physical and causal factors that would dominate the perception of observers, could rightly say 'No way do I intend to kill the baby' and 'It is no part of my purpose to kill the baby'. Of course, the lethal damage done to the baby by a craniotomy, being foreseen and voluntarily accepted, can be called 'deliberate' and/or 'intentional' in various uses of those words. But when the question is whether bringing about that lethal

[35] See e.g. *Sent.* II d.24 q.3 a.2c; d.40 q.1 a.1c and ad 4 and a.4 ad 2; d.42 q.1 a.1c; *ST* I–II q.20 a.3 ad 1 and a.6c; *De Malo* q.2 a.4 ad 7 and q.7 a.3c. See further essay 9, sec. III.

damage violates the commandment and moral norm that exceptionlessly excludes killing the innocent, the fact that bringing it about can in *those* senses be called intentional and deliberate is irrelevant. What matters is whether the killing is brought about as an end sought (obviously not) or *as a chosen means*—in other words, whether it is the *object*, in the sense defined in *Veritatis Splendor*, of the act of the surgeon who performs the craniotomy.[36]

(d) Craniotomy might well be physically indistinguishable from 'partial birth abortion'. But the proposals adopted by the two kinds of choices, and thus the objects of the two procedures, are entirely different. In partial birth abortion done for any of the purposes for which elective abortions are done, the object of the act is to kill the baby before the killing would be classed as infanticide. In craniotomy done for the purpose of saving at least the mother's life, the object of the act is to reduce the size of the baby's head so that the baby or its corpse can be removed from the birth canal. No partial-birth abortion would ever be performed if the baby were already dead. If the baby stuck in the birth canal were already dead, craniotomy would always be performed. This difference is an important sign of the difference between the two kinds of operations considered as *human acts* in the morally significant sense of that term.

(e) Though a craniotomy of the kind we have been discussing, in which the contents of the skull are emptied so that it can be crushed, is not a procedure that could be done to help *the baby*, there could be a form of craniotomy in which, though the usual outcome is the death of the baby, the surgeon nevertheless hopes that cutting and squeezing the skull without emptying its contents will not result in the baby's death. This, too, is a sign that the fact that craniotomy normally results in the baby's death does not suffice to settle what is or is not the object and therefore the moral species of the act. But that fact is relevant in a consideration of another important question: even if a craniotomy can be done without violating the commandment and moral norm that *exceptionlessly excludes* intentional killing, isn't it unfair to the baby, and as such wrongful, and therefore homicidal? That question is not considered in this essay, since it is not settled by what the acting person intends as an end or chooses as a means.[37]

(f) That craniotomy is repugnant and horrible is unquestionable. It is also unquestionably horrible and repugnant for doctors and nurses who

[36] That the relevant question concerns what is intended as an end or chosen as a means is clear from the Church's teaching about a kind of act that clearly does violate the norm excluding all killing of the innocent, namely direct abortion; see *Evangelium Vitae* no. 62 ('Pius XII excludes all direct abortion, i.e., every act tending directly to destroy human life in the womb "whether such destruction is intended as an end or only as a means to an end"'); likewise *CCC* 2271.

[37] The question is briefly considered by Grisez, *Living a Christian Life*, 503.

must stand by as both a mother and her baby die while they might be doing a craniotomy to increase the probability that at any rate one would survive. But in neither case can their repugnance and horror help them judge what they truly ought to do. If they correctly analyse the two options, they will see that the norm exceptionlessly excluding intentional killing does not exclude the option of performing a craniotomy, and that their judgment should accordingly be determined by considerations of fairness to both the mother and the baby.[38]

(g) Interpreting the Church's documents with precision, one finds that the Church has never taught that craniotomy is intentional killing or that performing a craniotomy is morally wrong. The three documents referring to craniotomy were responses published by the Holy Office, two of them with explicit papal approval, to questions raised by individual bishops. The first two questions (1884 and 1889) concerned craniotomy, but the response asserted only that it could not be safely taught in Catholic educational institutions to be licit. The third question (1895) concerned only premature expulsion of a non-viable fetus, and the response asserted only that such operations could not be safely done; and indicated that this response was in accordance with the earlier decrees that did refer to craniotomy.

To say that something cannot be safely taught or even that it cannot be safely done is not to assert that it is immoral. Rather, it is to provide pastoral guidance for the faithful fulfilment of one's responsibilities as a teacher, and for the formation of one's conscience. Receiving this advice, faithful and prudent teachers and doctors would have realized that, though craniotomy might possibly be morally acceptable, their moral responsibility was to proceed on the assumption that it was not. But a good deal of pastoral guidance wisely given in the nineteenth century could not

[38] Brock, *Action and Conduct: Aquinas and the Theory of Action*, 204–5 n. 17, says:

> Thomas's view would allow us to suppose that the surgeon is not aiming at the fetus's death, not crushing the skull *in order* that the fetus die. But—also on Thomas's view—regardless of his *further* aim, his act is aimed at producing the crushed skull of an innocent person; and surely it is to that extent unjust.... How unjust is it? Well, what is the value of an intact skull? The person's *life* depends on it.

But Brock fails to show that the *object* of the surgeon's chosen act is better described as 'producing the crushed skull of an innocent person' than as 'cranium-narrowing for the purposes of removal from the birth-canal'—a description he set aside as 'a merely abstract description' or 'redescribing'. (See n. 47 below and text at n. 63.) Still, Brock seems to be perhaps conceding, *sub silentio*, that the craniotomy need not be excluded by the exceptionless moral norm against killing the innocent, and therefore letting the assessment of its moral character rest on an assessment of its fairness, its justice. To support his view that it is unjust he quotes (but only in Latin) *ST* I–II q.73 a.8; but this quotation is not to the point, since it deals only with the way in which consequences, even though unintended, can aggravate the gravity of *what is already judged to be wrongful*. Note that whether and to what extent the life of the unborn child 'depends on' not being subjected to the craniotomy is far from clear in the obstetric emergency we are considering—a situation in which the child is expected to die no matter what is done.

be rightly followed today. These responses by the Holy Office effectively closed the debate among theologians of those days. However, since the Holy Office did not assert that craniotomy is immoral, its responses cannot ground a sound argument against a position such as ours,[39] based as it is upon an understanding of action thoroughly in line with the tradition and the contemporary magisterium—an understanding not articulated with sufficient clarity by nineteenth-century theologians.[40]

Still, although those Holy Office responses refrain from asserting the immorality of the procedures in question, the Church's teaching elsewhere, especially in the twentieth century, makes it perfectly clear that direct killing of the unborn, even to save the life of the mother, is always wrong. We regard this teaching as a truth of faith.[41] Our position is that a doctor could do a craniotomy, even one involving emptying the baby's skull, without intending to kill the baby—without the craniotomy being a direct killing.[†] Of course, even when bringing about a person's death is not direct killing, doing so is often gravely wrong. We do not deny that there might be reasons for condemning the practice of craniotomy other than that it is direct killing.[42]

Besides the seven points now considered, an argument has recently been proposed by Kevin L. Flannery SJ, that 'there is positive reason *not* to separate off' the death of the baby from 'the compass of the means' in the craniotomy.[43] Flannery, like virtually all Catholic moralists, holds that there is no direct killing in a case where, to save the life of the pregnant mother, her cancerous uterus is removed ('hysterectomy') along with the unborn baby within it, with the inevitable result that the baby promptly dies (perhaps many weeks earlier than it otherwise would). He also accepts that 'the bringing about of the death of the fetus is not conceptually related to the performance of the craniotomy'[‡] and that 'there is logical independence of this sort between the crushing of a skull and the fetus's death'.[44] But he contends that 'the two cases, craniotomy and hysterectomy,

[39] Our position is shared by some theologians completely faithful to the Church's teaching; see e.g. Zalba, '"Nihil prohibet unius actus esse duos effectus"... Numquid applicari potest principium in abortu therapeutico?' at 567–8.

[40] See e.g. Waffelaert, 'De Abortu et Embryotomia', especially the exegesis attempted at 165–71 of *ST* II–II q.64 a.7.

[41] See Grisez, 'The Definability of the Proposition: The Intentional Killing of an Innocent Human Being is Always Grave Matter'.

[42] Faithful Catholics who reject our account of intention and judge that craniotomy, or any other action, is direct killing certainly ought to form their consciences, in relation to such actions, by the Church's teaching that all direct killing of the innocent is gravely wrong. And, even if certain that a possible action would not be a direct killing, all faithful Catholics should form their consciences in the light of faith with regard to the requirements of both justice and mercy.

[43] Flannery, 'What is Included in a Means to an End?' at 510 et seq.

[44] *Ibid.* at 506.

have different logical structures'.[45] He points to two ways in which the cases differ 'logically'.

First, the hysterectomy is performed 'upon the woman', the craniotomy 'upon the fetus'. We reply: this difference does not show that craniotomy is direct killing. A counter-example makes this clear. All those acts of self-defence of the kind that Aquinas shows need involve no intent to kill and no direct killing are nonetheless performed 'upon' the person killed.[46] And in general, the fact that an act is done to (or 'upon') X for the sake of Y, or to Y for the sake of Y, provides no criterion for distinguishing between what is intended and what is accepted as a side effect.

Flannery's second 'logical' distinction: whereas in the hysterectomy 'the death of the fetus stands outside [the] description' of the act as 'a hysterectomy on a pregnant woman in order that she might regain her health', in the craniotomy, 'in order to separate off from the compass of the means the killing of the fetus, it is necessary to redescribe the act of craniotomy, calling it a cranium-narrowing operation'. Such separating off or redescription is, he says, 'artificial'.[47] This argument also fails. What counts for moral analysis is not what may or may not be included in various descriptions that might be given by observers, or even by acting persons reflecting on what they have done, but what is or is not included within a proposal developed in deliberation for possible adoption by choice. Only the truthful articulation of that proposal can be a description that specifies an act for the purposes of moral analysis. Our contention, which Flannery fails to discuss, much less refute, is that when someone chooses to do a craniotomy on a baby to save his or her mother's life in an obstetrical predicament, the morally relevant description of the act would not include killing the baby.

As shown in sec. II above, the act analysis we have just employed in refuting Flannery's argument is not simply a philosophical and anthropological view peculiar to us, but is rooted in the tradition, employed by the magisterium,

[45] *Ibid.* at 511.

[46] Note: in saying this we in no way suggest that the baby in the craniotomy is an unjust aggressor or any other kind of aggressor. (Indeed, we deny that the unborn baby is ever an aggressor.) Aquinas's analysis of the intention in self-defence does not depend upon there being an unjust aggression.

[47] *Ibid.* at 511–12. May, 'The Management of Ectopic Pregnancies' at 142, expresses his agreement with Flannery's article and at 140 expresses the thought that 'Grisez and Boyle are really *redescribing* the act in terms of its intended (in the sense of future, as distinct from *present* intentions) consequences'. In both contexts, the talk of 'redescription' amounts to no more than a rhetorical means of asserting, without argument, that the description of the act for which Grisez and Boyle have argued, re-articulated with further argument in the present essay, is unacceptable. *Pace* May at 142, it is not true that 'Grisez and Boyle prefer to call [craniotomy] a "cranium-narrowing" operation'. Its physical character as a lethal crushing and emptying is not evaded or softened in our discussions.

and explicitly taught in *Veritatis Splendor.* Flannery's insufficient grip on that act analysis is indicated by his claim, in a subsequent article, that if a hysterectomy on the cancerous womb is performed needlessly early, it 'becomes not merely performing a hysterectomy but also a direct killing'.[48] This is a significant confusion.[49] Performing a hysterectomy to save a woman from a slow-growing cancer, when her baby could have been saved by waiting a few weeks without much greater risk to her, is seriously wrongful killing in as much as it is unjust to the baby, and so can be called homicidal. But the injustice does not transform that homicide into direct killing; the baby's death is a side effect just as it would be if the operation were being done later and were justified.

It is worth adding another example of confusion about intention, object, proposals, and directness in Flannery's recent writings: where someone puts a bomb on an aircraft in order to collect insurance *on the aircraft itself* (*not* life insurance on its passengers or crew), Flannery rightly holds that 'it is not part of this proposal that anyone be killed', and that, unlike Mr G who walks into a restaurant and shoots down Mr H 'because he wants him dead', 'the aircraft bomber's intentions...extend only as far as destruction of the aircraft'.[50] But at the same time he says that 'both the aircraft bomber and Mr G. intend death' and both of them 'intend to violate' the basic human good of life, because 'destruction of the aircraft...in fact means death for the passengers'.[51] The two sets of statements contradict each other. What is true is that the passengers' deaths, being outside the proposal, are not intended by the bomber; and that the bomber's willingness to cause their deaths, and his doing so, is nevertheless gravely wrong. A soldier who leaps on a hand grenade to save his buddy also expects that this 'in fact means' death for himself, but does not on that account intend to violate the basic good of human life, for (as we noted at the beginning of sec. III above) he is not choosing to bring about his death.

IV

Jean Porter has recently devoted an article to arguing that the account of action and intention developed by Grisez (and the other authors of the

[48] Flannery, 'Natural Law *mens rea* versus the Benthamite Tradition' at 395.

[49] Flannery is also inaccurate in stating (*ibid.*) that

> in Thomistic terms, the end (which a person intends) *specifies* the act, but it is not part of the substance of the act [*ST* I–II q.7 a.3]: it is not part of what the person *is doing.* It is 'a sort of adjunct end.' [*aliquis finis adiunctus*—...I–II q.7 a.3]. (Italics and brackets in original.)

But in *ST* I–II q.7 a.3 [ad 3], Aquinas does not say that an act's specifying end is 'adjunct' (what Flannery calls 'not part of the act's substance'); rather he says that adjunct ends are to be contrasted with specifying ends.

[50] Flannery, 'Natural Law *mens rea*' at 393, 392, 396.

[51] *Ibid.*, 396.

present essay) fails to provide a cogent account of 'the distinction between direct and indirect action'. 'His applications of the distinction', she says, 'apparently reflect prior moral judgments which the distinction serves to justify after the fact'.[52]

Porter gives an apparently detailed and careful statement of Grisez's account of what is a *means* (that is, what is 'directly' chosen and intended) rather than a *side effect* (that is, what is only 'indirectly' willed and done) or an *end* (that is, the *further* intention(s) of the chooser). But she considers that his account 'is spelled out most fully' in an article published in 1970,[53] and that a key to his understanding of *means* is a concept important in that article, 'indivisibility of performance'. The bulk of Porter's article is devoted, in one way or another, to arguments attempting to show the unsatisfactoriness of indivisibility of performance as a 'criterion' of the unity of a human act to be morally evaluated (618) and/or a 'criterion for distinguishing between direct and indirect harms' (627). But 'indivisibility of performance' has not been used by Grisez in any of his writings on action since 1970, and it plays no part whatever in any of the work on act analysis on which we have collaborated. Though its irrelevance to our understanding of intention and action will have been evident to many careful readers of our work since 1970, it would have been helpful had we stated explicitly, somewhere, that the appeal to 'indivisibility of performance' in the 1970 article was a false step caused by failure to appreciate the decisive significance of 'the perspective of the acting person' and of the *proposal* an acting person develops in deliberation as a possibility for choice.

Porter says something true and important in her critique of indivisibility of performance. In the 1970 article Grisez said that: 'The very act of crushing and removing the baby, an act in fact destructive of its life, saves the mother from otherwise perhaps inevitable death.'[54] But as Porter rightly notes, the performance of the craniotomy is divisible: 'if the doctor were to walk away immediately after crushing the head of the child, the woman would almost certainly still die' (629).[55] This divisibility—and its irrelevance—is implicit in our discussion of craniotomy in sec. III above: the baby's death is

[52] Porter, '"Direct" and "Indirect" in Grisez's Moral Theory' at 612. (Parenthetical numbers in the text below signify page numbers in her article.) In n. 4 she states that the views expressed in the writings of Boyle and Finnis on these matters are not significantly different from Grisez's.

[53] Grisez, 'Toward a Consistent Natural-Law Ethics of Killing' at 88, 85.

[54] *Ibid.*, 94.

[55] Lombardi, 'Obstetrical Dilemmas and the Principle of Double Effect' at 205–9, also notes that doing a craniotomy does not by itself save the mother's life and that further actions are required, and infers that killing the baby necessarily is a bad means to the good end of saving the mother. But Lombardi refers not to Grisez's mistake about indivisibility of performance but to Boyle's mistake of denying that further actions are needed to save the mother: see Boyle, 'Double Effect and a Certain Type of Embryotomy' at 307.

a side effect of changing the dimensions of its skull, which is the means to the further actions that save the mother's life; and no side effect of a means is part of the means.[56]

What should be said about Porter's central claim, that our analysis of action lacks objectivity, and is controlled by prior moral judgments derived from 'other considerations' (631)? Her position is that the analysis common among post-Tridentine moralists (see sec. III above) has an advantage over ours, and that their assimilation of cause-effect with means-end 'provided an objective basis for assessing the intention of the agent' (620).

There is a sense of 'objective' that lends plausibility to her claim. Cause and effect in the physical world are observable. So, if killing is understood simply as bringing about death, one can observe John killing Mary just as one can observe a cat killing a mouse. But, as explained above, unless one adopts and steadily maintains the perspective of the acting person, one cannot provide or even recognize the only description of a moral act that is morally relevant and true, and so morally objective. Therefore, the objectivity Porter considers appropriate is not even morally relevant.

It is easy to understand why this irrelevant objectivity is invoked by Porter and many others. Though observers can often infer in some respects the morally objective description of another's act, his or her proposal never can be an observable object. So people with what Bernard Lonergan calls a naïve extroverted consciousness are always likely to think that the authentic objectivity of human acts is not really objective, and that the objectivity required for act analysis must be derived from external observations of causes and effects, or other factors entirely accessible to any and every observer.

Accordingly, Porter thinks that our distinction between means and side effects is merely subjective because it is not based on the sequence of cause and effects ('the causal structure of the act'):

> Without some such basis, the agent's intention could be described in terms of *whatever could be said* to be the agent's purpose or motive in acting. In that case it would be difficult to see how the doctrine of double effect would rule anything out, since any act *can be said* to be directed to some good or other, in terms of which the agent's intention could be described.... The question that arises is: Does Grisez's interpretation of the direct/indirect [sc. means/side effect] distinction similarly provide an objective criterion for determining what the agent's intention is? Or does it leave open the possibility of describing the agent's intention in terms of *whatever good purposes* motivate the act in question.[57]

[56] See also Grisez, *Living a Christian Life*, 502–3.

[57] '"Direct" and "Indirect" in Grisez's Moral Theory' at 620 (emphases added).

So Porter maintains that Grisez's account—which we have expounded in sec. I of this essay, and whose roots in the tradition we have shown in sec. II—provides no ground for an objective identification of what someone is doing, and thus leaves the moral evaluation of action at the mercy of arbitrariness or manipulation.

We have emphasized in the foregoing quotation the phrases that indicate the core of Porter's view. What 'could be said' about an action by people who observe its performance, and who speak about it for their multifarious purposes, is indeed, as Porter indicates, indefinitely various. Indeed, what 'can be said' about an action and its intentions by the very person whose act and intent they are is various, indefinite, and unstable, if that person is reflecting, as a kind of observer, on his or her purposes and motivations. And acting persons so reflecting on their actions and intentions, and representing them to others, are indeed likely to shape their account by reference to 'whatever good purposes' they have, and to suppress or misstate—perhaps even to themselves—both any other purposes that may be motivating them and any means they have adopted but would rather not think about and/or be known to have adopted. But none of this should obscure the fact that the truth about what is intended and being done is available, primarily if not exclusively, to the acting person *in* that acting—*in* that deliberating, choosing, and carrying out the choice—which constitutes the reality to which all accounts of intention and action must conform if they are to be true.

Each clear-headed and honest person knows what he or she is truly or objectively doing. Such persons know what end(s) they have in view, and what means they have reason, in view of such end(s), to choose, and are actually choosing in preference to alternatives. Roe knows, for example, that he saw an assailant's attack as an *opportunity to kill* a long-hated enemy (or: a person he had contracted for money to kill), and knows that in taking steps that any observer would reasonably judge to be intended only as self-defensive measures to stop the assailant's attack, he was really and truly—objectively—trying to kill in revenge (or: to fulfil the contract). Roe's self-knowledge is objective. So too in the converse case. Doe, a shopkeeper robbed many times may acquire a gun and—as a bluff—announce to the neighbourhood that she will kill the next robber in her store. When she sees a young tough move something suspiciously in his coat, she judges that she is about to be robbed at gunpoint, tries to shoot him in the shoulder, but hits his heart. To a jury, what happened may well seem to have been a straightforward intentional killing, carrying out her deterrent threat. But in truth and reality it was no more than a self-defensive act, chosen, without any intent to kill, to stop what she mistakenly believed was an assault.

The morally significant acts a person does are, objectively, what that person chooses to do for the reasons he or she has for making those choices. A true and morally objective description of such acts is the description they have, prospectively (as acts still to be done), in the proposals the acting person shapes in deliberation and adopts by choice(s). What an act objectively is, and can be known objectively to be, is not affected by what the acting person or others may say about it, or by what others may reasonably (though mistakenly) infer it to be. Nor is the reality of what an acting person is doing described adequately or objectively by describing it only in terms of the purposes that motivated it, omitting what the acting person chose to do as means of pursuing those purposes.

Failing to attend to the perspective of the acting person, Porter systematically fails to attend to chosen means (to what the tradition, retrieved and restated in *Veritatis Splendor*, calls the 'objects' of acts). Her accounts of actions reduce them to intended ends and outward behaviour—the 'immediate bodily movements' she calls 'primitive acts'. Even the accounts she offers of ends or motivations for action tend to overlook *reasons* for choosing *means*. We shall point out the oversight when commenting on her examples of types of act.

For now we illustrate Porter's misunderstanding of action by pointing simply to a notable instance that occurs when she is stating her position at the level of general theory. This instance occurs at the very moment when she—about halfway through the article—acknowledges that:

> Grisez could admit that there are indefinitely many correct descriptions for every act, and yet still hold that only one of these is morally relevant, namely, that which describes the act in terms of what the agent does in fact intend. (622)

She remarks at this point that 'this argument does not resolve the difficulty' that she thinks faces Grisez in trying to distinguish means from side effects. For:

> If one accepts the Thomistic principle that every action is directed knowingly towards the attainment of some good (as Grisez does), then it follows that every action can be described in terms of some good which the agent is voluntarily seeking. Why should the agent not describe his intention in terms of that good, relegating the harms which he brings about to foreseen but not chosen aspects of the act? (622)

The answer to her question is clear. If a young woman chooses to have her embryonic child suctioned from her uterus *as a means* to forestalling the unwelcome choice between giving her baby up for adoption and raising him or her, then a description—such as 'having the pregnancy terminated'—of this human action that omits her choice to have that done as a means to her end is objectively incomplete in an essential respect.

But instead of attending to the answer that our theory of action gives to her question, Porter imagines that Grisez would respond to it 'by claiming that the intention in question must be understood psychologically as well as logically' (623). By 'psychologically' she refers not to rational but to emotional motives: 'no amount of redescription can change the reality of what the agent *desires*' when 'desires' is understood (as she takes for granted) to refer to, for instance, 'hatred', 'desire for revenge', 'malice', 'envy', 'cruelty', 'or some similar motive' (620).

However, even though some such emotional factors do help motivate adult children to decide to bring about the death of their aged parent before the insurance moneys run out and the estate is consumed, still neither the emotional motives nor the prospect of financial gain *specify* what it is that the children choose and do. If those emotions and reasons motivate the children to think of a way to hasten their parent's death, and the children adopt that proposal, what they choose and do is hasten their parent's death. Even if the means they use cannot be recognized by outside observers as means of hastening death, the children's practical reasoning shaped their choice: *to hasten her death, as a means* to their ends, ends arising from emotional motives and/or rational considerations. Similarly, the parents of a newborn baby afflicted with Down's syndrome may consider terminating their child's life by withholding an easy, effective, and inexpensive operation, whatever emotional motivations drive that deliberation. If they decide to withhold the operation as a way of (means to) killing the child, then, whatever they tell themselves or others, they really ('objectively') intend to kill the baby. There is little or nothing to be gained by asking whether this truth about their intentions and actions is 'psychological' or 'logical'.[58] And it is entirely beside the point to ask (as Porter repeatedly does) whether, in cases such as these, 'the agent's will must necessarily[59] be focused on the killing, and not on the good which is sought' (623). An agent choosing to kill someone, for whatever good, necessarily and really focuses both on the end sought and the killing chosen as a means to it.

[58] If the question were pressed, we could point out that the structure of actions considered as the subject-matter of moral evaluation pertains to the third of the four types of order identified by Aquinas in the opening paragraphs of his *In Eth.*—the kind of order that one brings into one's own behaviour by deliberation and choice, as irreducibly distinct from (1) the order of nature (which includes much of what is called 'psychological'), (2) the order of logic, and (4) the order of arts and techniques. See e.g. Grisez, *Beyond the New Theism*, ch. 14; *Aquinas*, 20–3, 52, and index s.v. 'four orders'. So far forth, then, the structures considered in moral evaluation are neither 'psychological' nor 'logical', though there are psychological and logical, as well as ontological and technical, elements both in moral life and in reflection upon it.

[59] Porter (at 621) had introduced 'necessarily' into her lead-in to a quotation from Grisez in which 'necessarily' nowhere appears. She then went on to say: 'When Grisez says that an action with both good and bad effects is not defined by the bad effect unless it is necessarily included in the agent's intention...' and proceeded to speculate about what kind of necessity that might be, thus constructing a dialectic irrelevant to Grisez's moral theory.

Striving to press her claim that Grisez has no good way of distinguishing means from side effects, Porter takes up various kinds of cases. She asks, first, 'how Grisez can distinguish morally between killing in self-defense and euthanasia' (624). After trying to show that the two kinds of act cannot be distinguished in various ways, she at last notices that Grisez would say, and has everywhere said, that (to use her rendering) 'in the case of euthanasia, as opposed to killing in self-defense, the agent's act is aimed precisely at the death of the individual who is killed' (624). But instead of addressing this response, which provides precisely what she claims Grisez cannot provide, Porter changes the subject. She notices that Grisez has sometimes called attention to one *sign* or *manifestation* of the difference between engaging in lethal behaviour with intent to stop an attack (accepting the attacker's death as a side effect) and engaging in the same behaviour with intent to kill the attacker: that in the first case the acting person will desist from the lethal behaviour if the attack is broken off by the wounding or flight of the attacker, whereas in the second the acting person will or may well press on with the lethal behaviour, seizing the opportunity to finish off the attacker. Not attending to Grisez's analysis of the difference as chosen means between self-defence and euthanasia, she argues that that sign or manifestation of the difference is not an adequate criterion of it. Of course, we agree that it is not an adequate criterion, since it is no criterion at all.

In irrelevantly challenging the adequacy as a criterion of the sign, Porter considers the possibility that a woman using lethal force in self-defence against rape does not at once succeed in stopping her attacker, and says: 'then presumably she would try again to kill him' (625). By saying 'try again to kill', Porter inadvertently makes clear the irrelevance of her argument, for Grisez's analysis of morally acceptable lethal self-defence precisely is that it is *not* trying to kill. It would be logically impossible for a victim to 'try again' to kill an attacker if that victim's prior behaviour were genuine self-defence. Porter also considers the possibility that a doctor trying to euthanase a patient might desist if the first attempt unexpectedly 'somehow relieves the patient's suffering without killing him' (625). In this case she soundly points out that what usually is a sign of non-homicidal intent cannot be a criterion. But she overlooks the physician's first choice: having tried to kill her patient, the doctor has done an act of homicide whether or not she herself, in subsequent reflection, Porter, or anyone else recognizes that.

Another of Porter's sample cases, put forth to show that Grisez's account of action cannot (without covertly drawing upon prior moral judgments) distinguish means from side effects, is craniotomy. We have discussed this in the preceding section, but it is important now to see precisely how Grisez's view of craniotomy is handled by Porter. She invites the reader:

Consider the case of the doctor who saves the life of a woman in labor by performing a craniotomy on her child. Such an act is justified, in Grisez's view, because it is inseparably an act of killing and an act of saving the woman's life. (629)

Porter obviously is referring to Grisez's 1970 formulation of his view.[60] His more recent view is set out in *Living a Christian Life* (1993), which Porter cites elsewhere in her article. On the specific question being considered by Porter—the question whether ending the baby's life is intended ('direct') or rather accepted as a side effect ('indirect')—Grisez states his view without reference to inseparability:

...the baby's death need not be included in the proposal adopted in choosing to do a craniotomy. [Footnote citation omitted.] The proposal can be simply to *alter the child's physical dimensions and remove him or her*, because, as a physical object, this body cannot remain where it is without ending in both the baby's and the mother's deaths. To understand this proposal, it helps to notice that the baby's death contributes nothing to the objective sought; indeed, the procedure is exactly the same if the baby has already died. In adopting this proposal, the baby's death need only be accepted as a side effect.[61]

Ignoring this articulation of the doctor's proposal, Porter addresses Grisez's former idea about inseparability, and argues that the 'primitive acts' (immediate bodily movements) involved in craniotomy are in fact separable, since the doctor might walk away after crushing the baby's skull, omitting the further primitive acts needed to save the mother (pulling out the child, etc.). Since the same could be said of any surgical operation, 'it is hard to see how he [Grisez] could allow any medical procedure that requires a series of primitive actions, some of which are destructive in their immediate effects' (629). And that *reductio ad absurdum* would follow if Porter's interpretation of Grisez's position were sound. But it is not sound, and she concedes that 'perhaps what this example shows is that we are mistaken in assuming that the Davidsonian primitive act *is* Grisez's unit of moral analysis' (629). Her 'assuming' that the 'Davidsonian' or any other kind of 'primitive act' (immediate bodily movement) is or ever has been

[60] Even so, she misstates that position, which was not that inseparability justifies craniotomy but only that it is a necessary condition for its moral acceptability. Even in 1970, Grisez pointed out that it is not the only necessary condition for the act's uprightness.

[61] *Ibid.*, 502 (emphasis added).

Grisez's unit of moral analysis is groundless and plainly contrary to his account of acts in all the texts of his which she considers.[62]

Porter considers the possibility that 'primitive acts' are not Grisez's unit of analysis. But she does not abandon her attempts to attribute to Grisez an account of action that fails to adopt the perspective of the acting person and looks only to primitive movements plus overall intention, ignoring *chosen means*:

> Perhaps the explanation of the craniotomy example lies in the fact that the primitive act of crushing, taken together with a series of other acts, is informed by the agent's overall life-saving intention, especially since Grisez insists that what is morally significant is the will of the agent, as determined by the proposal he adopts. (629)

Porter's reference to 'the proposal he adopts' might suggest that she has grasped the central element of Grisez's analysis. However, she still fails to notice that proposals are not of primitive movements informed by an overall intention, but of actions understood as possible means. The act of craniotomy, whatever immediate physical movements it may involve, is the act accurately described by Grisez in the passage already quoted from his book: to alter the child's physical dimensions and remove him or her. Earlier on the same page of that book he had given another, equivalent description of the proposal/act: 'a craniotomy (an operation in which instruments are used to empty and crush the head of the child so that it can be removed from the birth canal)'. Both these formulations describe the same kind of act, and do so by identifying the 'object' of that act.[63] Both correspond to the ways the choice and act might be conceptualized in the deliberations of a doctor considering *whether or not* to perform the act, and in the deliberations of the child's parents or anyone else concerned in the decision-making.

Instead of giving her own moral evaluation of craniotomy—as she imagines Grisez understands it—Porter proceeds immediately to assert that the account of action she (mistakenly) attributes to Grisez would justify contraception by 'uniting the primitive actions of employing some contraceptive and engaging in sexual intercourse into one intention, say,

[62] In the 1970 article to which Porter gives (inappropriate) prominence, Grisez says:

> A means in the order of human action must be a single, complete human act...Now a human action derives its unity from two sources. One source is the unity of one's intention. (*'Intention' here refers not merely to intention of the end, but also to the meaning one understands his act to have when he chooses it as a means* to an intended end).

Or again: 'both *means* and end have a behavioral aspect (Aquinas's external act) *and an aspect of human meaning* (Aquinas's interior act)': 'Toward a Consistent Natural-Law Ethics of Killing' at 88, 85 (emphases added).

[63] See also response to Brock in n. 38 above.

an intention of expressing marital intimacy in a responsible fashion' (629). Here Porter unwittingly testifies to the ease with which people, well or ill disposed, can identify *means* for the purpose of morally significant deliberation and choice. For 'employing a contraceptive' is not the sort of thing she had been calling a 'primitive act'; it does not pick out any immediate bodily movement or set of such movements. The relevant bodily movements, after all, might be those involved in putting on a condom, or those involved in taking a pill, and so forth. Rather, *employing a contraceptive* is a kind of human act specified as a means to an end—that is, using something, anything whatever, to make an act of intercourse less likely than it otherwise would be to result in conception. In short, the very term 'contraception' which Porter uses here refers to a means as it would usually be identified in deliberating and shaping proposals to act for an end: to prevent conception.

Moreover, Porter's suggestion that our view allows an argument for contraception is incorrect. For, on our view, one cannot engage in what Porter calls 'expressing marital intimacy in a responsible fashion' without at some time or other having adopted *two proposals* by making *two choices*: (1) to employ a contraceptive, (2) to engage here and now in marital intercourse. Each is the choice and carrying out of a means to an end; each is identifiable as a distinct kind of act (however many bodily movements it may involve); and neither can be assessed morally without reference, in the first instance, to its characteristics as an act of *that kind*.

As noted at the beginning of this section, Porter's primary thesis is that Grisez is guilty of the same thing with which he charged Richard McCormick:[64] taking positions on moral issues and then finding reasons for them (631–2). Her article is an elaborate attempt to prove that charge against Grisez. We have shown that her account of Grisez's action theory, and her attempts to criticize it, fail radically. She also contends that our account of action is out of line with the tradition's, but we have shown both here and elsewhere that the main lines of our account are entirely traditional.

Still, Porter is right about one thing: our analysis of craniotomy is not defending a teaching of the Church. But that fact by itself is sufficient to falsify her primary thesis. Grisez's work has not been an effort to 'provide a systematic philosophical justification for the tenets of traditional Catholic morality' (611). If that had been his purpose, he surely would not have said what he consistently has about craniotomy, and capital punishment, and killing in war. He would never have taken the position that it is wrong to

[64] See *Christian Moral Principles*, 157.

try to kill a human being. He would have been satisfied instead to defend the thesis that he has argued is a truth of faith: the intentional killing *of the innocent* is always a grave matter. But as it is, he criticized traditional views of capital punishment and killing in warfare, and argued that capital punishment always is wrongful killing and that even the killing of enemy combatants can be justified only if the action that brings about their death is done without any intention to kill them.[65]

It is worth noting that the *Catechism of the Catholic Church*, most plainly in its revised edition—in relation to killing in capital punishment, and war, and in general if not on craniotomy (which is not mentioned)—has adopted a position like the one defended for thirty years by Grisez. Killing of human beings is justifiable only insofar as it is not intended.[66] This underlines the importance, for a sound understanding of the faith as well as for a sound philosophy, of understanding with precision and consistency just what it is to intend, to choose, and to act.

NOTES

† *Craniotomy need not be direct killing*...(p. 254 after n. 41). Another context in which to consider the issues of action theory, act analysis, and intention that are raised by craniotomy is the separation of conjoined ('Siamese') twins who share vital organs in such a way that (a) unless they are separated both will soon die because these organs cannot sustain both children, (b) the separation will result in the more or less immediate death of the twin who is separated from the vital organs necessary to the survival of each twin, and (c) the other, stronger twin is reasonably expected to survive the operation indefinitely. This situation was considered in September 2000 by the Court of Appeal in England in *Re A (Children) (Conjoined Twins: Medical Treatment)* [2001] Fam 147. (See endnote ‡ to essay 10.) The Archbishop of Westminster, Cardinal Murphy-O'Connor, submitted a brief arguing that the twins' parents were correct in judging the proposed separation morally unacceptable. The Archbishop's brief did not contend, however, that the operation involved an intent to kill. So far forth, the brief was compatible with the analysis of intention presented in these essays. But it did contend that the operation involved an intent to mutilate the weaker twin chosen for separation from the shared vital organs; likewise Watt, 'Conjoined Twins: Separation as Mutilation' at 243–5. That contention is inconsistent with the understanding of intention expounded in these essays. Grisez, *Difficult Moral Questions*, 290–1 (Q. 63), had earlier analysed the matter, both as a hypothetical and in relation to a similar separation performed some years earlier ('the Lakeberg twins'):

> I hold that directly killing an innocent human being is always wrong, provided direct killing is understood as killing intended as an end or chosen as a means to some other end.... I also grant that the attempt to separate the...twins involved the physically immediate causing of the weaker twin's death, so that the surgeon directly killed her in the sense that the surgery of itself straightaway brought about her death. However, there is no reason to think the surgeon intended the weaker twin's death as an end and there was no need to choose her death as a means. The shared heart and liver were not exclusively the organs of either twin; the chosen means to

[65] See e.g. *ibid.*, 220; *NDMR* 309–19.

[66] The revised *CCC*'s entire treatment of cases of justifiable killing is put under the aegis of Aquinas's distinction between the 'double effect' of lethal self-defensive actions that do not intend the killing of the aggressor: no. 2263 (and see nn. 28 and 34 above). Accordingly, punishment can only be lethal 'if this is the only way of effectively defending human lives against the unjust aggressor': no. 2267. And killing in war can be justifiable only as 'legitimate defence', i.e. where 'the defence of the common good requires that an unjust aggressor be rendered unable to cause harm', and the right to use arms is the right only 'to repel aggressors'.

> fashion an adequate heart for the stronger was to cut away the shared heart from the weaker and the chosen means to provide a liver from the stronger was to cut it away from the weaker. That, of course, resulted in her death, but her death was an effect of chosen means [, an effect] that in no way contributed to the end sought....
>
> To challenge [this]... someone might propose the following argument. Suppose identical twins who were not conjoined were born afflicted with similar heart defects, so that neither was likely to survive without heart surgery, and suppose the surgeon removed the weaker twin's heart and used it to fashion a more adequate heart for the stronger. Since the weaker baby's death, though an effect of removing his or her heart, would in no way contribute to the end sought, even this operation would not involve the intentional killing of an innocent human being. Yet, the argument would proceed, removing the weaker baby's heart surely would be intrinsically wrong; if not, there would be nothing wrong in transplanting vital organs from dying persons without waiting for them to die....
>
> I concede that on my analysis removing the weaker twin's heart and transplanting vital organs from dying persons would not necessarily involve intentional killing. But I maintain that such operations would be intrinsically wrong, since they would involve an intentional violation of functional bodily integrity. The surgery would involve two distinct procedures: (1) to take from certain persons organs needed for some function, and (2) to give those organs and their functioning to others. The first procedure would be chosen as a means, and the choice would include depriving persons of a function. By contrast, separating the Lakeberg twins involved only a single procedure: cutting away the stronger twin, together with the heart and liver both babies had shared, from her weaker sister. So, it seems to me, the operation did not involve intending the violation of the weaker twin's bodily integrity, but only accepting her being deprived of her share in organs that had been parts of both her sister and herself.

The Archbishop's brief in *Re A* spoke of a 'deliberate mutilating invasion', as if that were equivalent to an invasion intended to mutilate. But 'deliberate' extends to foreseen and accepted (albeit regretted) side effects. Aquinas's account of intention in self-defence applies as much to damaging as to killing, and holds that both damaging and lethal effects can be deliberately caused, without intent to damage or kill, where one's intent is to stop a threat to one's life of a kind which one has no obligation to accept. So if a baby, by falling asleep, will fall onto a button which will bring about the incineration of a school full of children, and the only way to stop the baby from falling is to shoot it so that it topples the other way, that can be done without intent to kill or injure even though the effect on the baby is mutilating or lethal and 'deliberate', that is, caused with full knowledge and control. (This is like the paradigmatic fat man in the cave, considered at length in essay 10, sec. II pp. 189–94; see also its third endnote.) Fundamentally different is the position of a person V whose presence or movements present no threat to X, but whose heart could benefit X; the intent to enter V's body to remove his heart is an intent to damage V and his bodily integrity, for the sake of X (and is as exceptionlessly wrong as acting with intent to kill).

‡ *Flannery accepts that craniotomy and death are not 'conceptually related'*...(p. 254 at n. 44). A hasty inference from our use of the word 'accepts' here seems the only basis for the interpretation of this essay (and, on that sole basis, of our entire theory of intention and action) offered by Cavanaugh, *Double-Effect Reasoning*, 66–71 and 90. According to Cavanaugh (90) we hold that one intends only those 'effects' that are included by 'conceptual necessity' in 'the words one employs to describe one's acts':

> Finnis, Grisez, and Boyle find ordinary language too restrictive for [double-effect reasoning]. In its place they propose conceptual necessity (treated more fully [on p. 90]). H.L.A. Hart considers such an account, saying, '[a] foreseen but unwanted outcome will be taken to be intended if it is of a kind so immediately and invariably connected with the kind of action done that the connection is regarded as conceptual rather than contingent' (Hart 1967). Following this line of reasoning, one violates the norm against killing the innocent when one cannot help but conceptualize one's act as killing. (*Ibid.*, 69.)

Cavanaugh then elaborates on the approach he (fantastically) ascribes to us. His discussion concludes with his critique on *ibid.*, 90:

> One intends more than that included in a conceptual analysis of the words one employs to describe one's acts. An agent's expression of intent leads us to *ask her why and how she plans to act, just as she herself has already addressed these very questions in her deliberations* concerning the act of which she speaks to us. I [Cavanaugh] now turn to these (why and how) questions...(Emphasis added.)

But this last passage states *our* position. We have no interest whatever in conducting an act analysis in terms of 'conceptual necessity' or 'conceptual relations'. We spoke of the 'conceptual' only in relation to Flannery and only because *he* is interested in conceptual or 'logical' necessity. Our understanding of intention and action is entirely in terms of the why and how questions that the acting person addressed in the deliberations that ended in choice and action. In turning to these, Cavanaugh forgets his baseless earlier claims (*ibid.*, 67) that our doing so is 'Cartesian' and refuted by Anscombe's *Intention* (a book whose approach we follow rigorously). He asks (*ibid.*, 70) whether our account really prohibits any killing; thus he provides further ground for the hypothesis that he has attended only to those parts of the essay that concern craniotomy (though even there overlooking what we say about 'partial birth abortion'), and has neglected Part I with its eight 'cases' culminating in *Case H.* Although he quotes the opening sentence of sec. II of the essay, his discussion ignores the reasons we offer, in that section, for adopting the perspective of the acting person, not *qua* describing his or her action for the purposes of persuasion (as Cavanaugh (68) suggests), but *qua* actually deliberating towards choice and action.

14

INTENTION IN DIRECT DISCRIMINATION*

It is direct discrimination on ethnic and therefore racial grounds for a school to give preference, in admissions, to children who are Orthodox Jews according to the Chief Rabbi's criteria of Orthodoxy; for, by those criteria, unless a boy be a convert to Orthodoxy, he is Orthodox only if, at his birth, his mother was Orthodox by conversion or matrilineal descent, and such matrilineality is ethnic in character. The Supreme Court of the United Kingdom so held, 5 to 4, in *R (E) v Governing Body of JFS*.[1] It was intentionality, rather than ethnicity, that occasioned the sharp division of opinion. The argument that prevailed is a variant of 'doing this just is doing that'.[2]

On intention in direct discrimination the dissenting minority had the better conclusion, but failed to find a decisive argument. All but one of the eight full judgments get off on the wrong foot by treating the meaning of 'discriminates on racial grounds' (direct discrimination) as either settled or demarcated by the Lords' decisions in *Birmingham City Council v Equal Opportunities Commission*[3] and *James v Eastleigh Borough Council*.[4] A better view is that the direct-discrimination issue in *JFS* was structurally quite different from the direct-discrimination issue in the unanimous and correctly decided *Birmingham*, and was structurally identical to that in *Eastleigh*, a 3 to 2 decision reversing a unanimous Court of Appeal on grounds that will continue to confuse the law and divide the judges until it is overruled. Unfortunately, counsel for the school in *JFS* did not invite the court to reconsider *Eastleigh*, and even the four dissenting Justices failed to note the structural contrast between *Birmingham* and *Eastleigh*, and the latter's radical unsoundness.

All three cases hold that the decision-maker treated some persons less favourably than others, unlawfully because 'on the ground of' their sex (*Birmingham* and *Eastleigh*) or 'on racial grounds' (*JFS*): under the relevant

* 2010a

[1] [2009] UKSC 15.

[2] See essay 10 at 189–93 above.

[3] [1989] 1 AC 1155.

[4] [1990] 2 AC 751.

statutes, no justification can be offered for such 'direct discrimination'. In *Birmingham* the decision-making council admitted girls to its selective single-sex schools only if their test papers scored significantly higher than the threshold score for boys. It had a reason for treating girls' scores and applications differently from boys': only thus could the number of girls admitted be kept to the number of places available for girls—many fewer places than for boys. Thus the council's reasoning, at more than one point, made overt reference to a child's sex as *the ground for* treating it less favourably than another child of the opposite sex. The unchallenged evidence that the council harboured neither animus against females nor prejudice in favour of males—a fact ineptly described in the Court of Appeal and House of Lords as having 'no intention to discriminate'—was rightly held immaterial. The impugned decision to set the threshold higher for girls treated girl applicant-examinees less favourably on the ground that they were girls, albeit only *as a means* of balancing admissions to places available. The Lords' ruling was right and ineluctable. It could fittingly have been (but was not) formulated thus: the council's decision-making involved, indeed on its face expressed, an intention (adopted as a means) to treat one sex less favourably than the other at the point of selection.

In *Eastleigh*, on the other hand, the council's ground (reason) for admitting persons of pensionable age to its swimming pools without charge had nothing to do with anybody's sex. It had as *end* (purpose, ground) the alleviation of the poverty presumptively experienced by pensioners, and as *means* the adoption (on grounds of ease of verification) of a criterion much more easily verifiable than being in receipt of a pension or being poor, namely pensionability: being of pensionable age. The fact that, as it happened, Parliament had discriminated between the sexes in fixing pensionable age (60 for women, 65 for men) played no part, whether overt or covert, in the council's reasoning and decision-making. Losing sight both of the phrase 'on the ground of', and of the decision-making subject (the council) whose grounds for 'treating' persons favourably or unfavourably are the issue in 'direct discrimination', the Lords' majority held that the selected criterion (pensionable age) '*itself*... treats women more favourably than men "on the ground of their sex"', that 'the expression "pensionable age" is no more than a convenient shorthand expression' for aged 60 (women) and aged 65 (men), that the council's 'determinative formula' was '*inherently* discriminatory' between men and women and was a condition 'which is itself gender-based'. The case was, said Lord Goff, 'no different from one in which the defendant adopts a *criterion which favours* widows against widowers, on the basis that the former are likely to be less well off'.[5]

[5] [1990] 2 AC 751 at 771F (emphasis added, here as elsewhere).

But if 'on the basis of' qualifies 'adopts' (rather than 'favours')—as it must if it is to match the anti-discrimination statute's relevant provision—Lord Goff's proposition is unsustainable; there was no reason at all to suppose that the council thought poverty runs with sex rather than with age.

Test it like this. Eastleigh Council's reasoning and policy, and its policy's formulation and operation, would doubtless have remained quite unchanged whether the councillors adopted and operated it: (1) quite unaware that pensionable age differs according to sex; or (2) at a time when pensionable age was uniform but subsequently changed by Parliament so as to become sex-based; or (3) at a time when the pensionable age was sex-based but subsequently changed to become uniform; or (4) during a period when Parliament's scheme discriminated between the sexes by explicitly providing, for each age cohort of the population between 60 and 70, (a) that a much higher proportion of women than of men would be declared of pensionable age, and (b) that the particular women and particular men to be declared pensionable would be settled by an annual birthdate lottery—with the result that for any particular person aged between 60 and 70, his or her 'being of pensionable age' could be determined only by production of a card issued on the basis of the lottery. As the four hypotheses just listed show, the majority's variously worded assertions that 'pensionable age' is 'inherently' sex-based or is 'shorthand for' sex-based differences can quite properly be simply denied. At best, those assertions are irrelevant to the statutory question of the *grounds* on which the council decided its charging policy, or on which the council's servants issued or refused free tickets for swimming. For the pool gatekeepers could ask for a card certifying pensionable age without even being aware that the cards are currently available to women at an earlier age (or, under the lottery scheme imagined in (4) above, are available to many more women than to men at each age between 60 and 65). In the relevant (grounds-related) sense of 'because', it cannot (with respect) be right to say, with Lady Hale in *JFS*, that 'the husband in [*Eastleigh*] was charged admission to the pool, when his wife was not, simply because he was a man'.[6] In short, *Eastleigh* was wrongly decided. Even after two decades, it would be right to overrule it, for no one can have relied on it to their own detriment, and its error deprives some decision-makers of their statutory right to show proportionate justification for their discrimination.

Instead, the majority in *JFS* adopted *Eastleigh*'s fallacious conflation of 'grounds' with 'criterion'. True, Lord Phillips PSC showed little sympathy for Lord Goff's proposal, in *Eastleigh*, that the question is whether the complainant 'would…have received the same treatment from the defendant

[6] [2009] UKSC 15 at para. [62].

but for his or her sex', a question which eliminates the statutorily mandated inquiry into the *defendant's grounds*, practical reasoning and deliberation, and intentionality, in favour of an inquiry (without statutory mandate) into the *causation* of the *complainant's outcome*. But the *JFS* majority all held that the school applied to applicants a criterion which, like (they said) the council's in *Eastleigh*, is 'inherently' or 'intrinsically' discriminatory—here ethnically and thus racially.

The structural similarity between *JFS* and *Eastleigh* is, one may respectfully suggest, a quite different one. It is this. In *Eastleigh* the council's adoption of the criterion of pensionable age had nothing to do with sex. But (whether or not the council was aware of it), a third party, Parliament, had made the criterion at least temporarily sex-based and sex-discriminatory. In *JFS* the school's adoption of the criterion (for preferential admission) of membership of the Orthodox Jewish religion had nothing to do with ethnicity: it was concerned—as emerges clearly from Lord Mance's discussion ([95]) of indirect discrimination—with encouraging or kindling the religious belief and practice of boys who (because already members of the religion) could thus be helped to adopt or conform to Orthodox Jewish belief and practice without having to enter that religion or undergo the extended formal processes of conversion to it. But (whether or not the school was aware of it), the third party to whom the school deferred in identifying applicants' membership of the religion, the Office of the Chief Rabbi (OCR), interpreted the criterion in such a way that persons of a certain descent ('ethnic origin', said the Supreme Court) would be counted as members of the religion even without evidence of their own or either of their parents' creed, religious practice, or conversion. This fundamental structural similarity between *Eastleigh* and *JFS* is not identified even in the dissenting judgments. The importance of the distinction—unregarded in *JFS*—between (a) the impugned decision-maker's grounds and (b) the grounds on which a third party such as Parliament or the OCR made a decision causally determining the result of the impugned decision can be seen by annotating a passage in the judgment of Lord Kerr, representative of the majority's approach:

> [a] The school refused entry to M because an essential part of the required ethnic make-up was missing in his case. [b] The reason that they took the decision on those grounds was a religious one—[c] OCR had said that M was not a Jew. But [d] the reason that he was not a Jew was because of his ethnic origins...[7]

The school's grounds for refusing are accurately stated in [b] and, above all, [c]. The third-party OCR's grounds for its pronouncement are stated,

[7] Para. [116].

rather simplistically but for present purposes accurately enough, in [d]; they are the grounds mentioned in [a]. But in [a] Lord Kerr, using the highly ambiguous term 'because', speaks as if those grounds can be predicated of the school simply because they are predicated of the OCR. This supposed entailment fails, however, for the reason which is so conspicuous in *Eastleigh* and is equally (albeit not so obviously) applicable here, as appears from the truth of [b] and [c]: the council's or the school's impugned decision-making, its *grounds* for decision, and its decision would be precisely the same even if these decision-makers were completely unaware of the criteria used by the third party in its ruling on pensionability or Orthodoxy—the criteria and ruling which make the *impact or effect* of the impugned decision turn out (in this respect like other cases of *indirect* discrimination) to be sex- or racially discriminatory.

Here as in many other areas of the law, nothing will go right while the courts neglect the basic structure of practical reasoning, intending, deciding, and acting. For the statutory distinction between direct and indirect discrimination has its foundation in that structure. The structure is not essentially problematic. But *seeing it whole* is what matters, and is all but universally neglected in our judicial jurisprudence. Aristotle's homely example will suffice to establish the essentials: What are you doing? I'm getting out of my armchair to go to the cupboard. Why? To get some herbs. Why? To mix a potion. Why? To lose weight. Why? Because that way I'll be healthy.[8] (It matters not whether your end here is health, or whether for you health is rather a means to being elected, and being elected is a means to becoming rich and becoming rich a means to buying women and old masters.) At each point, you are reporting your ground for exerting yourself to get up, your ground for going to the cupboard, your ground for getting herbs, and so on. At each point you are identifying your intention in so exerting yourself, walking, getting, etc. At each point you are identifying an end that is also (save perhaps for the very last one) a means, and are equally identifying a means that is also (save for the very first one) an end. At each point you are identifying your motive, as one of a whole sequence of motives,[9] your reason, as one of a whole sequence of reasons,

[8] *Physics* 2. 3: 194b35–195b1; *Metaphysics* 5. 2: 1013a35–b3. [See also essay 9 at pp. 158–9.]

[9] Of course, one can stipulate, as lawyers conventionally do, that 'motive' signifies an end which is at or near the end of the sequence furthest out from the acting person's immediate exertion. In *Birmingham* counsel and the courts quasi-stipulatively used 'intention' in this way. That is in line with the historic convention (pointed out by, e.g., Aquinas) that 'intention' signifies *end* rather than means. But this convention will mislead analysis unless one is equally aware (as Aquinas certainly is) that virtually all means are also ends—which entails that 'intention', 'intend', etc. apply just as well to 'go to the cupboard' as to 'get healthy', and just as well to 'set a score more favourable to boys (for whom we have more places)' as to 'to make selective education more available to boys than to girls (whose future, after all, is in the home or at the checkout)'.

your purpose(s) and your ground(s), as one of a whole sequence of purposes and grounds and intentions and ends which are also means. *Anything* which (even very reluctantly) you count—and *only* what you count—in favour of behaving the way you do appears (under the description it has in your actual practical reasoning) in the adequate account of your grounds = motives = intentions = ends = means (and thus of your action).[10]

So if an employer free from all racial prejudice rejects white job applicants because whites are unpopular with its customers, its ground for rejecting them—and its intention and indeed motive, end, and purpose in rejecting them—includes their race, not as an end in itself (racism) but *nonetheless* as a means (to customer satisfaction and business survival). If a council imposes higher standards on girl applicants because, for purely historical-accidental reasons, is has fewer girls' schools, it is acting on the grounds of sex. If a council animated by feminist chauvinism, or just concerned about *female* poverty, adopts pensionable age as a criterion for free swimming because the pensionable age for women is lower, it is deciding and acting on the grounds of sex. If other councils with swimming pools adopt that same criterion simply because it approximates to a poverty criterion and is readily verifiable, they are not deciding or acting on grounds of sex even though Parliament *was* when it set sex-differentiated pensionable ages. When so many judges speak as if these issues could be satisfactorily discussed by simple contrasts between, say, 'the motive' (or 'the intention') and 'ground(s)', it is hard to allay the suspicion that our judiciary lacks clear awareness of its need for an adequate analysis and synthesis of a set of concepts quite central to our law, not least to the statutory distinction between 'direct' (intended) and 'indirect' (side effect) discrimination.

[10] What you foresee as an effect of your behaviour, but do not in any way count in favour of so behaving, is a side effect—an *indirect* effect—outwith your intentions, not part of what you choose to do. (You are of course not free of moral and/or legal responsibility for it, but such responsibility is not intention-based.) Successful counsel in the Lords in *Eastleigh* appealed directly (755F) to the well-known passage in Lord Bridge's leading judgment *R v Moloney* [1985] AC 905 at 926:

> that intention is something quite distinct from motive or desire...can normally be quite simply explained...by some homely example. A man who, at London Airport, boards a plane which he knows to be bound for Manchester, clearly intends to travel to Manchester, even though Manchester is the last place he wants to be and his motive for boarding the plane is *simply to escape pursuit*. The possibility that the plane may have engine trouble and be diverted to Luton does not affect the matter. *By boarding the Manchester plane, the man conclusively demonstrates his intention to go there, because it is a moral certainty that that is where he will arrive.* (Emphases added.)

In reality, however, a man who, to escape his pursuers, boards the first plane he sees being boarded, simply because it gives him the best chance of eluding pursuit, need have no intention to go to Manchester even if, as he boards it, he sees (believes, 'knows') that that is the destination—the destination does not enter at all into his practical reasoning save under the description 'not London Airport'; the complete list of his intentions is: to elude pursuit, to take a plane, to get away from London Airport, to go into hiding in whatever turns out to be the plane's destination city. Though this appeal to *Moloney* was not alluded to by Lord Bridge, his mistakes about grounds in *Eastleigh* manifest the same failure of analysis as his paradigmatic mistake about intentions in *Moloney*.

The need for such an analysis will be no less when the Equality Act 2010 takes effect to replace 'on ... grounds ...' with 'because of'. For the new provision defining direct discrimination keeps the focus on the impugned action ('A treats') rather than on the action's impugned effect (on B):

13. Direct discrimination

(1) A person (A) discriminates against another (B) if, because of a protected characteristic, A treats B less favourably than A treats or would treat others.

The Explanatory Memorandum to the Bill stated that 'this change in wording does not change the legal meaning of the definition, but rather is designed to make it more accessible to the ordinary user of the [Act]'. Even without this assurance, the definition's concern with why ('because of' what) A treated B less favourably, rather than with what factors contributed to the impact of A's conduct on B, indicates that a decision-making body's treatment of B cannot rightly be judged direct discrimination unless at least one step in the body's actual, motivating reasoning towards decision refers to a protected characteristic.

Part Four

Persons Beginning and Dying

15

ORGANIC UNITY, BRAIN LIFE, AND OUR BEGINNING*

> ...*psychological* functioning is somehow of the essence of persons.... [I]t is in the mental or psychological dimension of the human organism that the unity and continuity of persons is to be sought.... What our identity actually consists in, I suggest, is, once again, whatever, as a matter of scientific or metaphysical fact, normally underlies these more superficial continuities [exhibited in consciousness and behavior, memory and so forth] and provides the deep explanation for them; and from a purely secular standpoint I should have thought that the overwhelmingly most favoured candidate was a continuity of organization within those parts of our brain that directly sustain those activities we think of as mental.... [C]onsiderations of identity firmly favour the view that before the brain has matured to the point of being able to sustain psychological functions, a human life has yet to begin.[1]

Philosophizing in Oxford from his 'purely secular standpoint', Michael Lockwood reports that he was 'somewhat taken aback to discover', after first writing up his '"brain life" conception of when human life begins', that the idea had for nearly twenty years had 'a wide currency amongst Catholic writers'.[2]

* Unpublished: 1988.

[1] Lockwood, 'Warnock versus Powell (and Harradine): When Does Potentiality Count?' at 204, 205, 207. Lockwood adds:

> (This notion of *brain life* has been in circulation in the literature since the mid 1960s—Singer and Wells have recently advocated it in their book *The Reproduction Revolution* [OUP, 1984, 97–8]—but other writers have not, to my knowledge, thought to tie it in with the question of what sustains the identity of a human person.)

[2] Lockwood, 'When Does a Human Life Begin?' at 213. He cites writings of 1966–74 by Bernard Häring, Rudolph Ehrensing, Roy U. Schenk, and Wilfried Ruff SJ.

I

The idea is presented as 'the symmetrical counterpart of the criterion of brain death, used for determining when a human being goes out of existence'.[3]

> Just as I shall live only as long as the relevant part of my brain remains essentially intact, so I came into existence only when the appropriate part or parts of my brain came into existence, or, more precisely, reached the appropriate stage of development to sustain my identity as a human being, with the capacity for consciousness.[4]

In short: human beings begin when capacity for consciousness begins, and end when it ends. Hence Lockwood's key general thesis: 'You and I are not human organisms'.[5] Each of us merely 'corresponds to',[6] and is 'ensconced in',[7] a human organism during a phase of that organism's life—a phase which begins when that organism develops a brain, or at least the relevant parts of a brain, and ends when it (irreversibly) loses (the functioning of) those parts.

In developing his symmetry thesis, Lockwood thought of brain death as the irreversible loss of function in the 'higher brain centers', a loss compatible with 'the continuation of such lower brain functions as are necessary to maintain respiration, circulation, and so forth', so that 'the living human organism remained, even though we were no more'.[8]

But in the statements on brain death which are normative for British medical practice, issued by the Conference of Medical Royal Colleges and their Faculties on 11 October 1976 and 15 January 1979, the key propositions are: (1) 'It is agreed that permanent functional death of the *brain stem* constitutes brain death'; and (2) 'brain death represents the stage at which the patient becomes truly dead, because by then *all the functions* of the brain have permanently and irreversibly ceased'.[9] The statements say nothing about loss of capacity for consciousness. A fair reading would treat them as founded on the idea of *loss of integrated organic functioning* (the functioning which *is* the life of an organism such as human persons are). Certainly, contemporary medical textbooks keep quite distinct what Lockwood treats as one and the same: (a) brain death; and (b) the 'persistent vegetative state' in which there is no cortical function but enough brain stem function to keep the person's integrated organic functioning and life going.[10]

[3] Lockwood, 'When Does a Life Begin?' at 20. [4] *Ibid.* at 23. [5] *Ibid.* at 11.
[6] *Ibid.* [7] *Ibid.* at 24. [8] *Ibid.* at 11.
[9] British Medical Journal, 13 November 1976, 1187; 15 January 1979, 332 (emphasis added).
[10] On the general question of 'brain death', and especially on integrated organic functioning, see Grisez and Boyle, *Life and Death with Liberty and Justice*, ch. 3 [and essay 18].

So, if one expects as a conceptual symmetry between the human being's loss of identity in death and the beginning of (the identity of) that being, one should look for the beginning of that integrated organic functioning which is lost in death.

II

That integrated organic functioning begins, in fact, at conception. Embryology is a science the central subject of which (its object of study) begins at fertilization. In mammals, this precedes by some weeks the development of a brain. During those weeks, factors other than the brain control the unified dynamism and organization of development. But once the developing organism, be it rat or human, equips itself with a brain, the factor by which it is *principally* integrated is the functioning of the brain. *Thereafter*, it is when the brain's function is altogether lost that the whole organism's *organic* unity is lost.

Lockwood displays no interest in the profound difference between the life, the being-in-continuity, of an organism and the existence and subsistence of any other system or state of affairs. He never attends to the differences between (a) complexity and distinction *within* a unitary being, and (b) diversity or multiplicity of beings, of substantial (not merely logical) subjects.

So he embraces the principle of a 'dilemma' which R.M. Hare, Peter Singer, Jonathan Glover, Michael Tooley, and other philosophers have proposed: whatever factors might support a duty not to kill the newborn child or the six-month fetus would support not only a duty not to kill the day-old conceptus *but also* a duty not to prevent a pre-conception system or state of affairs from resulting in conception.[11] True, Lockwood sets up the dilemma somewhat differently. These other philosophers draw the line between (a) the child after it has conscious desires and (b) all previous stages in the life of the child *and of the gametes from which it results.* Lockwood draws it between (a) the embryo/fetus/neonate at all stages after the emergence of its brain, and (b) the early conceptus and certain pre-conception states of affairs. But he shares with the other philosophers the refusal to acknowledge any relevant importance in the fact, event, reality of conception.

In reality, sperm, ovum, and conceptus—even when sperm and ovum are juxtaposed to each other in a manner conducive to fertilization, and

[11] See the texts cited by Lockwood, 'When Does a Life Begin?' at n. 29.

the conceptus (embryo)[12] is considered moments after conception—offer no analogy to the unity and continuity of human organic life. Sperm, ovum, and conceptus are (to use an old phrase) 'other and other': each quite distinct from the others. This otherness or distinctness is witnessed to by the fact that (a) the 'dilemma' to which Hare, Tooley, Glover, Singer, and Lockwood point *cannot even be stated in a clear and stable form*; and (b) Lockwood's main formulation of it is self-contradictory. Lockwood offers no less than six different statements about what it is that has, or what there are that have, or what it is that *is*, a reality equivalent to the reality of the early embryo:

(1) 'before the [early embryo's] brain comes into being... there is a potential for a human being. But then that is equally true of *a* sperm and an ovum before conception'[13]

(2) 'To say that both a sperm about to fertilize an ovum and a new-born child *have* the potential to become a person is to ignore a crucial distinction...'[14]

(3) 'neither a sperm-and-ovum-about-to-fuse, nor a new-born infant, actually possess*es* any of those attributes which...'[15]

(4) 'the sperm and ovum... *do* not *have* the potential ever to be a person...'[16]

(5) 'we were never week-old embryos, any more than we were sperm *or* ova'[17]

(6) 'individually [the ovum and sperm] don't [have the potential to develop into a human person], but considered jointly they do. If... one mixes sperm and ov*a* together in a Petri dish, with suitable nutrients, what the dish contains already has the potential for developing into at least one human person.... [T]he combined system comprising sperm and ov*a*, in a suitable medium, itself has an active potentiality for giving rise to a fertilized ovum.'[18]

Six statements, six different logical subjects: first Lockwood offers (1) a sperm and an ovum, whose unity or plurality is kept indeterminate by avoiding any verb and by using the locution 'there is a potential', thus

[12] Following the convention usual in bioethical discussion of the earliest stages of a human life, 'embryo' refers to the new organism (the unborn child) at all phases from its conception for its first sixty days or so, after which it is commonly called a fetus. (Complications arising in a very few cases from twinning are considered in essay 16.)

[13] Lockwood, 'When Does a Life Begin?' at 19 (emphasis added).

[14] *Ibid.* at 28 (emphasis added).

[15] *Ibid.* at 27 (emphasis added).

[16] *Ibid.* (emphasis added).

[17] *Ibid.* at 29 (emphasis added).

[18] 'Warnock versus Powell' at 196, 197 (emphasis added).

avoiding identifying what it is that has the potential. Then he offers three different specifications of a substantive subject of the potential: in (2) a sperm; in (3) a-sperm-and-ovum-about-to-fuse, hyphenated to warrant the singular verb that follows; in (4) the sperm and [the] ovum, distinct subjects because followed by a plural verb. Then he has (5) sperm *or* ova (translating the sentence from the first person plural to the first person singular, presumably a sperm *or* an ovum). Finally, we are offered (6) the multiple contents of a Petri dish, with plural subjects (including plural ova), singular verb, but perhaps plural product, 'at least one human person'. And the final and full-dress formulation contradicts both itself and the implicit thesis of the dilemma:

> [i] the sperm and ovum... do not have the potential ever to be a person, but only to become a person in the more oblique sense of turning into a human organism, comprising a brain capable of sustaining a human life. [ii] And that... goes for the early embryo as well. [iii] If it develops normally, it will, to be sure, one day be a mature human organism to which there corresponds a person. [iv] But persons, as I argued at the beginning of this paper, are not identical with human organisms.

In [i], Lockwood admits that sperm and/or ovum is or are not a human organism, and can only become a human person by first, each of them, *turning* (together) *into* (one) something else, a human organism. In [iii] he admits, tacitly, that the early embryo already is precisely that, a human organism, which can become (or, in his official theory, 'correspond to') a human person—*without turning into* any other human organism but simply by maturing.[19] Thus [iii] contradicts [ii], which asserted the supposed dilemma's principle: that what goes for sperm and ovum goes for the embryo. It is the tacit admission in [iii] that must survive this contradiction; for it does no more (and no less) than concede what all scientific and metaphysical study of early mammalian and human development treats, for good reason, as manifest: organic unity and (in the vast majority of cases) continuity, from fertilization.[20]

[19] This admission is even clearer in a later passage, in 'Hare on Potentiality: A Rejoinder' at 348, where Lockwood says of an embryo transferred to a surrogate's uterus, 'the chances that *it* will implant and *grow into a healthy child* are excellent' (emphasis added).

[20] The best that can be said for Lockwood on this matter is that he did not seek to cover over this indeterminacy of subject—of sperm/joint sperm-and-ovum singular/sperm and ovum plural/disjunctive sperm or ovum/disjunctive sperm and ova—with any such bizarre mock-naming ceremony as is performed by Hare, 'The Abnormal Child' at 369:

> I do not think that the harm you are doing to the foetus or the... new-born infant by killing them is greater than that which you are doing to *Andrew* by stopping *him* from being conceived...

Note, incidentally, that in his later 'When Does Potentiality Count? A Comment on Lockwood?' Hare argues (220–1) that newborn infants, since they have pleasures and desires, can themselves be

III

Let us return to the brain. The early embryo lacks the brain that will equip him or her with the capacity *to think*. But equally the early embryo already has the power to create precisely that capacity for itself (himself or herself), by the metabolic processes of ingestion and an internally directed organic maturing. And to be more precise, the human organism that came into being when I was conceived—or, in Lockwood's implausibly dualistic terms: the human organism which came into being with the conception of the organism to which now I correspond and in which now I am embodied or ensconced—already then had the unique capacity for having, that is, the potential for, *my* consciousness, my understanding, my choices, and my projects.

In short, the early embryo does have the capacity which Lockwood stipulates as definitive of the person, the 'capacity for conscious thought'.[21] It has this capacity rather as I have the capacity *for speaking* Norwegian; not the capacity *to speak* it, but the capacity to acquire that capacity by a kind of ingestion and metabolic change of external resources.[22] †

Underlying Lockwood's (and Hare's and others') lack of interest in organic constitution, unity, and continuity is a *dualism*. It is this dualism that prevents him (and them) from acknowledging that normal day-old human embryos, by being (as he concedes) human organisms, are equally human beings, each of them an individual for whom the development of its capacities would be a direct benefit. Such dualism's influence certainly goes far wider than Lockwood (and company) and the question of the status of embryonic human beings. The value of Lockwood's work is that it articulates with clarity the implications of thoughts which many people entertain—thoughts which one must be entertaining if one finds plausible the passage quoted at the head of this essay.

harmed, but that in the case of fetuses, embryos, and gametes 'no harm is in these cases done to the subject as such by destroying it' (224); gametes and, *pace* Lockwood, embryos and fetuses have no interests (224) and cannot be either benefited or harmed (216). An important part of Lockwood's argument is a sane protest against this sort of thing: see further his 'Hare on Potentiality: A Rejoinder'.

[21] 'A person is a being that is conscious, in the sense of having the capacity for conscious thought and experiences': Lockwood, 'When Does a Life Begin?' at 10. Note that Lockwood's later account of *person*, in his 'Warnock versus Powell' at 201–2, is more adequate:

> A sufficient condition for a sentient being to be a person is that it *belongs to a species* mature non-defective members of which [possess capacities such as self-awareness, rationality in the Aristotelian sense, etc.].

(But he does not explain why sentience is a necessary condition for a being of such a species to be a person. Nor does he say how the new references to species cohere with his continued objections to 'speciesism'.) See further n. 26 below.

[22] See, for helpful clarification of 'capacity', Iglesias, 'In Vitro Fertilization' at 35–6.

Lockwood wants us to distinguish as *other* and *other* (a) the human being or self which (even when unconscious and not yet able to have or form preferences or even desires) has interests[23] and (b) the human organism, which *even when fully mature* has no interests.[24] He does not address some relevant implications of his position.

One implication is this. It is not a human organism that performs bodily, intelligent, freely chosen, creative, and continuing human acts, such as my writing (or your reading) this essay on paper.

Lockwood's dualism suffers the fate of every account of our being, life, and activity which treats *human person* and *human life*, or *conscious self* and *human organism*, or *acts of the human organism* and *acts of the human person*, as other and other. That fate is to overlook, or render inexplicable, a unity which we know more intimately and thoroughly than any other unity in the world, indeed the very paradigm (for us) of substantial unity and identity through time. For this dualism renders inexplicable the unity (and continuity) in complexity, which one is aware of in each of one's conscious acts. Every dualism undertakes to be a theory of something (of *my personal identity* as a unitary and subsisting, *intermittently* self-conscious and freely self-directing organism), but ends up unable to pick out any *one* something of which to be the theory.[25]

Lockwood's theory involved him in a twofold dualism. For it identified and contrasted two realities, each of them contrasted with a third reality, the *human person*: neither the *human organism*, nor the *human being* (or self) is, he said, 'essentially' personal. But, sometime between 1985 and 1988, Lockwood abandoned one half of his twofold dualism, the contrast between *human person* and *human being*—without saying that he was doing so, but with definitive clarity.[26] Now he admits that to be a human being is to be a human person. He retains, unreconstructed, his equally needless and indefensible dualism of *human organism* and *human being*: 'You and I are not human organisms.'[27]

[23] 'When Does a Life Begin?' at 26. [24] *Ibid.* at 29.

[25] See further *NDMR* 308–9; Grisez and Boyle, *Life and Death with Liberty and Justice*, 71, 377–80, 402.

[26] In other words, there is a major, unadvertised change in position between 'When Does a Life Begin?' and 'Warnock versus Powell', even though the later paper refers its readers to the earlier for a fuller treatment. In the earlier paper (at 12–13), and in the version of the later paper which (as he records) was read to the Philosophical Society at Oxford in November 1985 (where I was the commentator), it was expressly denied that the human being or self is essentially personal. But in the published version of the later paper (at 201), 'human being' is defined as 'a person of the species homo sapiens', and we ourselves are said to be 'necessarily' persons.

[27] There is one point at which Lockwood offers to speak on behalf of a 'viewpoint' not 'purely secular'. He asserts that 'those who believe in the existence of an immortal soul' share his belief that we are not human organisms, 'because they believe that we continue to exist, even when the corresponding human organisms die, decay, and turn to dust'. The central western theological tradition can better speak through its own representative thinkers, whose teaching can be summarized in two

NOTES

See now, generally, George and Tollefsen, *Embryo*, especially 133–4 on the brain life/brain death argument; Lee and George, *Body-Self Dualism in Contemporary Ethics and Politics*, 119–30; Howsepian, 'Four Queries Concerning the Metaphysics of Early Human Embryogenesis'.

† *Capacity to acquire capacity naturally*… (at n. 22). The inherent and self-developing organic capacity to acquire capacity… is what in later writings I call radical [from *radix*, Latin for root] capacity: see e.g. essay 1, p. 35; essay 17, p. 297, and esp. III. 14 secs V, VI, and XI. This terminology is used and lucidly explained in George and Tollefsen, *Embryo*, 79–81. Olson, *The Human Animal*, 86 speaks equivalently of second-order capacities:

> Now there is one sense in which a human embryo or fetus lacks any mental capacities, in particular the capacity for rationality and self-consciousness. A five-month-old fetus cannot think or feel or remember because the neural structures needed to carry out those activities are not yet in place. But the fetus can *become* rational and self-conscious. It has the second-order capacity to acquire the first-order capacity to think and reason. Hence, there is a sense in which ordinary human fetuses, but not armchairs or oysters, have mental capacities, and in particular those mental capacities that distinguish people from non-people. Even if they have no first-order mental capacities, they have second-order mental capacities.

propositions. (1) The human organism's powers (e.g. of referring and meaning, and freely choosing) transcend the bodily, so that a dimension of one's being can be conceived as surviving the death of one's organism, as a mutilated remnant of it. (2) But that dimension is not oneself, and 'if only the soul finds salvation, I don't, nor any human person, any human being'. St Thomas: 'anima autem cum sit pars corporis hominis, non est totus hominis, et *anima mea non est ego*: unde licet anima consequatur salutem in alia vita, non tamen ego vel quilibet homo'. [In *I Cor.* XV lect ii; see also *ST* I q.75 a.4 obj. 2 and ad 2 (anima non potest dici hypostasis vel persona humana). See further Grisez, *Beyond the New Theism*, chs 14 and 23.]

16

WHEN MOST PEOPLE BEGIN*

Leaving aside real or supposed divine, angelic, and extraterrestrial beings, the one thing common to all who, in common thought and speech, are regarded as persons is that they are living human individuals. This being so, anyone who claims that some set of living, whole, bodily human individuals are not persons, and ought not to be regarded and treated as persons, must demonstrate that the ordinary notion of a person is misguided and should be replaced by a different notion. Otherwise the claim will be mere arbitrary discrimination. But no such demonstration has ever been provided, and none is in prospect.

Among the most serious attempts to provide a demonstration is Michael Tooley's argument that personhood is gradually acquired by development; he concludes that not only the unborn but also newborn babies are not persons.[1] But Tooley's argument begs the question by simply assuming two basic but unargued premises: (1) that abortion is morally acceptable, and (2) that an active potentiality or capacity which is not being actually exercised cannot be the defining property of personhood even when it is a capacity really possessed by an individual.[2]

Some contemporary neo-Aristotelians, notably Joseph Donceel, have argued that personhood is dependent on sense organs and a brain, and that the early embryo, though a living human individual, is only a pre-personal entity which changes into a person (is 'ensouled'), not gradually but by a sudden, substantial change that occurs when the brain first begins to develop; thereafter, the personal soul shapes the development of the whole entity.[3] (By 'substantial change' is meant the change which occurs when an individual entity of one kind changes into an individual entity of a different kind, as typically occurs, for example, in a chemical reaction.) But

* 1993a (part).

[1] Tooley, *Abortion and Infanticide*.

[2] Hurst, *Beginning Lives*, 107–11; Grisez, 'When Do People Begin?'; Atkinson, 'Persons in the Whole Sense'.

[3] Donceel, 'Immediate Animation and Delayed Hominization'.

Donceel's view, like its mediaeval predecessors, is inconsistent with the biological data and with itself.[4] The beginning of the brain's development does not yet provide a bodily basis for intellectual activities, but provides only the precursor of such a basis; so if this precursor is sufficient for 'ensoulment', there is no reason why earlier precursors should fail to suffice. In fact each embryonic human individual has from the outset the specific developmental tendency (involving a high degree of organization) which includes the epigenetic primordia of all its organs. The hypothesis of a substantial change by ensoulment at some time after the forming of the zygote is an unnecessary multiplication of entities, to be eliminated by Occam's razor, that is, the scientific principle of economy in explanations.

The biological basis for the mediaeval view that specifically human ensoulment takes place some weeks after conception has completely disappeared. Mediaeval Aristotelians such as Thomas Aquinas depended upon the biology then current, which taught that life originates from semen and menstrual blood, that neither of these is alive,[†] and that the very limited active instrumental power in the semen organizes the blood into a body which can begin to grow and nourish itself in a plant-like way and then in an animal-like way. If the mediaeval Aristotelians had known about the organic life which organizes the roughly one billion items of molecular information in the one-cell conceptus with a self-directing dynamic integration that will remain continuously and identifiably identical until death, they would have concurred with the view of their successors (and almost everyone else) since the eighteenth century.[5] On this later view the fertilized human ovum is specifically human (not merely vegetable), and even the youngest human embryo already has a body which in its already specified (but quite undeveloped) capacities, its epigenetic primordia, is apt for understanding, knowing, and choosing. Rather as you or I have the capacity to speak Tibetan or Icelandic, though we lack the ability to do so, so even the youngest human embryo already has the biological capacity appropriate to supporting specifically human operations such as self-consciousness, rationality, and choice (given only time and metabolic transformations of air, water, and other sustenance). The active potential which he or she already has includes the very capacities which are distinctive of persons.[6] So he or she is a human being and human person with potential, not a merely potential human person or potential human being.

[4] Grisez, 'When do People Begin?'; Ashley, 'A Critique of the Theory of Delayed Hominization'; Gallagher, 'Is the Human Embryo a Person?' at 22–6.

[5] Heaney, 'Aquinas and the Presence of the Human Rational Soul in the Early Embryo'.

[6] Wade, 'Potentiality in the Abortion Discussion'.

The most serious contemporary effort to show that there is no lasting human individual (and therefore no person) until about two weeks after conception, is by Norman Ford.[7] Unlike Tooley and Donceel, Ford holds that personhood begins when an individual with a truly human nature emerges. But the conclusions of his argument are so radically opposed to any biological understanding of human development that they turn out to offer no serious alternative to the standard view: an individual with a truly human nature begins at fertilization.[8] Still Ford's argument is worth tracing, because it attempts to take seriously certain claims often unreflectively uttered, such as that until implantation, or the formation of the primitive streak, or the loss of toti- or pluri-potentiality among the embryo's cells, or the end of the period during which twinning may naturally occur, the conceptus is 'not individuated'.

Ford proposes that at fertilization an ontologically individual and biologically human entity, the zygote, begins, but that (whatever biologists may think) this is never the same individual as the one which (with the same genetic constitution and gender) will begin about 16 days later and will thereafter survive as one and the same individual until death perhaps many decades later. For, according to Ford, the ontologically individual and human zygote is replaced at the first mitotic division by two ontologically individual beings, which in turn are replaced by four, the four by eight, the eight by 12 and 16, these by 32 and 64, and so forth, until by day 14 there are many thousands of ontologically entirely distinct individual human beings (even though biologists think there is still, unless there has been twinning, only one individual human being). Then these thousands of individuals all suddenly cease to exist when God forms them into 'one living body'.

What drives Ford towards this remarkable conclusion is, on the one hand, his imagination, which finds nothing that looks human in shape until the spatial axes of future somatic development emerge around day 15 and, on the other hand, the classic puzzle about twinning and mosaics (hypothetical combination of two embryos into one). However, his own theory makes twinning unintelligible, since it occurs at a time, around day 6 or 7, when, on his view, there is not one individual to become two, but hundreds to become... how many? (Ford does not even try to apply his theory to the facts about twinning, facts which he has earlier treated as decisive against the standard view.)

[7] Ford, *When Did I Begin?*

[8] For detailed analysis, refutations, and bibliography see Grisez, 'When Do People Begin?'; Fisher, 'Individuogenesis and a Recent Book by Fr Norman Ford'; Fisher, '"When Did I Begin?" Revisited'.

What, then, should be said about twinning, and about the assumed possibility of human mosaics? Simply that, biologically, one always finds just individuals. If these split, or combine to form a mosaic, one then simply finds one or more different individuals. Twinning is an unusual way of being generated; the relationship between the earlier and the later generated individuals is an unusual form of parentage. Being absorbed into a mosaic would presumably be an unusual way of dying. Common thought and language has not had to categorize these events, but there is little or no intrinsic difficulty in doing so.

Nor should one here substitute one's imagination for one's reason. Domination of thought and argument by imagination and conventional associations occurs at various places in the debate. Many people, for example, allow themselves to be dominated by the assumption that no single organ can be larger than all the other organs of an animal, and/or that no major organ can be transient and disposable; they therefore refuse to take seriously the biological data and philosophical considerations which establish that the placenta is an organ of the embryo. Or again, many people (not least some theologians) argue that personhood or ensoulment cannot begin at conception, because they feel it is intolerable to suppose that a high proportion of human persons never get beyond the earliest stage of existence as persons. But it is not intolerable to reason, for: (a) in every era hitherto, infant mortality has been very high, often as high as the rate of pregnancy losses in modern western society; (b) many pregnancy losses are due to chromosomal defects so severe that the losses are not of human beings, but only of beings which (like hydatidiform moles) had a human genome but lacked the epigenetic primordia of a human body normal enough to be the organic basis of at least some intellectual act; and (c) as Ford himself reflects,[9] it is presumptuous to suppose that we know how God provides for those who never have any intellectual life, and what are the limits of his provision.

Any entity which, remaining the same individual, will develop into a paradigmatic instance of a substantial kind already is an instance of that kind. The one-cell human organism originating with the substantial change which occurs upon the penetration of a human ovum by a human sperm typically develops, as one and the same individual, into a paradigmatic instance of the rational bodily person, the human person; in every such case, therefore, it is already an actual instance of the human person. In the atypical case where a genetically human zygote lacks the epigenetic primordia needed to develop any brain, there is no human being and so

[9] See Fisher, 'Individuogenesis and a Recent Book by Fr Norman Ford' at 181.

no human person, no unborn child.[10] And there is another atypical range of cases: some people, including some or all identical twins, were never activated ova, because their life began during the two or three weeks after fertilization, by others dividing or perhaps also others combining.

In all this, what is decisive is not the possession of a unique human genome, but rather the organic integration of a single, whole bodily individual organism. That organic integration, whether the developing organism has one cell or many and whether those cells are toti-potential, pluri-potential or fully specialized, is found from the inception of fertilization. On all biologically and philosophically pertinent criteria that event marks substantial change (in the sense explained above), and no subsequent development or event can be identified plausibly as a genuine substantial change.[‡] If there remain biologically and/or philosophically unresolved questions about identity (individuation) in the exceptional cases of embryos which are about to twin, this no more affects the identity of the remaining 97 per cent of embryos than the puzzles about the identity of some adult Siamese twins affect the identity of the rest of us.

Of course, our imagination balks at equating the intelligent adult with a one-cell zygote smaller than a full stop and weighing only 2 mg. But imagination also balks at differentiating between a full-term child just before and just after birth. And reason can find no event or principle or criterion by which to judge that the typical adult or newborn child or full-term or mid-term unborn child is anything other than one and the same individual human being—human person—as the one-cell, 46-chromosome zygote the emergence of which was the beginning of the personal history of that same child and adult.

In short, scientific and philosophical considerations converge on two conclusions. Every living human individual must be regarded as a person. And most people begin at fertilization; that is, most of us were once zygotes.[§]

NOTES

† *In mediaeval biology neither semen nor menstrual blood is alive*...(p. 288). This goes too far. Neither was thought to have animal life, but Aristotle, *Generation of Animals*, II.3: 736b3, taught that 'nobody would put down the embryo as soulless or in every sense bereft of life (since both the semen and the embryo of an animal have every bit as much life as a plant)' (trans. Arthur Platt, 1910, rev. Jonathan Barnes, 1984).

‡ Anscombe, 'The Early Embryo' in her *Faith in a Hard Ground*, expresses the view that for a 'very short period' the early embryo, though human, is not *a* human [being]. She works with the thought of Aristotle (*Generation of Animals*, II.3: 736b) and Aquinas (*ST* I q.119 a.2c) that there is 'a stage of

[10] Suarez, 'Hydatidiform Moles and Teratomas Confirm the Human Identity of the Preimplemantation Embryo'.

living with animal life without being e.g. a man or a horse', a thought she rightly describes as quite astonishing. At the same time she rejects (218) their thought that the transition from vegetative to animal life is a substantial change, and appears to regard the change from living an animal life to living the life of an animal as not an instance of substantial change. Her reasons for doubting that the human zygote is a human are not stated more definitely than that it lacks the 'outward form and...the human organs' (at 217) and that, though a natural whole (not a separated part like a heart kept alive), it has a 'a certain lack of determinateness' (220), which in turn has something to do, perhaps, with the possibility of twinning (215–16) and with the possibility that it might become, e.g. a cancer or a carneous mole (221).

But against these doubts, it must be said that Aristotle's reason for saying that some living being can be animal without being an animal of a definite species is, as he immediately says, that 'the end is developed last, and the peculiar character of the species is the end of the generation in each individual'. Anscombe accepts that often enough 'formal and final cause are the same' (220) and that as soon as one is really justified in saying 'this is a human' it will be 'an individualised actual form' that operates to govern development. Her thought that before then development is governed by the mysterious 'form that is to be' (final cause) seems incompatible with our understanding of organic development, in which actual form fully intelligible as human (not mouse or beetle or ape) governs the development of the zygote in an individualised but species-specific way.

§ See generally George and Tollefsen, *Embryo*, especially chs 2 and 6. Olson, *The Human Animal*, 92–3, adopts Ford's position, substantially on the faith of Ford's reinterpretation of embryology: until the end of the second week after conception, the cells

> adhere together only loosely, and their growth and other activities are not coordinated in the way that the activities of an organism's cells are coordinated. Until the end of the second week after fertilization, the cells are all alike, or totipotent: they do not have specialized tasks, and each can be the ancestor of any kind of human cell. Most of those cells in fact develop into the placenta and other supporting structures and not into the embryo proper. Each functions independently of the others, metabolizing and dividing at is own rate.

So, Olson thinks, there is no multicellular organism until about two weeks, just a 'mass' or 'clump' (eventually of thousands of organisms, that more or less suddenly become one—Olson does not articulate his thesis so clearly, but that is what it is). This, he says, is what 'embryologists tell us'. No doubt more than one embryologist can be found to say this, but Olson cites only J.J. Diamond's article in *Theological Studies* and the Rev Norman Ford's book, in which Ford accepts that 'most embryologists and biologists' (115) think that the zygote is the very same individual as the three-week embryo, the eight-month fetus and the 40-year-old man; Ford's opposing view relies upon 'inductive philosophical reasoning' (173) dependent on an unexplained distinction between 'biological identity' and 'ontological identity'. Ford concedes that throughout the two or three weeks after conception there is, 'biologically' just one (or two..., if twinning has taken place), but 'ontologically' there emerge, he opines, many complete and distinct individuals. Similarly, the placental tissues developed by the embryo, though biologically an organ of the embryo, are 'ontologically' no part of the individual (or of the mother—nor yet do they constitute an individual—they seem to exist in an ontological limbo). Ford's account of biological identity fails to notice that what biologists are interested in is not genetic constitution alone, nor inherent capacity alone, but the conjunction of these with dynamic and teleologically directed organic integration of parts and processes. Ford's, and derivatively Olson's, accounts of embryonic life minimize or eliminate the distinctively biological, in favour of a picture drawn from the non-biological, static analogy of a bag of (sticky) marbles. His denial that there is evidence of intrinsic unity and a multicellular individual neglects the immensely complex and directional processes by which the embryo's dividing cells, at the very stage to which he and Olson are referring, are becoming differentiated between 'inner' and 'outer' and are linked to one another by countless patterned processes characteristic of unified organic development. Ford arbitrarily declares (149) that 'directedness and finality [signs of which he concedes] are said to be intrinsic only if they appear within *what is already known* to be a definitely established given individual and for its benefit' (emphasis added). He thus constructs a vicious-circle barrier to protect his position against the best biological and ontological evidence of established individuality.

17

ON PRODUCING HUMAN EMBRYOS*

I

Some cloning is of cell lines, or is a matter of tissue culture. The cells thus produced are histologically identical to the cell or cells (for example skin or liver cells) from which they have been cloned. The new cells are like the antecedent cells: they lack the genetic primordia for self-directed development as a self-sustaining whole organism organized for development into a mature individual and member of a sexually reproducing animal species. Even when the cells are parts of, or derivative from parts of, a *human* organism, cloning of this kind does not involve the intrinsic ethical issues which I shall point to in relation to production of embryos by cloning. There arise of course all the incidental issues that pertain to experimentation, consent, commercialization, unwanted sequelae and iatrogenic illness, and so forth. But the development of cell cloning is, in itself, to be encouraged for its promise of significant medical advances.

Some cloning is of embryos. In the term 'embryo' I include the zygote, the morula, the blastocyst, and the embryo *stricto sensu* (not to mention the fetus)—that is to say, every instance (whether comprising one cell, two, or many) of an organism that has the genetic primordia for development into a mature individual member of an animal species. In using the term 'embryo' thus, I follow the example of the pioneers of IVF (in vitro fertilization), who though well aware of the conventional terms and distinctions which I just recalled, used 'embryo' to refer to even the earliest conceptus. That is how R.G. Edwards described 'the beginnings of life', for example of Louise Brown in the first minutes or hours after her conception in his Petri dish. He said, for example, that

> resistance to injury is a property of the earliest stages of embryonic life, that this resistance lasts to the blastocyst stage and perhaps further, before fading *after* the embryos become implanted in the womb...[1]

* 2000b (Address, 'Some Fundamental Evils in Generating Human Embryos by Cloning', 26 November 1999, Conference at European University Institute, Florence, on the Ethics of Biological Research).

[1] Edwards and Steptoe, *A Matter of Life*, 111.

Referring to 'the early stages of human life'[2] and 'the earliest period of human embryo growth'[3] as the period of a day or two before and after the one-cell embryo divides into two, Edwards says:

> the embryo is passing through a critical period in its life of great exploration: it becomes magnificently organised, switching on its own biochemistry, increasing in size, and preparing itself quickly for implantation in the womb.[4]

Recollecting (at her birth) his appreciation of Louise Brown as one or two cells in his Petri dish, Edwards added: 'She was beautiful then and she is beautiful now.' There is much to be deplored in decisions of the kind which Edwards made then, and which thousands of other medical technologists have since made, but Edwards has the great merit of frankness. Discussing his initial agreement in 1968 to work in vivo with the surgeon Patrick Steptoe, Edwards remarks:

> Ethical concerns hardly entered into our conversation.... We were... aware that our work would enable us to examine a microscopic human being—one in its very earliest stages of development...[5]

During the late 1990s a vocabulary was devised and popularized according to which there are two kinds of cloning to produce human embryos, embryo-cloning which is *reproductive* and embryo-cloning which is *therapeutic*. This vocabulary should be rejected as politicized and manipulative. Production of embryos by cloning is always reproductive, for it is always and necessarily reproduction—generation of one human being from another—even when the further aim is that the embryo so produced shall later be destroyed rather than proceed to independent life as a breathing child. And all uses of embryos as sources of organs, tissues, and cell lines for experimental study, or for use to improve the health of another human being, are *non*-therapeutic. In the use of the term 'therapeutic' which has been universal and well understood until the propagandist manipulations of 1998/9, a therapeutic intervention is an intervention directed towards the well-being *of the individual on whom the intervention is conducted.*

In short, what is being called 'therapeutic' as opposed to 'reproductive' cloning is *always* reproductive, and de facto is *never* therapeutic. Whatever our ethical disagreements, we should reject the misappropriation of well-understood words to disguise the reality of what is being proposed, debated, and chosen.

[2] *Ibid.*, 97. [3] *Ibid.*, 95. [4] *Ibid.*, 97. [5] *Ibid.*, 83.

We should be aware that both the aim and the structure of the current manipulation of language are precisely the same as the manipulation by which the British Government continued, throughout the Second World War, to assure its people, most solemnly, that the targets of its air operations were all 'military', even after it had adopted the precise, formal, and internally documented operational policy of selecting for destruction civilian houses and their civilian inhabitants in preference to factories producing war *matériel.* In choosing the wording of their public statements, the British authorities relied upon the conventional, well-understood distinction according to which a *military* target consists of persons or equipment engaged or preparing to engage in military operations, and the term 'military targets' does not include hostages or other civilians even when their destruction would have beneficial military effects by discouraging military personnel, blocking the roads with refugees, and so forth. The structure of the propagandistic manipulation consisted precisely in using the well-understood words in a way which—as the audience were more or less unaware—would be appropriate (accurate) only if they were understood in a different way: viz., our targets are all military just because our ultimate *aim* in targeting them is military victory, and all our operations are directed towards that aim. In *that* aim-dominated application of the word 'military' the statements of the British Government were substantially true, but the Government could not of course reveal that that was the way it was applying the word 'military'. Its statements were intended to be *understood* by their audience as referring not to the ultimate aims of the bombing but to the kinds of persons and things being attacked, since the audience wanted to be reassured that their Government was *not* pursuing its aim by illicit means, that is, that there was no policy of attacking civilians as hostages whose destruction could hasten the ultimate aim of victory. But that indeed was the policy, from February 1941 to April 1945, as I show in detail in my book with Joseph Boyle and Germain Grisez, *Nuclear Deterrence, Morality and Realism.*[6] Similarly, the recent use by governmental agencies of the terms 'reproductive' and 'therapeutic' manipulates its audience by replacing the conventional uses of those terms with a new application which would be appropriate (accurate) only if attention is diverted from the kinds of things being chosen and done—the means—to the ultimate aims for which they are being chosen and done.

So-called 'therapeutic' cloning is reproductive, but is all or in virtually all cases non-therapeutic. It consists in reproducing human beings for

[6] *NDMR* 38–44.

the purpose of being consumed in experimentation intended immediately or remotely for the benefit of other human beings, for whose sake the individuals produced by cloning are to be sacrificed—without of course the possibility of their consenting or appealing. It will be said, of course, that they are also too young to notice their destruction. And that is true. But the question whether a human being who has been selected for destruction will be aware of his or her fate is never decisive for an ethical judgment on the question whether his or her rights are being violated by the choice to destroy him or her.

II

In the wake of the war in which the major powers all, in their various ways, systematically violated human rights as a matter of high policy, the World Health Organization and the Council for International Organizations of Medical Sciences, reflecting on the abuses of science in the practice of the principal defeated powers, adopted the Declaration of Helsinki. (With due respect to our chairman, Prof Mazzoni, the need for *rules* limiting *freedom of research* is in no way a novelty.) The Declaration's key provisions were:

> I.5 ...Concern for the interests of the subject of biomedical research must always prevail over the interest of science and society.
>
> III.4 In research on man, the interest of science and society should never take precedence over considerations related to the well-being of the subject.

So-called 'therapeutic' cloning, since it is essentially non-therapeutic, that is, is entirely unconcerned with, or prepared to sacrifice totally, the well-being of the human subject directly affected, is a gross violation of those principles, and of a fundamental principle of just governance and social life.

It will be denied that there is a human subject here. But the denial is quite vain. You have only to scrutinize the language, the thoughts, the awareness, and the decisions of those who want their baby to survive and flourish, and of those who use their skills for that objective, to see that when people's interests do not conflict with the interests of the embryo, they are perfectly well aware that they are dealing with an individual human being, a him or a her, a subject, a who not a what, as irreplaceable as a baby immediately before or after birth.

It will be said that the early embryo is not a subject because it might be divided by natural monozygotic twinning or by artificially induced splitting during toti- or early pluri-potency. And indeed it might be so divided. But so what? One subject has been replaced by two (or more). The question whether one of the two (or more) is parent of the other (or others) because continuous with the initial embryo, or whether the initial embryo's life has simply been superseded by the new life of two, is of some theoretical interest. But its answer cannot affect the fact that the initial embryo had interests and rights as a human subject, and that the successor embryo or embryos equally have such interests and rights. It is a mistake to suppose that the possibility of twinning or splitting is evidence that the early embryo is not an integral organism, self-directing and fully equipped with all the radical capacities which, by their actuation in development, will be exercised in the activities, including the thought, speech, laughter, etc. of that individual whose life began at syngamy and will typically continue, without break or irruption for, say, ninety hours, or weeks, or months, or years.

People might say that the early human embryo is not a human subject, because it is very small. And indeed it is. But science and civilization make progress by substituting the reign of imagination and image-dominated sentiments to reasonable judgment. And by every standard of reasonable judgment the fact that you in the first days of your life, and I in the first days of mine, were very *small* has no tendency at all to show that that very embryo which *you* were was not you, or that that very embryo, that small embryo, was not *me*. Each of us was even then and there equipped with our genetic constitution—do not say genetic *blueprint*; we were and are three-dimensional, not two-dimensional—the whole genetic constitution which made you you and me, for better or worse, me…

We all know this. If it were not *useful*, we would not dream of denying it. Arguments of the kind I'm criticizing are not, I'm afraid, attempts to find out the truth of the matter, but rather are rationalizations of a result, an outcome, a product that is beneficial to many.

It will be said that the criterion I am using to distinguish between production of cell lines, on the one hand, and of embryos, on the other, is unsound. The criterion is whether the new cell has the genetic primordia for self-directing development into a mature individual of an animal species, and it will be said that the notion of a species has been cancelled out, or soon will be, by advances in DNA-related science and techniques. I accept that there probably will emerge cases where it is debatable whether a collection of cells has the genetic primordia, the radical capacities, the organizing principle which is the only basis for judging human beings to be fundamentally *equal* despite their manifest differences in every *other* dimension. There will probably be cases where it is not easy to say whether we have here a wounded human individual, misshapen and defective (perhaps by reason of his or her predecessors' decisions and desires), or rather a creature which, like a hydatidiform mole, is human in origin but not in nature, lacking those genetic primordia. But the existence of borderline cases should not make us hesitant about the manifold other cases where the fact is that we have a subject with the vigorously self-protecting and self-restoring animal *specificity* that we heard R.G. Edwards referring to.

III

I have been considering so-called therapeutic cloning, which must be judged *non*-therapeutic because it intends for its subject neither the benefit of life after birth nor the benefit of a healthier existence before birth—but rather: consumption, exploitation, and destruction. What then should we say about so-called reproductive cloning? This, as I have said, is reproductive only in the extended sense that it intends that the reproduction involved in all production of embryos by cloning shall in this instance extend, by the will or permission of the producers, to *life after birth* (provided it is not terminated earlier by their decision to abort it as defective or as in some other way inauspicious or unwanted, or contrary to a woman's (or some other person's) 'right to choose'. So, let me call this cloning for maturity.

For the sake of analysis, let us consider the case where all concerned are resolved to respect the life of any embryo generated by cloning at least as fully as if he or she were a born child. What then should we say about this 'pure case' or 'ideal case' of human cloning—cloning for maturity without quality control by termination of life?

I think we should say this. Generation of embryos by cloning, whether by splitting or somatic cell nucleus transfer, is a matter of asexual reproduction. The fact that cloning is *copying* is, biologically speaking, only an implication of that fact of non-sexuality in reproduction. As I have already emphasized, the embryo produced is a child as fully human, as incommunicably unique a person, as any ordinary twin or, indeed, as any other person. But the conditions or character of his or her generation by production *dramatize* something to be found, if less dramatically, in all generation of children in vitro, something that makes all these kinds of generation morally wrong, fundamentally or intrinsically. This moral significant fact is *not* of course the fact that technology is being put to use; still less is it the fact that what is being done is statistically or biologically abnormal. No, it is rather the fact that what is being chosen and done is precisely an act of production. (Please don't translate 'production' as it appeared in the Italian translation of my synopsis, as 'riproduzione'. It's 'produzione'!) The aim of this choice and act is precisely to supply someone with a baby by trying to produce a baby by the in vitro procedures which, in the case on which we are focusing, are one or other of the procedures of cloning.

How does this make the choosing act wrong? The answer is that products as such are assigned their meaning and value by the human makers who produce them, and the consumers who use them, and so the status of any product precisely as such is *sub*personal. That initial relationship, of those who choose to *produce* babies with the babies they produce, is inconsistent with, and so inherently impedes, the communion which is appropriate in any relationship among persons concerning the basic aspects of their personal well-being, their fundamental good.[7]

In short, the relation of producers to product is a relationship of domination, which in itself is contrary to the dignity and equality which is appropriate to the parent-child relationship.

In procreation by marital intercourse, on the other hand, one and the same act of choice, made by each spouse, governs both the union (in which they experience and actualize their marital commitment) and the procreation of the child. The intentionality of this act remains governing even in a case when procreation depends on supplementing that act of intercourse by some technical means to assist the intra-corporeal union of gametes. So the child comes into being, in such cases, as a kind of gift *supervening* upon an act chosen for expressing the parents' union and common life, and as a kind of incarnation of that act, of that union, and so as a kind of partner in that common life, and thus with a fundamental parity or equality with the parents whose procreative act expressed, by its structure as mutual giving and receiving, their mutual commitment to each member of their partnership, to serve that partner *through* the whole lottery of a lifetime.

Of course those who choose to produce a baby—to generate one in vitro, by cloning or otherwise—make that choice only as a means to an ulterior end. And that end may well include receiving the baby into an authentic child-parent relationship of communion, befitting those who share in personal dignity. If this intention is realized, it will be good for the baby as well as for the parents. But it remains that the choice to *produce* the baby is the choice of a morally bad means to a good end, because the baby's initial status as a *product* is subpersonal. The significance of that status is most clear when the laboratory's defective products are discarded and its surplus products used for lethal experiments or exploitation and consumption.

The character of IVF as essentially *production* is only more emphatic in generation by cloning. The radical separation of IVF from the act of marital union is only more radical and dramatic in generation by cloning which neither incarnates that union, as procreation does, nor even reproduces

[7] See essay III.17; 1983e; *LCL* 267. [The relationship referred to is the relationship between the producers and the produced in the proposal to produce, and in the proposal's carrying through to the time, at least, when the baby is ratified as acceptable and implanted.]

both father and mother, as sexual generation even in vitro does, but instead replicates a single person (who of course may or may not be the mother who supplies an egg, or the mother who supplies the womb, or the mother who undertakes the care for the child after birth).

I have been sketching some main lines of the philosophical analysis which shows that the moral character of the choice and act of IVF, and *a fortiori* the moral character of generation by cloning, is essentially the same as slavery (which like IVF has its relatively benevolent forms, the benevolence and benefits of which—good motives and effects—do not cancel out its fundamental evil). The question is thus one of equality in dignity, and of choices and acts which are disrespectful of that equality because (a) they do not conform to the Golden Rule that one must not do to others what one would not have done to us, or (b) they set the will of the choosing person directly against some basic aspect of the good of a human person.

IV

We heard Jürgen Simon say, twice, that the principle of respect for human dignity is 'modified by the years'.[8] His phrase reminded me of the famous passage in the main teaching instrument of Roman law, Justinian's *Institutes*, where the slave-owning Roman jurists declare that by nature, and from the outset, all human beings are born equal, but then slavery *arose*:[9] as Professor Simon might say, the principle of equality was 'modified by the years'—in truth, of course, the principle of equality came to be unacceptable, and so was systematically, for millennia, *violated by* those who had power—powerful democracies as well as autocracies.

In our philosophical and juristic discussions, we must not think that anyone can rationally derive ethical or other normative conclusions from

[8] Cf. Simon, 'Human Dignity as a Regulative Instrument for Human Genome Research' at 43–4:

> The Christian and philosophical ideas form the picture of the human being for the German Constitution, and the intellectual basis from which the guarantee of the human dignity derives. This picture has been modified over the years.... Human dignity... is not a static notion, but rather follows the dynamic of the developing picture of the human being, so that the sense of human dignity is modified over the years.... The actual discussion of [the demands of animal rights activists that the dignity of animals should be recognized] shows how far the concept of human dignity has already been modified, and how far it could be modified.... [T]he conception of human dignity inside the German Constitution has already been intensively discussed on the issue of abortion.... and is incapable of carrying the burden of proof in complex questions of medical ethics and legislation...

[9] [Inst. I.ii. 2:

> Wars arose, and in their train followed captivity and then slavery, which is contrary to the law of nature; for by that law all human beings are originally born free {bella etenim orta sunt et captivitates secutae et servitutes quae sunt iuri naturali contrariae; iure enim naturali ab initio omnes homines liberi nascebantur}.]

sheer facts about people's opinions, from facts such as that many powerful people *want* to own slaves, or that many German or English politicians and voters *want* to make abortion widely available, whatever the Constitution may or may not say; or *want* and fight for the protection of certain subhuman animals *more* than they want the protection of unwanted human subjects. Nor may we think that the fact that a supposed moral or legal principle or rule is 'open' is always a rational argument for preferring it to a more restrictive principle or rule. Nor should we think that the fact that certain arguments are 'knockdown' shows that they are weak or fallacious or 'emotional',[10] though some undoubtedly are.

Let me conclude by saying that the position in German law, which Professor Simon described to us with obvious signs of regret, is morally, that is to say rationally, superior in almost every dimension to the British position which he wanted us—as I understood him—to think superior to the German. There can be little doubt, of course, that the British position, or rather the even more laissez-faire position of the United States, or Korea, is the position which will prevail in the medium term. But that is not an argument in its favour.

The future is foreshadowed for us by the experience of the pioneer of IVF, Robert Edwards. For years his research was frowned upon by the ethical authorities of the medical profession and the scientific research-granting bodies. But as soon as he had achieved his technological success, the same persons who had ostracized him rose to their feet, *en masse*, to applaud him, and to open their doors and their purses to his work. We should recognize that the crowd, including the crowd of the learned, follow power and technical opportunity. But we don't have to applaud, and we don't have to do likewise.

[10] Cf. Simon, 'Human Dignity as a Regulative Instrument for Human Genome Research' at 37:

In German law even the embryo is protected by the human dignity requirement, with the consequence that no use is allowed even though the embryo may be sacrificed for the benefit of human life. By this procedure human embryos would become an object and this is an offence to human dignity in Germany. In this case the general emotional appeal to human dignity is used in the form of a knock-down argument....

18

BRAIN DEATH AND PETER SINGER*

I

Peter Singer's paper identifies its three aims. The first is to show that it is a mistake to think that the ready acceptance of brain death as a criterion of death resulted from an improved scientific understanding of the nature of death. In this aim he partly succeeds, I think, and partly fails. He easily shows that some people—notably, the people he identifies as associated with the emergence of the Harvard criteria—'readily accepted' the new 'criterion of death' for reasons that had little to do with 'scientific understanding of the nature of death' and a lot to do with relief from the burdens of caring for the irreversibly comatose, and with making their organs available to others. But Singer fails to show that the only other people he names in this connection, the philosophers Grisez and Boyle, accepted the new criterion or definition of death for these or any similar reasons; and he fails because he has misstated—that is to say, both substantially misquoted and thoroughly misunderstood—their conclusion and their reasoning. Or so I shall argue.

Singer's second aim is 'to show that there are serious problems with accepting brain death as a criterion of death'. I think he succeeds in this aim. He would have succeeded even more clearly, I shall argue, had he adopted the logical clarifications introduced by Grisez and Boyle, and also their theoretical (that is, conceptual and metaphysical) understanding of what Singer calls 'the nature of death'—that is to say, their differentiated answers to Singer's eventual but still undifferentiated 'first question': 'When does a human being die?'

When one makes the necessary clarifications, and then attends to data most of which was unavailable to Grisez and Boyle in the late

* Comment, given at a meeting of the Oxford University Philosophy Society (14 May 1998), on a draft paper presented by Peter Singer: 'Brain Death and the Sanctity of Life Ethic'. Singer's paper incorporated main elements of chs 2, 3, and 4 of his *Rethinking Life and Death*.

1970s—including some data which even Singer has not yet become aware of—one has good reason to reject Grisez and Boyle's conclusion that one dies 'when there is complete and irreversible loss of the functioning of [one's] entire brain'.[1] I shall later say a little about this data, relying on the work of an American paediatric neurologist who for many years used arguments along the lines of Grisez and Boyle to give public scientific support to the thesis that brain death is death, and who now regards their primary definition of death as entirely sound but incompatible with their conclusion that brain death is death. Like this neurologist, I had already changed my mind about the conclusion while retaining the *theoretical* (conceptual and metaphysical) premises which Grisez and Boyle adopt, defend, and rely upon.

Peter Singer's third and final aim is 'to point to a better way forward'. He adduces little indeed in the way of argument that his way forward is better, rather than a lot worse. I shall do little more than observe that while he offers 'frankness' as a principal merit of his 'route to... a good outcome', he could and I think should have been a lot franker.

II

Singer's methodological framework is articulated in the debate he stages between those—like (he suggests) Grisez and Boyle, and the 'ill-advised' Pius XII—who treat the nature and time of death as a matter of 'science, not ethics' and those who, like Singer himself, judge it to be an 'ethical issue'. He quotes Grisez and Boyle as saying

> that death is 'the irreversible loss of integrated organic functioning' and that this is a definition of death [which] is 'in factual terms... without any radical shifts in meaning, arbitrary stipulations, or subjective evaluations'.

But this is in substance a misquotation and certainly a thoroughgoing misunderstanding of Grisez and Boyle. They begin their discussion, fifteen pages earlier, with a set of distinctions, marked by stipulative definitions, to which they rigorously adhere throughout—distinctions which would have helped Singer get clearer about the whole matter as well as about what Grisez and Boyle themselves, in the passage he paraphrased, were saying:

> It... should be noticed that death can be defined in various ways. A definition of death in *theoretical* terms will tell what happens when an organism dies when this matter is considered within the framework of a general theory of life. A definition

[1] Grisez and Boyle, *Life and Death with Liberty and Justice*, 77.

of death in *factual* terms will tell what observable or inferable state of affairs obtains if the theoretical concept of death is satisfied. A definition of death in *operational* terms will tell how to establish that the factual state of affairs obtains.[2]

This threefold distinction is employed and illustrated in the section from which Singer is quoting, beginning a page and a half before the sentence on which his eye fell. In brief: Singer treats some remarks about the *operational* definition as if they were about the *factual* definition (the subject of the sentence[3] from which he has chopped some hunks), and fails to notice that his 'ethics not science' debate is about neither operational nor factual definitions, but rather about what Grisez and Boyle call *theoretical* definition (or theoretical clarification).

To set the record straight, and to think more clearly about death and the brain, let's follow Grisez and Boyle through their 'new proposal for defining death'. They begin by saying that there is need to 'refine the concept of death', since the problem thrown up by modern methods of intensive care is 'one of vagueness in the concept'. The old operational criteria of cessation of respiration and heartbeat were 'taken to be significant' because 'everyone observes the difference between a living body and a dead body, between a dying body and a decomposing body', and everyone notices that

the process which is characteristic of a dead and decomposing body correlates very well with traditional criteria... Clearly, something happened before the body began decomposing, at or about the time when breathing and circulation ceased. This 'something' was the turning point at which a living body became a dead body. The turning point was called 'death'.[4]

Grisez and Boyle now begin their move towards the first and most basic of their three definitions of death, the 'theoretical' as distinct from 'factual' or 'operational'.

If we look at this situation from the point of view of biological theory, we can understand more clearly what the turning point is. Life often is said to be—in general—a certain kind of physiochemical process, and the life of an organism a collection of such processes. But an organism is more than a collection of processes; it is a coordinated system. From a thermodynamic point of view an organism is an unstable open system, but it continues because it is maintained in dynamic equilibrium by homeostatic controls. These controls are of various kinds, but in an organism which is complex enough to have a nervous system, this [nervous] system coordinates and integrates the other control systems. This system is dispersed but centred in the brain; without some brain functioning, the whole system cannot be maintained. Thus when the whole brain ceases to

[2] *Life and Death*, 63 (emphasis added). [3] See at n. 6 below. [4] *Ibid.*, 76.

function, the dynamic equilibrium is lost, the materials which were unified in the system begin behaving without its control, and decomposition begins.

These considerations suggest a definition of death *in theoretical terms* ...: Death is the irreversible loss of integrated organic functioning.[5]

I pause to make two remarks. This is, I think, a fine example of what can be meant by *conceptual clarification*, or if you like *philosophy*, which does its work with full attention to empirical facts, and enriches our knowledge of those facts with further *understanding* of them, better conceptualizations of them. Secondly: as Singer rightly remarks: '"Dead" is a term applied much more widely than human beings, or conscious beings.' Singer says this in order to oppose attempts to produce a 'revisionist redefinition of a term in common use'. 'Why fiddle with a term that we all understand quite well' so as to be able to say that 'warm, supple, spontaneously breathing human beings are dead'? Quite so. But the issue is not about terms and fiddling with them. It's about facts—realities—and the best way to understand them. The way proposed by Grisez and Boyle is controlled by a range of data going 'much more widely than human beings, or conscious beings'; as they remark a couple of sentences later, 'Even a carrot lives and dies'. There is no trace anywhere here of an 'ethical decision' or, in Singer's unfriendly terms, of 'trying to disguise an important ethical decision as a matter of scientific fact'. Let's see if we can catch them out in this sort of subterfuge as their argument moves from the theoretical to the *factual* (in their stipulated sense of 'factual') and from there to the *operational*. Here's what they say:

If death is understood in theoretical terms as the permanent termination of the integrated functioning characteristic of a living body as a whole, then one can see why death of higher animals is usually grasped in factual terms by the cessation of the vital functions of respiration and circulation, which correlates so well with bodily decomposition.... However, considering the role of the brain in the maintenance of the dynamic equilibrium of any system which includes a brain, there is a compelling reason for defining death in factual terms as that state of affairs in which there is complete and irreversible functioning of the entire brain. To accept this definition is not to make a choice based on one's evaluation of various human characteristics, but is to assent to a theory which fits the facts.[6]

Then, in the four sentences immediately preceding the one mangled in Peter Singer's paper they respond to the objection that 'the integrating function of the brain could be replaced by a computer':

When the respirator maintains the organism, it is questionable whether there is complete and irreversible loss of the functioning of the *entire* brain. But this

[5] *Ibid.*, 76–7. [6] *Ibid.*, 77.

> is a question to be settled by empirical inquiry, not philosophy. Philosophically, we answer the objection by saying that if the functioning of the brain is the factor which principally integrates any organism which has a brain, then if that function is lost, what is left is no longer as a whole an *organic* unity. If the dynamic equilibrium of the remaining parts of the system is maintained, it nevertheless *as a whole* is a mechanical, not an organic system.[7]

Then the sentence mined by Singer; it refers to the final move needed to complete the trilogy of definitions:

> If death can be correctly defined *in factual terms* as the complete and irreversible loss of the functioning of the entire brain, then this definition can be accepted and translated into *operational* and legal terms without any radical shifts in meaning, arbitrary stipulations, or subjective evaluations.[8]

Grisez and Boyle offer some criticisms of the operational criteria proposed by the Harvard committee, for example of the sufficiency of three minutes off the respirator as a test for inability to breathe spontaneously.[9] But like Singer, and long before him, and more stringently than him, they criticize the 1968 Harvard committee's whole approach to their task. Their criticism is summed up in its concluding words:

> Even if it is correct to maintain—as we shall argue—that an individual whose entire brain is dead is no longer a living person, the Harvard committee's approach seems to have involved a method in principle unacceptable: A private group here consciously attempted to effect the legal nonpersonhood of a class of individuals.[10]

In that attempt, Peter Singer is, as we have seen, a true successor of the Harvard committee, however rightly scornful he is of the route they chose to the common goal.

III

Singer thinks that Pius XII handed the issue of the definitions of death and the moment of death over to medical specialists because he failed to see that that very issue is an 'ethical issue'. Whatever the views of Pius XII about the competence of anaesthesiologists and other doctors, the question of brain death was taken up in 1989 by a working group of the Pontifical Academy of Science, which issued a report favouring (like a 1985 working group of the Academy) the thesis that brain death (given a suitable factual definition and operational criteria) is death. There was one dissentient, the Austrian-American philosopher Josef Seifert. An important member of the

[7] *Ibid.*, 77 (emphases in original). [8] *Ibid.*, 78. [9] *Ibid.*, 66–7. [10] *Ibid.*, 66.

group was the American clinical paediatric neurologist Alan Shewmon. Now however, Shewmon has published in the first 1997 issue of the *Linacre Quarterly* a preliminary account[11] (prior to full elaboration in medical-scientific journals)[12] of his reasons for thinking that he and the rest of the majority of the 1989 group, like most of the medical-scientific community during the past quarter century, were badly mistaken in accepting the thesis.

Shewmon accepted in 1989 and still firmly accepts a theoretical, metaphysical or conceptual definition of death identical to the one we have seen offered by Grisez and Boyle. His decisive change of mind concerns the minor premise in their argument for the 'factual definition' of death as brain death, namely the premise they expressed in the words 'considering the role of the brain in the maintenance of the dynamic equilibrium of any system which includes a brain'. Shewmon, for physiological reasons, has come to reject what he calls 'the axiom that the brain is the "central integrating organ" of the body'.

It is worth noting that before 1989 Shewmon accepted and defended a neocortical approach rather like the one defended by Jeff McMahan in the work criticized (or, rather, set aside) by Singer. Like Singer, and McMahan as reported by Singer, Shewmon—the working child neurologist on the faculty of UCLA Medical School since 1981—took for granted that (in Singer's words) 'an anencephalic human infant is a living human organism without a mind' because the 'babies... without cerebral hemispheres' (though with brain stems) 'can never become conscious'. Shewmon gives a graphic account of his shock upon learning in 1989 of the existence of three anencephalic infants being raised by a former paediatric nurse, one of them 12, another 5 years old; one of these older two had weak but undeniable vision and both were able to hear, touch, smell, and discriminate between strangers and familiars, and respond appropriately to music with facial expressions, vocalization, and bodily movement. The children's neurologist (at Boston Children's Hospital) collaborated with Shewmon in a brief paper they published as a communication to the 1990 meeting of the International Child Neurology Society, speculating that at least in the *congenital* absence of cortex, developmental plasticity may allow the brain stem to assume certain otherwise cortical functions.[13]

[11] Shewmon, 'Recovery from "Brain Death": A Neurologist's Apologia'.

[12] [See now Shewmon, '"Brainstem Death", "Brain Death" and Death: A Critical Re-evaluation of the Purported Equivalence'; 'Chronic "Brain Death": Meta-Analysis and Conceptual Consequences'; 'The Brain and Somatic Integration: Insights into the Standard Biological Rationale for Equating "Brain Death" with Death'.]

[13] *Ibid.* at 57–8; Shewmon and Holmes, 'Brainstem Plasticity in Congenitally Decerebrate Children'. [See now Shewmon, 'The ABC's of PVS: Problems of Definition' at 217.]

I have to cut a long and fascinating story short. Having been forced by the observation of his own eyes to abandon one of the axioms of his post-Harvard medical education, Shewmon moved on to re-examining another axiom, that the brain is the central integrator of the body. It proved easy to see that the 1976 British factual definition of brain death as the irreversible destruction of the brain stem is a non-starter: a German neurologist in 1977 reported success in using electrical stimulation to arouse to undeniable consciousness patients in deep coma from discrete brain stem lesions.[14] (This is essentially the case that Singer takes up from McMahan, where a person's lack of capacity for consciousness is contingent—'for example [says McMahan, as Singer reports], when it is a result of a problem with the support mechanisms in the brain stem', though Singer and McMahan, unlike the curious German, content themselves with the postulate that this is 'irreversible' and that it would take a 'miracle' to reverse it.)

And there are some diseases and pathologies, notably Guillain-Barré Syndrome in its most severe form, which have the result that 'no information can enter or leave the central nervous system, creating a total locked-in syndrome externally mimicking "brain death"'[15] while the patient, if supported by intensive care well short of the heroic, remains fully conscious (and in due course can make a full recovery). The patient's body completely lacks the integrating influence of the brain. Though the patient needs technological assistance with breathing, blood pressure regulation, fluids and nutrition, and so forth, this substitutive technology is less than is required by many patients in intensive care. So it seems, as Shewmon's reflections on this kind of case conclude, that

> the brain's role vis à vis somatic integration is more one of modulating and fine-tuning a structurally and metabolically unified body than of constituting a 'central integrator' without which the body lacks unity and ceases to be a body.[16]

Peter Singer's paper summarizes some of the other relevant considerations, which Shewmon has amply documented in medical-scientific work prepared for early publication in the medical-scientific literature—for example, the facts about survival of brain dead patients for periods ranging up to nine months, in some cases with rather light support of a kind given in a modern American nursing home.[17] To put the present state of play most briefly and bluntly: facts unknown to or unconsidered by Grisez and Boyle in 1978 seem

[14] Shewmon, 'Recovery from "Brain Death"' at 51. [15] *Ibid.* at 65.

[16] *Ibid.* at 66–7.

[17] *Ibid.* at 67–9. [See now Shewmon, '"Brainstem Death" "Brain Death" and Death' at nn. 34–6, reporting the case of TK: and concluding:

> There is no question that he became 'brain dead' [and that the entire brain, including the brainstem, ha[s] been replaced by ghost-like tissues and disorganized proteinaceous fluids] at age four; neither is there any question that he is still alive at age nineteen.]

to make it clear that one can have dynamic, organic integration of the body without the contribution of the brain; and facts unknown to or unconsidered by Singer in 1998 make it clear that one can have consciousness at quite a high level without the cortex, at least if one is decerebrate congenitally and is given appropriate social stimulation of a kind usually denied to such children; and what is known about pain makes it highly likely that one can have certain sorts of pain (hunger, thirst, nausea, satiety, visceral pain, etc.) in the condition of cortical destruction now commonly known as PVS;[18] and there has been no demonstration whatever, nor could there be, that such patients are not conscious, in a kind of super-locked-in state.[19] There is, then, much to be said for Shewmon's revised conception (factual cum operational definition) of death, informed as it is by a theoretical conception identical to Grisez's and Boyle's: since the brain is not demonstrably, and perhaps demonstrably is not, the necessary source of organic integration in even the post-embryonic human individual, we should say that

> death occurs when failure of multiple vital systems and bodily processes (including the brain) progresses beyond a systems-dynamical point of no-return, ordinarily (in the absence of protective therapies) presumably some 20–30 minutes or so after nomothermic circulatory arrest. Although some 'brain-dead' patients may be truly dead, it is not because their brains are dead but rather because of supra-critical multi-system damage; the remaining subset of 'pure braindead' patients (with intact other organ systems) are not yet dead but are rather fatally injured and in a deep coma.[20]

[18] Shewmon, 'Recovery from "Brain Death"' at 59. [19] *Ibid.* at 59–60.

[20] *Ibid.* at 32; also the main conclusion of Shewmon, '"Brainstem Death" "Brain Death" and Death':

> But if 'brain death' is not death, what is? We orient once again to the three conceptual levels: definition, anatomical criterion, and clinical tests.
>
> Now, the basic definition remains precisely what we have been discussing all along: the loss of integrative unity of the body.
>
> The anatomical criterion, however, shifts from a single locus (the brain) to the entire body and consists in a critical degree of molecular-level damage (not yet grossly detectable) throughout the body, beyond a thermodynamical 'point of no return.' The body's intrinsic tendency to active, anti-entropic self-development and self-maintenance (of the essence of 'life') is irretrievably lost, so that physico-chemical processes now follow the path of increasing entropy characteristic of inanimate things (i.e., decay). This does not require supracritical damage of every single cell in the body, but rather supracritical damage of enough cells of enough different types that the body as a whole loses its intrinsic ability to counteract entropy (and thus, in principle, would continue to 'dis-integrate' even if hypothetically forcibly perfused mechanically by oxygenated blood).
>
> The clinical tests correspondingly shift from those implying loss of brain function to those implying thermodynamically supracritical microstructural damage diffusely throughout the body. Now a sine qua non of the opposition to entropy is energy, generated by chemical respiration, and a sine qua non of somatic integration is the circulation of blood, by means of which the body parts mutually interact. A clinical test for the 'point of no return' is therefore sustained cessation of circulation of oxygenated blood. The critical duration of cessation depends greatly on body temperature; under ordinary circumstances (i.e., normal temperature), an educated guess is that twenty to thirty minutes probably suffice to surpass the 'point of no return'.

IV

Since Singer neither supports nor tries to argue against McMahan's dualism,[21] I shall say no more than a word about it. Though spectacular in the clarity of its formulation, it is of course no more than a kind of codifying articulation of ways of thinking and talking which have become rather common. The fundamental philosophical objection to it is briefly stated in a book I wrote with Grisez and Boyle in 1987:

A theory which divides the unitary being of the person into two realities... is at odds with the very starting-point of the course of reflection from which it has emerged. For example, a body-spirit dualist cannot identify the I who undertakes reflection and philosophical discussion as either the *spirit-person* or the *mere living body* which dualism distinguishes and opposes to one another. For if the I be identified with the spirit-person, [then] the living organism recognized by others as the reality whose behaviour constitutes philosophical communication is not identical with the person excogitating the reflections communicated. And if the I be identified instead with the living organism whose behaviour communicates those reflections, [then] the spirit excogitating the reflections is not identical with the only reality recognizable as the person communicating them. Spirit-person and mere living human body [McMahan's two substances in the cot, but also at McMahan's writing desk][22] are philosophical constructs neither of which refers to the unified self who had set out to explain his or her own reality [experienced as an awareness of oneself as a unitary being]; both of [these constructs] purport to refer to realities other than the unified self but somehow, inexplicably, related to it.[23]

McMahan's spectacularly overt two-substance dualism[24] is only a special case of the dualism entailed by any willingness to treat person and life as other and other. Singer says: 'Of course, the death of those parts of the

[21] [See nn. 22 and 24 below. And see now McMahan, *The Ethics of Killing*, ch. 1, e.g. 93:

there are two conscious entities present where I am. My organism is conscious only in a derivative sense, only by virtue of having a conscious part [sc. the mind, person, I].

For commentary on the foundations of McMahan's position, see Lee and George, *Body-Self Dualism in Contemporary Ethics and Politics*, 44–9.]

[22] Singer's paper said:

Here is what McMahan says about anencephalic infants: 'Since you and I and all others of our kind are essentially minds, anencephalic infants are a fundamentally different sort of thing from us. They are simply organisms—permanently unoccupied human organisms. Whereas *in a normal infant's cot there are two substances*—a human organism and the infant mind or self that will eventually become a person—there is only one substance in the cot of an anencephalic infant.' (Emphasis added.)

[23] *NDMR* 308–9.

[24] [By 2002, McMahan rejected strict two-substance ('radical') dualism in favour of the two-entity dualism articulated at n. 21 above; his motivation was to be 'more respectful of commonsense': *The Ethics of Killing*, 92. But he accepts that his account still has the 'unsettling implication that there are two conscious entities occupying my chair at the moment' and hopes that what his part-whole thesis does is 'elucidate [this implication] in a way that makes it less bizarre'.]

brain required for consciousness is also the end of everything that matters about a person's life.' Nurses and others who maintain solidarity with patients in so-called PVS, like Anthony Bland, have a very different view of what matters about persons and their life.[25] They feel, think, and act, commonly enough, on the basis that Grisez and Boyle and I try to defend philosophically: that a person's life is nothing other than the reality of the person, and people in conditions such as PVS are simply gravely and even fatally wounded people who, however, continue to matter—to be lovable, each in his or her own way—until death.

V

Singer treats the sanctity of life ethic, mentioned in his title, as a position far beneath a philosopher's real attention. He articulates his proposal to intentionally kill persons such as I have just been discussing (along with a *sotto voce* proposal by some if not by him to *experiment* on such persons in all sorts of ways, and perhaps even to bury them alive while still breathing, as one of these experiments). That done, he need not entertain any ethical objection, even for a moment. No, 'the only serious objection I can see to this proposal is the claim that...it stands no chance of success'. For the purposes of his paper, at least, politics has completely ousted ethical dialogue. I am not interested in the tactical problems he worries about on his 'way forward' along the route to a 'better outcome'. So I find nothing to comment upon in his ethics save his claim that by promoting his proposal to kill anencephalics, and people in PVS, and whoever else's life we may judge not to 'matter', 'we would have made our ethical judgment transparent, thus advancing public discussion of the issues involved'. I think those who appeal to frankness should be a tad more frank than he has been. What is doing duty for ethical reflection and argument in his paper is the imagery of the march, 'moving on', the route, the way forward which we are all pursuing in a quasi-deterministic fashion such that (rather like in a Leninist fantasy or the gloomiest reactionary Catholic prophecies of doom) there are only questions of timing and tactics: the best way to get to where we simply want to go. The 'traditional sanctity of life doctrine', he says, 'is increasingly being abandoned by both medical practice and the law'. His star witnesses are the Law Lords in *Bland*, and a fine muddle they did indeed embroil themselves in by struggling to draw a distinction between action and omission which cuts across the well-established law of murder as killing (by act or omission) with intent to kill.[26] His prime witness

[25] See essay 19, p. 320. [26] See essay 19, pp. 315–7.

amongst the Lords is Lord Mustill, reflecting that the law thus declared is 'both morally and intellectually misshapen'. No one should disagree. But I think it would have been fair to note that Lord Mustill subsequently played a leading part in the Select Committee which considered proposals such as Singer's and unanimously reaffirmed the main principles and tenets of the ethic which Singer calls 'sanctity of life' but I prefer to call the ethics of equality in right to life. The Committee's central conclusions were framed in terms of the distinction between killing with intent and causing death as a foreseen side effect of acts intended to relieve suffering, and the Committee's fundamental principle was framed in terms of this equality of right:

> society's prohibition of intentional killing... is the cornerstone of law and social relationships. It protects each one of us impartially, embodying the belief that all are equal.[27]

Of course Singer may be right that this ethic will at some time be widely abandoned. But I hold to the philosophical thesis which Grisez, Boyle, and I have defended for decades, and find at the basis of the classical philosophical work which makes sense of our law: the thesis that (to put it without more nuance than I think the occasion requires) you can't get an ought from an is, not even the *is* of *is going to be* widely believed and acted upon by those who have the power to act on it, and *is going to* happen to those who apparently are irrevocably unconscious and to others whose lives no longer matter to those in charge.

NOTE

A brief up-to-date review of the issues is Lee and George, *Body-Self Dualism in Contemporary Ethics and Politics*, 163–9, concluding that

> since (it seems) the majority of neurologists are still not convinced that an individual can actually survive (or actually has survived) brain death, we ourselves are not certain which side is correct.... The standard definition of death—the irreversible cessation of the integrated functioning of the organism as a whole—remains valid. If the brain death criterion is incorrect, then Shewmon's circulatory-respiratory criterion appears to be the only valid alternative, but that would leave intact the definition of death as the irreversible loss of integrative function of the organism as a whole.

They say that this would not preclude organ transplantation in cases where a patient has (independently of transplant concerns) directed 'Do Not Resuscitate' and undergoes asystole (cardiac standstill); since attempts to restart the heart are on these hypotheses lawfully and ethically forbidden, extracting organs will not hasten death and can be done without intending death even as a means (and, they might have added, without subjecting the patient to the enslavement discussed in essay 10, pp. 193–4 and third endnote). For a fuller consideration, accepting Shewman's physiological findings, see President's Council on Bioethics, *Controversies in the Determination of Death*. Most recent, and against the drift of sec. III above: Lee and Grisez, 'Total Brain Death: A Reply to Alan Shewmon'.

[27] House of Lords Select Committee on Medical Ethics, *Report*, para. 237; Keown, *Euthanasia Examined*, 102.

19

INTENTIONALLY KILLING THE 'PERMANENTLY UNCONSCIOUS'*

Lord Goff of Chieveley's speech in *Bland*[1] mentions

> the Rubicon which runs between on the one hand the care of the living patient and on the other hand euthanasia—actively causing his death to avoid or end his suffering.

In the view of all nine judges hearing these proceedings in the Family Division, Court of Appeal, and House of Lords, the declarations sought and granted—primarily that, despite the inability of the defendant Bland to consent thereto, the hospital and physicians responsible for attending on him might lawfully discontinue all life-sustaining treatment and medical-support measures designed to keep him alive in his persistent vegetative state including the termination of ventilation, nutrition, and hydration by artificial means—were rightly granted and leave the law still safely north of the Rubicon. In another view, the judges were willy-nilly in mid-stream, wading south. Their predicament is most clearly discerned by Lord Browne-Wilkinson:

> the conclusion I have reached will appear to some to be almost irrational. How can it be lawful to allow a patient to die slowly, though painlessly, over a period of weeks from lack of food but unlawful to produce his immediate death by a lethal injection, thereby saving his family from yet another ordeal... ? I find it difficult to find a moral answer to that question. But it is undoubtedly the law...

Joining in that *cri de coeur*, Lord Mustill described the foundations of the courts' unanimous decision as 'morally and intellectually misshapen'.

Foundations morally and legally better were in fact available. But they were never, it seems, put forward by counsel or identified for consideration in the judgments, searching and thoughtful though these are.

* 1993b ('*Bland*: Crossing the Rubicon?').

[1] *Airedale NHS Trust v Bland* [1993] AC 789.

When Bland was 17, in 1989, his lungs were crushed in the Hillsborough crowd disaster: his breathing ceased and his brain was deprived of oxygen. By the time his breathing was restored, his cerebral cortex (the upper brain's outer layers) but not the lower brain or brain stem had been severely and irreversibly damaged; subsequent scans revealed no evidence of electrical activity in the cortex. Thereafter, despite intensive care in Airedale General Hospital, he remained in a profound unconsciousness, a state of chronic wakefulness without awareness, now commonly called a 'persistent vegetative state' to distinguish it from sleep-like 'coma'. (A patient in PVS responds in a reflex way, for example to sounds.) He breathed unaided. He could not swallow and so was fed by pumping nutritive fluids down a nasogastric tube; he was evacuated by enema and catheter; frequent infections were treated by antibiotics. Thus cared for, he was far from dying and seemed likely to live for years. Four months after the accident, his doctor thought that feeding and antibiotics should be discontinued. But on consulting the coroner responsible for Hillsborough disaster fatalities he was advised that this might result in criminal proceedings. Three years later, the hospital applied for the declaration stated above and other declarations, notably that no medical treatment need be furnished 'except for the sole purpose of enabling A.B. to end his life and [to] die peacefully with the greatest dignity and the least distress'. (The significant 'to' here bracketed appears in the original and reported versions of Sir Stephen Brown P's judgment but not in any later judgment.)

It is desirable, said the President on granting the foregoing two declarations, that the court's approval be sought in 'similar' cases, and essential where (unlike here) family opinion is divided. The desirability was reaffirmed by the appellate courts: partly to reassure the public, such application should be made as a matter of routine, at least for the time being. But Lord Goff hoped that this 'requirement' might soon be relaxed. Doubtless it will be. For it hardly coheres with what the Lords, unlike the courts below, identified as the true juridical position, viz. that discontinuance of life-sustaining measures is not merely permissible but indeed the *duty* of physicians who, in line with a body of reputable medical opinion, consider 'invasive' life-sustaining measures no longer in their patient's best interests. The Lords perhaps did not measure the full implications of their analysis. How can the court's 'approval' be required to discontinue what, on this analysis, has already become a tort if not a crime?

What are 'similar' cases? That will depend on which unconscious or other unconsenting patients some reputable body of medical opinion comes to consider unable to be benefited (overall, net) by life-sustaining measures.

May it also depend on what measures are judged 'invasive'? The latter concept makes no appearance in the judgments below, but in treating it as important the Lords did not dissociate themselves from Butler-Sloss LJ's suggestion that no line need be drawn among 'different forms of feeding such as spoonfeeding a helpless patient or inserting a tube through the nose'. That was her reason for preferring to call such feeding 'medical care' rather than 'medical treatment', and the Lords all considered 'medical treatment *or* care' the appropriate description for the life-supporting steps whose discontinuance they judged the law authorized (and required). Thus, despite the wording of the declarations and incidental dicta, the artificial aspects of Bland's regime of feeding are probably no necessary part of the argument justifying the permission (and duty) articulated by *Bland*; the supply of nutrients may in a proper case be discontinued, whatever the means of supply.

What is novel and gravely significant is that in the view of the majority, at least, of the Lords, such discontinuance may be proper even when decided upon precisely with the intention of terminating life. Now by 'intention' (and its cognates) none of the judges meant the academic lawyer's gratuitously artificial notion that one's intentions must include whatever effects of one's conduct one foresees as certain—a notion foreign to common sense, sound philosophy, and much recent judicial authority.[2] Their synonyms make this clear:

> the proposed conduct has the aim... of terminating the life of Anthony Bland by withholding from him the basic necessities of life... [T]he conduct... is intended to be the cause of death. (Lord Mustill)

It was

> a course of action designed to produce certain death... What is proposed... is to adopt a course with the intention of bringing about Anthony Bland's death... [T]he whole purpose of stopping artificial feeding is to bring about the death of Anthony Bland. (Lord Browne-Wilkinson)

And per Lord Lowry:

> the intention to bring about the patient's death is there.

Two questions arise. Whence this finding or assumption of fact? And why is a 'course of action' or 'conduct' with such an intention and effect not murder?

[2] See White, *Misleading Cases*, ch. 4, and Lord Goff's convincing 'The Mental Element in the Crime of Murder'. [Also essay 10.]

As to the first. While recording the 'principal submission' of Mr Munby QC for the guardian ad litem, that the proposed withholding was the doing of an act intended to lead to Bland's death, the President's judgment made neither finding nor comment on the issue. Nor was it addressed in the Court of Appeal judgments. Lord Goff (Lord Keith of Kinkel agreeing) rejected Mr Munby's contention that discontinuance of artificial feeding is equivalent to cutting a mountaineer's rope or a diver's air pipe. If that contention sought to justify an inference that there was here an intent to bring about death, it was rightly rejected. The British climber in the Andes who, some years ago, finally cut the rope on which his friend was dangling, lest he himself be dragged over the precipice, and who later found (to his amazed delight) that the friend he had thought *certain* to be killed had fallen unscathed into deep snow, had no intent to bring about death or any lesser harm.[†] Similar incidents might occur with tangled air-pipes. One intends to bring about X if and only if the bringing about of X is either an end or a means in the proposal which one shapes by deliberation (however rapidly formed or habitually executed) and chooses to adopt. So if one withdraws life-sustaining measures precisely because that has been requested by a competent patient on grounds of their burdensomeness, one need not be purposing, aiming at, or intending the patient's foreseeably certain death. One's purpose and intent is to honour the patient's wish to be relieved of (or free others from) the burden of those measures. One does, on the other hand, intend to bring about death (as a means) if one withdraws nutrition because it is the one sure way of ensuring, through death, that benefits will be paid under a term life insurance policy, or that a régime of nursing care which threatens to last for years will be terminated and the costs applied instead to recarpeting, or that parents will be relieved of their grief at the spectacle of their child's hopeless disability. In the absence of findings by the trial judge (and, apparently, of cross-examination designed to elicit—as in a criminal trial—the responsible physician's deliberations and thus intentions), the appellate courts should have proceeded on the basis that there may well have been, but perhaps was not, an intention to terminate Bland's life.

Secondly, then: Would such an intention, if it existed, make the proposed withdrawal an offence (murder)? The majority of the House, neither followed nor challenged by Lord Keith and Lord Goff, thought not. The whole House agreed that withdrawal is an omission, not a positive act of commission, and so would be unlawful only if there were, as there here was not, a duty to take the steps omitted. On this point, the House like the Court of Appeal silently rejects the submission developed before the latter court by the amicus curiae appointed by the Attorney General and instructed by the Treasury Solicitor, a submission not mentioned in the judgments (and existing reports), that:

> The issue is not whether the withdrawal of treatment is an act or a deliberate omission, but whether such withdrawal is lawful... Thus, no relevant distinction is to be drawn between, *e.g.* the administration of a lethal dose to an incompetent patient and the withholding of a necessary nutrient or medicine from such a patient.

But by relying *simply* on the distinction between an action (or 'positive action') and an omission, the rejection of this remarkable submission, though welcome, leaves the law confessedly 'misshapen' and 'almost irrational'. And unnecessarily.

For there was available, but not it seems argued, a better development of the rule articulated in *R v Bubb*[3] and *R v Gibbins and Proctor*.[4] Those cases, not cited to the President and not orally cited to or mentioned by the Court of Appeal, establish that one who undertakes the charge of caring for a dependent person (for example a young child) and omits to supply necessary food or raiment with the intention of causing death or serious bodily injury is guilty of murder. They do not, of course, confront the argument successfully raised in *Bland*, that one who has undertaken a duty of care may yet have no duty to exercise that care so as to sustain life. But the proper application or extension of their rule to meet that argument was surely this: those who have a duty to care for someone may never exercise it in a manner intended to bring about that person's death.

What is misshapen and indefensible is a law that treats as criminal a harmful 'act' while treating as lawful (and indeed compulsory) an 'omission', with the very *same intent*, by one who has a duty to care for the person injured. There is nothing misshapen about a law treating acts and omissions alike when deliberately adopted with the same intention. And the settled legal (not moral) doctrine that harmful intent by itself does not make an omission criminal should not govern when the omission is by one who admittedly has a legal duty to protect the party harmed against that type of harm.

The judges in *Bland* proceed, of course, on the basis that the responsible physicians no longer had any duty to prevent Bland's death. His death would be for him no harm or loss. Or as they put it, neither continued life nor the measures necessary to keep him alive were of any benefit to him, or in his best interests. That is of the *ratio* of the case.

[3] (1850) 4 Cox CC 455. [4] (1918) 13 Cr App R 134.

The Law Lords other than Lord Mustill reached this judgment wholly or very largely by applying the doctrine in *Bolam*[5] (somewhat as in *Re F*[6]): there is a responsible medical opinion that life in a persistent vegetative state with no prospect of recovery is of no benefit. It happens that on the same day as the President gave judgment in *Bland* (19 November 1992), the High Court of Australia, in a case of duty to warn of risk, unanimously disapproved the entire *Bolam* principle.[7] But even if that principle has some appropriate sphere, its application or extension to the question who has a life worth sustaining (and protecting against intentional termination), and who does not, seems radically unsound. No comfort can be derived from Lord Lowry's unsupported statement that he 'reject[ed] the idea…that informed medical opinion in these respects is merely a disguise for a philosophy which, if accepted, would legalise euthanasia'. The issue is not one of disguise or sincerity, but of the true implications of principles and notions being put into practice by a group of citizens whose medical qualifications, experience, and ethos confer no standing to settle for the whole community such issues of meaning, consistency, humanity, and justice.

Still, the judges whose responsibility it was to settle those issues were apparently in full accord with the principles and notions implicit in the medical opinion to which they deferred. The judgments all suggest a dualistic distinction between Bland himself and his body: for example, 'his spirit has left him and all that remains is the shell of his body' (Sir Stephen Brown P); 'his body is alive, but he has no life…He is alive but has no life at all' (Hoffmann LJ). This sort of dualism, which thinks of the body as if it were some kind of habitation for and instrument of the real person, is defended by few philosophers indeed (religious or otherwise). It renders inexplicable the unity in complexity which one experiences in everything one consciously does. It speaks as if there were two things, other and other: a non-bodily person and a non-personal living body. But neither of these can one recognize as oneself. One's living body is intrinsic, not merely instrumental, to one's personal life. Each of us has a human life (not a vegetable life plus an animal life plus a personal life); when it is flourishing that life includes all one's vital functions including speech, deliberation, and choice; when gravely impaired it lacks some of those functions without ceasing to be the life of the person so impaired.

People in PVS are gravely damaged (at least for the time being; 'persistent' does not mean permanent, and quite a few of them, as the scholarly medical

[5] *Bolam v Friern Hospital Management Committee* [1957] 1 WLR 582.

[6] *Re F (Mental Patient: Sterilisation)* [1990] 2 AC 1.

[7] *Rogers v Whitaker* (1992) 175 CLR 479.

literature shows, recover substantially after months or even years in PVS). But since human bodily life is not a merely instrumental good, extrinsic to the reality and value of the human person, their inability to participate in any other basic human good does not nullify their participation in the good, the benefit, of human life—not even when that participation is wounded and deficient as hopelessly as Bland's.

Does that entail that they must be given all the medical treatments which would be provided to a patient in better shape and with better prospects—say, heart bypass or kidney transplant (as Mr Munby unfortunately contended)? Surely not. Even in an affluent society such as ours there must be limits to medical treatment and it is reasonable to decide that no one should be sustained indefinitely by costly medical régimes. Similarly it is reasonable to treat medicine's objectives as limited, generally, to (a) the maintenance and restoration of health (the well functioning of the human organism as a whole) or some desirable approximation to health, and (b) the palliation of suffering. For patients such as Bland the first objective is unattainable,‡ and the second is irrelevant; such a patient stands to benefit in only a very limited way from many sorts of medical treatment, and these treatments may reasonably be restricted to people who will benefit from them more.

But not all that doctors do in the care of patients is directed to achieving the objectives of medical *treatment*. The judgments all seem to embrace a fallacious inference, that if tube-feeding *is* part of medical 'treatment or care', tube-feeding is therefore *not* part of the non-medical (home or nursing) care which decent families and communities provide or arrange for their utterly dependent members. The non-sequitur is compounded by failure to note that although nasogastric tube-feeding will not normally be established without a doctor's decision, no distinctively medical skills are needed to insert a nasogastric tube or maintain the supply of nutrients through it.

To desist from medical treatments designed to prevent, retard, or cure illness, on the ground that for invalids such as Bland these treatments will achieve a benefit too limited to warrant this resort to medical resources, need involve neither intent to terminate life nor a will to cease caring for such invalids. But to desist from providing at least food and basic hygiene to invalids whose death is not imminent, and to whom the processes involved are no significant burden, seems to be either (a) to intend and bring about their death as a means, for example to saving the other costs involved in their continued existence, or (b) to make a choice (however hidden by benign sentiments and palliative accompaniments) to cease providing care for them. And in an affluent society—unlike a society, for example after a nuclear attack, where attending to the needs of the able-bodied might reasonably be preferred—the latter is willy-nilly a choice to deny the personhood of these invalids by breaking off human solidarity with them at its root.

The foregoing line of thought is not perceptible in *Bland*. But the judgments almost all propose a contrary argument (derived immediately from dissents in *Cruzan*[8] and developed in writings by Ronald Dworkin acknowledged by Hoffmann LJ): Bland's continued existence was not merely no benefit but actually a harm to him, a source of indignity, violation of his wish to be remembered well, humiliation.

This argument undermines Hoffmann LJ's own hopeful dictum that, because Bland's condition differed 'in kind' from that of a severely handicapped but conscious person, *Bland* has no 'eugenics' implications. Epithets about indignity and humiliation could easily be applied (as in recent history) to various classes of severely handicapped people, many of whom, moreover, cannot exercise the distinctively human or 'personal' forms of understanding and response. And the judicial application of such epithets to Bland's existence and/or to the care provided for him depends on an equivocation clearly evident in Hoffmann LJ's judgment, where the argument is most amply developed. This judgment early on describes the principle of respect for individual dignity: 'quite irrespective of what the person concerned may think about it, it is wrong for someone to be humiliated or treated without respect for his value as a person', whether by self-demeaning actions or by the disrespectful actions of others. But later it states that discontinuing feeding Bland will 'put an end to the humiliation of his being', of his being 'grotesquely alive', etc. Thus the judgment slides from one, moral sense of (in)dignity and humiliation to quite another, emotional sense which would be better captured by the word 'undignified'.

The fact that Bland could indeed have been subjected to indignities, for example by being treated as a sex object or thrown, living, into the hospital rubbish, confirms that he remained a person, with some interests, and could be harmed, or benefited. But, *pace* the courts' incautious rhetoric, the nurses' devoted care for him did not humiliate or demean him or treat him without respect for his value as a person. On the contrary. As Lord Mustill acknowledged, the proposed discontinuance of care was going to require them to act 'contrary to all their instincts, training and traditions'. Their relationship to Bland was one of (largely unreciprocated) human solidarity between persons; as such it benefited both them and him. Failure

[8] *Cruzan v Director Missouri Dept of Health* 497 US 261 (1990). [See now essay III.16 (1998b), n. 7.]

to distinguish being subjected to indignities from being (or being put) in an undignified condition (or position) is a deeply unsettling aspect of *Bland*. Many are those who might be rescued from undignified conditions by benevolent termination of their life.

The judges identified *Bland* as a case in which sanctity of human life should yield to self-determination or best interests. Regrettably, no judgment attempted to *state* the much mentioned 'principle of sanctity of life'. A principle is a proposition which can guide deliberation, and any plausible articulation of this principle would exclude all choices intended to terminate (innocent) human life. The 'principle of self-determination' in giving or withholding consent to medical care was, however, often stated, in the quasi-absolute form canonized in *Sidaway*[9] which conspicuously fails to address the case where a refusal is known to be suicidal (for example motivated exclusively by concern to ensure payment of term life insurance benefits; or pursuant to an open suicide pact). Lord Goff alone adverted to suicide, but quite ambiguously. And he approved Hoffmann LJ's dictum that suicide's decriminalization 'was a recognition that the principle of self-determination should in that case [suicide] prevail over the sanctity of life'.

The sponsors of the Suicide Act 1961 repudiated rather than recognized the 'principle of self-determination'.[10] Indeed, the Act's severe penalties for complicity in suicide entail a rejection of the supposed primacy of self-determination and attest the law's acceptance, hitherto, that civilized relationships should have no truck with choices intended to terminate the lives of innocent people.

NOTES

† *The climber who cut the rope* (p. 316)...Simon Yates, who cut the rope suspending his friend Joe Simpson at 17,000 feet in the Peruvian Andes in the spring of 1985, said in an interview published in the *Independent on Sunday* (London) on 23 February 1997 that when he cut the rope he thought this 'was likely to kill Joe'; but a little later in the interview he says 'if I hadn't cut the rope I would certainly have died'. So 'likely' was doubtless an understatement; and in any event 'kill Joe' meant result in Joe's death.

‡ *Restoration of health 'is unattainable'*...(p. 319). The essay's position here seems to presume that it was sufficiently clear that Bland's condition of PVS was not one of the kind that, as was mentioned in the preceding paragraph, is compatible with significant recovery. The essay's position hereabouts also presumes that this was not a case of 'super-locked-in syndrome' (a condition that Alan Shewmon has argued—see essay 18 at n. 19—cannot be demonstrated not to be the condition of at least some PVS patients).

[9] *Sidaway v Board of Governors of the Bethlem Royal Hospital* [1985] AC 871 at 904–5.

[10] See e.g. HC Deb. 19 July 1961, cols 1425–6 .

BIBLIOGRAPHY OF THE WORKS OF JOHN FINNIS

1962	a		'Developments in Judicial Jurisprudence', Adelaide L Rev 1: 317–37
	b		'The Immorality of the Deterrent', Adelaide Univ Mag: 47–61
1963			'Doves and Serpents', The Old Palace 38: 438–41
1967	a	**I.17**	'Reason and Passion: The Constitutional Dialectic of Free Speech and Obscenity', University of Pennyslvania L Rev 116: 222–43
	b	**IV.8**	'Blackstone's Theoretical Intentions', Natural L Forum 12: 63–83
	c		'Punishment and Pedagogy', The Oxford Review 5: 83–93
	d		'Review of Zelman Cowen, *Sir John Latham and Other Papers*', LQR 83: 289–90
1968	a	**III.10**	'Old and New in Hart's Philosophy of Punishment', The Oxford Review 8: 73–80
	b		'Constitutional Law', *Annual Survey of Commonwealth Law 1967* (Butterworth), 20–33, 71–98
	c		'Separation of Powers in the Australian Constitution', Adelaide L Rev 3: 159–77
	d		Review of Neville March Hunnings, *Film Censors and the Law*, LQR 84: 430–2
	e		'Natural Law in *Humanae vitae*', LQR 84: 467 71
	f		Review of H. Phillip Levy, *The Press Council*, LQR 84: 582
	g		'Law, Morality and Mind Control', Zenith (University Museum, Oxford) 6: 7–8
1969	a		'Constitutional Law', *Annual Survey of Commonwealth Law 1968* (Butterworth), 2–15, 32–49, 53–75, 98–114
	b		Review of Herbert L. Packer, *The Limits of the Criminal Sanction*, Oxford Magazine, 86 no. 1 (new series), 10–11
1970	a	**I.6**	'Reason, Authority and Friendship in Law and Morals', in Khanbai, Katz, and Pineau (eds), *Jowett Papers 1968–1969* (Oxford: Blackwell), 101–24
	b		'Natural Law and Unnatural Acts', Heythrop J 11: 365–87
	c		i. 'Abortion and Legal Rationality', Adelaide L Rev 3: 431–67 ii. 'Three Schemes of Regulation', in Noonan (ed.), *The Morality of Abortion: Legal and Historical Perspectives* (HUP)
	d		'Constitutional Law', *Annual Survey of Commonwealth Law 1969* (Butterworth), 2–4, 27–34, 37–50, 65–81
	e		Review of H.B. Acton, *The Philosophy of Punishment*, Oxford Magazine, 87 (new series) (13 April)
	f		Review of Colin Howard, *Australian Constitutional Law*, LQR 86: 416–18

1971	a	**IV.21**	'Revolutions and Continuity of Law', in A.W.B. Simpson (ed.), *Oxford Essays in Jurisprudence: Second Series* (OUP), 44–76
	b		'The Abortion Act: What Has Changed?', Criminal L Rev: 3–12
	c		'Constitutional Law', *Annual Survey of Commonwealth Law 1970* (Butterworth), 2–4, 17–31, 33–42, 51–60
1972	a	**III.11**	'The Restoration of Retribution', Analysis 32: 131–5
	b	**IV.18**	'Some Professorial Fallacies about Rights', Adelaide L Rev 4: 377–88
	c		'The Value of the Human Person', Twentieth Century [Australia] 27: 126–37
	d		'Bentham et le droit naturel classique', Archives de Philosophie du Droit 17: 423–7
	e		'Constitutional Law', *Annual Survey of Commonwealth Law 1971* (Butterworth), 2–5, 11–25, 28–41
	f		'Meaning and Ambiguity in Punishment (and Penology)', Osgoode Hall LJ 10: 264–8
1973	a	**III.3**	Review of John Rawls, *A Theory of Justice* (1972), Oxford Magazine 90 no. 1 (new series) (26 January)
	b	**III.18**	'The Rights and Wrongs of Abortion: A Reply to Judith Jarvis Thomson', Philosophy & Public Affairs 2: 117–45
	c		'Constitutional Law', *Annual Survey of Commonwealth Law 1972* (Butterworth), 2–8, 23–56, 62–6
1974	a		'Constitutional Law', *Annual Survey of Commonwealth Law 1973* (Butterworth), 1–66
	b		'Commonwealth and Dependencies', in *Halsbury's Laws of England*, vol. 6 (4th edn, Butterworth), 315–601
	c		'Rights and Wrongs in Legal Responses to Population Growth', in J.N. Santamaria (ed.), *Man—How Will He Survive?* (Adelaide), 91–100
	d		Review of R.S. Gae, *The Bank Nationalisation Case and the Constitution*, Modern L Rev 37: 120
1975			'Constitutional Law', *Annual Survey of Commonwealth Law 1974* (Butterworth), 1–61
1976	a		'Constitutional Law', *Annual Survey of Commonwealth Law 1975* (Butterworth), 1–56
	b		Chapters 18–21 (with Germain Grisez), in R. Lawler, D.W. Wuerl, and T.C. Lawler (eds), *The Teaching of Christ* (Huntingdon, IN: OSV), 275–354
1977	a	**I.3**	'Scepticism, Self-refutation and the Good of Truth', in P.M. Hacker and J. Raz (eds), *Law, Morality and Society: Essays in Honour of H.L.A. Hart* (OUP), 247–67
	b		'Some Formal Remarks about "Custom"', in International Law Association, Report of the First Meeting [April 1977] on the Theory and Methodology of International Law, 14–21
1978	a		'Catholic Social Teaching: *Populorum Progressio* and After', Church Alert (SODEPAX Newsletter) 19: 2–9; also in James V. Schall (ed.), *Liberation Theology in Latin America* (San Francisco: Ignatius Press, 1982)

b 'Conscience, Infallibility and Contraception', The Month 239: 410–17

c 'Abortion: Legal Aspects of', in Warren T. Reich (ed.), *Encyclopedia of Bioethics* (New York: Free Press), 26–32

1979 V.18 'Catholic Faith and the World Order: Reflections on E.R. Norman', Clergy Rev 64: 309–18

1980 a *Natural Law and Natural Rights* (OUP) (425 pp)
Legge Naturali e Diritti Naturali (trans. F. Di Blasi) (Milan: Giappichelli, 1996)
Ley Natural y Derechos Naturales (trans. C. Orrego) (Buenos Aires: Abeledo-Perrot, 2000)
Prawo naturalne i uprawnienia naturalne (trans. Karolina Lossman) Klasycy Filozofii Prawa (Warsaw: Dom Wydawniczy ABC, 2001)
自然法与自然权利 ([Mandarin] trans. Jiaojiao Dong, Yi Yang, Xiaohui Liang) (Beijing: 2004)
Lei Natural e Direitos Naturais (trans. Leila Mendes) (Sao Leopoldo, Brazil: Editora Unisinos, 2007)

b 'Reflections on an Essay in Christian Ethics: Part I: Authority in Morals', Clergy Rev 65: 51–7: 'Part II: Morals and Method', 87–93

c V.19 'The Natural Law, Objective Morality, and Vatican II', in William E. May (ed), *Principles of Catholic Moral Life* (Chicago: Franciscan Herald Press), 113–49

1981 a [*British North America Acts: The Role of Parliament*: Report from the Foreign Affairs Committee, House of Commons Paper 1980–81 HC 42 (21 January) (87 pp)]

b 'Observations de M J.M. Finnis' [on Georges Kalinowski's review of *Natural Law and Natural Rights*], Archives de Philosophie du Droit 26: 425–7

c [Foreign Affairs Committee, *Supplementary Report on the British North America Acts: The Role of Parliament*, House of Commons Paper 1980–81 HC 295 (15 April) (23 pp)]

d [Foreign Affairs Committee, *Third Report on the British North America Acts: The Role of Parliament*, House of Commons Paper 1981–82 HC 128 (22 December) (17 pp)]

e 'Natural Law and the "Is"-"Ought" Question: An Invitation to Professor Veatch', Cath Lawyer 26: 266–77

1982 a (with Germain Grisez) 'The Basic Principles of Natural Law: A Reply to Ralph McInerny', American J Juris 26: 21–31

b Review of Anthony Battaglia, *Towards a Reformulation of Natural Law*, Scottish J Theol 35: 555–6

1983 a 'The Responsibilities of the United Kingdom Parliament and Government under the Australian Constitution', Adelaide L Rev 9: 91–107

b *Fundamentals of Ethics* (OUP; Washington DC: Georgetown University Press) (163 pp)

c 'Power to Enforce Treaties in Australia—The High Court goes Centralist?', Oxford J Legal St 3: 126–30

	d		'The Fundamental Themes of *Laborem Exercens*', in Paul L. Williams (ed.), *Catholic Social Thought and the Social Teaching of John Paul II* (Scranton: Northeast Books), 19–31
	e		['In Vitro Fertilisation: Morality and Public Policy', Evidence submitted by the Catholic Bishops' Joint Committee on Bio-ethical Issues to the [Warnock] Committee of Inquiry into Human Fertilisation and Embryology, May, 5–18]
1984	a	I.10	i. 'Practical Reasoning, Human Goods and the End of Man', Proc Am Cath Phil Ass 58: 23–36; also in ii. New Blackfriars 66 (1985) 438–51
	b	IV.2	'The Authority of Law in the Predicament of Contemporary Social Theory', J Law, Ethics & Pub Policy 1: 115–37
	c		['Response to the Warnock Report', submission to Secretary of State for Social Services by the Catholic Bishops' Joint Bioethics Committee on Bio-ethical Issues, December, 3–17]
	d		'IVF and the Catholic Tradition', The Month 246: 55–8
	e		'Reforming the Expanded External Affairs Power', in Report of the External Affairs Subcommittee to the Standing Committee of the Australian Constitutional Convention (September), 43–51
1985	a	III.1	'A Bill of Rights for Britain? The Moral of Contemporary Jurisprudence' (Maccabaean Lecture in Jurisprudence), Proc Brit Acad 71: 303–31
	b	IV.9	'On "Positivism" and "Legal-Rational Authority"', Oxford J Leg St 3: 74–90
	c	IV.13	'On "The Critical Legal Studies Movement"', American J Juris 30: 21–42; also in J. Bell and J. Eekelaar (eds), *Oxford Essays in Jurisprudence: Third Series* (OUP, 1987), 145–65
	d		'Morality and the Ministry of Defence' (review), The Tablet, 3 August, 804–5
	e		'Personal Integrity, Sexual Morality and Responsible Parenthood', Anthropos [now Anthropotes] 1: 43–55
1986	a		'The "Natural Law Tradition"', J Legal Ed 36: 492–5
	b		'The Laws of God, the Laws of Man and Reverence for Human Life', in R. Hittinger (ed.), *Linking the Human Life Issues* (Chicago: Regnery Books), 59–98
1987	a	I.9	'Natural Inclinations and Natural Rights: Deriving "Ought" from "Is" according to Aquinas', in L. Elders and K. Hedwig (eds), *Lex et Libertas: Freedom and Law according to St Thomas Aquinas* (Studi Tomistici 30, Libreria Editrice Vaticana), 43–55
	b	II.8	'The Act of the Person' *Persona Veritá e Morale*, atti del Congresso Internazionale di Teologia Morale, Rome 1986 (Rome: Cittá Nuova Editrice), 159–75
	c	III.2	'Legal Enforcement of Duties to Oneself: Kant v. Neo-Kantians', Columbia L Rev 87: 433–56
	d	IV.4	'On Positivism and the Foundations of Legal Authority: Comment', in Ruth Gavison (ed.), *Issues in Legal Philosophy: the Influence of H.L.A. Hart* (OUP), 62–75

e IV.12 'On Reason and Authority in Law's Empire', Law and Philosophy 6: 357–80

f Germain Grisez, Joseph Boyle, and John Finnis, 'Practical Principles, Moral Truth, and Ultimate Ends', American J Juris 32: 99–151 (also, with original table of contents restored, in 1991d)

g *Nuclear Deterrence, Morality and Realism* (with Joseph Boyle and Germain Grisez) (OUP) (429 pp)

h 'Answers [to questions about nuclear and non-nuclear defence options]', in Oliver Ramsbottom (ed.), *Choices: Nuclear and Non-Nuclear Defence Options* (London: Brasseys' Defence Publishers), 219–34

i 'The Claim of Absolutes', The Tablet 241: 364–6

j ['On Human Infertility Services and Bioethical Research', response by the Catholic Bishops' Joint Committee on Bioethical Issues to the Department of Health and Social Security, June, 3–12]

1988 a V.21 'The Consistent Ethic: A Philosophical Critique', in Thomas G. Fuechtmann (ed.), *Consistent Ethic of Life* (Kansas: Sheed & Ward), 140–81

b V.20 'Nuclear Deterrence, Christian Conscience, and the End of Christendom', New Oxford Rev [Berkeley, CA] July–August: 6–16

c 'Goods are Meant for Everyone: Reflection on Encyclical *Sollicitudo Rei Socialis*', L'Osservatore Romano, weekly edn, 21 March, 21

d '"Faith and Morals": A Note', The Month 21/2: 563–7

e Germain Grisez, Joseph Boyle, John Finnis, and William E. May, '"Every Marital Act Ought to be Open to New Life": Toward a Clearer Understanding', The Thomist 52: 365–426, also in Grisez, Boyle, Finnis, and May, *The Teaching of Humanae Vitae: A Defense* (San Francisco: Ignatius Press); Italian trans. in Anthropotes 1: 73–122

f 'Absolute Moral Norms: Their Ground, Force and Permanence', Anthropotes 2: 287–303

1989 a II.5 'Persons and their Associations', Proc Aristotelian Soc, Supp. vol. 63: 267–74

b IV.3 'Law as Coordination', Ratio Juris 2: 97–104

c V.11 'On Creation and Ethics', Anthropotes 2: 197–206

d 'La morale chrétienne et la guerre: entretien avec John Finnis', Catholica 13: 15–23

e 'Russell Hittinger's Straw Man', Fellowship of Catholic Scholars Newsletter 12/2: 6–8 (corrigenda in following issue)

f 'Nuclear Deterrence and Christian Vocation', New Blackfriars 70: 380–7

1990 a I.12 'Aristotle, Aquinas, and Moral Absolutes', Catholica: International Quarterly Selection 12: 7–15; Spanish trans. by Carlos I. Massini-Correas in Persona y Derecho 28 (1993), and in

A.G. Marques and J. Garcia-Huidobro (eds), *Razon y Praxis* (Valparaiso: Edeval, 1994), 319–36

b **IV.16** 'Allocating Risks and Suffering: Some Hidden Traps', Cleveland State L Rev 38: 193–207

c 'Natural Law and Legal Reasoning', Cleveland State L Rev 38: 1–13

d **IV.17** 'Concluding Reflections', Cleveland State L Rev 38: 231–50

e **V.16** 'Conscience in the Letter to the Duke of Norfolk', in Ian Ker and Alan G. Hill (eds), *Newman after a Hundred Years* (OUP), 401–18

f Joseph Boyle, Germain Grisez, and John Finnis, 'Incoherence and Consequentialism (or Proportionalism)—A Rejoinder' American Cath Phil Q 64: 271–7

g 'The Natural Moral Law and Faith', in Russell E. Smith (ed.), *The Twenty-Fifth Anniversary of Vatican II: A Look Back and a Look Ahead* (Braintree, MA: Pope John Center), 223–38; discussion (with Alasdair MacIntyre), 250–62

1991 a **II.9** 'Object and Intention in Moral Judgments according to St Thomas Aquinas', The Thomist 55: 1–27; rev. version in J. Follon and J. McEvoy (eds), *Finalité et Intentionnalité: Doctrine Thomiste et Perspectives Modernes*, Bibliothèque Philosophique de Louvain No. 35 (Paris: J. Vrin, 1992), 127–48

b **II.10** 'Intention and Side-effects', in R.G. Frey and Christopher W. Morris (eds), *Liability and Responsibility: Essays in Law and Morals* (CUP), 32–64

c *Moral Absolutes: Tradition, Revision and Truth* (Washington DC: Catholic University of America Press) (115 pp) *Absolutos Morales: Tradición, Revisión y Verdad* (trans. Juan José García Norro) (Barcelona: Ediciones Internacionales Universitarias, EUNSA SA) *Gli assoluti morali: Tradizione, revisione & verità* (trans. Andrea Maria Maccarini) (Milan: Edizioni Ares, 1993)

d 'Introduction', in John Finnis (ed.), *Natural Law*, vol. I (International Library of Essays in Law and Legal Theory, Schools 1.1) (Dartmouth: New York University Press), xi–xxiii

e 'Introduction', in John Finnis (ed.), *Natural Law*, vol. II (International Library of Essays in Law and Legal Theory, Schools 1.2) (Dartmouth: Aldershot, Sydney), xi–xvi

f 'A propos de la "valeur intrinsèque de la vie humaine"', Catholica 28: 15–21

g 'Commonwealth and Dependencies', in *Halsbury's Laws of England*, vol. 6 re-issue (4th edn, London: Butterworth), 345–559

1992 a **I.14** 'Natural Law and Legal Reasoning', in Robert P. George (ed.), *Natural Law Theory: Contemporary Essays* (OUP), 134–57

b **III.7** 'Commentary on Dummett and Weithman', in Brian Barry and Robert E. Goodin, *Free Movement: Ethical Issues in the Transnational Migration of People and of Money* (University Park, Pennsylvania: University of Pennsylvania Press), 203–10

c III.15 'Economics, Justice and the Value of Life: Concluding Remarks', in Luke Gormally (ed.), *Economics and the Dependent Elderly: Autonomy, Justice and Quality of Care* (CUP), 189–98

d V.9 *'Historical Consciousness' and Theological Foundations*, Etienne Gilson Lecture No. 15 (Toronto: Pontifical Institute of Mediaeval Studies) (32 pp)

e V.17 'On the Grace of Humility: A New Theological Reflection', The Allen Review 7: 4–7

1993 a II.16/ III.19 'Abortion and Health Care Ethics', in Raanan Gillon (ed.), *Principles of Health Care Ethics* (Chichester: John Wiley), 547–57

b 'The Legal Status of the Unborn Baby', Catholic Medical Quarterly 43: 5–11

c II.19 '*Bland*: Crossing the Rubicon?', LQR 109: 329–37

d 'Theology and the Four Principles: A Roman Catholic View I' (with Anthony Fisher OP), in Raanon Gillon (ed.), *Principles of Health Care Ethics* (Chichester: John Wiley), 31–44

e 'The "Value of Human Life" and "The Right to Death": Some Reflections on *Cruzan* and Ronald Dworkin', Southern Illinois University LJ 17: 559–71

1994 a II.12 'On Conditional Intentions and Preparatory Intentions', in Luke Gormally (ed.), *Moral Truth and Moral Tradition: Essays in Honour of Peter Geach and Elizabeth Anscombe* (Dublin: Four Courts Press), 163–76

b 'Law, Morality, and "Sexual Orientation"', Notre Dame L Rev 69: 1049–76; also, with additions, Notre Dame J Law, Ethics & Public Policy 9 (1995) 11–39

c 'Liberalism and Natural Law Theory', Mercer L Rev 45: 687–704

d '"Shameless Acts" in Colorado: Abuse of Scholarship in Constitutional Cases', Academic Questions 7/4: 10–41

e Germain Grisez and John Finnis, 'Negative Moral Precepts Protect the Dignity of the Human Person', L'Osservatore Romano, English edn, 23 February

f 'Beyond the Encyclical', The Tablet, 8 January, reprinted in John Wilkins (ed.), *Understanding* Veritatis Splendor (London: SPCK), 69–76

g Germain Grisez, John Finnis, and William E. May, 'Indissolubility, Divorce and Holy Communion', New Blackfriars 75 (June), 321–30

h '"Living Will" Legislation', in Luke Gormally (ed.), *Euthanasia, Clinical Practice and the Law* (London: Linacre Centre), 167–76

i 'Unjust Laws in a Democratic Society: Some Philosophical and Theological Reflections', in Joseph Joblin and Réal Tremblay (eds), *I cattolici e la società pluralista: il caso delle leggi imperfette: atti del I Colloquio sui cattolici nella società pluralista: Roma, 9–12 Novembre 1994* (Bologna: ESP), 99–114

1995 a II.11 'Intention in Tort Law', in David Owen (ed.), *Philosophical Foundations of Tort Law* (OUP), 229–48 b III.14 'A Philosophical Case against Euthanasia', 'The Fragile Case for Euthanasia: A Reply to John Harris', and 'Misunderstanding the Case against Euthanasia: Response to Harris's First Reply', in John Keown (ed.), *Euthanasia: Ethical, Legal and Clinical Perspectives* (CUP), 23–35, 46–55, 62–71

c 'History of Philosophy of Law' (465–8), 'Problems in the Philosophy of Law' (468–72), 'Austin' (67), 'Defeasible' (181), 'Dworkin' (209–10), 'Grotius' (328), 'Hart' (334), 'Legal Positivism' (476–7), 'Legal Realism' (477), 'Natural Law' (606–7), 'Natural Rights' (607), in Ted Honderich (ed.), *Oxford Companion to Philosophy* (OUP)

1996 a III.5 'Is Natural Law Theory Compatible with Limited Government?', in Robert P. George (ed.), *Natural Law, Liberalism, and Morality* (OUP), 1–26

b III.13 'The Ethics of War and Peace in the Catholic Natural Law Tradition', in Terry Nardin (ed.), *The Ethics of War and Peace* (Princeton University Press), 15–39

c IV.7 'The Truth in Legal Positivism', in Robert P. George (ed.), *The Autonomy of Law: Essays on Legal Positivism* (OUP), 195–214

d 'Unjust Laws in a Democratic Society: Some Philosophical and Theological Reflections', Notre Dame L Rev 71: 595–604 (a revised version of 1994i)

e I.13 'Loi naturelle', in Monique Canto-Sperber (ed.), *Dictionnaire de Philosophie Morale* (Paris: Presses Universitaires de France), 862–8

1997 a 'Natural Law—Positive Law', in A. Lopez Trujillo, I. Herranz, and E. Sgreccia (eds), *'Evangelium Vitae' and Law* (Libreria Editrice Vaticana), 199–209

b I.15 'Commensuration and Public Reason', in Ruth Chang (ed.), *Incommensurability, Comparability and Practical Reasoning* (HUP), 215–33, 285–9

c III.21 'Law, Morality and "Sexual Orientation"', in John Corvino (ed.), *Same Sex: Debating the Ethics, Science, and Culture of Homosexuality* (Lanham: Rowman & Littlefield), 31–43

d III.22 'The Good of Marriage and the Morality of Sexual Relations: Some Philosophical and Historical Observations', Am J Juris 42: 97–134

1998 a I.16 'Public Reason, Abortion and Cloning', Valparaiso Univ LR 32: 361–82

b III.16 'Euthanasia, Morality and Law', Loyola of Los Angeles L Rev 31: 1123–45

c V.3 'On the Practical Meaning of Secularism', Notre Dame L Rev 73: 491–515

d *Aquinas: Moral, Political, and Legal Theory* (OUP) (xxi + 385 pp)

e 'Public Good: The Specifically Political Common Good in Aquinas', in Robert P. George (ed.), *Natural Law and Moral Inquiry* (Washington DC: Georgetown University Press), 174–209

f 'Natural Law', in Edward Craig (ed.), *Routledge Encyclopaedia of Philosophy*, vol. 6 (London: Routledge), 685–90

1999 a I.2 'Natural Law and the Ethics of Discourse', American J Juris 43: 53–73; also in Ratio Juris 12: 354–73

b III.12 'Retribution: Punishment's Formative Aim', American J Juris 44: 91–103

c IV.20 'The Fairy Tale's Moral', LQR 115: 170–5

d V.6 'The Catholic Church and Public Policy Debates in Western Liberal Societies: The Basis and Limits of Intellectual Engagement', in Luke Gormally (ed.), *Issues for a Catholic Bioethic* (London: Linacre Centre), 261–73

e 'What is the Common Good, and Why does it Concern the Client's Lawyer?', South Texas L Rev 40: 41–53

2000 a II.1 'The Priority of Persons', in Jeremy Horder (ed.), *Oxford Essays in Jurisprudence, Fourth Series* (OUP), 1–15

b II.17 'Some Fundamental Evils of Generating Human Embryos by Cloning', in Cosimo Marco Mazzoni (ed.), *Etica della Ricerca Biologica* (Florence: Leo S. Olschki Editore), 115–23; also in C.M. Mazzoni (ed.), *Ethics and Law in Biological Research* (The Hague, London: Martinus Nijhoff; Boston: Kluwer, 2002), 99–106

c 'Abortion, Natural Law and Public Reason', in Robert P. George and Christopher Wolfe (eds), *Natural Law and Public Reason* (Washington DC: Georgetown University Press), 71–105

d 'On the Incoherence of Legal Positivism', Notre Dame L Rev 75: 1597–611

e 'God the Father', in Peter Newby (ed.), *Occasional Papers from the Millennium Conferences at the Oxford University Catholic Chaplaincy* No. 1 (Oxford), 24–6

2001 a II.13 '"Direct" and "Indirect": A Reply to Critics of Our Action Theory' (with Germain Grisez and Joseph Boyle), The Thomist 65: 1–44

b III.6 'Virtue and the Constitution of the United States', Fordham L Rev 69: 1595–602

c 'Reason, Faith and Homosexual Acts', Catholic Social Science Review 6: 61–9

2002 a IV.5 'Natural Law: The Classical Tradition', in Jules Coleman and Scott Shapiro (eds), *The Oxford Handbook of Jurisprudence and Philosophy of Law* (OUP), 1–60

b V.22 'Secularism, the Root of the Culture of Death', in Luke Gormally (ed.), *Culture of Life—Culture of Death* (London: Linacre Centre)

c 'Aquinas on *jus* and Hart on Rights: A Response', Rev of Politics 64: 407–10

d Patrick H. Martin and John Finnis, 'The Identity of "Anthony Rivers"', Recusant History 26: 39–74

e —— and —— 'Tyrwhitt of Kettleby, Part I: Goddard Tyrwhitt, Martyr, 1580', Recusant History 26: 301–13

2003 a III.8 'Natural Law & the Re-making of Boundaries', in Allen Buchanan and Margaret Moore (eds), *States, Nations, and Boundaries: The Ethics of Making Boundaries* (CUP), 171–8

	b	**IV.1**	'Law and What I Truly Should Decide', American J Juris 48: 107–30
	c	**V.10**	'Saint Thomas More and the Crisis in Faith and Morals', The Priest 7/1: 10–15, 29–30
	d		'Secularism, Morality and Politics', L'Osservatore Romano, English edn, 29 January, 9
	e		'Shakespeare's Intercession for *Love's Martyr*' (with Patrick Martin), Times Literary Supplement, no. 5220, 18 April, 12–14
	f		'An Intrinsically Disordered Attraction', in John F. Harvey and Gerard V. Bradley (eds), *Same-Sex Attraction: A Parents' Guide* (South Bend: St Augustine's Press), 89–99
	g		'Nature and Natural Law in Contemporary Philosophical and Theological Debates: Some Observations', in Juan Correa and Elio Sgreccia (eds), *The Nature & Dignity of the Human Person as the Foundation of the Right to Life: The Challenges of Contemporary Culture* (Rome: Libreria Editrice Vaticana), 81–109
	h		Patrick H. Martin and John Finnis, 'Tyrwhitt of Kettleby, Part II: Robert Tyrwhitt, a Main Benefactor of John Gerard SJ, 1599–1605', Recusant History 27: 556–69
	i		—— and —— 'Thomas Thorpe, "W.S." and the Catholic Intelligencers', Elizabethan Literary Renaissance, 1–43
	j		—— and —— '*Caesar*, Succession, and the Chastisement of Rulers', Notre Dame L Rev 78: 1045–74
	k		'Commonwealth and Dependencies', in *Halsbury's Laws of England*, vol. 6 re-issue (4th edn, London: Butterworth), 409–518
	l		'Abortion for Cleft Palate: The Human Fertilisation and Embryology Act 1990', Sunday Telegraph, 7 December
	m		'An Oxford Play Festival in 1582' (with Patrick Martin), Notes & Queries 50: 391–4
2004	a	**II.18**	'Per un'etica dell'eguaglianza nel diritto alla vita: Un commento a Peter Singer', in Rosangela Barcaro and Paolo Becchi (eds), *Questioni Mortali: L'Attuale Dibattito sulla Morte Cerebrale e il Problema dei Trapianti* (Naples: Edizioni Scientifiche Italiane), 127–39
	b	**IV.22**	'Helping Enact Unjust Laws without Complicity in Injustice', American J Juris 49: 11–42
2005	a	**I.1**	'Foundations of Practical Reason Revisited', American J Juris 50: 109–32
	b	**I.4**	'Self-referential (or Performative) Inconsistency: Its Significance for Truth', Proceedings of the Catholic Philosophical Association 78: 13–21
	c	**II.2**	'"The Thing I Am": Personal Identity in Aquinas and Shakespeare', Social Philosophy & Policy 22: 250–82; also in Ellen Frankel Paul, Fred. D. Miller, and Jeffrey Paul (eds), *Personal Identity* (CUP), 250–82
	d	**IV.6**	'Philosophy of Law' (Chinese trans.), in Ouyang Kang (ed.), *The Map of Contemporary British and American Philosophy* (Beijing: Dangdai Yingmei Zhexue Ditu), 388–413

	e		'On "Public Reason"', in *O Racji Pulicznej* (Warsaw: Ius et Lex), 7–30 (Polish trans.), 33–56 (English original); <http://ssrn.com/abstract=955815>
	f		'Restricting Legalised Abortion is not Intrinsically Unjust', in Helen Watt (ed.), *Cooperation, Complicity & Conscience* (London: Linacre Centre), 209–45
	g		'A Vote Decisive for . . . a More Restrictive Law', in Helen Watt (ed.), *Cooperation, Complicity & Conscience* (London: Linacre Centre), 269–95
	h		'Aquinas' Moral, Political and Legal Philosophy', Stanford Encyclopedia of Philosophy; <http://plato.stanford.edu/entries/aquinas-moral-political/>
	i		Patrick H. Martin and John Finnis, 'Benedicam Dominum: Ben Jonson's Strange 1605 Inscription', Times Literary Supplement, 4 November, 12–13
	j		—— and —— 'The Secret Sharers: "Anthony Rivers" and the Appellant Controversy, 1601–2', Huntingdon Library Q 69/2: 195–238
2006	a	V.4	'Religion and State: Some Main Issues and Sources', American J Juris 51: 107–30
	b		'Observations for the Austral Conference to mark the 25th Anniversary of *Natural Law and Natural Rights*', Cuadernos de Extensión Jurídica (Universidad de los Andes) no. 13: 27–30
2007	a	III.9	'Nationality, Alienage and Constitutional Principle', LQR 123: 417–45
	b	IV.10	'On Hart's Ways: Law as Reason and as Fact', American J Juris 52: 25–53; also in Matthew Kramer and Claire Grant (eds), *The Legacy of H.L.A. Hart: Legal, Political & Moral Philosophy* (OUP, 2009), 1–27
	c		'Natural Law Theories of Law', Stanford Encyclopedia of Philosophy; <http://plato.stanford.edu/entries/natural-law-theories/>
2008	a	I.5/ II.7/V.8	'Reason, Revelation, Universality and Particularity in Ethics', AJJ 53: 23–48
	b	II.6	'Universality, Personal and Social Identity, and Law', address, Congresso Sul-Americano de Filosofia do Direito, Porto Alegre, Brazil, 4 October 2007; Oxford Legal Studies Research Paper 5; <http://ssrn.com/abstract=1094277>
	c	III.20	'Marriage: A Basic and Exigent Good', The Monist 91: 396–414
	d	[V.13]	'Grounds of Law & Legal Theory: A Response', Legal Theory 13: 315–44
	e		'Common Law Constraints: Whose Common Good Counts?', Oxford Legal Studies Research Paper 10; <http://ssrn.com/abstract_id=1100628>
	f		*Humanae Vitae*: A New Translation with Notes (London: Catholic Truth Society) (31 pp)
2009	a	II.3	'Anscombe's Essays', National Catholic Bioethics Q 9/1: 199–207
	b	IV.11	'H.L.A. Hart: A Twentieth Century Oxford Political Philosopher', American J Juris 54: 161–85

c V.1 'Does Free Exercise of Religion Deserve Constitutional Mention?', American J Juris 54: 41–66

d V.2 'Telling the Truth about God and Man in a Pluralist Society: Economy or Explication?', in Christopher Wolfe (ed.), *The Naked Public Square Revisited: Religion & Politics in the Twenty-First Century* (Wilmington: ISI Books), 111–25, 204–9

e 'Endorsing Discrimination between Faiths: A Case of Extreme Speech?', in Ivan Hare and James Weinstein (eds), *Extreme Speech and Democracy* (OUP), 430–41

f 'Discrimination between Religions: Some Thoughts on Reading Greenawalt's *Religion and the Constitution*', Constitutional Commentary 25: 265–71

g 'Commonwealth', in *Halsbury's Laws of England*, vol. 13 (5th edn, London: LexisNexis), 471–589

h 'Why Religious Liberty is a Special, Important and Limited Right', Notre Dame Legal Studies Paper 09–11; <http://ssrn.com/abstract=1392278>

i 'The Lords' Eerie Swansong: A Note on *R (Purdy) v Director of Public Prosecutions*', Oxford Legal Studies Research Paper 31; <http://ssrn.com/abstract=1477281>

j 'The Mental Capacity Act 2005: Some Ethical and Legal Issues', in Helen Watt (ed.), *Incapacity & Care: Controversies in Healthcare and Research* (London: Linacre Centre), 95–105

k 'Debate over the Interpretation of *Dignitas personae*'s Teaching on Embryo Adoption', National Catholic Bioethics Q 9: 475–8

2010 a II.14 'Directly Discriminatory Decisions: A Missed Opportunity', LQR 126: 491–6

b 'Law as Idea, Ideal and Duty: A Comment on Simmonds, *Law as a Moral Idea*', Jurisprudence 1: 247–53

OTHER WORKS CITED

Ames, J.B. (1905), 'How Far an Act May be a Tort Because of the Wrongful Motive of the Actor' Harv L Rev 18: 411

Anscombe, G.E.M. (ed.) (1953), Ludwig Wittgenstein, *Philosophical Investigations* (Oxford: Blackwell)

——([1957] 1985), *Intention* (Oxford: Blackwell; HUP)

——(1963), 'Events in the Mind', in *The Collected Philosophical Papers of G.E.M. Anscombe*, vol. 2, 57–63

——([1965] 1981), 'Thought and Action in Aristotle', in *The Collected Philosophical Papers of G.E.M. Anscombe*, vol. 1, 66–77

——(1971), 'Causality and Determination', in *The Collected Philosophical Papers of G.E.M. Anscombe*, vol. 2, 133–47

——(1976), 'Soft Determinism', in *The Collected Philosophical Papers of G.E.M. Anscombe*, vol. 2, 163–72

——(1981), *The Collected Philosophical Papers of G.E.M. Anscombe*, vol. 1, *From Parmenides to Wittgenstein* (Oxford: Basil Blackwell; Minneapolis: University of Minnesota Press)

——(1981), *The Collected Philosophical Papers of G.E.M. Anscombe*, vol. 2, *Metaphysics and the Philosophy of Mind* (Oxford, Blackwell, 1981; Minneapolis: University of Minnesota Press)

——(1981), *The Collected Philosophical Papers of G.E.M. Anscombe*, vol. 3, *Ethics, Religion and Politics* (Oxford: Basil Blackwell; Minneapolis: University of Minnesota Press)

——(1982), 'Action, Intention and "Double Effect"', Proc Am Cath Phil Ass 12–25

——([1991] 1995), 'Ludwig Wittgenstein', Philosophy 70: 395–407

——(2008), *Faith in a Hard Ground: Essays on Religion, Philosophy and Ethics by G.E.M. Anscombe* (eds Mary Geach and Luke Gormally) (Charlottesville, VA and Exeter, UK: Imprint Academic)

Ashley, Benedict O.P. (1976), 'A Critique of the Theory of Delayed Hominization', in D.G. McCarthy and A.S. Moraczewski (eds), *An Ethical Evaluation of Fetal Experimentation: An Interdisciplinary Study* (St Louis: Pope John XXIII Medical-Moral Research and Education Center), 113–33

Atkinson, G.M. (1977), 'Persons in the Whole Sense', AJJ 22: 86–17

Belmans, Th.G. (1980), *Le sens objectif de l'agir humain* (Vatican City: Libreria Editrice Vaticana)

Boyle, Joseph M. (1977), 'Double Effect and a Certain Type of Embryotomy', Irish Theological Q 44: 304–18

——(1978), '*Praeter intentionem* in Aquinas', Thomist 42: 649–65

——(1980), 'Toward Understanding the Principle of Double Effect', Ethics 90: 527–38

——(1991), 'Who Is Entitled to Double Effect?', J of Medicine & Philosophy 16: 475–94

——and Sullivan, Thomas D. (1977), 'The Diffusiveness of Intention Principle: A Counter-Example', Phil Studies 31: 357–60

——, Grisez, Germain, and Tollefsen, Olaf (1976), *Free Choice: A Self-Referential Argument* (Notre Dame: University of Notre Dame Press)

Braine, David (1992), *The Human Person: Animal and Spirit* (Notre Dame and London: University of Notre Dame Press)
Brock, Stephen L. (1998), *Action and Conduct: Aquinas and the Theory of Action* (Edinburgh: T. & T. Clark)
Broderick, Patrick A. (1985), 'Conditional Objectives of Conspiracies', Yale LJ 94: 895–908
Cartwright, J.P.W. (1990), 'Conditional Intention', Phil Studies 60: 233–55
Castañeda, Hector-Neri (1982), 'Conditional Intentions, Intentional Action and Aristotelian Practical Syllogisms', Erkenntnis 18: 239–60
——(1983), 'Reply to Wilfrid Sellars: Intending and the Logic of Intentions', in James E. Tomberlin (ed.), *Agent, Language and the Structure of the World* (Indianapolis: Hackett), 419–34
Cavanaugh, T.A. (2006), *Double-Effect Reasoning: Doing Good and Avoiding Evil* (OUP)
Chisholm, Roderick (1970), 'The Structure of Intention', J of Philosophy 67: 636
Clerk, J.F. and Lindsell, W.H.B. (1989), *Torts* (eds R.W.M. Dias et al.) (16th edn, London: Sweet & Maxwell)
Daube, David (1969), *Roman Law: Linguistic, Social and Philosophical Aspects* (Edinburgh: Edinburgh University Press)
Davidson, Donald (1980), 'Intending', in *ibid., Essays on Actions and Events* (OUP)
Davis, Henry S.J. ([1935] 1946), *Moral and Pastoral Theology* (4th edn, London: Longman)
Diamond, James J. (1975), 'Abortion, Animation and Hominization', Theological Studies 36: 305–24
Donagan, Alan (1982), 'Thomas Aquinas on Human Action', in N. Kretzmann, A. Kenny, and J. Pinborg (eds), *The Cambridge History of Later Medieval Philosophy* (CUP), 642–54
Donceel, J.F. (1970), 'Immediate Animation and Delayed Hominization', Theological Studies 31: 76–105
Duff, R.A. (1986), 'The Obscure Intentions of the House of Lords', Crim LR 771–81
——(1990), *Intention, Agency and Criminal Liability: Philosophy of Action and the Criminal Law* (Oxford: Basil Blackwell)
Dworkin, Ronald (1977, 1978), *Taking Rights Seriously* (rev. edn with reply to critics) (HUP; London: Duckworth)
——(1978), 'Political Judges and the Rule of Law', Proc Brit Acad 44: 259–87
——(1981), 'Do We Have a Right to Pornography?', Oxford J Legal Studies 1: 177
——(1985), *A Matter of Principle* (HUP)
——(1986), *Law's Empire* (HUP; London: Fontana)
——(1993), *Life's Dominion* (New York: Alfred A. Knopf; London: Harper Collins)
Edwards, Robert G. and Steptoe, Patrick (1981), *A Matter of Life: The Story of a Medical Breakthrough* (London: Sphere Books)
Fisher, Anthony OP (1991), 'Individuogenesis and a Recent Book by Fr Norman Ford', Anthropotes: Rivista di Studi sulla Persona e la Famiglia [1991] no. 2: 199–244
——(1991), '"When Did I Begin?" Revisited', Linacre Q, August, 59–68
Flannery, Kevin L. SJ (1993), 'What is Included in a Means to an End?', Gregorianum 74: 499–513
——(1995), 'Natural Law *mens rea* versus the Benthamite Tradition', AJJ 40: 377–400
Fleming, John G. (1987), *The Law of Torts* (7th edn, Sydney: Law Book Co.)
Fletcher, George P. (1978), *Rethinking Criminal Law* (Boston and Toronto: Little, Brown)
Foot, Philippa (1978), *Virtues and Vices* (OUP)
Ford, Norman M. (1988), *When Did I Begin?* (CUP)

Forsythe, Clark D. (1998), 'Human Cloning and the Constitution', Valparaiso U L Rev 32: 469 at 497–502
Fraser, Russell (ed.) (1985), *All's Well That Ends Well* (CUP)
Freeman, Samuel (2006), 'Distributive Justice and the Law of Peoples', in Rex Martin and David A. Reidy (eds), *Rawls's Law of Peoples: A Realistic Utopia?* (Malden, MA and Oxford: Blackwell), 243–60
Fuchs, Joseph SJ (1970), *Human Values and Christian Morality* (Dublin: Gill & Macmillan)
Gallagher, J. (1985), 'Is the Human Embryo a Person?', *Human Life Institute Reports*, No. 4 (Toronto: Human Life Research Institute), 22–6
Garrigou-Lagrange, Reginald OP (1951), *De Beatitudine, de actibus humanis et habitibus. Commentarius in Summam theologicam S. Thomae, Ia-IIae, q. 1–54* (Torino: Berrutti)
Gavison, Ruth (ed.) (1987), *Issues in Contemporary Legal Philosophy: The Influence of H.L.A Hart* (OUP)
Geach, Mary and Gormally, Luke (eds) (2005), *Human Life, Action and Ethics: Essays by G.E.M. Anscombe* (Charlottesville, VA and Exeter, UK: Imprint Academic)
—— and —— (2008), *Faith in a Hard Ground: Essays on Religion, Philosophy and Ethics by G.E.M. Anscombe* (Charlottesville, VA and Exeter, UK: Imprint Academic)
Geach, Peter (1961), 'Conscience in Commission', in Walter Stein (ed.), *Nuclear Weapons and Christian Conscience* (London: Merlin Press)
—— (1969), *God and the Soul* (London: Routledge & Kegan Paul)
—— (1977), *The Virtues* (CUP)
George, Robert P. and Tollefsen, Christopher (2008), *Embryo: A Defense of Human Life* (New York: Doubleday)
Gierke, Otto von ([1934] 1950), *Natural Law and the Theory of Society 1500 to 1800* (ed. Ernest Barker) (CUP)
Gilby, Thomas OP (ed.) (1970), *Summa Theologiae*, vol. 17 (London and New York: McGraw-Hill)
Goff, Robert (Lord Goff of Chieveley) (1988), 'The Mental Element in the Crime of Murder' LQR 104: 30
Gormally, Luke (ed.) (1994), *Euthanasia, Clinical Practice and the Law* (London: Linacre Centre)
——, Kietzmann, C., and Torralba, J.M. (2009), *Bibliography of Works by G.E.M. Anscombe*, <http://www.unav.es/filosofia/jmtorralba/anscombe>, 5th version.
Grisez, Germain (1970), 'Toward a Consistent Natural-Law Ethics of Killing', AJJ 15: 64–96
—— (1975), *Beyond the New Theism: A Philosophy of Religion* (Notre Dame and London: University of Notre Dame Press) (republished with a new introduction, as *God? A Philosophical Preface to Faith* (St Augustine's Press, 2004))
—— (1977), 'Choice and Consequentialism', Proc Am Cath Phil Ass 51: 144–52
—— (1983), *The Way of the Lord Jesus*, vol. 1, *Christian Moral Principles* (Chicago: Franciscan Herald Press)
—— (1985), 'Public Funding of Abortion: A Reply to Richard A. McCormick, SJ', Homiletic and Pastoral Rev 85.9 (June): 32, 45–51
—— (1987), 'The Definability of the Proposition: The Intentional Killing of an Innocent Human Being is Always Grave Matter', in *Persona Veritá e Morale: Atti del Congresso Internazionale di Teologia Morale (Roma, 7-12 aprile 1986)* (Rome: Cittá Nuova), 291–313
—— (1989), 'When Do People Begin?', Proc Am Cath Phil Ass 63: 27–47

——(1993), 'Revelation versus Dissent,' *The Tablet*, 16 October 1993, 1329–31, reprinted in John Wilkins (ed.), *Understanding Veritatis Splendor* (London: SPCK, 1994), 1–8
——(1993), *The Way of the Lord Jesus*, vol. 2, *Living a Christian Life* (Quincy: Franciscan Press)
——(1997), *The Way of the Lord Jesus*, vol. 3, *Difficult Moral Questions* (Quincy: Franciscan Press)
—— and Joseph Boyle (1979), *Life and Death with Liberty and Justice* (Notre Dame: University of Notre Dame Press)
Hallett, Garth (1983), *Christian Moral Reasoning: An Analytic Guide* (Notre Dame and London: University of Notre Dame Press)
Hare, R.M. (1976), 'The Abnormal Child: Moral Dilemmas of Doctors and Parents,' in S. Gorowitz (ed.), *Moral Problems in Medicine* (Engelwood Cliffs: Prentice-Hall), 364–9
——(1988), 'When Does Potentiality Count? A Comment on Lockwood', Bioethics 2: 213–26
Hart, H.L.A. (1968), *Punishment & Responsibility: Essays in the Philosophy of Law* (ed. John Gardner) (2nd edn, OUP)
——([1968] 2008), *Punishment and Responsibility: Essays in the Philosophy of Law* (2nd edn, OUP)
——(1979), 'Between Utility and Rights', Columbia L Rev 79: 828–46
——(1983), *Essays in Jurisprudence and Philosophy* (OUP)
—— and Honoré, Tony ([1959] 1985), *Causation in the Law* (2nd edn with new Preface, OUP)
Heaney, S.J. (1992), 'Aquinas and the Presence of the Human Rational Soul in the Early Embryo', Thomist 56: 19–48
Hohfeld, Wesley N. (1923), *Fundamental Legal Conceptions as applied in Judicial Reasoning* (ed. W.W. Cook) (New Haven: Yale University Press)
Holmes, Oliver Wendell Jr (1894), 'Privilege, Malice, and Intent', Harv L Rev 8: 1–14
Honoré, A.M. (1987), *Making Law Bind: Essays Legal and Philosophical* (OUP)
House of Lords Select Committee on Medical Ethics (1994), *Report of the Select Committee on Medical Ethics*, HL Paper 21-I of 1993–4 (London: HMSO)
Howe, Mark De Wolfe (1941), *Holmes-Pollock Letters: The Correspondence of Mr Justice Holmes and Sir Frederick Pollock, 1874–1932* (HUP)
Howsepian, A.A. (2008), 'Four Queries Concerning the Metaphysics of Early Human Embryogenesis', J of Medicine & Philosophy 33: 140–57
Hurst, G. (1977), *Beginning Lives* (Oxford: Basil Blackwell/Open University)
Iglesias, Teresa (1984), 'In Vitro Fertilization: The Major Ethical Issues', J Medical Ethics 10: 32–7
Iwan, Wilhelm ([1931] 1995), *Because of Their Beliefs* [*Um des Glaubens willen nach Australien*] (trans. David Schubert) (Adelaide: H Schubert)
Kavka, Gregory (1978), 'Some Paradoxes of Deterrence', J of Philosophy 75: 285
Keenan, James F. SJ (1992), *Goodness and Rightness in Thomas Aquinas's* Summa Theologiae (Washington, DC: Georgetown University Press)
Kelley, Patrick J. (1983), 'A Critical Analysis of Holmes's Theory of Torts', Washington U LQ 61: 681
——(1990), 'Who Decides? Community Safety Conventions at the Heart of Tort Liability', Cleveland State L Rev 38: 315
Kelsen, Hans (1945), *General Theory of Law and State* (trans. Anders Wedb) (HUP)
——(1991), *General Theory of Norms* (trans. Michael Hartney) (OUP)
Kenny, Anthony J.P. (1975), *Will, Freedom and Power* (OUP)

——(1977), 'Intention and *Mens Rea* in Murder', in P.M.S. Hacker and J. Raz (eds), *Law, Morality and Society* (OUP), 161–74
——(1989), *The Metaphysics of Mind* (OUP)
Keown, John (1995), *Euthanasia Examined: Ethical, Climical and Legal Perspectives* (CUP)
Landes, William M. and Posner, Richard A. (1987), *The Economic Structure of Tort Law* (HUP)
Lee, Patrick (1981), 'Permanence of the Ten Commandments ...', Theological Studies 42: 422
——and George, Robert P. (2008), *Body-Self Dualism in Contemporary Ethics and Politics* (CUP)
——and Grisez (2010), 'Total Brain Death: A Reply to Alan Shewmon', Bioethics 24/9: 1
Linacre Centre (1982), *Euthanasia and Clinical Practice: Trends, Principles and Alternatives*, A Report of a Working Party (London: Linacre Centre) (republished as Book One of Luke Gormally, *Euthanasia, Clinical Practice and the Law* (1994))
Lockwood, Michael (1985), 'When Does a Human Life Begin?', in Michael Lockwood (ed.), *Moral Dilemmas in Modern Medicine* (OUP), 199–215 at 213
——(1988), 'Warnock versus Powell (and Harradine): When Does Potentiality Count?', Bioethics 2: 187–213
——(1988), 'Hare on Potentiality: A Rejoinder', Bioethics 2: 343–52
Lombardi, Joseph (1992), 'Obstetrical Dilemmas and the Principle of Double Effect', AJJ 37: 197–211
Lonergan, Bernard J.F. (1958), *Insight: A Study of Human Understanding* (London and New York: Longmans)
——(1966), *Collection* (New York: Herder & Herder)
Mackie, John (1977), *Ethics: Inventing Right and Wrong* (Harmondsworth: Penguin)
——(1980), 'The Transcendental "I"', in Baas van Straaten (ed.), *Philosophical Subjects* (OUP), 48–61
Mahoney, John SJ (1981), *Seeking the Spirit* (London: Sheed & Ward)
Maritain, Jacques (1951), *Man and the State* (Chicago: University of Chicago Press)
Martin, Christopher F.J. (1993), 'Thomas de Aquino y la Identidad Personal', Anuario Filosófico 26: 249–60
May, William E. (1994), 'The Management of Ectopic Pregnancies: A Moral Analysis', in Peter J. Cataldo and Albert S. Moraczewski OP (eds), *The Fetal Tissue Issue: Medical and Ethical Aspects* (Braintree, MA: The Pope John Center), 121–47
McCormick, Richard SJ (1978), 'Notes on Moral Theology 1977', Theological St 39: 76
——(1984), 'Medicaid and Abortion', Theological St 45: 715–21
——(1985), 'Notes on Moral Theology: 1984', Theological St 46: 50–114
——(1994), 'Some Early Reactions to *Veritatis Splendor*', Theological St 55: 481–506
——and Ramsey, Paul (eds) (1978), *Doing Evil to Achieve Good* (Chicago: Loyola University Press)
McMahan, Jeff (2002), *The Ethics of Killing: Problems at the Margins of Life* (OUP)
Meiland, Jack W. (1970), *The Nature of Intention* (London: Methuen)
Montgomery, George R. (ed.) (1902), *Leibniz: Discourse on Metaphysics, Correspondence with Arnauld, Monadology* (Open Court)
Moore, Michael (1987), 'Intentions and *Mens Rea*', in Ruth Gavison (ed.), *Issues in Contemporary Legal Philosophy: The Influence of H.L.A. Hart* (OUP), 245–70
Morris, Harry (1985), *Last Things in Shakespeare* (Tallahassee: Florida State University Press)
Moya, Carlos J. (1990), *The Philosophy of Action: An Introduction* (Oxford: Polity/Blackwell)
Müller, Jan-Werner (2007), *Constitutional Patriotism* (Princeton: Princeton University Press)

Nagel, Thomas (1979), *Mortal Questions* (CUP)

O'Connell, Timothy E. (1978), *Principles for a Catholic Morality* (New York: Seabury Press)

Olson, Eric T. (1997), *The Human Animal: Personal Identity without Psychology* (OUP)

Paulson, Stanley L. (1998), 'Four Phases in Hans Kelsen's Theory? Reflections on a Periodization', 18 Oxford J Legal Studies 18: 154–66

Pears, David (1980), 'Intentions as Judgements', in Z. van Straaten (ed.), *Philosophical Subjects: Essays Presented to P.F. Strawson* (OUP), 223–37

Peschke, K.-H. (1988), 'Tragfähigkeit und Grenzen des Prinzips der Doppelwirkung', Studia Moralia 26: 101–17

Pinckaers, Servais OP (1962), Notes to St Thomas d'Aquin, *Somme Théologique: Les Actes Humaines* (Paris: Desclée)

Pink, T.L.M. (1991), 'Purposive Intending', Mind 100: 343

Porter, Jean (1996), '"Direct" and "Indirect" in Grisez's Moral Theory', Theological St 57: 611–32

Posner, Richard A. (1971), 'Killing or Wounding to Protect a Property Interest', J Law & Econ 14: 201

——(1977), *Economic Analysis of Law* (2nd edn, Boston and London: Little, Brown)

President's Council on Bioethics (2008), *Controversies in the Determination of Death* (Washington, DC)

Price, Anthony W. (1989), *Love and Friendship in Plato and Aristotle* (OUP)

Price, Joseph G. (1968), *The Unfortunate Comedy: A Study of* All's Well That Ends Well *and Its Critics* (Liverpool University Press/Toronto University Press)

Rawls, John ([1993] 1996), *Political Liberalism* (New York: Columbia University Press)

——(1999), *The Law of Peoples* (HUP)

Raz, Joseph (1986), *The Morality of Freedom* (OUP)

——(1994), *Ethics in the Public Domain* (OUP)

——(1998), 'Multiculturalism', Ratio Juris 11: 193–205

——(2009), *Between Authority and Interpretation: On the Theory of Law and Practical Reason* (OUP)

Rhonheimer, Martin (1987), *Natur als Grundlage der Moral* (Innsbruck and Vienna: Tyrolia)

Scheer, Richard (1989), 'Conditional Intentions', *Philosophical Investigations* 12: 52–62

Schüller, Bruno SJ (1978), 'The Double Effect in Catholic Thought: A Reevaluation', in R. McCormick and P. Ramsey, *Doing Evil to Achieve Good* (Chicago: Loyola University Press), 165–91

——(1980) 'La moralité des moyens', Recherches de Science Religieuse 68: 204–24

Scruton, Roger (1989), 'Corporate Persons', Proc Aristotelian Soc Supp 63: 239–66

Sellars, Wilfrid (1983), 'Conditional Promises and Conditional Intentions (Including a Reply to Castañeda)', in James E. Tomberlin (ed.), *Agent, Language and the Structure of the World* (Indianapolis: Hackett), 195–221

Shewmon, D. Alan (1997), 'Recovery from "Brain Death": A Neurologist's Apologia', Linacre Q 64: 30–96

——(1998), '"Brainstem Death", "Brain Death" and Death: A Critical Re-evaluation of the Purported Equivalence', Issues in Law & Medicine 14: 125–45

——(1998), 'Chronic "Brain Death": Meta-Analysis and Conceptual Consequences', Neurology 51: 1538–45

——(2001), 'The Brain and Somatic Integration: Insights into the Standard Biological Rationale for Equating "Brain Death" with Death', J of Medicine & Philosophy 26: 457–78

——(2004), 'The ABC's of PVS: Problems of Definition', in Calixto Machado and D. Alan Shewmon (eds), *Brain Death and Disorders of Consciousness* (New York and London: Kluwer Academic/Plenum)

——and Holmes, G.L. (1990), 'Brainstem Plasticity in Congenitally Decerebrate Children' [abstract] Brain and Development 12(5): 1773–81

Sidgwick, Henry ([1874] 1907), *The Methods of Ethics* (7th edn, London: Macmillan)

Simon, Jürgen W. (2002), 'Human Dignity as a Regulative Instrument for Human Genome Research', in Cosimo Marco Mazzoni (ed.), *Ethics & Law in Biomedical Research* (The Hague: Martinus Nijhoff), 35–45

Singer, Peter (1995), *Rethinking Life and Death: The Collapse of our Traditional Ethics* (OUP)

Smith, Sydney ([1839] 1859), *The Works of the Rev. Sydney Smith* (London: Longman), vol. I

Sokolowski, Robert (2003), 'Language, the Human Person, and Christian Faith', Proc Am Cath Phil Ass 76: 27–38

Strawson, P.F. (1959), *Individuals: An Essay in Descriptive Metaphysics* (London: Methuen)

Suarez, A. (1990), 'Hydatidiform Moles and Teratomas Confirm the Human Identity of the Preimplemantation Embryo', J of Medicine & Philosophy 15: 627–35

Taylor, Gary (2003), 'The Cultural Politics of Maybe', in *Theatre and Religion: Lancastrian Shakespeare* (eds Richard Dutton, Alison Findlay, and Richard Wilson) (Manchester and New York: Manchester University Press), 242–58

Tillyard, E.M.W. (1961), *Shakespeare's Problem Plays* (London: Chatto & Windus)

Tooley, Michael (1983), *Abortion and Infanticide* (OUP)

Voegelin, Eric (1957), *Plato and Aristotle*, vol. 3 of *Order and History* (Chapel Hill: Louisiana State University Press)

——([1944] 1997), 'The Middle Ages to Aquinas', in *The Collected Works of Eric Voegelin*, vol. 20 (ed. Peter von Sivers) (Columbia and London: University of Missouri Press)

Wade, F.C. (1975), 'Potentiality in the Abortion Discussion', Review of Metaphysics 29: 239–55

Waffelaert, J. (1884), 'De Abortu et Embryotomia', Nouvelle Revue Théologique 16: 160–79

Walter, James J. (1988), 'Response to John Finnis: A Theological Critique', in Thomas G. Fuechtmann (ed.), *Consistent Ethic of Life* (Kansas City: Sheed & Ward)

Watt, Helen (ed.) (2001), 'Conjoined Twins: Separation as Mutilation', Medical L Rev 9: 237–45

White, Alan (1985), *Grounds of Liability: an Introduction to the Philosophy of Law* (OUP)

——(1991), *Misleading Cases* (OUP)

Wiggins, David (2001), *Sameness and Substance Renewed* (CUP)

Williams, Bernard (2002), *Truth and Truthfulness: An Essay in Genealogy* (Princeton: Princeton University Press)

Williams, Glanville (1958), *The Sanctity of Life and the Criminal Law* [Carpentier Lectures at Columbia, 1956] (London: Faber & Faber)

——(1961), *Criminal Law: The General Part* (2nd edn, London: Stevens)

——(1965), *The Mental Element in Crime* (Jerusalem and Oxford: Magnes Press, Hebrew University)

——(1983), *Textbook of Criminal Law* (2nd edn, London: Stevens)

——(1987), 'Oblique Intention' [1987] CLJ 46: 417–38

——(1989), 'The *Mens Rea* of Murder: Leave It Alone', LQR 105: 387

Wilson, George (2008), 'Action', *The Stanford Encyclopedia of Philosophy* (Fall 2008), Edward N. Zalta (ed.), <http://plato.stanford.edu/archives/fall2008/entries/action>

Wojtyla, Karol (1979), *The Acting Person* (Dordrecht, Boston, and London: Reidel)
—— (Pope John Paul II) (2005), *Memory and Identity* (London: Weidenfeld & Nicolson)
Wright, George T. (2001), *Hearing the Measures: Shakespearean and Other Inflections* (Madison: University of Wisconsin Press)
Wright, John J. (1943), *National Patriotism in Papal Teaching* (Westminster, MD: Newman Bookshop)
Yowell, Paul (2007), 'A Critical Examination of Dworkin's Theory of Rights', AJJ 53: 93–137
Zalba, Marcellino SJ (1977), '"Nihil prohibet unius actus esse duos effectus" (*Summa theologiae* 2-2, q.64, a.7) Numquid applicari potest principium in abortu therapeutico?', in *Atti del Congresso Internazionale (Roma-Napoli—17/24 Aprile 1974) Tommaso D'Aquino nel suo settimo centenario*, vol. 5, *L'Agire Morale* (Naples: Edizioni Domenicane Italiane), 557–68

ACKNOWLEDGEMENTS

The following essays were originally published as indicated:

Essay 1: 'The Priority of Persons', in Jeremy Horder (ed.), *Oxford Essays in Jurisprudence, Fourth Series* (OUP, 2000), 1–15

Essay 2: '"The Thing I Am": Personal Identity in Aquinas and Shakespeare', Social Philosophy & Policy 22: 250–82

Essay 3: 'Anscombe's Essays', National Catholic Bioethics Q 9/1: 199–207

Essay 5: 'Persons and their Associations', Proceedings of the Aristotelian Society, supplementary volume 63, 267–74

Essay 7: 'Reason, Revelation, Universality and Particularity in Ethics', American Journal of Jurisprudence 53: 23–48

Essay 8: '"The Act of the Person" *Persona Veritá e Morale*, atti del Congresso Internazionale di Teologia Morale', Rome 1986 (Rome: Cittá Nuova Editrice), 159–75

Essay 9: 'Object and Intention in Moral Judgments according to St Thomas Aquinas', The Thomist 55: 1–27

Essay 10: 'Intention and Side-effects', in R.G. Frey and Christopher W. Morris (eds), *Liability and Responsibility. Essays in Law and Morals* (CUP, 1991), 32–64

Essay 11: 'Intention in Tort Law', in David Owen (ed.), *Philosophical Foundations of Tort Law* (OUP, 1995), 229–48

Essay 12: 'On Conditional Intentions and Preparatory Intentions', in Luke Gormally (ed.), *Moral Truth and Moral Tradition: Essays in Honour of Peter Geach and Elizabeth Anscombe* (Dublin: Four Courts Press, 1994), 163–76

Essay 13: '"Direct" and "Indirect": A Reply to Critics of Our Action Theory' (with Germain Grisez and Joseph Boyle), The Thomist 65: 1–44

Essay 14: 'Directly Discriminatory Decisions: A Missed Opportunity', Law Quarterly Review (Sweet and Maxwell) 126: 491–6

Essay 16: 'Abortion and Health Care Ethics', in Raanan Gillon (ed.), *Principles of Health Care Ethics* (John Wiley, 1993), 547–57

Essay 17: 'Some Fundamental Evils of Generating Human Embryos by Cloning', in Cosimo Marco Mazzoni (ed.), *Etica della Ricerca Biologica* (Leo S. Olschki Editore, 2000)

Essay 19: '*Bland*: Crossing the Rubicon?', Law Quarterly Review (Sweet and Maxwell) 109: 329–37

INDEX

The manufacturer's authorised representative in the EU for product safety is Oxford University Press España S.A. of El Parque Empresarial San Fernando de Henares, Avenida de Castilla, 2 - 28830 Madrid (www.oup.es/en or product.safety@oup.com). OUP España S.A. also acts as importer into Spain of products made by the manufacturer.
Printed and bound by CPI Group (UK) Ltd, Croydon, CR0 4YY
14/09/2026
02216304-0012